FUNDAMENTALS *of* COLLECTION DEVELOPMENT *&* MANAGEMENT

Peggy Johnson

American Library Association

Chicago   2004

Composition and design by ALA Editions in Avenir and Sabon using QuarkXPress 5.0 for the PC

Printed on 50-pound white offset, a pH-neutral stock, and bound in 10-point coated cover stock by Victor Graphics

The paper used in this publication meets the minimum requirements of American National Standard for Information Sciences—Permanence of Paper for Printed Library Materials, ANSI Z39.48-1992. ∞

Library of Congress Cataloging-in-Publication Data

Johnson, Peggy, 1948-
    Fundamentals of collection development and management / Peggy Johnson.
        p. cm.
    Includes bibliographical references and index.
    ISBN 0-8389-0853-5 (alk. paper)
    1. Collection development (Libraries) 2. Collection management
(Libraries) 3. Collection development (Libraries)—United States.
    4. Collection management (Libraries)—United States. I. Title.
    Z687.J64 2004
    025.2'1—dc22   2003016815

Printed in the United States of America

08 07 06   5 4 3

CONTENTS

FIGURES   *v*

ACKNOWLEDGMENTS   *vii*

PREFACE   *ix*

1   Introduction to Collection Management and Development   *1*

2   Organization and Staffing   *32*

3   Policy, Planning, and Budgets   *65*

4   Developing Collections   *101*

5   Managing Collections   *138*

6   Marketing, Liaison, and Outreach Activities   *172*

7   Electronic Resources   *199*

8   Cooperative Collection Development and Management   *235*

9   Collection Analysis: Evaluation and Assessment   *268*

APPENDIX: SELECTION AIDS   *299*

GLOSSARY   *307*

INDEX   *327*

▎ FIGURES

3-1 Collection Development Policy: Geography *81*

3-2 Budget Planning Cycle *93*

4-1 Online Order Request Form *112*

4-2 Approval Plan Notification Slip *114*

5-1 Simple Treatment Decision Form *143*

5-2 Detailed Treatment Decision Form *144*

6-1 Faculty Profile *188*

7-1 E-Resources Decision-Making Flowchart *213*

8-1 The Three Components of Successful Cooperation *237*

9-1 Collection Analysis Methods *270*

ACKNOWLEDGMENTS

This book could not have been written without the support of many. My thanks go to Marlene Chamberlain, my editor, for her persistence and encouragement during the time it took to get this book from concept to reality; to my colleagues and confidantes Bonnie MacEwan and Barbara Allen, who were always supportive; and to my parents, who kept asking if I was done yet. I also wish to acknowledge Bonnie MacEwan's contributions to chapter 3, especially the section on budgets. I owe the most to Lee, my best friend, for his patience, love, and inspiration.

PREFACE

Writing a book on collection development and management offers two challenges—what to include and what to exclude, not unlike the practice of collection development and management itself. Entire books can be and have been written on the topics addressed in each chapter in this book. Within the limitations of a single book, my goal is to introduce the theory and practice of collection development and management and to present each of the responsibilities that fall within it. In addition, chapters contain a brief history of how these responsibilities and topics have evolved along with the major influencing factors.

Collection development and management are the meat and potatoes of libraries. If you don't have a collection, you don't have a library. In the earliest libraries, people concentrated on building collections and locating materials to add, though the need for preservation has been with us for the duration of libraries. Medieval monks often spent their entire lives copying manuscripts to preserve them—and creating questions about the mutability of content similar to those that trouble us today.

By the late 1970s, the idea of collection development and management as a professional specialization and as more than "selection" (if ever it was just that) was gaining acceptance. Over the last thirty years, collection development and management have come to encompass a suite of responsibilities. This book aims to address this breadth of responsibilities. Chapter 1 presents an introduction to and an overview of collection management and development. Chapter 2 addresses the organization and assignment of collection development and management responsibilities within libraries. Chapter 3 looks at planning activities, including policies and budgeting. Chapter 4, "Developing Collections," introduces various topologies for defining types of materials and explores the selection process and criteria, sources for identifying titles and acquisition options, and selection challenges.

"Managing Collections," chapter 5, examines the responsibilities that come into play after an item is added to a collection: decisions about weeding, storage, preservation and conservation, serials cancellation, and protecting materials from theft and damage. The very important responsibilities of reaching out to and understanding a library's user community are the topics of chapter 6. Electronic resources are addressed in every chapter; however, their special nature and the unique challenges as well as opportunities they present are considered in chapter 7. Chapter 8 considers library cooperation and its increasing importance to those with collection development and management responsibilities. The final chapter covers collection evaluation (Is it a "good" collection?) and assessment (Does it serve the community for which it is intended?). Two appendixes provide suggested "Selection Aids" and a library-centered "Glossary" of terms used in this book.

The work of collection development and management is being profoundly changed by the Internet and increasing options for resources in digital format. Librarians select print materials that will be digitized, remote e-resources to which they will subscribe, e-books and CD-ROMs that they will purchase, and free web resources to which they will direct their library community. Decisions about e-resources cannot be separated from the decisions that librarians make on a daily basis—selecting, budgeting, planning, assessing and evaluating, canceling and withdrawing, and so on. To that end, I have aimed to integrate digital with more familiar, traditional formats in each chapter. Nevertheless, e-resources continue to present unique challenges, and a separate chapter addressing these remains necessary.

Collection development and management does not exist in a vacuum. It is done well only when its practitioners interact constantly with others within a library and with the collection's users and potential users. Librarianship, regardless of the speciality or range of responsibilities or the library in which it is practiced, cannot be separated from other areas of professional research and theory. To reiterate that point, I have sought to introduce the reader to relevant theories and resources outside the traditional literature of librarianship and information management. References are made to experts and their research in sociology, organizational behavior, communications, history of science and technology, and business and management. A list of suggested readings accompanies each chapter. For the most part, I have recommended more recent resources, electing not to provide literature reviews unless a landmark article or book provides a historical context for current discussion.

Each chapter, excluding the first one, concludes with a case study. The reader is presented with a fictional library situation that illustrates the topics covered in that chapter. Each case includes pertinent facts needed to analyze the issue and make recommendations or solve a problem. The reader should consult materials presented in the chapter's "Suggested Readings" for additional resources that will assist in responding to the problems presented in the case study. My intent is to ground theory and recommended practices in the reality of situations librarians encounter every day and to foster analysis either through group discussion or individual exploration. To this end, questions, outlined in an "Activity" section, accompany each case.

All URLs referenced in this book were valid as of late summer 2003. The URLs at the web site of the American Library Association are continuing to change; therefore, I have provided directions (a sequence of steps) for locating sources within this web site.

This book is intended for those with little experience in collection development and management—students preparing to enter the field of librarianship and experienced librarians with new or expanded responsibilities. I hope that the combination of history, theory, current thinking, and practical advice also will be of interest to seasoned selectors, who may value a work that aims to present a contemporary perspective on important issues.

CHAPTER 1

Introduction to Collection Management and Development

This chapter begins with an introduction to terms and concepts, followed by a capsule history of the practice of collection development, focusing on the United States. A brief look at the history of collection work is useful because contemporary practice builds on that of the past. Selectors work with library collections that have been created over time in accordance with past understandings and conventions. This chapter also considers trends in and affecting collection development and what the future may bring for collection development librarians. Topics introduced in this chapter are explored in more depth in subsequent chapters.

The first issue to be addressed in a book devoted to collection development and management is an understanding of what this phrase means. *Collection development* came into wide use in the late 1960s to replace *selection* as a more encompassing term reflecting the thoughtful process of developing a library collection in response to institutional priorities and community or user needs and interests. Collection development was understood to cover several activities related to the development of library collections, including selection, the determination and coordination of selection policy, assessment of the needs of users and potential users, collection use studies, collection analysis, budget management, identification of collection needs, community and user outreach and liaison, and planning for resource sharing. In the 1980s, the term *collection management* was proposed as an umbrella term under which collection development was to be subsumed. In this construct, collection management includes collection development and an expanded suite of decisions about weeding, canceling serials, storage, and preservation. Also of concern in collection management are the organization and assignment of responsibilities for its practice.

Collection management and *collection development* now often are used synonymously or in tandem, a practice followed in this book. For example, the professional organization within the American Library Association's (ALA) Association for Library Collections and Technical Services that focuses on this topic is called the Collection Management and Development Section. The tasks, functions, and responsibilities now understood to be the portfolio of collection development librarians include selection of materials in all formats, collection policies, collection maintenance (selection for weeding and storage, preservation, and serials cancellation), budget and finance, assessment of needs of users and potential users, liaison and outreach activities related to the collection and its users, collection use studies, collection assessment and evaluation, and planning for cooperation and resource sharing.

A literature sampling provides a clearer understanding of how collection development and management are understood by practitioners.

"Simply put, collection management is the systemic, efficient and economic stewardship of library resources."[1]

"The goal of any collection development organization must be to provide the library with a collection that meets the appropriate needs of its client population within the limits of its fiscal and personnel resources. To reach this goal, each segment of the collection must be developed with an application of resources consistent with its relative importance to the mission of the library and the needs of its patrons."[2]

"Collection management is defined as a process of information gathering, communication, coordination, policy formulation, evaluation, and planning. These processes, in turn, influence decisions about the acquisition, retention, and provision of access to information sources in support of the intellectual needs of a given library community. Collection development is the part of collection management that primarily deals with decisions about the acquisition of materials."[3]

"Collection development is a term representing the process of systematically building library collections to serve study, teaching, research, recreational, and other needs of library users. The process includes selection and deselection of current and retrospective materials, planning of coherent strategies for continuing acquisition, and evaluation of collections to ascertain how well they serve user needs."[4]

Those who practice collection management are called variously selectors, bibliographers, collections librarians, subject specialists, collection development librarians, collection managers, and collection developers. This book uses these terms interchangeably to mean a library staff member who is responsible for developing, managing, and teaching about collections. The responsibilities that comprise collection management include one or more of the following: selecting materials for acquisition and access, weeding, storage, and preservation; writing and revising collection development policies; promoting, marketing, and interpreting collections and resources; evaluating and assessing collections and related services; community liaison and outreach responsibilities; managing budgets; liaison with other libraries and cooperative collection development; and soliciting funding to supplement allocated collection development funds. Although their assignment and importance will vary from library to library, these elements are universal in the practice of collection management. For that reason, this book does not contain separate chapters for various types of libraries.

All these responsibilities imply a knowledge of the library's user community and its fiscal and personnel resources, mission, values, and priorities along with those of the library's parent organization. Collection management cannot be successful unless it is integrated within all library operations and the responsible librarian has an understanding of and close relationship with other library operations and services. Important considerations for the collection management librarian include who has access to the collection on-site and remotely, circulation policies, types of interfaces the library supports, quality of bibliographic records and the priority given to their creation, and the extent to which local catalog records reflect access to remote resources. A constant theme throughout this book is the importance of the environment, both internal and external, to the library, within which the collection management librarian practices his or her craft.

Historical Overview

Selection of materials for libraries has been around as long as libraries have, though records of how decisions were made in the ancient libraries of Nineveh, Alexandria, and Pergamum are nonexistent. One can assume that the scarcity of written materials and their value as unique records made comprehensiveness, completeness, and preservation guiding principles. Libraries served primarily as storehouses rather than as instruments for the dissemination of knowledge. Comprehensiveness, completeness, and preservation have continued as library goals through the growth of commerce, the Renaissance, invention of movable type, expanding lay literacy, the Enlightenment, the public library movement, and the proliferation of electronic resources. Size continues today to be a common, though only one, measure of a library's greatness.

Systematic philosophies of selection are rare until the end of the nineteenth century, though a few early librarians gave written attention to selection. Gabriel Naudé, hired by Cardinal Mazarin to manage his personal library in the early 1600s, addressed selection in the first modern treatise on the management of libraries. He stated, "It may be laid down as a maxim that there is no book whatsoever, be it never so bad or disparaged, but may in time be sought for by someone."[5] However, completeness as a goal has been balanced by a desire to select the best and most appropriate materials. In 1780, Jean-Baptiste Cotton des Houssayes stated that libraries should consist only of books "of genuine merit and of well-approved utility," with new additions guided by "enlightened economy."[6] Appropriate criteria for selectivity has been a continuing debate between librarians and library users for centuries.

Collection Building in the United States

Libraries developed first in the American colonies as private collections and then within higher education institutions. These early libraries were small for three reasons: relatively few materials were published in the New World, funds were limited, and acquiring materials was difficult. Even as late as 1850, only 600 periodicals were being published in the United States, up from 26 in 1810.[7] Monographic publishing was equally sparse, with most works being religious in nature.

Academic Libraries

Academic libraries seldom had continuing budget allocations, and selection was not a major concern. Most support for academic libraries' collections came from gifts of books or donations to purchase them. Less than a tenth of the holdings of colonial American college libraries were added through direct purchase.[8] Most gifts were gladly accepted. Any institutional funds came from the occasional actions of the trustees or boards of regents rather than from recurring allocations. Student library fees were charged at several institutions, either on a per annum or a per use basis.[9] Even by 1856, when John Langdon Sibley became librarian of Harvard, the total fund for library acquisitions and binding was only $250 per year.[10] Even with funds in hand, acquiring materials was challenging. Everything had to be purchased on buying trips to book dealers in large East Coast cities and Europe.

Collections grew slowly. By 1790, Harvard's library had reached only 12,000 volumes. It had averaged 82 new volumes per year in the preceding 135 years. William and Mary's library collection numbered only 3,000, and it was the second largest. The academic libraries added, on the average, only 30 to 100 volumes per year before 1800. Most additions, because they were donations, were irrelevant to the educational programs of the time.[11] By 1850, only one U.S. academic institution had a collection larger than 50,000 volumes: Harvard College collections had reached 72,000 volumes.[12] At the middle of the century, total holdings for the approximately 700 colleges, professional schools, and public libraries in the United States totaled only 2.2 million volumes.[13]

College libraries reflected American education's priories of the time: teaching rather than study, students rather than scholars, and maintaining order and discipline rather than promoting learning and research. Reflective thinking and theoretical considerations were unusual in any college discipline before the Civil War. As a consequence, academic libraries had only limited significance in their institutions and still functioned as storehouses.

Following the Civil War, academic libraries and their parent institutions began a period of significant change. Libraries gained greater prominence as universities grew. The period from 1850 to 1900 witnessed a fundamental change in the structure of American scholarship, influenced by the ideas and methods imported from German universities, which had become centers for advanced scholarship. The move to lectures and seminars as replacements for textbooks, memorization, and recitation and the increasing importance of research had far-reaching consequences for libraries. Passage of the Morrill Act in 1862, which created the land-grant universities, introduced the concept that universities were obligated to produce and share knowledge that would advance society. A direct result was a tremendous increase in scholarly journals and monographs. The needs and working habits of the professionalized and institution-centered scholars were quite different from those of their predecessors. Scholars' attitudes toward the academic library experienced a basic reorientation. The institutional academic library became a necessity. The scholarly profession was no longer confined to those who had the private wealth to collect extensive personal collections. A mounting flood of publications meant that even those few scholars with private means could not individually keep up with and manage all the new information available. They needed the institutional library to consult and use the materials necessary for research. As the library became increasingly important to higher education, the process of creating collections gained a higher profile.

Well into the 1900s, most selection in academic libraries was handled by faculty members. When Asa Gray was hired as an instructor at the University of Michigan in 1838, he went first to Europe to acquire books for the library. The president at Ohio Wesleyan traveled to New York and Europe in 1854 to purchase library books.[14] German university libraries were unique in placing selection as the direct responsibility of librarians and staff, with less faculty input. A primary advocate of the role of librarians in the development of library collections was Christian Gottlob Heyne, the librarian at the University of Göttingen in Germany from 1763 to 1812.[15] In 1930, faculty members in the United States still were selecting as much as 80 percent of total university library acquisitions, and librarians were choosing 20 percent.[16] This ratio began to shift in the 1960s and had reversed by the late 1970s. The change can be linked to an increasing professionalism among librarians, the burgeoning volume of publications, a growing number of librarians with extensive subject training, and the expanding pressure on faculty of other responsibilities, including research and publication. As the responsibility for building library collections shifted from faculty to library staff, selection emphasis changed from selecting materials primarily to meet the needs and interests of specific faculty members to building a unified collection to meet both current and future institutional priorities.

Public Libraries

Academic libraries preceded public libraries in the United States. Established in 1833, the Peterborough Town Library in New Hampshire usually is identified as the first free, publicly owned and maintained library in the United States.[17] A library established in Franklin, Massachusetts, through funds from Benjamin Franklin to purchase 116 volumes, was opened to all inhabitants of the town in 1790.[18] Though public, it was not supported by public funding. Social libraries, limited to a specific clientele and supported by subscriptions, had existed in the colonies for more than 100 years. One of the more well known is the Philadelphia Library Company, founded by Benjamin Franklin in 1731 and supported by fifty subscribers to share the cost of importing books and journals from England. Other social libraries were established and supported by philanthropists and larger manufacturers to teach morality, provide a more wholesome environment, and offer self-education opportunities to the poor and uneducated drawn to cities. Circulating libraries were commercial ventures that loaned more popular materials, frequently novels, for a fee. When considered together, these early libraries were furnishing the collections that libraries provide today—materials that are used for information, education, and recreation.

Boston was the first major community to establish a public library, in 1852. The trustees defined the purpose of the public library as education, and though they had no plans to acquire novels, they were willing to include the more popular respectable books. In their first report, the trustees wrote, "We consider that a large public library is of the utmost importance as the means of completing our system of public education."[19] The responsibility of libraries to educate their users and to bring them to the better books and journals has been a theme guiding selection in public libraries since their establishment, and the definition of appropriate materials has been the source of constant debate.

Trustees or committees appointed by trustees selected materials in early public libraries. By the end of the 1800s and as librarianship evolved as a profession, John Cotton Dana was advising that book selection should be left to the librarians, directed by the trustees or a book committee.[20] The present practice of assigning collections responsibility to librarians is the result of a slow transformation. In the United States, public librarians generally acquired selection responsibilities before those in academic libraries. The shift happened in public libraries earlier because the faculties of colleges and universities retained a more active interest in library collections than did the members of public library boards or trustees. The rise of library schools and the professionalization of librarianship led librarians to expect expanded responsibilities for selection and made trustees and, ultimately, faculty members more willing to transfer them to librarians.

Following the Second World War, increased funding for education and for public libraries led to a period of unparalleled expansion in all types of library collections. The seemingly endless possibilities for growth broadened the librarian's collection responsibilities. Moving beyond individual book evaluation and selection, librarians begin to view building coherent collections as an important responsibility. Librarians began to seek and acquire materials from all over the world. The scope of collections expanded to include Asia, Africa, the Middle East, and Eastern Europe as well as Western Europe.[21]

Collections theory began to focus on who should be selecting materials for the library, how selection decisions were made and the appropriate criteria, and alternatives to individual title selection for building collections. During the 1950s, vendors and jobbers began offering services that freed librarians from ordering directly from the publisher. Many of these service agencies began supplying materials through approval and blanket plans, freeing selectors to concentrate on identifying and obtaining more esoteric resources. The emphasis during this period was on growth and how to handle it effectively. Fremont Rider made his famous statement that research library collections were doubling every sixteen years.[22] In 1953, Kenneth J. Braugh wrote that the mission of Harvard's library was the "collection and preservation of everything printed."[23]

Fiscal Stringency

By the 1970s, library budgets in all types of libraries began to hold steady or to shrink. Libraries were unable to keep pace with rapidly increasing costs and growing numbers of publications. Librarians began to look for guidance in how they could make responsible decisions with less money. The goal of comprehensive, autonomous, self-sufficient collections became less realistic. Interest grew in developing guidelines for downsizing serials collections and mechanisms for increasing library cooperation. Collection development policy statements became more common as libraries sought guidance in managing limited financial resources amid conflicting demands. The Research Libraries Group was founded in 1974 as a "partnership to achieve a planned, coordinated interdependence in response to the threat posed by a climate of economic retreat and financial uncertainty."[24]

Financial stringency has had a profound impact on the growth of library collections. Between 1986 and 2002, the Association of Research

Libraries documented only a 9 percent increase in serials purchased and a 5 percent decline in monographs purchased by its member libraries. During that same period, serial unit costs increased 227 percent while expenditures increased 227 percent and monograph unit costs increased 75 percent and expenditures for monographs increased 62 percent.[25] Interlibrary lending became essential in response to libraries' inability to meet users' needs. Librarians began to debate ownership versus access via interlibrary loan and document delivery. The older idea of building comprehensive collections "just-in-case" a particular item might be needed lost favor. Some librarians suggested a more responsible use of budgets might be supplying materials to meet users' needs "just-in-time." In 1988, Maurice B. Line wrote, "Before World War 2, interlending was regarded as an optional extra, a grace and favour activity, to be indulged in sparingly; any research library considered it an admission of failure to have to obtain any item from elsewhere. Now every library, however large, accepts that it cannot be self-sufficient, and some of the largest obtain the most from elsewhere."[26]

Several pressures, external and internal, buffeted libraries in the last twenty-five years of the twentieth century. Rapid changes in user community expectations and the makeup of those communities, the publishing industry, telecommunication technology, copyright law, and scholarly communication are among the most significant. Collections librarians in all types of libraries are seeking to cope with scarce financial resources, preservation and conservation needs, cooperation in collection building and resource sharing, serials cancellation projects, and weeding and storage decisions. In 1982, Patricia Battin described academic libraries as beset by "space constraints, soaring labor costs, a horrifying recognition of the enormous preservation problem in our stacks, increasing devastation of our collections by both casual and professional theft and continuing pressure from scholars for rapid access to a growing body of literature."[27] Financial austerity, which has characterized libraries since the early 1980s, coupled with the need to readjust priorities continually is a primary reason the term *collection management* has become more meaningful to the profession.

Another challenge for libraries emerged in the late 1980s—electronic information. Some academic libraries had been acquiring data files on magnetic tapes and punched cards for a number of years, but widespread adoption of microcomputers presented libraries of all types with a variety of information resources on floppy disks, followed soon by CD-ROMs.

The growth of the Internet and ubiquitous access added remote resources to the choices to be considered. Librarians selecting electronic resources faced new decisions about software, technical support, operating systems, interfaces, and hardware. User expectations about ease of access and ubiquity have continued to increase. Purchasing the rights to access remote electronic resources has meant that collection management librarians have had to master the language of contracts and license agreements. Much of the literature at the turn of the twentieth century has focused on the problems libraries face operating in both print and electronic environments simultaneously.

Theories of Selection

The origins of collection management and development can be traced to theories of selection. Until the 1960s, most theories of selection promoted in the United States focused on choosing materials for public libraries. Libraries of all types have experienced a continuing tension between demand and value, and much of the literature on selection has focused on this tension between what people want and what librarians believe is good for them. This has been particularly true in public libraries, which have seen the education of citizens as a primary goal. Part of the demand-value controversy has been the question of what to do about fiction. The public's preference for novels was troubling to early library leaders, in part because of the long-term effects of Puritan condemnation of fiction reading. Many early librarians took a paternalistic and high, even elitist position about selection and collection building.

Librarians as Arbiters of Quality

Such early legends in American librarianship as Melvil Dewey, John C. Dana, Herbert Putnam, and Ainsworth Spofford insisted that libraries' primary role as educator meant that their responsibility was to provide only the highest-quality materials—with *quality* defined, of course, by librarians. Many librarians were proud of their role as censors, by which they meant arbiters of quality. Arthur E. Bostwick explained the positive role of public librarians as censors in his 1908 ALA presidential address. He stated that they had a responsibility to censor anything that was not Good, True, and Beautiful.[28] Among those supporting the selection and provision of more popular materials were William F. Poole, Justin Winsor, and Charles Cutter.

One of the most powerful, early statements in support of popular reading materials in public libraries was written by Poole, first head of the Chicago Public Library. He voiced the still widely held view that reading less sophisticated materials will lead readers to more cultivated works. In 1876, Poole wrote, "To meet, therefore, the varied wants of readers there must be on the shelves of the library books which persons of culture never read, although it is quite probable they did read such books in some stage of their mental development. Judged from a critical standpoint, such books are feeble, rudimentary, and perhaps sensational; but they are higher in the scale of literary merit than the tastes of the people who seek them; and, like primers and first-readers in the public schools, they fortunately lead to something better."[29]

Not all librarians were confident they could select the Good, True, and Beautiful or identify the primers that would lead readers to a higher level. As the profession of librarianship developed, librarians turned to their professional associations and librarian authorities for guidance in selecting individual titles. A number of reviewing tools appeared in the early 1900s to help select the best books. These include *ALA Booklist* (1905), *Book Review Digest* (1906), and *Fiction Catalog* (1908). The first edition of *Guide to the Study and Use of Reference Books* (now *Guide to Reference Books*) was published in 1902 by the ALA.

Despite the theoretical debate among the library leaders over value versus demand, the volume of fiction in American public libraries continued to increase. By 1876, practically all American public libraries offered at least some fictional materials, though it was often of the "better" kind. During the First World War, those opponents of fiction in U.S. public libraries felt that the serious mood of the country provided a logical argument against the frivolity of popular fiction. Cornelia Marvin, state librarian of Oregon, suggested a new librarian's slogan, "No new fiction during the war."[30] However, many librarians selected materials for military camp libraries and were not hesitant about choosing fiction to entertain and distract the troops.[31]

Following the First World War, the controversy about the role of fiction in public libraries continued. Many wanted libraries to be as attractive as possible to returning soldiers. Nevertheless, with the Great Depression resulting in a declining economy and reduced library funding, fiction continued as a point of contention among librarians. Some library leaders felt that the 1930s were a time for libraries to focus on educational reading. Carl B. Roden of the Chicago Public Library asked, "Who among us would not rather supply the books and competent guidance for ten self-students than the latest novels for a thousand fiction readers?"[32] Others felt that libraries had an obligation to provide fiction as part of their public mission. The debate over suitable library materials is documented in Esther Jane Carrier's two volumes on fiction in U.S. public libraries and gives a detailed picture of the arguments for and against fiction and its rise as part of collections.[33]

Evolution of Selection Theory

The first comprehensive American works on book selection were textbooks written by Francis K. W. Drury (1930) and by Helen Haines (1935).[34] These early works on book selection are both a reflection of their times with statements such as "Consider what books mean in individual development: in the formation of character, in the activation of intelligence, in the enrichment of resources, and in the deepening of sensitivity" and a testament to the continuity of guiding principles in collection management.[35] Drury's goals have relevance today, with a few exceptions that seem amusingly dated. He stated that the purposes of a course in book selection and, by implication, the goals of selectors were

- to analyze the nature of a community;
- to recognize the various uses to which books of varied types are to be put;
- to consider the character and policy of a library in adding books;
- to cultivate the power of judging and selecting books for purchase, with their value and suitability to readers in mind;
- to become familiar with the sources of information;
- to renew acquaintance with books and writers from the library angle;
- to develop the ability to review, criticize, and annotate books for library purposes;
- to decide where in the library organization book selection fits;
- to learn how to perform the necessary fundamental tasks of book selection; and
- to scrutinize the mental and personal fitness of the selector.[36]

Drury stated that "a qualified selector, acquainted with the demand from his community and knowing the book and money resource of his library, chooses the variety of books he believes will be used, applying his expert knowledge."[37]

The continuing tension between demand and value was a recurring theme in the professional literature on selection. A vigorous proponent of value was Leon Carnovsky, who framed his position by saying that public libraries should provide materials that were true.[38] Before the Second World War, he offered a scholarly position supporting internal censorship. He held a strong conviction that the public library should be a force for truth on vital issues. He advocated censorship of local prejudice and opinion and said the library is "acting democratically when it sets up the authority of reason as the censor."[39] The political implications of World War II, combined with a loss of confidence in librarians' knowledge and ability to choose what is true and what is not, caused Carnovsky to moderate his position in the 1950s and 1960s.

The debate over popular materials in public libraries has continued through much of the twentieth century. The Public Library Inquiry of the late 1940s once again raised serious questions about the place of light fiction. Funded by the Carnegie Corporation and conducted by the Social Science Research Council, the inquiry focused on describing libraries, their services, collections, and users. Bernard Berelson wrote the summary volume, in which he held to an elitist view of public libraries, recommending the library's purpose should be "serious" and its proper role might be to serve the culturally alert community members rather than to try to reach all people.[40]

Other librarians responded that a public library's duty was to supply its users with the books of most interest to them. They believed that democratic principles should operate in libraries as well as society. These librarians were increasingly conscious of the importance of the freedom to read and the right of each reader to find what he or she liked best. In 1939, the ALA adopted the first "Library Bill of Rights" to provide an official statement against censorship and to oppose pressures on the freedom of citizens to read what they wished. Lester Asheim, in his 1953 paper, "Not Censorship but Selection," stressed the concept of selection as choosing good books instead of excluding the bad ones.[41] Librarians in the second half of the twentieth century began promoting the ideal that subjects should be covered evenly or equally within collections. Balanced coverage has meant seeking to select materials representing all viewpoints on important and controversial issues. Librarians have become increasingly aware of their responsibilities to be attentive to both content and format in selection of library materials.

Collection Development and Management as a Specialization

A preconference held before the ALA Annual Conference in Detroit in 1977 is often identified as the landmark event recognizing collection development as a new specialization in librarianship. Conducted by the then new Collection Development Committee of the Resources Section of ALA's Resources and Technical Services Division (RTSD), the preconference and the section were created and organized by a group of forward-looking librarians including Juanita Doares, Sheila Dowd, Hendrik Edelman, Murray Martin, Paul H. Mosher, and David Zubatsky.

The volume of new publications was increasing rapidly, the publishing world was becoming more complex, and steady acquisitions budgets had slowed libraries' expansion. Part-time faculty selectors and librarians without special expertise could no longer manage selection adequately. The planners, who were primarily academic librarians, of the 1977 preconference saw a need to develop research collections in a more solid, conscious, planned, and documented manner. They called this new specialization "collection development" to distinguish it from acquisitions. The goal of the 1977 preconference was to educate the library profession about this new subdiscipline of collection development, its nature, components, and functions. The first *Guidelines for Collection Development,* published by the Collection Development Committee, RTSD, ALA, followed soon after the preconference.[42] This 1979 publication has been revised and published as several numbers with narrower foci in the Collection Management and Development Guides series.

The first Collection Management and Development Institute, sponsored by RTSD's (now Association of Library Resources and Technical Services) Collection Development Committee, was held at Stanford in 1981. Planners increasingly were aware that the management of collections—not just their development and growth—was the primary issue for the future of this new specialization. They focused on boundary-spanning aspects, including the integration of collection management with acquisitions and other internal library operations and services, and working closely with interested constituents. They sought to define collection management in ways that had meaning to librarians in all types of libraries.

Many professional groups were focusing on collection development and management in the early 1980s. The Public Library Association sponsored a preconference in 1984.[43] The Association of Research Libraries established a Collection Development Committee, the Research Libraries Group initiated a Collection Management and Development Committee, and other divisions within ALA, including the Reference and Adult Services Division (now Reference and User Services Association) and the Association of College and Research Libraries, formed committees that concentrated on collection development and management. While collection development always has been closely associated with acquisitions, these two functions began to be separated, with acquisitions more typically associated with technical services units and collection development and management as separate or, perhaps, allied with public services.

In the late 1970s and 1980s, the profession took up collection management as a cause célèbre. Numerous textbooks, manuals, overviews, and journal articles were published. Specialized journals, including *Collection Management* (1976), *Collection Building* (1983), and *Library Collections, Acquisitions and Technical Services,* previously *Library Acquisitions: Practice and Theory* (1977), began publication. Several textbooks on collection development, which was more broadly defined than acquisitions or selection, appeared in the 1970s. Research in the field was summarized in the important publication *Collection Development in Libraries: A Treatise.*[44]

By the mid-1980s, most professional library schools were offering one or more courses focusing on collection development and management. Richard Kryzs identified the topics covered in a basic collection development course of the time.[45] These included historical background of books and libraries, types of libraries and their communities, library materials, publishers and publishing, selection of materials, acquisition of material, and collection evaluation, which covered storage, weeding, preservation, and replacement decisions. In 1991, a final step in the definition of collection development and management as a distinct speciality occurred when the Resources Section in ALA's Association for Library Collection and Technical Services split into the Acquisitions Section and the Collection Management and Development Section.

Trends and the Future of Collection Management

Earlier sections in this chapter have described the forces at work on and in libraries as the twenty-first century began. Predicting the future is risky, especially in times of rapid change. This is particularly perilous when the most powerful influences at work are rapidly evolving technologies for creating, organizing, storing, delivering, and retrieving information resources. Suggesting how librarians and their libraries might and should seek to shape their roles in that hazy future is a combination of guessing and hoping, based on what is known now.

Evolving Technologies

Librarians are preoccupied with the impact of electronic information on library operations, collections, and services. More significant for library planning are the cultural and psychological consequences of mass media and technology on society because society shapes libraries more than librarians do. Marshall McLuhan was an early student of the role of the information explosion on societal change.[46] He compared the effects of the wide and inexpensive distribution of information made possible after the appearance of the printing press in 1456 with those resulting from mass media in the middle of the twentieth century. Just as the printing press made possible consistencies in language, literature, law, religion, and education never before experienced, McLuhan predicted a unified and uniform global society resulting from worldwide access to the same media.

While the advent of television programming broadcast via satellites and global phone, fax, and Internet services have eliminated time and distance as barriers, a global society as envisioned by McLuhan remains far from reality. One result of electronic communication becomes communication for and by increasingly specialized groups. Scholars in arcane disciplines can work with colleagues nearly anywhere in the world. Individuals with narrow and specialized interests (from fans of a particular rock band to collectors of salt and pepper shakers) can locate and chat with like-minded persons. Fanzines are published electronically for readers groups of three individuals. Very small communities with shared interests are possible in the digital era.

Simultaneously, the ease of communication and distribution of information facilitates the crossing of traditional boundaries in scholarship, culture, and politics. Interdisciplinary research is much easier. New social, political, cultural, and educational coalitions and partnerships are possible and developing constantly. Age, race, sex, and physical traits are not obvious when mediated by computers. Novice and professional, student and teacher can meet as equals. Only economic condition currently places limits on computer-based access to information and communication. During the Clinton administration, the U.S. government provided funding to overcome disparity through increasing availability of computers and Internet access in schools, public libraries, and community centers.

The Digital Divide

Government reports produced by the National Telecommunications and Information Administration (NTIA) in the 1990s and 2000s have used U.S. Department of Commerce Census Bureau data to track the extent to which computer availability and access to the Internet are changing. Reports during the Clinton administration were titled *Falling through the Net* and focused on the need to bridge what was called the digital divide.[47] U.S. census data show significant changes in just the three years between 1997 and 2000. During this period, homes with computers went from 36.6 percent to 51 percent, and homes with Internet access went from 18 percent to 41.5 percent.[48] In September 2001, 56.5 percent had personal computers in the home, and 50.5 percent had Internet access in the home.[49] However, this means that many people have Internet access only outside the home, either through work (which excludes children) or a community access center, such as a school or library.

One area in which federal legislation has positively influenced connectivity is in the rapid increase in Internet access in U.S. schools. The U.S. government set a goal of Internet access in all schools by the year 2000. Data reported by the National Center for Education Statistics, an agency of the federal government, show this goal was nearly achieved.[50] In 1994, 35 percent of public schools in the United States provided Internet access. By the fall of 2000, 98 percent had access to the Internet. A second goal, to have every instructional room connected to the Internet, showed an increase from 3 percent in 1994 to 77 percent in 2000. Connectivity increased in schools with the highest concentration of poverty (up to 60 percent) and in schools with the highest minority enrollment (up 64 percent). The increase in Internet access through the schools over the years was aided by the allocation of funds through the Education rate (Erate) program. The Erate program was established by the Telecommunications Act of 1996 to make services, Internet access, and internal connections available to schools and libraries at discounted rates based upon the income level of the students in their community and whether their location is urban or rural. As of February 28, 2001, $5.8 billion had been committed to Erate applicants throughout the nation.

In early 2002, the Bush administration sought to strip more than $100 million in public investments previously available annually for community technology grants and information technology training programs. A nationwide study, *A Nation Online*, the successor to the *Digital Divide* reports, was intended to show that the digital divide was no longer a concern.[51] However, while documenting increased connectivity, the report showed that gaps in technology access among citizens of different educational, income, racial, and geographic backgrounds were not abating, and gaps between the poorest and the wealthiest households expanded dramatically. Among people with low family incomes, 75 percent of households with an income less than $15,000 and 66.6 percent of households with incomes between $15,000 and $35,000 are without access. Further, 87.2 percent of adults with less than a high school education, 68.4 percent of all Hispanics, and 60.2 percent of blacks are without access. These are the people who depend on Internet access through public agencies— schools, libraries, and community centers.

In response to the Bush administration's stance, the Leadership Conference on Civil Rights Education Fund and the Benton Foundation released a report that concluded continued federal leadership to be essential in bringing the nation online, given the significant technology gaps that remain for those in specific economic, racial, and geographic groups.[52] This report stated that libraries play a critical role in Internet access for low-income families and cites data in the NTIA study showing that 10 percent of Internet users' only access to the Internet is at a public library. Reliance on Internet access at public libraries is more common among those with lower incomes than those with higher incomes. Slightly more than 20 percent of Internet users with household family incomes of less than $15,000 a year depend on public libraries. Among racial and ethnic groups, 12.7 percent of whites, 19.4 percent of blacks, and 16 percent of Hispanics using the Internet at libraries do not also access the Internet from home, work, or school. Schools and libraries are helping to equalize the disparities that would otherwise exist in computer and Internet use among various household income categories and racial groups.

Library Users

Mary Louise Pratt developed the theory of "contact zones" to refer to social spaces where cultures meet, clash, and grapple with each other.[53] Pratt's contact zones are characterized by highly asymmetrical relations of power. She emphasizes the conditions of difficulty and struggle under which literatures from different cultures come together and the tendency of the dominant culture to be restrictive and egocentric, while the subordinate culture appropriates from the dominant culture and responds in creative ways. Parallels can be found in the ways libraries are grappling with the changing society of which they are a part. Power as access to information resources is still asymmetrical. While librarians cannot control what emanates from the dominant culture, librarians can decide what gets absorbed into libraries. Ethnographers call this *transculturation*—both a complex mixing of cultures and the process by which members of subordinated groups select and invent from materials transmitted by the dominant culture. Librarians should look at the changing society of which their libraries are a part and concentrate on it as well as on the force for change, technology.

Several librarians have written about the role of libraries and their collections as transmitters of culture.[54] Library collections document and preserve viewpoints, perceptions, and interpretations and are social, artistic, and political expressions. Though librarians espouse unbiased selection, each decision reflects a personal perspective, made within the context of the dominant or dominating cultures. Sensitivity to changes in those cultures is essential for effective libraries.

Librarians must know their communities and continually assess user expectations and needs so they can reach the proper balance of traditional and innovative collections and services. The impact of computers and telecommunication results in several characteristics that define contemporary library users and the potential user community. Rapid bibliographic access is creating a parallel desire for rapid resource delivery. Users do not want to wait for information resources. They want the elimination of barriers between themselves and the information they seek and between information formats. They expect online literature to be fully searchable and complete with high-quality color graphics, tables, and equations. Access to all resources should be easy, efficient, timely, and transparent. Users consider remote access as an acceptable alternative to local ownership if that access is speedy. Advances in hardware, software, and connectivity suggest that local ownership will become increasingly less relevant. Users are not seeking information independence to the extent some have predicted. Users continue to want mediated services and expect more help, either face-to-face or online, locating and obtaining the resources they seek. Users want easy access to electronic information, and they want to continue to find print materials.

How will librarians respond to these needs and expectations? They will play an aggressive role in providing effective intellectual access. They will help develop extensive navigational tools that integrate access to traditional and electronic resources. They will take greater responsibility in selecting and pointing to digital resources via web pages and ensuring that traditional cataloging provides hyperlinks to the resources themselves. They will be comfortable with collections and services that reach beyond a library's physical location. Librarians will become heavily involved in developing standards for future information formats and their organization. Academic and research librarians will play a major role in integrating scholarship in the online environment.

Demographic, social, and economic characteristics and the ways in which they are changing will be of critical importance. Librarians who shape collections must be sensitive to such trends as increasing ethnic and cultural diversity, an aging population, greater disparity in educational and income levels, popularity of distance education programs, and changes in family composition. User communities are becoming more heterogeneous, and collections librarians must develop and manage collections in response.

Publishing Trends

Commercial journal and monographic publishers are growing larger as they buy and absorb competitors. They are less likely to publish items that are perceived to appeal to limited audiences. The volume of publications worldwide is continuing to increase. New information providers appear with great frequency. Evolving technologies mean that any individual can self-publish or disseminate a work at low cost and quickly. The means of distribution are altering. Some scholars are reclaiming publication of scholarly journals from the commercial sector. Interoperability standards, which facilitate sharing of data between different hardware configurations and software, are increasingly important to commercial publishers, who aim to protect their investments, and to scholars and researchers, who seek wider access to digital resources. Commercial publishers, scholarly societies, and university presses are moving rapidly to electronic publications, particularly journals, indexing and abstracting sources, and reference sources. The volume of electronic information will continue to grow. Publishers will continue to grapple with pricing models for electronic information as they learn more about the cost of publishing and the market. More scholarly journals will shift to electronic distribution only.

Publishers, information service vendors, and others in the commercial and academic sectors are becoming aggregators of digital information collections and services. They offer packages of indexing and abstracting tools and full-text collections of current literature, government documents, journal articles, and journal back runs and combinations of documents with indexes and abstracts. They combine electronic access to these collections with document delivery services. Centralized document delivery systems and the services they provide will continue to increase. Libraries will increase use of these combinations of online catalogs and indexing and abstracting tools with full-text documents and document delivery services.

Scholars will make progress toward regaining publication control of their research. Academic libraries, working with academic presses and campus computing centers, will begin to assume responsibility for disseminating scholarly information. Various libraries will take primary responsibility for certain disciplines, building electronic files of documents vetted by peers for worldwide use. Librarians will have a principal role in the organization of these databases and their intellectual access.

Legal Issues

The ownership rights to information are being questioned and revised. Publishers and authors are seeking revisions in copyright law and new interpretations of fair use to protect intellectual property. Copyright holders' efforts to strengthen and enforce their rights will continue. As more journals are canceled and fewer monographs are purchased, collections librarians will need to pay closer attention to changes in the law of copyright and its effects. Publishers and distributors of electronic information are using the law of contracts to reinforce ownership and control of their products. Because electronic text can be used in various forms, sold and resold by various vendors, and manipulated by various users, licensing and contracts become critically important to authors, publishers, distributors, and libraries. Negotiating contracts and license agreements will become an increasingly important duty of collections librarians.

Telecommunication and Computing Power

The percentage of the population with personal computers and remote access capabilities will continue to increase. The ability to escape the traditional constraints of distance and time means that libraries will have a growing number of users, both remote and on-site. Remote users will search online catalogs and learn about collections. Use of print materials will increase because more people will learn about specific libraries' holdings. Librarians will allocate financial resources for interlibrary loan staff, mail budgets, fax equipment, and digital document transmission to satisfy remote users. They will face decisions about how best to preserve and conserve all types of collections as use increases.

The opening of library catalogs to remote users, along with access to an endless variety and number of files outside library collections and their catalogs, creates a role for librarians as information guides or mediators. Librarians must be prepared and willing to guide users to files, no matter where they are stored, and ready to advise on retrieving them. Librarians have a mission to provide access to information and sources that have been inaccessible and unknown.

Librarians must be sensitive to specialization and to cross-disciplinary initiatives. They need to learn new vocabularies and become comfortable providing services to a variety of users. Librarians must move toward collaboration across disciplinary divisions within the library and recognize that more and more resources become relevant.

Costs and Funding

Materials costs and publication volume will continue escalating faster than library budgets. The boom years that followed the Library Services Act of 1956 and the Higher Education Act of 1965 will not return. Libraries will continue to be unable to acquire all the materials they would like to own locally to support user needs and wants. Digital information will not save libraries money. Librarians will become even more selective about what they acquire and to which they provide remote access. Librarians will reallocate budgets continually to meet users' needs, cope with rising demands, and adapt to new business models in the publishing industry.

Libraries will begin to charge for some services, passing on to users the costs. Just as the profit sector will continue to unbundle services and products and charge separately for them, so too will libraries. These may include rush processing and notification of material availability, document delivery, sophisticated reference services, recalling materials in response to user requests, and local printing of information delivered electronically.

Selection

The role of selection will become increasingly important in libraries because of the hard choices caused by the economic situation, growth in the output of information resources, and the need to build two libraries simultaneously, a digital one and a traditional one. Libraries will continue to acquire materials for the foreseeable future, but they will balance more systematically what is acquired locally with what is accessed remotely and borrowed from other libraries. Librarians will need to know more about their users' needs to purchase those materials needed on-site. Access and just-in-time delivery will increase in importance, and collections librarians will guide decisions about budget allocation to support these services. Current criteria for selection and collection management decisions will be refined and applied to all materials, regardless of format. Collections librarians will spend more time and energy focusing on cost and benefits and product effectiveness. They will work closely with automation librarians to compare interfaces, security models, response time, and local hardware and software capabilities. They will make choices about how to deliver electronic information based on user preferences, selecting, for example, digitized page images or marked-up text as appropriate. Collections librarians will make better use of analysis data collected from their local systems—circulation, use of online resources, and so forth—to guide their selection. Collection assessment and evaluation and user analysis will increase in importance as librarians make difficult choices about what to acquire locally, access remotely, purchase when requested, preserve, store, cancel, and withdraw.

Collaboration and Partnerships

Cooperative collection development will attain its promise. Librarians will be forced to coordinate local collection building with regional and national cooperative collection development programs to ensure that access to comprehensive national collections is maintained. Libraries will increase their participation in consortia and partner with local, statewide, regional, and national groups of libraries both to assign collecting and preserving responsibilities and to obtain buying-group discounts for electronic resources. Collections librarians will take on responsibility for developing subject-based web pages within these consortia, dividing the work of identifying and organizing digital information resources.

Preservation

The continuing deterioration of print collections and new problems maintaining digital resources will make conservation and preservation unavoidable concerns for collections librarians. Ensuring digital information integrity will be compounded by the speed with which technologies will become out-of-date. Preserving digital resources will remain labor-intensive and costly. Every library will face decisions about what to conserve and what to preserve and how to fit these priorities within an already strained budget. Cooperation among libraries to address preservation will increase more rapidly than in other areas. Partnerships will expand to include publishers, the federal government, funding organizations, and other information providers. Publishers will cease to see older back files of journals as major revenue sources and be more willing to work with libraries to preserve and make them accessible to users. Collections librarians will work with publishers and producers in identifying priorities for conversion of print-based resources to digital format and work together to develop and market these products.

Staffing for Collection Development and Management

The number of librarians who have only collection development and management responsibilities will continue to decline. Librarians who build and manage collections will have additional responsibilities. They will work across traditional organizational boundaries in the library because of the complexities of developing and managing collections that are both digital and print-based. Individuals will select in a number of subject areas. They will implement new methods of creating collections, purchasing materials, borrowing materials, and purchasing the right to on-demand access to materials.

Good collection development and management will be more difficult, take more time, and require broader expertise as librarians work with limited funding, various formats, and an increasing volume of publications. Collections librarians will become active managers of knowledge, more proactively involved in the processes of locating, acquiring, managing, and delivering information to users. They will have an active role in bringing order to the chaos of the Internet. The ease of accessing all types of information through the Internet will bring increased attention to libraries' roles as gatekeepers and censors. Librarians will have greater responsibility to understand and comply with legislation dealing with issues, such as copyright and fair use and Internet filtering.

Libraries will develop new organizational structures and collection development, and management units may include interlibrary loan and document delivery. The separation between selectors and acquisitions staff members will blur again as selectors work directly with vendor and publisher databases. They will initiate orders as part of the process of identifying materials for acquisition and access. Business and accounting skills, including cost-benefit analysis and performance measurement, will grow in importance as budgets become more complicated and collections librarians are required to demonstrate accountability. Outsourcing will increase in importance as vendors develop the capability to offer approval plans for consortia and as librarians rely on aggregators to provide collections of digital resources. Collections librarians in libraries of all types will be comfortable functioning in a dual environment—one that is simultaneously digital and print-based.

Summary

The theory and practice of collection development and management have its origins in the selection of materials for library acquisition. In early U.S. libraries, a combination of limited budgets and a small volume in publications caused selection per se to receive little attention. Decisions about what to acquire were in the hands of faculty and trustee boards. As acquisitions budgets and the number of materials being published increased and librarianship developed as a profession in the second half of the nineteenth century, selection responsibilities shifted to librarians in public libraries. Following the Second World War, the same transition occurred in academic libraries.

A tension between collecting as much as possible and collecting only the best and most appropriate has been a constant feature of library selection. This is coupled with defining what is good and appropriate and balancing user demand against librarians' perception of value. Public librarians have struggled with the role of popular fiction in their collections and how to fulfill their mission as a public institution, funded to serve the public interest. Much early theory of selection for public libraries focused on the responsibilities of libraries to lead their readers to the "better" works. In the twentieth century, librarians began to consider the implications of intentional and unintentional censorship and libraries' responsibilities for guaranteeing intellectual freedom and the right to read what one wishes. Librarians began to strive for broad and even coverage in collections. Balancing immediate need and long-term responsibilities to develop collections remains a troubling issue.

Collection development and management as a speciality can be traced to the 1970s, when professional associations, conferences and institutes, and professional literature began focusing on a variety of collections responsibilities in addition to selecting materials. Collection development and management is now understood to include selection; the determination and coordination of selection policy; assessment of the needs of users and potential users; collection use studies; collection analysis; budget management; identification of collection needs; community and user outreach and liaison; planning for resource sharing; decisions about weeding, storage, and preservation; and the organization and assignment of responsibilities for its practice.

Tremendous and continuing growth in worldwide publications, rapidly inflating prices for information in all formats, and library budgets unable to accommodate either have stressed libraries and collections librarians since the late 1970s. Simultaneously, deteriorating print collections are requiring decisions about appropriate preservation expenditures within already strained budgets. These pressures have been compounded by the electronic information explosion and user expectations about the services, collections, and access that libraries should provide.

The future of collection development will be influenced by the rapid spread of digital technology both as a means for information creation, access, and delivery and as a primary influence on society. Electronic formats are leading to libraries that extend beyond their physical walls and see their collections as drawing from all the information sources that can be found and used without regard to location or time. The global network is creating a new community of resources and information and of seekers after resources and information. The intrinsic nature of society and how it defines and perceives itself is changing. This is the contact zone on which librarians should concentrate and the direction in which their future lies.

Collections librarians will serve a primary role in developing this collection and adapting current collection development and management tools and methods to this new environment. The practice of building and maintaining collections will change while the mission of libraries will remain constant—ensuring that the carriers of recorded knowledge and information of all kinds are acquired, organized, made accessible, and preserved while simultaneously seeking to save users' time and effort and maximize library cost-effectiveness. The future of collection development and management will depend on how successfully librarians mediate the new world of information for users and the extent to which users perceive this success.

REFERENCES

1. Paul H. Mosher, "Collection Development to Collection Management: Toward Stewardship of Library Resources," *Collection Management* 4, no. 4 (winter 1982): 45.
2. Bonita Bryant, "The Organizational Structure of Collection Development," *Library Resources and Technical Services* 31 (1987): 118–29.
3. Charles B. Osburn, "Collection Development and Management," in *Academic Libraries: Research Perspectives*, ed. Mary Jo Lynch, ACRL Publications in Librarianship, no. 47 (Chicago: American Library Assn., 1990), 1.
4. Michael R. Gabriel, *Collection Development and Evaluation: A Sourcebook* (Lanham, Md.: Scarecrow, 1995), 3.
5. Gabriel Naudé, *Advice on Establishing a Library*, with an introduction by Archer Taylor (Berkeley: Univ. of California Pr., 1950), 17.
6. Jean-Baptiste Cotton des Houssayes, *The Duties and Qualifications of a Librarian*, English translation (Chicago: A. C. McClurg, 1906), 43.
7. Howard Clayton, "The American College Library, 1800–1860," *Journal of Library History* 3 (April 1968): 132.
8. Louis Shores, *Origins of the American College Library, 1638–1800* (Nashville, Tenn.: George Peabody College, 1934), 109.
9. Arthur T. Hamlin, *The University Library in the United States* (Philadelphia: Univ. of Pennsylvania Pr., 1981), 19.
10. Orvin Lee Shiflett, *Origins of American Academic Librarianship* (Norwood, N.J.: Ablex, 1981), 29–31.
11. Shores, *Origins of the American College Library, 1638–1800*, 51–56.
12. George Livermore, *Remarks on Public Libraries* (Cambridge, Mass.: Bolls and Houghton, 1850), 17.
13. Michael K. Buckland, "The Roles of Collections and the Scope of Collection Development," *Journal of Documentation* 45 (Sept. 1989): 215.
14. Shiflett, *Origins of American Academic Librarianship*, 29–31.
15. Margaret Ann Johnson, *Christian Gottlob Heyne as Librarian* (master's thesis, Univ. of Chicago Graduate Library School, 1973).
16. U.S. Office of Education, Bulletin, 1930. No. 9, *Survey of Land-Grant Colleges and Universities*, 2 vols. (Washington, D.C.: Govt. Print. Off., 1930), 1:651.

17. Jesse H. Shera's *Foundations of the Public Library: The Origins of the Public Library Movement in New England 1629–1855* (Chicago: Univ. of Chicago Pr., 1949) is the classic history of public libraries and the source of information presented here.

18. James C. Baughman, "Sense Is Preferable to Sound," *Library Journal* 111 (Oct. 1986): 44.

19. Boston Public Library, *Upon The Objects to Be Attained by The Establishment of a Public Library: Report of The Trustees of The Public Library of the City of Boston, July, 1852* (1852; reprint, Boston: Hall, 1975), 8–9.

20. John Cotton Dana, *A Library Primer* (Chicago: Library Bureau, 1899), 39.

21. Edward G. Holley, "North American Efforts at Worldwide Acquisitions since 1945," *Collection Management* 9 (summer/fall 1987): 89–111.

22. Fremont Rider, *The Scholar and the Future of the Research Library* (New York: Hadham, 1944), 3–19.

23. Kenneth J. Braugh, *Scholars Workshop: Evolving Concepts of Library Service* (Urbana: Univ. of Illinois Pr., 1953), 99.

24. Jeanne Sohn, "Cooperative Collection Development: A Brief Overview," *Collection Management* 8, no. 2 (summer 1986): 4.

25. Association of Research Libraries, "Monograph and Serial Costs in ARL Libraries, 1986–2002," available at http://www.arl.org/stats/arlstat/graphs/2002/2002t2.html. Information at this site is updated annually as ARL member libraries statistics are added.

26. Maurice B. Line, "Interlending and Document Supply in a Changing World," in *Interlending and Document Supply: Proceedings of the First International Conference Held in London, November, 1988,* ed. Graham P. Cornish and Alison Gallicao (Ballston Spa, England: IFLA Office for International Lending, 1989), 1.

27. Patricia Battin, "Libraries, Computers and Scholarship," *Wilson Library Bulletin* 56, no. 8 (April 1982): 580.

28. Arthur E. Bostwick, "Librarian as a Censor," *Library Journal* 33 (July 1908): 257–59.

29. William F. Poole, "The Organization and Management of Public Libraries," in *Public Libraries in the United States: Their History, Condition, and Management,* Part I (Washington, D.C.: Govt. Print. Off., 1876), 479–80.

30. Cornelia Marvin, "No New Fiction during the War," *Public Libraries* 22 (Dec. 1917): 409.

31. American Library Association, "Our Libraries and the War," *Library Journal* 42 (Aug. 1917): 606–11.

32. Carl B. Roden, "The Library in Hard Times," *Library Journal* 56 (Dec. 1, 1931): 986.

33. Esther Jane Carrier, *Fiction in Public Libraries, 1876–1900* (New York: Scarecrow, 1965) and her *Fiction in Public Libraries, 1900–1950* (Littleton, Colo.: Libraries Unlimited, 1985). For explorations of the manner in which librarians' cultural and social attitudes and biases have affected their theories of selection and service, *see* Lee Garrison, *Apostles of Culture: The Public Librarian and American Society, 1876–1920* (New York: The Free Press, 1979); and Evelyn Geller, *Forbidden Books in American Public Libraries, 1879–1939: A Study in Cultural Change* (Westport, Conn.: Greenwood, 1984).

34. Francis K. W. Drury, *Book Selection* (Chicago: American Library Assn., 1930); Helen Haines, *Living with Books: The Art of Book Selection* (New York: Columbia Univ. Pr., 1935).
35. Haines, *Living with Books*, 3.
36. Drury, *Book Selection*, xii–xiii.
37. Ibid., 2.
38. Leon Carnovsky, "The Role of the Public Library: Implications for Library Education," in *The Intellectual Foundations of Library Education*, ed. Don R. Swanson (Chicago: Univ. of Chicago Pr., 1965), 13–23.
39. Leon Carnovsky, "Community Analysis and the Practice of Book Selection," in *The Practice of Book Selection*, ed. Louis R. Wilson (Chicago: Univ. of Chicago Pr., 1940), 27.
40. Bernard Berelson, *The Library's Public* (New York: Columbia Univ. Pr., 1949), 148.
41. Lester Asheim, "Not Censorship but Selection," *Wilson Library Bulletin* 28 (Sept. 1953): 63–67. *See also* his "Selection and Censorship: A Reappraisal," *Wilson Library Bulletin* 58 (Nov. 1983): 180–84.
42. David L. Perkins, ed., *Guidelines for Collection Development* (Chicago: Collection Development Committee, Resources and Technical Services Division, American Library Assn., 1979).
43. Judith Serebnick, ed., *Collection Management in Public Libraries: Proceedings of a Preconference to the 1984 ALA Annual Conference, June 21–22, 1984, Dallas* (Chicago: American Library Assn., 1986).
44. Robert D. Stueart and George B. Miller Jr., eds., *Collection Development in Libraries: A Treatise*, 2 vols., Foundations in Library and Information Science, v. 10 (Greenwich, Conn.: JAI Pr., 1980). A new collection of essays updated this publication—Charles B. Osburn and Ross Atkinson, eds., *Collection Management: A New Treatise*, 2 vols., Foundations in Library and Information Science, v. 26 (Greenwich, Conn.: JAI Pr., 1991).
45. Richard Kryzs, "Collection Development Courses," in *Internationalizing Library and Information Science Education: A Handbook of Policies and Procedures in Administration and Curriculum*, ed. John F. Harvey and Frances Laverne Carroll (New York: Greenwood, 1987), 201–14. More recent studies of curricula have been conducted by John M. Budd and Patricia L. Brill, "Education for Collection Management: Results of a Survey of Educators and Practitioners," *Library Resources and Technical Services* 38, no. 4 (Oct. 1994): 343–53; and Paul Metz, "Collection Development in the Library and Information Science Curriculum," in *Recruiting, Educating, and Training Librarians for Collection Development*, ed. Peggy Johnson and Sheila S. Intner, 87–97 (Westport, Conn.: Greenwood, 1994).
46. Marshall McLuhan, *The Gutenberg Galaxy: The Making of Typographic Man* (Toronto: Univ. of Toronto Pr., 1962), and his *Understanding Media: The Extensions of Man* (New York: McGraw-Hill, 1964).
47. U.S. Dept. of Commerce and National Telecommunications and Information Administration, *Falling through the Net* reports 1 through 4 were issued in 1995, 1998, 1999, and 2000, available at http://www.ntia.doc.gov/ntiahome/digitaldivide/.

48. U.S. Census Bureau, *Computer Use and Ownership,* available at http://www. census.gov/population/www/socdemo/computer.html.
49. National Telecommunications and Information Administration and the Economics and Statistics Administration, *A Nation Online: How Americans Are Expanding Their Use of the Internet* (Feb. 2002), available at http://www. ntia.doc.gov/ntiahome/dn/index.html.
50. National Center for Education Statistics, *Internet Access in U.S. Public Schools and Classrooms: 1994–2000* (2001), available at http://nces.ed.gov/pubs2001/ InternetAccess/2.asp.
51. National Telecommunications and Information Administration and the Economics and Statistics Administration, *A Nation Online.*
52. *Bringing a Nation Online: The Importance of Federal Leadership* (Benton Foundation and Leadership Conference on Civil Rights Education Fund), available at http://www.benton.org/publibrary/nationonline/bringing_a_nation.html. *See also* Norris Dickard, *Federal Retrenchment on the Digital Divide: Potential National Impact,* Policy Brief, no. 1 (March 18, 2002), issued by the Benton Foundation, available at http://www.benton.org/publibrary/policybriefs/ brief01.html.
53. Mary Louise Pratt, "Acts of the Contact Zone," *Profession* (1991): 33–40.
54. *See* Michael Harris, "State, Class, and Cultural Reproduction: Toward a Theory of Library Service in the United States," *Advances in Librarianship* 14 (1986): 211–52; and Marlene Manoff, "Academic Libraries and the Culture Wars: The Politics of Collection Development," *Collection Management* 16, no. 4 (1992): 1–17.

SUGGESTED READINGS

Atkinson, Ross. "Contingency and Contradiction: The Place(s) of the Library at the Dawn of the New Millennium." *Journal of the American Society of Information Science and Technology* 52, no. 1 (2001): 3–11.

Bobinski, George S. "Public Librarianship: An Appreciation and a Profile." *Public Libraries* 28 (Nov./Dec. 1989): 355–57.

Branin, Joseph. "Shifting Boundaries: Managing Research Library Collections at the Beginning of the Twenty-first Century." In *Cooperative Collection Development: Significant Trends and Issues,* edited by Donald B. Simpson, 1–17. New York: Haworth, 1998. Also published in *Collection Management* 23, no. 4 (1998).

Branin, Joseph, Frances Groen, and Suzanne Thorin. "The Changing Nature of Collection Management in Research Libraries." *Library Resources and Technical Services* 44, no. 1 (Jan. 2000): 23–32.

Budd, John M., and Bart M. Harloe. "The Future for Collection Management." In *Collection Management for the Twenty-first Century: A Handbook for Librarians,* edited by G. E. Gorman and Ruth H. Miller, 3–28. Contributions in Librarianship and Information Science, no. 96. Westport, Conn.: Greenwood, 1997.

Carrigan, Dennis P. "Toward a Theory of Collection Development." *Library Acquisitions: Practice and Theory* 19 (spring 1995): 97–106.

Cassell, Kay Ann, and Elizabeth Futas. *Developing Public Library Collections, Policies, and Procedures.* New York: Neal-Schuman Publishers, 1991.

Clayton, Peter, and G. E. Gorman. *Managing Information Resources in Libraries: Collection Management in Theory and Practice.* London: Library Assn. Pub., 2001.

Garrison, Dee. *Apostles of Culture: The Public Librarian and American Society, 1876–1920.* New York: The Free Press, 1979.

Hanson, Eugene R. "College and University Libraries: Traditions, Trends, and Technology." *Advances in Library Administration and Organization* 7 (1988): 209–44.

Holley, Edward G. "Academic Libraries in 1876." *College and Research Libraries* 37, no. 1 (Jan. 1976): 15–47.

Jenkins, Clare, and Mary Morley, eds. *Collection Management in Academic Libraries.* 2d ed. Aldershot, Hampshire, England, and Brookfield, Vt.: Gower, 1999.

Johnson, Peggy, and Bonnie MacEwan, eds. *Virtually Yours: Models for Managing Electronic Resources and Services: Proceedings of the Joint Reference and User Services Association and Association for Library Collections and Technical Services Institute, Chicago, Illinois, October 23–25, 1997.* ALCTS Papers on Library Technical Services and Collections, no. 8. Chicago: American Library Assn., 1999.

Nilsen, Kirsti S. "Collection Development Issues of Academic and Public Libraries: Converging or Diverging?" *Collection Building* 13, no. 4 (1994): 9–17.

Osburn, Charles B. "Toward a Reconceptualization of Collection Development." *Advances in Library Administration and Organization* 2 (1983): 175–98.

Osburn, Charles B., and Ross Atkinson, eds. *Collection Management: A New Treatise.* 2 vols. Foundations in Library and Information Science, v. 26. Greenwich, Conn.: JAI Pr., 1991.

Pankake, Marcia. "From Book Selection to Collection Management: Continuity and Advances in an Unending Work." *Advances in Librarianship* 13 (1984): 185–220.

Raber, Douglas. *Librarianship and Legitimacy: The Ideology of the Public Library Inquiry.* Contributions in Librarianship and Information Science, no. 90. Westport, Conn.: Greenwood, 1997.

Zhou, Yuan. "From Smart Guesser to Smart Navigator: Changes in Collection Development for Research Libraries in a Network Environment." *Library Trends* 42, no. 4 (spring 1994): 648–60.

| Organization and Staffing

Introduction

This chapter considers, in general terms, the tasks that make up collection development and management and the place of collection development and management within the library organization. Various tasks, functions, and responsibilities are explored in greater depth in subsequent chapters. Also addressed in this chapter are desired competencies, ethical issues associated with the practice of collection development and management, the effects of automation of the work of collections librarians, a phenomenon known as deskilling, on-site training for collections librarians, and performance evaluation.

Responsibilities and Their Assignment

Collection development and management encompass a suite of activities. Not all collections librarians have all responsibilities that can fall under the heading of collection development and management. However, most librarians who have a title of or an assignment as selector, bibliographer, subject or area specialist, collection development or collection management librarian, or collections librarian will perform several of these functions. The usual list of responsibilities follows:

Selecting:
- Choosing current materials in one or more formats for acquisition and access
- Selecting access methods for digital resources
- Deciding upon retrospective materials for acquisition and access
- Choosing which gift materials to accept
- Selecting materials to withdraw, store, preserve, digitize, and cancel

Budgeting:
- Requesting and justifying budget allocations
- Managing budgets
- Working with donors and potential donors of in-kind and cash gifts
- Grant proposal writing and grants management

Planning and organizing:
- Coordinating collection development and management activities with others within the library
- Monitoring and reviewing approval plans
- Monitoring and reviewing exchange agreements
- Evaluating and assessing collections and related services
- Initiating and monitoring cooperative collection development activities
- Writing and revising collection development policies

Communicating and reporting:
- Serving on internal and external committees dealing with collections issues
- Promoting, marketing, and interpreting collections and resources
- Performing liaison and outreach responsibilities
- Acting as liaison with other libraries and librarians

One possible responsibility not listed in this summary is the preparation of bibliographies, once routinely taught in library school courses. Although some collections librarians do prepare both analytical and enumerative bibliographies of varying lengths, this function is not as common as those identified above.[1] Developing a library web site that is subject- or user-based and that lists and points to related resources is beginning to replace the preparation of bibliographies.

Assignment of responsibilities and placement of collections activities within the organization vary with the size of the library and its budget, its mission, and its user community. In small libraries, all activities may be handled by one individual. In very large libraries, responsibilities may be highly centralized or widely dispersed according to subject responsibility, user community, physical location of staff members, or subset of functions within the many that are considered collection development and management activities.

The contemporary understanding of collection development and management as an inclusive set of coherent activities mandates close coordination between activities when they are handled by different individuals or by different units. When a single individual does not perform all functions identified in the list above, he or she usually works closely with those who handle these related tasks. For example, a preservation unit may identify items in need of treatment and recommend alternatives but rely on the collection management librarian to decide if the item should be withdrawn, replaced, preserved, or conserved. Choosing an approval plan vendor may be the joint responsibility of the acquisitions unit and the collection development unit. A collections librarian cannot develop and manage a collection effectively without in-depth knowledge of everything affecting that collection.

Subject Specialists

The idea of subject specialist positions responsible for portions of the collection was developed in Germany in the 1800s. German academic libraries began the practice of placing selection in specific fields in the hands of library staff with academic credentials in those areas.[2] U.S. libraries did not begin to employ subject specialists (sometimes called area specialists) widely until after the Second World War, when selection in academic libraries began to shift from faculty members to academic librarians.[3] Subject specialists were seen to be most appropriate in libraries with complex bibliographic, linguistic, acquisition, and processing problems that required specialized expertise to solve. Some have seen the shift of selection decision making from teaching faculty to librarians as both a force toward and an indication of the professionalization of librarianship.[4] For a time, the phrase *subject specialist* or *subject bibliographer* was understood to mean a librarian who was assigned full time to collections activities. This has changed, and now a librarian who is called a subject specialist or bibliographer may have additional library responsibilities, such as reference service or cataloging, using his or her unique language expertise.

In many smaller academic libraries, faculty continue to play a major role in selecting materials, though collection management activities are generally handled by librarians. Teaching faculty may identify new materials for acquisition through their work in a discipline, through review of approval plan slips, and review of new approval plan receipts. They may make recommendations with final authority for approving orders residing with the library. Smaller libraries seldom have the breadth and depth of specialized subject expertise found in larger libraries, and relying on the proficiency of faculty members active in the field is logical. The success of faculty-based selection depends on faculty members' interest in and involvement with the library. In such environments, librarians typically will have responsibility for reference collection development and management and, perhaps, more general materials.

The evolving nature of subject specialists mirrors a trend in academic libraries of all sizes toward assigning librarians at least one other primary responsibility along with collection development and management. A 1994 study of eighty-six Association of Research Libraries (ARL) member libraries found that the most frequent model was a decentralized staff composed, in part or wholly, of librarians having responsibilities in collection development as well as other areas.[5] More than half the responding libraries in this survey reported having no full-time staff members assigned to collection development. Part-time selectors are now found in most types of libraries.

Expanding Responsibilities

Traditionally, dual assignments have combined reference services and collection development and management. Although subject specialists or bibliographers often have provided specialized reference service, they now more frequently serve as part of a reference unit with assigned reference desk hours and bibliographic instruction responsibilities. An additional trend in large research libraries is to assign collections responsibilities to staff members from nonpublic service units, such as cataloging.[6] The result is that many librarians in academic libraries now are doing some selection and collection management. It may be either a major or a minor assignment among many responsibilities. Regardless of the number of librarians handling collections responsibilities, all activities must be carefully coordinated or the collection will lose focus and coherence.

A debate continues in large academic, research, and public libraries over the advantages and disadvantages of full-time bibliographers compared to using librarians with part-time collections responsibilities. Full-time selectors (used here to cover the full range of collection development and management functions) are championed because this model is seen to assure that collections responsibilities are not subordinated to other library responsibilities. Full-time academic bibliographer positions were, from their beginning, perceived as a special class of scholar-librarians, intended both to replace faculty selectors and to appease faculty members with appropriate replacements within the library.[7] This model is promoted as more effectively positioning selectors to establish formal communication with teaching faculty members because of their credibility as scholars. Without distractions such as assigned reference desk hours or a backlog of cataloging, the full-time selector is seen as better able to focus on building and managing the collection. Louis Pitschmann has written that the larger the library's collection budget and the broader the span of collection development functions, the greater the justification and need for at least some full-time selectors.[8]

The full-time selector model has been criticized as elitist and distanced from everyday library services, concerns, and problems. Full-time academic bibliographers have the potential of becoming too closely affiliated with the departments or schools they support. Any full-time bibliographer faces the risk of losing sight of the overall goal of building and maintaining a balanced collection. The independent nature of full-time bibliographer work can result in internal cultural and organizational problems and in positions that do not fit comfortably into the library's organizational structure.[9] Even if a library has moved from a traditional bureaucratic organizational structure to a flattened, less rigid model, the solitary character of full-time selections work can isolate the bibliographer.[10] Other staff members may perceive the full-time bibliographer as uninvolved and outside the collaborative interaction that has come to characterize library planning and problem solving.

The alternative to full-time selectors is positions in which collection development and other duties are shared. This model stresses the value of regular contact with collection users that occurs through reference service. This contact can provide direct information about user interests and needs. A front-line librarian has firsthand experience with and under-standing of the importance of continually balancing needs and reassessing priorities. Catalogers with in-depth subject background and language expertise may have more knowledge and skills in certain areas than other librarians on the staff. Assigning collections responsibilities to such capable individuals can be the best use of staff resources and lead to outstanding collections. However, having many librarians with collections responsibilities can make coordination more challenging. The primary criticism of part-time selectors is that collections work has a tendency to become a secondary responsibility and can be slighted as librarians try to fit it in among the constant pressures of other daily activities.

Public Libraries and School Library Media Centers

Public libraries and large school systems may use full-time or part-time collections librarians or a combination of both types of assignment. Large public libraries may have a centrally located collections coordinator or collection development officer (CDO) who manages the collections budget and either coordinates or directly supervises the work of several subject specialists located in a central library and larger branches, if they exist. In general, public library collections librarians also have responsibilities for reference work and may manage a major subject- or user-based unit (for example, music, children's services, or a branch library). Subject specialists have, as in academic libraries, responsibility for monitoring review aids in their speciality. Some large public libraries have one or two individuals who handle all selection work, while collection management is handled at the service points. Many public libraries have a selection committee with rotating membership. In public libraries in which selection responsibilities are widely distributed, the centrally located coordinator is usually responsible for monitoring and circulating reviews, acquiring review copies, and coordinating approval plans.

Catherine Gibson has suggested that many public libraries are moving toward more use of centralized selection.[11] This permits redirecting additional staff time to public services. Her justification for this reassignment of responsibility is based on research studies showing that the variations between user interests and circulation at different branches is minimal because so much of contemporary reading is influenced by popular media—which reaches a wide audience. Centralized selection and ordering of multiple copies can speed the delivery of new materials to the branches, increase branch collection diversity, and reduce biases in individual collections. Research conducted in 1995 by Ann Irvine in ninety-one public libraries reported that 81 percent of libraries with budgets over $100,000 and 43 percent of libraries with budgets less than $100,000 had centralized a portion of the selection process.[12] In these libraries, branches continue to make recommendations and, occasionally, to make some selection decisions locally.

All librarians are more likely to participate in collection development and management in medium-sized and smaller public libraries in order to distribute the work and take advantage of librarians' formal education and interest areas. Selection and collection management typically are coordinated by the head librarian, who has direct budgetary responsibility. Of course, the smaller the budget, the less that will be expended on collections, though selection decisions will require more scrutiny. In the smallest public library, collection development and management is normally handled by a single individual, usually the head librarian. In the past, a small acquisitions budget also meant limited access to print review sources. Now, if the library has Internet access, a host of online review sources can be at the librarian's fingertips.

The assignment of collections responsibilities in school library media centers mirror those found in public libraries. Large systems usually have a district coordinator who supervises the activities of librarians in the several schools that comprise the system. Each individual librarian has responsibility for developing collections that match the needs of his or her school's teachers and students. Normally, verification of orders, order placement, and processing are handled at the district office. If the school librarian is not part of a system or works in a school system without a district office, then these responsibilities fall to the individual.

Understanding the User Community

Special libraries present a unique environment for collection development and management for several reasons. First, special libraries have a very clear idea of their mission and user community. Second, they may be staffed by only one librarian, who is responsible for all functions. Third, collection building may consist primarily of placing orders submitted by the special library's users. Even in larger special libraries with several librarians, each librarian typically will have a clear and narrow area of specialization within which he or she manages the collection.

Collection development and management in all types of libraries requires close contact with users, and this may be reflected in the assignment of selection responsibilities. Special libraries, as noted above, rely primarily on their users to identify new acquisitions. Academic libraries serving smaller academic institutions often rely heavily on faculty for selection decisions. School library and media centers may rely on committees composed of librarians, teachers, administrators, and sometimes students and parents. Coordination, communication, and cooperation are always essential.

The need to balance collections responsibility assignments between librarians and multiple responsibility assignments within a single position has motivated the profession to try to determine the time or staffing levels needed to expend budgets and manage collections. Several authors have said such calculations are impossible because collections work is too complex and neither objective nor observable.[13] Bonita Bryant noted the "difficulties in measuring the results of collection development and management qualitatively and in measuring the process itself quantitatively."[14] One solution to this dilemma is to make clear the priorities assigned to various tasks.

Paul Metz, however, wrote about a successful project to develop a pragmatic, objective, and quantitative means of estimating collection development workload in a library with part-time bibliographers.[15] Metz proposed a formula of weighted parameters, with weights to be assigned different values according to the library in which the formula was applied. The five parameters are (1) number of academic departments and key centers for which a bibliographer is responsible, (2) number of full-time tenure-track faculty in assigned departments or centers, (3) number of orders in all the bibliographer's firm order budget accounts for the previous fiscal year, (4) call number responsibilities measured as total inches in the shelf list or via automated title count, and (5) the number of standing orders and continuations in all the bibliographer's accounts. Although no one has been able to figure out how much time it takes to be a successful selector, Metz has suggested four significant components that make up collections work in academic libraries: outreach and liaison, selecting items to order, managing an existing collection, and managing serials, continuations, and standing orders.

Technology's Influence on Skills

Harry Braverman introduced the concept of deskilling and explored it in his book, *Labor and Monopoly Capital*.[16] He suggested that capitalism, combined with technology, results in degradation of work by pushing the skills necessary for doing a job down in the organization or the profession. Capitalism is, according to Braverman, geared toward profit and finding more economical ways of delivering goods and services. The increasingly sophisticated responsibilities assigned to nurse practitioners and physician's assistants, who handle many medical practices previously performed only by physicians, might be presented as one example. Braverman's work has been the source of extensive research, numerous articles, and endless debate by economists, sociologists, and historians.[17] Many analyses on the effects of new, computerized technology on work have tended to characterize them as a continuation of the deskilling process described by Braverman. However, some analysts see new technologies as having enskilling effects as well—that is, automation changes the nature of a position by requiring more sophisticated knowledge and skills.[18]

Understanding the nature of skill and distinguishing between skill in individuals and the skill required in particular positions are two aspects of the debate surrounding Braverman's thesis. Individuals can learn the skills needed to perform routine tasks through experience and on-the-job training. However, different degrees of awareness are required to perform certain activities. Advanced education and extensive experience prepare individuals to cope with unfamiliar situations for which existing routines are inadequate. Even in environments in which automation is causing significant changes, autonomous, skilled employees continue to have an important role.

The blurring of distinctions that have separated professional librarians from library support staff or paraprofessionals might be seen as deskilling. Over the last twenty years, paraprofessionals have taken on more diverse and higher levels of responsibilities.[19] Complex activities are moving downward in the library hierarchy. One distinguishing aspect of a profession is the ability of its practitioners to exercise control over the knowledge base of the field, including control over the criteria for entering that field.[20] Librarians and their professional associations have been unable to maintain exclusive control over the qualifications needed to perform library work. This is caused, in part, by shrinking staffs and the need of libraries to use effectively all current employees. In addition, automation has broadened the skill base needed to work in libraries. In the area of collection development and management, the increasing use of approval plans and automation have reduced the emphasis on selecting individual titles in many libraries.

Nevertheless, most libraries continue to assign certain collections responsibilities to professional staff members. Selection at the individual title level has traditionally remained the purview of professional librarians—at least in academic libraries—but this distinction is not as rigorously maintained as previously. Academic libraries may assign selection to a staff member without a graduate library degree if that individual has extensive subject knowledge gained either through formal study in the discipline or extensive experience with the local collections and their users. The collections-related areas that remain the responsibility of librarians are distinguished by their complex and abstract nature, significant impact on the future of the library, and influence on how the library is perceived by its user community, stakeholders, partners, and services and materials providers. Allen B. Veaner has called these programmatic responsibilities.[21] Such areas include collection development program planning and articulation, budget allocation, collection development policy preparation and revision, departmental and community liaison, and work with suppliers, vendors, and consortia.

Organizational Models

Who performs various functions or activities, how these individuals are coordinated, and how they communicate between themselves and with others both within and outside the library defines the library's collection development and management organizational structure. Much of the professional literature on organization of collections activities addresses academic libraries and, specifically, large academic and research libraries. This focus reflects the greater tendency of libraries with larger staffs, collections, and budgets to develop large, complex, and variant organizational structures.

No single collection development organizational model predominates. Defining the components of an optimal structure that assures successful accomplishment of goals has proved impossible. No specific model is perfect. Variations, as with the assignment of collections responsibility, are influenced by the size of existing collections, staffing levels, budget, local assumptions about the goals of collection management and development, and the preferences of the current library administrators.

Bonita Bryant suggested that one or more of three conditions make some sort of collection management organizational structure necessary.[22] These are when the decision of what to purchase and the responsibility for expenditure of the materials budget is no longer the direct responsibility of the library director, when the library acknowledges that neither technical services (where funds have been managed) nor public services (where selection and user liaison have occurred) allow the necessary combination of fund management and patron contact for systematic collection development and management, and when inconsistencies among collection growth, collection use, and patron needs are discovered.

Libraries handle reporting lines and assignment of responsibilities in various ways, depending on their size, history, and individuals on their staffs. Two models predominate. They can be seen as two ends on a continuum, with variations falling in between. In the functional model, staff members with collection development and management responsibilities are grouped in a single organizational unit. This unit may be called a department, division, or team. The bibliographers, who may or may not be full time, may then be subdivided into subunits according to subject responsibilities, user community, or physical location of their offices, collections, or libraries.

In the geographic or client-based model, collection development librarians are part of a unit that consists of staff members with various responsibilities who are grouped according to the user community they serve or a common geographic location shared by members of the unit. Again, the librarians may be assigned full or part time to collections work. As with the functional model, members of a geographic or client-based unit may be subdivided into smaller units. In this case, the smaller units may be functional or subject-based.

The functional model has the advantage of improved communication and coordination among librarians with similar responsibilities. This can enhance the development of a coherent collection and make working on shared projects, such as serials cancellations or collection analysis, easier. The role of the CDO is less complicated because he or she has direct authority as well as responsibility for the collections librarians. Disadvantages include the potential of isolation from other librarians and distance from the user community.

The geographic or client-based model can be particularly effective in focusing on the needs and expectations of a specific user group. In addition, collections librarians work more closely with staff members, including catalogers, circulation units, and interlibrary loan, whose work is integral to effective collections work. Planning and problem solving may be easier. The main difficulty with this model is in coordinating collections activities across a large library with many geographic- or client-based units. Balancing needs and goals can be a challenge.

Few libraries are organized into either of these "pure" models. Most fall somewhere between them. A large academic library may have a functional unit of full-time bibliographers under an assistant director or assistant university librarian for collection development and a client-based unit with part-time selectors under an assistant director for science and engineering. A large public library system may have a central division of collection development librarians with systemwide responsibilities and several branch libraries with librarians who have multiple responsibilities including collection development and management. These hybrid models can have all the advantages of each of the pure models and all of their problems as well. Regardless of the organizational structure employed, the most important consideration is coordination of collection activities and their proper attention within the library's mission and priorities.

Many medium-sized and larger libraries have one or more standing committees to improve communication across departmental or divisional lines. Typical committees are a general collection development and coordinating committee, a serials review committee, a discipline- or user-based committee (e.g., a committee of science selectors or of children's librarians), and a committee that addresses electronic resources. Many of these committees will include staff members from other library units because of the boundary-spanning nature of collections work. A general coordinating committee may include, for example, representatives from the library's fiscal office, cataloging unit, or interlibrary loan operation. Committees that deal with electronic resources almost always include members from throughout the library—acquisitions and cataloging staff members, automation librarians, reference librarians, an individual charged with managing and monitoring contracts—whose expertise is essential in making responsible, informed decisions about acquisition and access. Ad hoc committees may be appointed to address a finite issue or project, such as choosing a new serials or approval plan vendor. The goal of all these committees is to improve communication and decision making by drawing together the individuals and library units with appropriate expertise and who will be affected by the decisions.

Collection Development Officers

Libraries in which several staff members have collections responsibilities generally have an individual who coordinates their activities. By 1994, 82 percent of ARL member libraries responding to a survey reported they had a senior CDO reporting directly to the head librarian.[23] This person may be called coordinator, team leader, head or director of collection development, assistant or associate librarian for collection development and management, chief collection development officer, or a variation of one of these. A separate senior position is found most commonly in large and medium-sized public, academic, and research libraries. The CDO generally coordinates collection development activities, manages the overall collections budget, and may or may not have direct supervisory responsibility for all staff members with collection management and development assignments.

In large libraries, the collections officer often has senior administrative responsibility for additional operations or services, such as information services, public services, technical services, reference, planning, document delivery and interlibrary loan, development of external funding sources, all aspects of electronic resources, or preservation. A direct linkage with acquisitions, either through placing acquisitions within the collection development and management division or combining senior administrative responsibility for technical services (of which acquisition is a subunit) and collection development and management, is seen frequently.[24] This arrangement provides direct control over budget expenditures. These realignments reflect both the boundary-spanning nature of collection development and management and a reduction in the number of senior administrators through consolidation of responsibilities. The CDO is often a member of the library's administrative group and participates in library-wide policy development and planning. He or she works with other administrators and unit heads to develop mutually agreed-upon processing priorities.

The CDO's role varies depending on his or her span of control and responsibilities within the library and the library's collection development and management operation. As the administrator responsible for library-wide collection development and management, the CDO is normally charged with preparing budget requests for staffing and collections and allocating and monitoring the funds. He or she manages the collection development staff. This may involve direct responsibility for full-time bibliographers or responsibility for the collections work of part-time bibliographers. These responsibilities normally include recruitment, training, assignment of responsibilities to staff members, supervision, and evaluation of that portion of work assignments considered under his or her purview.

The collections officer overseas all aspects of collection building and management for all formats. Under this heading will fall creating and revising the collection development policy, ensuring the policy is upheld, collection assessment and evaluation, preservation and conservation decisions, and withdrawals, transfers, and journal cancellations. The CDO is one of several library administrators who may be charged with negotiating contracts and licenses for acquisition of and access to electronic resources. Primary responsibility for and coordination of cooperative collection development and consortial activities and fund-raising through development activities and grant writing are usually assigned to the CDO. He or she may negotiate with individual donors and review gifts and exchanges. The collection officer frequently represents the library's collection development program to user groups, governing agencies, and in external forums.

Jasper G. Schad has stressed the leadership role of the CDO. He lists team building, articulation of vision and values, continuous formal and informal training, and controlling workload as the four key challenges for a CDO.[25] These four responsibilities, when effectively executed, enable selectors to know what to do, how to do it, realize why it is important, help reduce frustration, and enhance feelings of competence. The CDO, whether managing a full-time staff or coordinating the work of part-time selectors, has an important role in helping set a realistic agenda that allows selectors to establish priorities, regulate work flow, and accomplish their work. Communication and interpersonal skills are particularly important.

In some libraries, the CDO may serve a coordinating function. As coordinator of collection development management, he or she may have all the responsibilities outlined above but no direct line responsibility for multiple responsibility selectors. In this environment, the selectors report to another administrator, such as the associate university librarian (AUL) for technical services or public services. The CDO, however, may have line responsibility for a major unit within the library, such as special collections and archives or preservation and conservation.

Ethical Issues

Ethics are the principles of conduct or standards of behavior governing an individual or profession. These standards can be legal or moral, personal or institutional, and deal with what is right or wrong, good or bad. A value is an explicit conception of what an individual or group regards as desirable. Ethical considerations influence how collections librarians interact with materials sellers, suppliers, and service agents as well as with their user community and with their coworkers.

Ethical behavior is the result of an internal or personal code and an external context provided by institutional and professional principles. A personal code of ethics may develop out of civic and religious convictions. People do what makes them feel good about themselves and avoid what makes them feel bad. They also are influenced by the frame of reference for behavior developed by the groups of which they are members. In other words, behavior can be a consequence of how one feels others around him or her perceive this behavior. People understand and react to what happens according to the particular frame of reference they are using for ethical behavior.

Lee G. Bolman and Terrence E. Deal identify three principles found in ethical judgments. These are mutuality (all parties to a relationship are operating under the same understanding about the rules of the game), generality (a specific action follows a principle of conduct applicable to all comparable situations), and caring (this action shows care for the legitimate interests of others).[26] As Bolman and Deal state, "Such questions raise issues that should be part of an ongoing dialogue about the moral dimension of management and leadership."[27] Taking a stance on values, ethical choices, and appropriate behavior is a reflection of principled judgment.

Professional ethics is an additional frame of reference for behavior and the decisions a librarian makes on a daily basis. Professional ethics is behavior set forth, either formally or informally, by the profession of librarianship. The American Library Association (ALA) provides a *Code of Ethics.*[28] The Association for Library Collections and Technical Services (ALCTS) has developed a set of guidelines for its members to supplement the ALA *Code of Ethics.*

Guidelines for ALCTS Members to Supplement the American Library Association Code of Ethics

Within the context of the institution's missions and programs and the needs of the user populations served by the library, an ALCTS member:

1. strives to develop a collection of materials within collection policies and priorities;
2. strives to provide broad and unbiased access to information;
3. strives to preserve and conserve the materials in the library in accordance with established priorities and programs;
4. develops resource sharing programs to extend and enhance the information sources available to library users;
5. promotes the development and application of standards and professional guidelines;
6. establishes a secure and safe environment for staff and users;
7. fosters and promotes fair, ethical and legal trade and business practices;
8. maintains equitable treatment and confidentiality in competitive relations and manuscript and grant reviews;
9. supports and abides by any contractual agreements made by the library or its home institution in regard to the provision of or access to information resources, acquisition of services, and financial arrangements.[29]

Rare book, manuscript, and special collections librarians have also developed a set of standards for ethical conduct, as has the Acquisitions Section of ALCTS.[30]

An individual's response to situations is guided by a mix of standards or principles from various frames of reference. When these frames lack coherence with one another, the individual experiences conflict and must decide which code should predominate and guide behavior. When different sources or frames of reference for ethical behavior suggest different decisions or responses, the librarian must resolve the conflict in order to act. This is an individual decision. There are times when one must take an ethical stand that conflicts with one's employer. Situations in which the parent institution or community prescribes censorship and the librarian believes that intellectual freedom is being compromised are examples of personal and professional ethics taking precedence over institutional ethics.

Working with Suppliers and Vendors

An area in which collections librarians can face ethical issues is their relationship with suppliers and vendors. Librarians often develop a congenial relationship with supplier and vendor representatives, fostered by pleasant lunches and conference receptions. This is one reason why many libraries and their parent institutions prohibit or place financial limits on the gifts and personal benefits librarians may accept. Librarians should not permit a personal desire to be "nice" to representatives interfere with an ethical obligation to manage institutional resources as effectively as possible. While librarians have an obligation to be honest and fair and to act in good faith with suppliers, they have no obligation to help them succeed. Librarians should keep the financial and service interests of their libraries foremost, seeking to obtain the maximum value for each purchase, license agreement, and service contract.

Another frame of reference may be explicitly or implicitly provided by the library and its parent institution. One university has issued a document called "Ethical Negotiating," which makes explicit the institution's expectations and values when negotiating with an external supplier. This document states, "Whenever you contact a vendor to work out the price, delivery, and terms for goods or services you need to buy, you are negotiating with that vendor. . . . When you negotiate as a University representative, you are accountable for a higher level of negotiating conduct. You are negotiating for the long term benefit of the University." Implicit guidance supplements explicit guidelines and codes and is modeled through the behavior of administrators, managers, and peers. Values are conveyed through actions as well as written statements.

A binder who cannot provide quality binding at market prices should not be retained as the library's binder, no matter how long the relationship has continued. A serials agent who has a cash flow problem and fails to pay publishers is not a reliable serials agent with a promising future. A history of friendly relations between librarian and vendor is not the issue. Each service and purchase agreement must be reviewed while evaluating all available information. Each agreement must be continually assessed as a business decision, and the needs of the library must be placed first.

A librarian must keep in mind the long-term interests of the communities that his or her decisions affect. One must have the ethical convictions and courage to place these interests above any personal short-term preoccupations. No matter how gracious and charming a service agency's representatives are and how competently the agency has performed in the past, future performance and financial viability are the deciding factors.

Librarians' ethical obligations are twofold: to conduct business with mutual respect and trust and to serve their own organizations as best they can. Explicit and implicit codes aim for high standards of professional conduct and integrity and value honesty, trustworthiness, respect, and fairness in dealing with other people and loyalty toward the ethical principles, values, policies, and procedures espoused by a librarian's institution. Librarians have an obligation to consistently demonstrate and carefully maintain a tradition of ethical behavior.

Collection Development Activities and Evolving Technologies

Automation and new information technologies are affecting how collections librarians do their work as well as the resources with which they work. Library automation and access to bibliographic networks and Internet resources support collections activities such as selection of materials, individual item verification, order preparation, claiming, collection evaluation and assessment, budget management, and communication with library staff members and others outside the library, including publishers, vendors, and other suppliers. In-house automated library systems often can produce various useful reports and provide information on demand about fund balances, unit and cost information, circulation activity, supplier performance, and other statistical compilations that can be manipulated on personal computers.

Some libraries and librarians are creating web-based resources specifically to aid in the practice of collection development and management. Linda A. Brown describes such a site as a customized toolkit for selectors.[31] A locally developed site for collections librarians typically provides links to useful external sites prepared by other librarians, such as home pages of vendors and publishers frequently used by the library and links to local policies, procedures, and forms. AcqWeb is a web site that provides links to resources of interest, including verification tools and directories of publishers and vendors, to acquisitions and collection development librarians.[32] Some local sites include links to bibliographic tools, like *Books in Print,* to which the library has contractual access, and to relevant professional association pages. Other types of information often provided are budgets and fund allocation, a selectors' directory with their subject responsibilities, a currency converter, and management and statistical data. Contributing to and, perhaps, maintaining a local selectors' home page is now a common selector's responsibility.

Working with electronic information resources requires different skills and expertise. Collections librarians must understand licensing and contract negotiation for electronic resources, copyright in the digital environment, and new types of consortial agreements for cooperative purchasing. More library staff members may be involved in evaluation and selection decisions because of the boundary-spanning nature of managing and servicing both local and remotely accessed electronic information.

Skills and Competencies

Libraries expect newly hired librarians to have certain skills and competencies that they learned in a graduate school program. These are supplemented with on-the-job training and experience gained through the practice of collection development and management over time. Library and information schools provide the conceptual learning. These are the skills, principles, and concepts of librarianship and provide the building blocks or mental models for its practice. They represent the theory that lies behind the practice of collection development and are important to the master as well as the novice. For the master, they are points of reference that aid in continually refining practice and in explaining it to others. For the novice, they give an understanding of the rationale that guides collection development and management.

A library school curriculum should include basic functional principles. George I. Soete has called these "assumed competencies."[33] These include

- the reasons for building library collections and a commitment to resource sharing,
- the importance of knowing the library's users,
- the factors that make for effective selection and collection management decisions,

- the tenets of intellectual freedom and respect for diverse points of view, and
- the importance of building and preserving collections for the future as well as the present.

Conceptual learning includes skills and practices. These basics are as important as the philosophical underpinnings. A selector needs knowledge of the subject, formats, and users for whom he or she will select. He or she needs a basic understanding of the targeted user community and knowledge of the techniques to learn about the specific local community being served. This means, at a minimum, expertise in the literature if the selector is not an expert in the subject or discipline. Ideally, a subject specialist will be familiar with specialized terminology, understand the basic concepts and importance of the field, be aware of current controversies, recognize the names of prominent researchers and authors, know of historical milestones and the names associated with them, and understand how the field relates to other fields and disciplines. A librarian who plans to work with collections used by children and teenagers will be familiar with the history of children's fiction and nonfiction, understand children's interest and reading levels and the types of materials that match these, be aware of current theories about the use of literature in the curriculum, and know the names of prominent authors, illustrators, and award-winning books.

A library expects a new selector to understand the publishing industry and the factors a publisher considers in making decisions about what to publish, the types of materials in which major publishers specialize and the quality of their publications, and major publishers' reliability, pricing practices, and general reputation. The new selector should have studied publishing trends, production statistics, and pricing behavior. Equally important is how materials are provided to libraries. This includes distribution and acquisitions mechanisms (vendors, agents, scholarly societies, approval plans, firm orders, standing orders, and so forth). The student should have a basic understanding of intellectual property rights, copyright law, and licensing agreements and the role they play in acquisition of and access to resources. Those who plan to become academic librarians should understand the changing nature of scholarly communication and academic research.

John M. Budd and Patricia L. Bril found that collection development practitioners ranked the ability to identify and use key materials as selection sources as the most important skill gained in graduate education.[34]

The new selector should have a firm grasp of sources of information (book reviews, bibliographies, publishers' catalogs, web pages, publishers' reputations, key authors) for selecting resources and how to find authoritative reviews when needed.

Additional Competencies

Various authors have identified additional competencies that new librarians should bring to their first jobs.[35] These are

- the ability to control information bibliographically;
- the ability to understand the community to be served;
- the knowledge of assessment and evaluation techniques;
- the understanding of collection development policy and procedures;
- the knowledge of financial analysis and budget management;
- the knowledge of currency fluctuations around the world and world market forces;
- abilities in critical analysis, problem solving, and critical decision making;
- negotiation skills;
- managerial and supervisory skills;
- salesmanship;
- the understanding of organizational behavior, power, and politics;
- the understanding of administrative practices; and
- knowledge of grant writing and administration.

Many of these competencies are not normally part of a library school curriculum. Students should consider taking courses in other professional school programs, such as a business school, education department, or public policy program, to gain the skills needed in contemporary collection development and management practice.

Nancy M. Cline, a university librarian, has provided a set of desired attributes she views as essential for collections librarians and that supplement the competencies that should be learned through formal study. Collection development and management librarians should have

- commitment to change;
- the ability to think innovatively, creatively, and strategically;

- commitment to quality services;
- commitment to professionalism;
- skills in analytical reasoning;
- adaptability, flexibility, and resilience;
- vision;
- resourcefulness;
- intellectual curiosity;
- excellent communication and interpersonal skills;
- a keen sense of political contexts; and
- the ability to tolerate ambiguity.[36]

The previous paragraphs have identified a set of core or assumed competencies consisting of principles, concepts, and skills that libraries expect a newly hired collection development and management librarian to have learned in a course of graduate study. Certain ingredients in successful collections work cannot be taught in library school. These are always specific to the individual's library and are learned once he or she begins a new position. These include the selector's responsibilities, which will depend on his or her job description, and local procedures. In the latter category are how to prepare orders, how to interact with various library units, and how the local budget and financial system operates. To this can be added learning about the local culture or organizational environment, including what is acceptable behavior and what is not, how decisions are made, and how autonomously individuals operate.

Learning and Mastery

Peter M. Senge has explored the difference between learning and mastery.[37] Successful collections work can be mastered only by practice—by actually doing the work. The distinction rests on the difference between theory, which can be learned, and practice. Practices are the most evident aspect of any profession in the sense that they are what define the field to those outside it. Practices are also the primary focus of individuals when they begin to follow a new career or discipline. The novice requires "discipline" in the sense of conscious and consistent effort because following the practices is not yet second nature. The new selector working with mental models of how to develop and manage a collection will have to make an effort to identify the assumptions he or she is making and the skills and competencies that guide them. Over time and with experience, the practices of a discipline become more and more automatic. This is why it is sometimes hard for an experienced selector to explain what goes into a selection or collection management decision and how one weighs pros and cons to select or not to select, replace, withdraw, or cancel a title.

The novice is tempted to think that understanding certain principles means one has learned all about the discipline. This confuses intellectual understanding with mastery. A student of the French language may know French grammar and vocabulary but has not mastered the language until he or she speaks French automatically and without first mentally translating every word from English to French. Senge calls this the essence of a discipline. These essences in learning a discipline cannot be gained by focusing conscious attention and effort on them. The essences of a discipline are the state of being that is experienced naturally by individuals with high levels of mastery in the discipline.

This suggests that the successful collection development librarian *is* a collection developer instead of one who *does* collection development. It means moving from a linear understanding (knowing the building blocks) to a nonlinear, internalized understanding of collection development as a whole. This is the mastery that cannot be learned in library school. The new collections librarian has learned everything he or she can through an educational program, but only through experience does the whole become greater than the sum of its parts. Practice gives meaning to theory, refines performance, and builds mastery.

Training On-Site

If fortunate, a newly hired selector is provided with a formal on-site training program, supported by a bibliographer's manual. Although library and information science education teaches the elements of collection development and management, each library has unique practices and expectations. A librarian, even one who has worked in another library, comes to a new position equipped with collection development and management principles, guidelines, and typical procedures but must learn how to operate in a new environment. Among the ARL libraries, only 78 percent reported that they provided local training for collections development, and several noted that their training was minimal, informal, or handled one-on-one.[38] Most new collections librarians learn the details of a new position through individual instruction, mentoring, and on-the-job experience.

A manual provides the documentation necessary for carrying out collection development and management activities in a specific library.[39] It documents local practices in a systematic way and provides a planning tool for individual selectors to measure progress of their work or improve its quality. Other in-house training materials may include library-specific collection development policies, procedures for the acquisition process, guidelines for collection analysis, procedures for using an automated library system, and goals for collection development work.

A collections librarian should be prepared to develop his or her own training program. Without a formal local program, the new librarian might consult the *Guide for Training Collection Development Librarians*, which lays out the skills and expertise specific to a library in which a new librarian will need training.[40] Even with a formal on-site program, a newly hired selector should develop a personal self-education plan in consultation with his or her supervisor. It will include learning

- how the library and its parent organization are organized and the scope and emphasis of its programs;
- who the library's staff members are and what they do;
- the individuals and groups outside the library with whom he or she will work;
- the library's holdings and their strengths and weaknesses;
- how patrons use the collections;
- how the materials budget is allocated, monitored, and spent;
- reports available from the local automated system or generated manually;
- the library's collection development policies;
- any cooperative collection development agreements;
- how the library chooses, uses, and evaluates vendors and the vendors used; and
- the local procedures for selection, ordering, and processing materials.

As libraries move to dual or multiple responsibility assignments, many librarians who have not handled collections responsibilities previously are being asked to assume them. This is a particular challenge for two reasons. The librarian may have completed his or her graduate library school program some time ago, and even if he or she remembers the content of collection management courses, the information likely will be out-of-date. Secondly, supervisors and coworkers may assume the new selector has a familiarity with in-house policies, procedures, and performance expectations that does not exist. A carefully designed training program is as important for existing staff who assume collections responsibilities as it is for a newly hired librarian.

Effective performance of collection management and development activities requires continual learning, both in the theories and practices of this speciality and in the areas for which one is responsible. A commitment to self-education along with intellectual curiosity, energy, and time are essential.

Performance Evaluation

An important aspect of any position is regular evaluation of performance. This may involve an annual formal performance review and should include frequent informal contacts with a supervisor that address performance goals, accomplishments, and problems. This continuous dialogue ensures the librarian has a clear understanding of expectations and the extent to which they are being met. Performance appraisals, whether formal or informal, should provide constructive guidance. Ideally, performance evaluation begins with an individual's job description, which reflects the relative importance of and anticipated percentage of time devoted to collection activities. The job description may be responsibility-based (what the person does) or outcome-based.

Evaluations of collection development librarians are complicated because of difficulty in developing performance standards and measuring outcomes. If the librarian has multiple assignments and multiple supervisors, compiling and preparing the evaluation can be challenging. If more than one supervisor is involved, the librarian and supervisors must be in agreement about the priorities of multiple assignments and effort to be devoted to each. The librarian being reviewed should be provided with explicit goals within each review period and a clear understanding of performance criteria and what is being measured.

Academic libraries may use peer reviews in place of or in addition to supervisor reviews. The newly hired collection development librarian should know from his or her first day on the job how performance evaluation is handled. Many libraries require supporting documentation, and the librarian should be assembling this information on an ongoing basis. Some libraries require monthly reports prepared by the staff member and may solicit comments from faculty in academic departments.[41] Part of the annual review process may be the preparation of a self-review reporting on the individual's success or failure in meeting certain specific goals agreed upon at the beginning of the review cycle.

Performance expectations should be consistent with the library's overall mission and goals. They may be very specific and delineate every area of the job description such as quantity and quality of liaison contacts with users, success in managing budget allocations, quality of new acquisitions, and contributions to the library as a whole. Librarians in academic libraries also may have performance expectations that must be met in order to be promoted and granted tenure or continuous appointment. Typically, these are similar to those of teaching faculty and will involve research, publication, instruction, and contributions to the profession. Because most tenure and promotion decisions are based on a cumulative history of performance, the new librarian must work closely with his or her supervisor and the tenure committee or its equivalent to begin building a persuasive dossier from the point of hire.

Summary

Any library activity that relates to library collections both on-site and accessed remotely may be assigned to the collection development and management librarian. Assignment of responsibilities and placement of collections activities within a library will vary depending on the library's size, budget, mission, and user community. In small libraries, all activities may be handled by one individual. In very large libraries, responsibilities may be highly centralized or widely dispersed according to subject responsibility, user community, physical location of staff members, or a subset of functions. The trend is toward combining collections responsibilities with others, though full-time collection development and management librarians are found in larger libraries. Many functions that were once the purview of professional librarians have migrated to paraprofessionals. Those that remain solely the responsibility of collections librarians are programmatic in nature because they have the potential to change the library's direction, create new programs, and influence how the library's constituents perceive it.

Larger libraries of all types often have a senior CDO. This individual may have direct line responsibility for all librarians with collection development and management responsibilities or may serve a coordinating function. The CDO usually has budgetary authority and provides the guidance essential for coherent, coordinated collection development and management. Many libraries also have committees with permanent or rotating membership that provide coordination, consistency, and help with problem solving by virtue of members representing various units, branches, or divisions.

Ethics are the principles influencing how collections librarians interact with materials sellers, suppliers, and service agents as well as with their user community and with their coworkers. Collections librarians have ethical obligations in how they conduct business with vendors and suppliers and how they serve their libraries in all aspects of performing their responsibilities. Honesty, trustworthiness, respect, and fairness in dealing with other people and loyalty toward the ethical principles, values, policies, and procedures espoused by a librarian's institution are essential.

Library automation and new technologies for delivering and accessing information are affecting the work of collections development librarians. Computerization is making the identification of resources, placement of orders, and provision of management information faster and easier. Digital information provides new challenges through complex licensing, new interpretations of copyright and fair use, and the complexities of accessing and servicing different formats. The expansion of electronic information reinforces the importance of cooperation and coordination within library operations and services.

The skills and competencies that a new librarian brings to the practice of collection management and development are extensive. Ranging from knowledge of factors that make for effective selection and collection management decisions and how to analyze a user community to management practices for budgeting, planning, and critical decision making, these skills can be learned and form the building blocks for beginning a career. Other aspects of collections work can only be learned through on-site training and practice. A collections librarian must work closely with his or her supervisor to set performance and mastery goals. Whether newly hired or newly assigned collections responsibilities, a collection development and management librarian must take personal responsibility for his or her professional goals, accomplishments, and career.

| CASE STUDY |

Molly Bekins is a newly hired librarian in the Newley County Public Library System. Newley County is in a major metropolitan area, and the system has thirteen branch libraries. Molly is assigned to the Melba Branch Library, one of the four main branch libraries. She reports to the branch librarian and is the second of two professionals assigned to this branch library. In this position, her responsibilities include general reference and managing the children's and young adult collections along with service programs directed toward children and teens. The Newley County Public Library System has two bibliographers, or collections librarians, responsible for systemwide selection, located in the main library. One, Max, is responsible for adult collections, and the other, Ralph, is responsible for children's and young adult collections. The Newley County Public Library System uses a combination of an approval plan and firm orders to acquire new books. Although Max and Ralph make decisions about new titles to be acquired for the system, they rely on the staff members in the branch libraries to manage the branch collections and to make decisions about added copies and replacements and to provide information about special interests and foci in each branch collection. The two systemwide collection librarians accept purchase recommendations from all their colleagues. Molly reports to her branch head and also, for collections responsibilities, to the children's and young adult collections "central" collection development librarian, who has input to her annual evaluations. The Newley County Public Library System has no formal training program for new librarians, though it provides informal training in basic procedures in submitting new purchase orders.

Activity

Prepare a list of the competencies that Molly should have gained in her graduate library and information science program that prepare her for this position. Develop a twelve-month schedule for Molly that lays out what she needs to learn about the collections, operations, services, and users in the Melba Branch Library and the Newley County Public Library System and the sequence and time frame in which she should master this knowledge. Prepare a list of contacts Molly should make in the library system and in the region as part of her training program.

REFERENCES

1. *See* Robert B. Harmon, *Elements of Bibliography: A Guide to Information Sources and Practical Applications,* 3d ed. (Lanham, Md.: Scarecrow, 1998), for an introduction to the art of bibliography.
2. J. Periam Danton, "The Subject Specialist in National and University Libraries, with Special Reference to Book Selection," *Libri* 17 (1967): 51.
3. Russell Duino, "Role of the Subject Specialist in British and American University Libraries: A Comparative Study," *Libri* 29 (1979): 16.
4. Raven Fonfa, "From Faculty to Librarian Materials Selection: An Element in the Professionalization of Librarianship," in *Leadership and Academic Librarians,* ed. Terrence F. Mech and Gerard B. McCabe (Westport, Conn.: Greenwood, 1998), 35.
5. Gordon Rowley, comp., *Organization of Collection Development,* SPEC Kit, no. 207 (Washington, D.C.: Assn. of Research Libraries, 1995).
6. James E. Bobick, *Collection Development Organization and Staffing in ARL Libraries,* SPEC Kit, no. 131 (Washington, D.C.: Assn. of Research Libraries, 1987).
7. John Haar, "Scholar or Librarian? How Academic Libraries' Dualistic Concept of the Bibliographer Affects Recruitment," *Collection Building* 13, no. 1/2 (1993): 19.
8. Louis A. Pitschmann, "Organization and Staffing," in *Collection Management: A New Treatise,* ed. Charles B. Osburn and Ross Atkinson, Foundations in Library and Information Science, v. 26 (Greenwich, Conn.: JAI Pr., 1991), 136.
9. Eldred R. Smith, "The Impact of the Subject Specialist Librarian on the Organization and Structure of the Academic Research Library," in *The Academic Library: Essays in Honor of Guy R. Lyle,* ed. Evan Ira Farber and Ruth Walling (Metuchen, N.J.: Scarecrow, 1974), 71–81.
10. The traditional bureaucratic organizational structure, as defined by Max Weber, is hierarchical and places decision making and responsibility at the top of the organization. Diminishing amounts of authority are delegated in prescribed portions to lower levels in the organizational pyramid. *See* Max Weber, "Bureaucracy," in *From Max Weber: Essays in Sociology,* trans. H. H. Gerth and C. Wright Mills (New York: Oxford Univ. Pr., 1962), 196–244.
11. Catherine Gibson, "'But We've Always Done It This Way!' Centralized Selection Five Years Later," in *Public Library Collection Development in the Information Age,* ed. Annabel K. Stephens (New York: Haworth, 1998), 33–40. Also published in *The Acquisitions Librarian,* no. 20.
12. Ann Irvine, "Is Centralized Collection Development Better? The Results of a Survey," *Public Libraries* 34 (July/Aug. 1995): 216.
13. *See,* for example, Anthony W. Ferguson, "University Library Collection Development and Management Using a Structural-Functional Systems Model," *Collection Management* 8 (spring 1986): 1–14; and Dan C. Hazen, "Modeling Collection Development Behavior: A Preliminary Statement," *Collection Management* 4 (spring 1982): 1–14.
14. Bonita Bryant, "The Organizational Structure of Collection Development," *Library Resources and Technical Services* 31 (1987): 111.
15. Paul Metz, "Quantifying the Workload of Subject Bibliographers in Collection Development," *Journal of Academic Librarianship* 17, no. 5 (1991): 284–87.

16. Harry Braverman, *Labor and Monopoly Capital: The Degradation of Work in the Twentieth Century* (New York: Monthly Review, 1974).

17. *See* a special issue of *Monthly Review* 46, no. 6 (Nov. 1994), commemorating Harry Braverman's *Labor and Monopoly Capital,* and *The Degradation of Work? Skill, Deskilling, and the Labour Process,* ed. Stephen Wood (London: Hutchinson, 1982).

18. Shoshana Zuboff, *In the Age of the Smart Machine: The Future of Work and Power* (New York: Basic Books, 1988).

19. Ron Ray, "Paraprofessionals in Collection Development; Report of the ALCTS/CMDS Collection Development Librarians of Academic Libraries Discussion Group," *Library Acquisitions: Practice and Theory* 18 (fall 1994): 6–10.

20. Nina Toren, "Professionalization and Its Sources," *Sociology of Work and Occupations* 2 (spring 1975): 323–27.

21. Allen B. Veaner, "Paradigm Lost, Paradigm Regained? A Persistent Personnel Issue in Academic Librarianship, II," *College and Research Libraries* 55 (1994): 393–94.

22. Bryant, "The Organizational Structure of Collection Development," 113–14.

23. Rowley, *Organization of Collection Development,* from unpaged prefatory materials.

24. *See* Nancy Courtney and Fred W. Jenkins, "Reorganizing Collection Development and Acquisitions in a Medium-Sized Academic Library," *Library Acquisitions: Practice and Theory* 22, no. 3 (1998): 287–93; and Kathleen Wachel and Edward Shreeves, "An Alliance between Acquisitions and Collection Management," *Library Acquisitions: Practice and Theory* 16 (1994): 383–89.

25. Jasper G. Schad, "Managing Collection Development in University Libraries That Utilize Librarians with Dual-Responsibility Assignments," *Library Acquisitions: Practice and Theory* 14, no. 2 (1990): 169.

26. Lee G. Bolman and Terrence E. Deal, *Reframing Organizations: Artistry, Choice, and Leadership,* 2d ed. (San Francisco: Jossey-Bass, 1997), 192.

27. Ibid., 193.

28. "Code of Ethics of the American Library Association," adopted by the American Library Assn. Council, June 28, 1995, available at ALA's Office for Intellectual Freedom web site; click "Our Association" on the top navigation bar of the ALA home page (http://www.ala.org), click "Offices" on the left navigation bar, click "Intellectual Freedom" under that heading, and click "Statements and Policies."

29. "Guidelines for ALCTS Members to Supplement the American Library Association Code of Ethics," developed by the ALCTS Task Force on Professional Ethics and adopted by the ALCTS Board of Directors, Midwinter Meeting, Feb. 7, 1994, available at the ALCTS web site (http://www.ala.org/alcts); click "Resources" on the left navigation bar.

30. "Standards for Ethical Conduct for Rare Book, Manuscript, and Special Collections Librarians, with Guidelines for Institutional Practice in Support of the Standards, 2d edition, 1992," *College and Research Library News* 54, no. 4 (April 1993): 207–15. "Statement on Principles and Standards of Acquisitions Practice," developed by the ALCTS Acquisitions Section Ethics Task Force,

endorsed by the ALCTS Acquisitions Section and adopted by the ALCTS Board of Directors, Midwinter Meeting, Feb. 7, 1994, available at the ALCTS web site (http://www.ala.org/alcts); click "Resources" on the left navigation bar.

31. Linda A. Brown, "The Acquisitions Workstation—Collection Development Style," *Against the Grain* 11, no. 2 (April 1999): 1+; and Julie L. Rabine and Linda A. Brown, "The Selection Connection: Creating an Internal Web Page for Collection Development," *Library Resources and Technical Services* 44, no. 1 (Jan. 2000): 44–49.

32. AcqWeb [WWW home page of AcqWeb, produced by librarians at Vanderbilt University]. Available [Online]: http://acqweb.library.vanderbilt.edu/.

33. George I. Soete, "Training for Success: Integrating the New Bibliographer into the Library," in *Recruiting, Educating, and Training Librarians for Collection Development,* ed. Peggy Johnson and Sheila S. Intner (Westport, Conn.: Greenwood, 1994), 165.

34. John M. Budd and Patricia L. Bril, "Education for Collection Management: Results of a Survey of Educators and Practitioners," *Library Resources and Technical Services* 38, no. 4 (Oct. 1994): 349.

35. Maria Otero-Boisvert, "The Role of the Collection Development Librarian in the 90s and Beyond," in *Catalysts for Change: Managing Libraries in the 1990s,* ed. Gisela M. von Dran and Jennifer Cargill (New York: Haworth, 1993): 159–70; also published in *Journal of Library Administration* 18, no. 3/4 (1993); Patricia Battin, "Managing University and Research Library Professionals: A Director's Perspective," *American Libraries* 14, no. 1 (Jan. 1983): 22–25; and Edward G. Holley, "Defining the Academic Librarian," *College and Research Libraries* 46 (Nov. 1985): 462–77.

36. Nancy M. Cline, "Staffing: The Art of Managing Changes," in *Collection Management and Development: Issues in an Electronic Era,* ed. Peggy Johnson and Bonnie MacEwan, ALCTS Papers on Library Technical Services and Collections, no. 5 (Chicago: American Library Assn., 1994), 25.

37. Peter M. Senge, *The Fifth Discipline: The Art and Practice of the Learning Organization* (New York: Doubleday, 1990).

38. Rowley, *Organization of Collection Development,* from unpaged prefatory materials.

39. Collection Management and Development Committee, Resources and Technical Services Division, American Library Assn., *Guide for Writing a Bibliographer's Manual,* Collection Management and Development Guides, no. 1 (Chicago: American Library Assn., 1987).

40. Susan L. Fales, ed., *Guide for Training Collection Development Librarians,* Collection Management and Development Guides, no. 8 (Chicago: Assn. for Library Collections and Technical Services, American Library Assn., 1996).

41. Jack Siggins, comp., *Performance Appraisal of Collection Development Librarians,* SPEC Kit, no. 181 (Washington, D.C.: Assn. of Research Libraries, 1992).

SUGGESTED READINGS

Biery, Susan S. "Team Management of Collection Development from a Team Member's Perspective." *Collection Management* 25, no. 3 (2001): 11–22.

Bryant, Bonita. "Staffing and Organization for Collection Development in the New Century." In *Collection Management for the Twenty-first Century*, edited by G. E. Gorman and Ruth H. Miller, 191–200. Westport, Conn.: Greenwood, 1997.

Eckwright, Gail S., and Mary K. Bolin. "The Hybrid Librarian: The Affinity of Collection Management with Technical Services and the Organizational Benefits of an Individualized Assignment." *Journal of Academic Librarianship* 27, no. 8 (Nov. 2001): 452–56.

Finks, Lee W., and Elisabeth Soekefeld. "Professional Ethics." In *Encyclopedia of Library and Information Science*, edited by Allen Kent, 52, Supplement 15, 301–21. New York: Marcel Dekker, 1993.

Fisher, William. "Impact of Organizational Structure on Acquisitions and Collection Development." *Library Collections, Acquisitions, and Technical Services* 25, no. 4 (winter 2001): 409–19.

Frazier, Kenneth. "Collection Development and Professional Ethics." In *Collection Development in a Digital Environment*, edited by Sul H. Lee, 33–46. New York: Haworth, 1999. Also published in *Journal of Library Administration* 28, no. 1.

Gorman, Michael. *Our Enduring Values: Librarianship in the Twenty-first Century.* Chicago: American Library Assn., 2000.

Guide for Writing a Bibliographer's Manual. Collection Management and Development Guides, no. 1. Chicago: Collection Management and Development Committee, Resources and Technical Services Division, American Library Assn., 1987.

Harris, Roma M. "Information Technology and the Deskilling of Librarians." In *Encyclopedia of Library and Information Science*, edited by Allen Kent, 53, Supplement 16, 182–202. New York: Marcel Dekker, 1994.

Hazen, Dan. "Twilight of the Gods? Bibliographers in the Electronic Age." *Library Trends* 48, no. 4 (spring 2000): 821–41.

Hill, Joanne Schneider, William E. Hannaford Jr., and Ronald H. Epp, eds. *Collection Development in College Libraries.* Chicago: American Library Assn., 1991.

Johnson, Peggy, and Sheila S. Intner, eds. *Recruiting, Educating, and Training Librarians for Collection Development.* New Directions in Information Management, no. 33. Westport, Conn.: Greenwood, 1994.

Kennedy, John. "Education for Collection Management: Ending before It Ever Really Started, or Only Just Beginning?" *Education for Information* 16 (1998): 45–56.

Koehler, Wallace C., and J. Michael Pemberton. "A Search for Core Values: Towards a Model Code of Ethics for Information Professionals." *Journal of Information Ethics* 9, no. 1 (spring 2000): 26–54.

Metz, Paul. "Quantifying the Workload of Subject Bibliographers in Collection Development." *Journal of Academic Librarianship* 17, no. 5 (1991): 284–87.

Mosher, Paul H. "Collection Development to Collection Management: Toward Stewardship of Library Resources." *Collection Management* 4 (1983): 41–48.

Mouw, James R. "Changing Roles in the Electronic Age—The Library Perspective." *Library Acquisitions: Practice and Theory* 22, no. 1 (spring 1998): 15–21.

Munroe, Mary, John Haar, and Peggy Johnson. *Guide to Collection Management Administration, Organization, and Staffing.* Collection Management and Development Guides, no. 10. Lanham, Md.: Scarecrow and the Assn. for Library Collections and Technical Services, 2001.

Neville, Robert, James Williams, and Caroline C. Hunt. "Faculty-Library Teamwork in Book Ordering." *College and Research Libraries* 59, no. 6 (Nov. 1998): 524–33.

Rabine, Julie L., and Linda A. Brown. "The Selection Connection: Creating an Internal Web Page for Collection Development." *Library Resources and Technical Services* 44, no. 1 (Jan. 2000): 44–49.

Rowley, Gordon, and William K. Black. "Consequences of Change: The Evolution of Collection Development." *Collection Building* 15, no. 2 (1996): 22–30.

Rubin, Richard R., and Thomas Froehlich. "Ethical Aspects of Library and Information Science." In *Encyclopedia of Library and Information Science,* edited by Allen Kent, 58, Supplement 21, 33–52. New York: Marcel Dekker, 1996.

Sorgenfrie, Robert, and Christopher Hooper-Lane. "Book Selection Responsibilities for the Reference Librarian: Professional Benefit or Burden?" *Library Collections, Acquisitions, and Technical Services* 25 (2001): 171–78.

Webb, John. "Collections and Systems: A New Organizational Paradigm for Collection Development." *Library Collections, Acquisitions, and Technical Services* 25, no. 4 (winter 2001): 461–68.

Wengert, Robert G. "Some Ethical Aspects of Being an Information Professional." *Library Trends* 49, no. 3 (winter 2001): 486–509.

Wicks, Don A., Laura Bairdiella, and David Swords. "Four Birds with One Stone: Collaboration in Collection Development." *Library Collections, Acquisitions, and Technical Services* 25 (2001): 473–83.

Winters, Barbara J. "Ethics in Acquisitions Management." In *Understanding the Business of Library Acquisitions,* 2d ed., edited by Karen A. Schmidt, 335–45. Chicago: American Library Assn., 1998.

CHAPTER 3 | # Policy, Planning, and Budgets

Introduction

Formal or systematic planning and goal-setting activities, along with assessment and evaluation techniques to measure progress toward those goals, have become standard practice in many libraries. Planning would not be necessary in a static environment, but the environment in which every library exists is changing constantly. These changes are on many fronts—sociological, educational, economic, political and governmental, technological, and institutional. This chapter will introduce planning as an organizational responsibility and examine collection development policies and budgeting, two of the most commonly used formal planning tools in libraries.

Planning in Libraries

Planning is one of many responsibilities librarians have. Formal planning should not be viewed only as the responsibility of managers and administrators. Planning should be part of all activities in the library. Planning means devising a method for accomplishing something. Planning occurs every day because outcomes are sought, decisions are made to reach those outcomes, and actions are taken based on those decisions. The distinction is between informal planning, which people do daily, and formal planning, which has a structure within which conscious, intentional planning occurs.

Peter Drucker has written that formal planning is improving the "futurity" of decisions.[1] In an environment of rapid change, formal continuous planning becomes more important. Libraries need to anticipate change and decide how to handle it. Formal planning examines both the probable and the possible future. Ideally, a library will identify several possible futures and then decide which are the most probable. The future is unpredictable, and alternatives need to be on hand so that plans can be modified as needed. Uncertainty is the reason planning is a continuous process.

Consider, for example, the impact of information in digital formats. Librarians recognize its pervasiveness and costs along with increasing user expectations to access it through libraries. A librarian should consider several possible futures. What percentage of information resources will be available electronically five, ten, twenty years from now? What is the impact on the current and projected acquisitions budget? What percentage of the budget might be spent on electronic resources five, ten, twenty years from now and how will this affect acquisition of other formats? Given the forces at play, where would the library like to go and what does it need to do to get there? Laying out alternative scenarios allows the librarian to project alternative funding needs, collection development policies, and service implications.

Formal planning is a form of organizational learning. Planning for the future requires understanding what the library is doing now, what it would like to be doing in the future given certain probable conditions, and choosing the most reasonable path to that future. People involved in planning—and, ideally, planning is broad-based in an organization—learn a tremendous amount about their library, their parent organization, and the external environment.

Planning is also a communication tool. Information is shared within the library as part of the planning process. Equally important, information about present services and programs and future needs, expectations, and hopes is both gathered and shared with the library's clientele and funding bodies. Planning sets a course for the future. It provides a mechanism to inform people about that future and an opportunity for them to buy into it.

George Keller has identified several caveats to consider when planning.[2] Planning is not the production of a blueprint to be followed rigorously. A formal plan is not a set of platitudes and buzzwords. It should not be the personal vision of one individual nor a statement by a particularly vocal individual or group. Planning does not work if it is an attempt to avoid or outwit the future. Plans do not eliminate risks, nor are they a surrender to external forces. Planning should not be limited to a once-a-year organizational exercise. Planning will not solve all an organization's problems, and it cannot address all issues at once. Formal planning is a library's guide for continuity. It provides a structured way to envision and move toward a future, anticipate change, maximize its positive effects, and minimize its negative ones.

Planning Models

No single style, method, or model of planning is best. Several types of planning may be in use simultaneously in the same library. The following discussion presents various popular planning approaches, but is not exhaustive. *Budgeting* is a traditional planning process through which many program-planning decisions are made. It is discussed later in this chapter. Budgeting often is a component of the planning approaches described below.

Master planning is top-down planning that begins in the administrative offices. In a college or university, the president's or provost's office begins with an institutional mission and sets out goals, objectives, and time lines with which each academic unit must adhere. City government, through the mayor's office, or the school district, through the superintendent's office, can take the same approach. Unit plans are prepared consistent with the master plan. This model is simple because responsibility for planning is not dispersed and nothing changes unless mandated by the governing body or administrative office. Units and individuals within the organization or institution are seldom satisfied with such an approach. Their knowledge and expertise does not contribute to the planning process, and plans may be crafted in isolation from the reality in which librarians work.

Contingency planning is directed specifically toward preparing for one possible and usually undesirable future. For example, libraries prepare disaster contingency plans. Such a plan begins by identifying the possible disaster, such as a flood, and consequences for facilities, services, and collections. Contingency plans identify appropriate steps to respond to those circumstances. Collection development librarians should ensure that a disaster response plan is prepared and kept up-to-date for the library collection.

Formal democratic planning is a cyclic planning process in which all units are requested to formulate their plans for program development on a regular schedule. Plans are reviewed simultaneously to arrive at a complete and coherent plan for the library, college or university, school system, city government, and so on. In this style, the source of ideas rests primarily with individuals and individual units. Contributing units and individuals may be given one or more themes or priorities on which to focus.

Strategic planning has an external focus and requires continual scanning to monitor changes in the environment. Environmental scanning is an important component of strategic planning but equally useful in all types of planning. Strategic planning constantly reviews external conditions, as well as changing internal conditions, and devises an appropriate response. It usually begins with a vision of the organization's future that serves as a guide to planning the goals, objectives, and strategies that form the plan. Strategic planning is broadly participative and often uses small groups to generate strategies that are incorporated into a coherent plan. Strategic planning, although it may look at one- or three- or five-year increments, does not produce a final, static plan. It remains an open-ended, continuous process that seeks to keep the organization in step with its environment. Collection development activities are defined and planned in terms of the environment.

In *scenario planning*, the library develops scenarios describing alternative futures and formulates plans or strategies for the library in those various futures. Scenario planning can be used in strategic planning and in more focused planning as well. It provides an opportunity to be creative in envisioning the library's future and to consider what is probable, possible, and preferable.

Entrepreneurial planning, also called opportunistic planning, is a laissez-faire, individual approach to program planning that relies on individuals to come forward whenever they have an idea for altering or expanding programs. There are no planning constraints, no timetables, and no formal requests for ideas. It implies acting immediately while the opportunity presents itself. The process of choosing remote electronic resources in libraries is often entrepreneurial. If a new resource is suddenly available and the price is favorable, the library may choose to purchase access, even though that particular resource or subject focus was not identified as a priority in library planning.

Incentive planning has not been as prevalent in nonprofit organizations as in the corporate sector, though it is being seen more often in higher education, where it is may be called responsibility centered management. The institution is viewed as an economic organization. Institutional leaders develop performance benchmarks and an incentive structure that rewards particular types of activities. Each unit or department selects programs to be developed based on the incentive structure. For example, units may retain revenue generated through tuition or sales. Academic units may be taxed to support the library. In this scenario, the academic library faces pressures to justify its contributions to the institution.

Environmental Scanning

Environmental scanning, a formal methodology developed in the for-profit sector, can gather information and enhance understanding of the library's environment. It is a key component of strategic planning. Environmental scanning has been defined as "a methodology for coping with external social, economic, and technological issues that may be difficult to observe or predict but that cannot be ignored and will not go away."[3] Its purpose is to detect, monitor, and analyze trends and issues in the environment, both internal and external, in which an organization operates. It is a key component in planning because it positions an organization to set goals and make plans within the framework of an emerging future.

Environmental scanning first received widespread attention in the late 1960s as businesses sought a way to avoid unexpected crises and to prepare for startling and increasingly rapid change. The American auto industry did not anticipate the consequences of smaller families, increasing fuel prices, and declining interest in new car models as status symbols. Consequently, U.S. companies were years behind foreign car manufacturers in entering the small car market. They realized a need to prepare for significant changes in their market and the forces that governed that market. This evolved into an awareness that tracking external forces and issues that have great impact on an organization can provide a competitive advantage. An organization that analyzes alternative futures and effectively monitors potential threats and opportunities can take advance action. It can modify present decisions and adapt quickly.

Environmental scanning is distinguished from simple monitoring by a systematic approach. The four elements are scanning, analyzing, reporting, and crafting an appropriate organizational response. Formal environmental scanning requires the creation of a scanning team, which collects and analyzes information. The team selects the resources to scan, chooses criteria by which to scan, and develops categories of trends to monitor. Team members have individual scanning assignments and meet regularly to review trends. After selecting key trends, they interpret these trends' strategic importance to the organization. The team is responsible for producing reports and briefings that can inform planning and decision making.

The corporate sector continues to rely on formal environmental scanning, but it is less widely used in nonprofit organizations because its complexities can be overwhelming. C. Davis Fogg maintains that strategic planning is impossible without environmental analysis.[4] Environmental scanning is not an all-or-nothing proposition. A modified approach can provide benefits to the library. Recognizing trends and analyzing their impact can position libraries to assign priorities and make decisions about budget, personnel, and facilities before crises force them into a corner. As planning for alternative futures becomes increasingly important, libraries need all the resources they can marshal to make informed decisions. Anticipating future user community needs, wants, and demands helps the library to design collections and services to meet them.

Libraries and Environmental Scanning

Many libraries already monitor their internal and external environments, using techniques that can be applied more widely. These monitoring techniques can to be combined with analysis and a commitment to link this analysis to planning activities. Typical techniques are reading source materials, monitoring electronic discussion lists, and tracking issues through personal contacts. Some libraries assemble and route "reading files" of relevant materials to staff members. These files may include newsletters and reports from peer and local libraries; pertinent articles and editorials; announcements and newsletters from the college or university, school district, or local and national government; federal and foundation grant announcements; vendor announcements; and publications from consortia, organizations, and agencies with whom the library has regular contact. Many library science journals have sections devoted to tracking important developments and issues of interest to librarians.

These information sources should be seen as more than a source for current awareness. Classic environmental scanning includes developing a set of categories or a mental model within which trends or issues are organized. This helps draw together dispersed information to form a more complete picture of trends on the horizon. Categories should be tied to organizational concerns. Librarians often already use mental models as they scan the information that crosses their desks. For example, the children's librarian in a public library will pay particular attention to information in the local newspaper regarding the increase in day-care homes or changes in competency requirements for advancing to the next elementary grade. He or she will note which books are on banned book lists or the focus of school-parent conflict. Tracking popular topics for local school assignments and local trends in school-age population or growth in non-English-speaking families are important in library planning.

An important aspect of environmental scanning often neglected in libraries is analysis. The question is, What do these trends mean for our programs, services, and collections? Trend analysis does not have to be addressed by a special team with the permanent responsibility of collecting and analyzing information. Individuals or small groups of staff members can prepare briefings that will guide planning and goal setting. In addition, occasional meetings of the management team and other library committees or teams can be devoted to a review and analysis of hot topics that should be monitored and incorporated into planning.

The goal of environmental scanning is to identify and analyze trends that can inform planning. Just as the corporate sector seeks a competitive advantage through environmental scanning, so too libraries can better position themselves to meet a changing future. Identifying the trends, events, and ideas on which the library can capitalize can guide in managing financial and personnel resources. Simultaneously, libraries can identify possible events outside their control that are threats and for which they need to plan and seek ways to mitigate. If issues and trends are identified early, librarians can incorporate them in planning. Recognizing and reacting to environmental change before it becomes a crisis is the goal of environmental scanning.

Why Undertake Formal Planning?

The earlier an issue is identified and analyzed, the more successful the response. Planning does not eliminate uncertainty. It does suggest ways in which the organization can prepare for and respond to possibilities. Foresight, manifested in a plan, can lead to organizational actions that may prevent problems and provide positive opportunities for the organization. Refusing to prepare or delaying preparation of plans does not delay the future or minimize its impact. Such behavior only hinders the ability to respond effectively. Planning should not be viewed only as contingency planning for worst-case scenarios. Proactive planning gives the library a measure of control over the future. Planning offers an opportunity to influence the environment. Preparing plans is more than being prepared.

Planning, by focusing on goals along with the objectives or steps to reaching those goals, provides desired outcomes against which to measure progress. Accountability is increasingly important in nonprofit organizations like libraries. The library must be in a position to demonstrate and document how it is using its financial resources effectively. By pointing to what it has accomplished, the library can justify continued and perhaps increased funding. Library plans often have subtitles such as "The Library in the Twenty-first Century" or "A Vision for the Future." These should not be seen as grandstanding. A final plan with goals, objectives, and strategies is only one result of formal planning. The process of systematic planning creates its own benefits by creating a vision of the library and engaging people to share that vision.

Any planning activity in a library will have impact on collection development, and collection development planning must occur within the context of the library's overall planning. A collection development policy statement can be written and revised within various planning models. A collection policy is most effective if it has aspects of democratic planning—it should be prepared by the individuals who best understand the issues and will apply the plan.

Collection Development Policy Statements

Libraries without collection development policies are like businesses without business plans. Without a plan, an owner and his employees lack a clear understanding of what the business is doing now and what it will do in the future, and potential investors have little information about the business's prospects. The owner has no benchmarks against which to measure progress. Daily decisions are made without context. Even a library with written policy statements suffers if those statements are not reviewed, revised, and updated regularly. Selection, deselection, and priority setting throughout the library occur in isolation and without coordination if the library has no recorded rationale for decisions.[5]

Paul H. Mosher has written that collection development is a process that "should constitute a rational documented program guided by written policies and protocols and should reflect, in a sense, a contract between library users and library staff as to what will be acquired, for whom and at what level."[6] A collection development policy describes the collection (on-site and remote access) as it is now and as it will be developed while defining the rules directing that development. It is a systematic document, both comprehensive and detailed, that serves multiple purposes as a resource for public planning, allocation, information, administration, and training.[7]

Written collection policies became more widespread, particularly in academic libraries, following World War II and the tremendous growth of academic libraries' collections. In the decades that followed, libraries of all types began to prepare polices that documented practices and goals. By the mid-1950s, the American Library Association (ALA) recommended that every public library have a written selection and collection maintenance policy. In 1961, the American Association of School Librarians published *Policies and Procedures for the Selection of School Library Materials.*[8]

Policy statements are not general, idealistic, theoretical, or vague, but they are not so detailed that they become unusable. Policy statements are not static. Preparing, reviewing, and revising policy statements are continuous processes because the community served, the financial resources available, and the information resources produced are always changing. No policy, however well written, is a substitute for good collection development and management. A policy statement defines a framework and provides parameters, but it never tells how to select or reject a specific title. No matter how specific and detailed the collection development policy statement is, personal judgment is still necessary.

Purposes and Audience

The many purposes that collection policies serve can be divided into two broad purposes: to inform and to protect. The audience being informed must also be considered when creating a policy.

INFORMATION

Collection development policy statements inform by describing current collections in terms of strengths and weaknesses and setting future goals. By identifying future collection levels, policies provide a benchmark against which to measure success in reaching those levels. To the extent that they match collections to mission, policies can guarantee that the collection being developed serves the educational, entertainment, and research mission of the parent institution or community. This presupposes a clear understanding of the institution's mission and that of the library. Collection policies provide the information needed to establish priorities for the library. Priorities for collection development and management are an obvious result. In addition, collection policies can inform decisions about cataloging, retrospective conversion, space allocation, budgeting, and fund-raising priorities. They can guide those individuals responsible for managing personnel, fiscal resources, space, and other resources in support of collections. By establishing collection priorities, policy statements guide libraries in establishing staffing needs and allocating available personnel.

Policy statements help with budgeting by providing information for external and internal budget preparation and allocation. A well-crafted policy informs a library's governing and funding body about the library's directions and provides a clear and carefully articulated rationale for its collection. It demonstrates accountability by presenting a plan for careful management of fiscal resources and describing the results of funding decisions. A good policy statement can improve the library's ability to compete for resources within a complex and competitive institutional or government environment. A policy can provide supporting information for the preparation of grant proposals, budget requests, and fund-raising and development plans. Policy statements can be used in responding to accreditation surveys and to inquiries about the impact of new academic and research programs or new service mandates.

Policy statements serve as a vehicle for communication with the library's staff, administration, and constituencies. While describing the library collection and its strengths and weaknesses, they also formally document practice. They are contracts documenting the library's commitment, and they express this commitment in writing. Within the library, policy statements serve to coordinate selection when responsibility for selection is dispersed among many selectors and geographically among several physical locations. Policies provide control and consistency.

Because they are used to educate and train librarians responsible for collections, collection development policy statements must not become outdated. As new selectors are hired and selecting responsibilities reassigned, policy statements serve as a training tool. The new selector will have a baseline of information from which to begin managing the collection if the policy statement is current in describing community service priorities, academic programs and research interests, criteria for selection and deselection, collecting levels, and so forth.

Policy statements serve a particularly important function to the extent they document and support cooperative collection development. The policy statement should explicitly identify all current cooperative programs in which the library participates: collection building, resource sharing, regional storage, shared contribution and access to electronic resources, and so on. By documenting what the library does and what it plans to do with collecting levels by discipline or user group, a policy can facilitate cooperative collection development and resource-sharing programs. Using the same policy format and descriptive measures or terms within a consortium or other resource-sharing group can expedite cooperation and coordination.

PROTECTION

Collection development policy statements protect the library against external pressures. Policy statements can serve to protect intellectual freedom and prevent censorship. Many libraries' statements repeat or reference the "Library Bill of Rights" and other intellectual freedom statements.[9] Librarians should give care to this significant area, especially with so much public attention focused on library access to the Internet. A library is best served by preparing a statement that is tailored to its own environment. The policy may include the procedures for handling a complaint against material held by a library. This does not mean that a statement about censorship is totally negative. The policy can be written so that it is a statement that affirms the library's commitment to intellectual freedom. The process of creating a statement on intellectual freedom provides library staff members with the opportunity to think through these issues and to clarify their position. When the library is challenged, librarians are prepared to respond. They have, in effect, rehearsed their response through the writing of a policy.

At the same time that a policy resists the exclusion of certain materials, it can protect against pressure to include inappropriate and irrelevant materials. A statement can protect against undue special interest pressure from those who demand that the library accept gifts or purchase certain materials. A policy makes clear that materials are rejected because of collection guidelines, not because of who may or may not wish their acceptance.

Policies can protect by guiding the handling of gifts. The policy specifies the conditions under which the library accepts and rejects gifts. The gift policy should address the economic, social, and political situation in which a library exists. Libraries are advised not to appraise gifts, but to refer potential donors to one or more external appraisers. By defining policy and procedures for accepting or declining, appraising, accessioning, acknowledging, and processing gifts, both the library and the potential donor are protected legally and practically.

In times of decreasing budgets and increasing materials costs, libraries need protection as they plan weeding, deselection, and serials cancellations. Making clear the operating principles under which these decisions are made protects the library from charges of bias and irresponsible behavior. A policy should define the process through which materials identified for withdrawal and cancellation are reviewed and evaluated and by whom. Any processes for involving members of the user community should be described. This portion of the policy statement should include guidelines for disposal of unneeded materials.

A policy statement can identify issues of confidentiality. By specifying the types of information—for example, about donors, budgets, costs and value of materials—that are private, a policy protects the library and its users, the parent institution, and donors.

AUDIENCE

Just as collection development policy statements serve many purposes, they serve many audiences. The library's collection policy usually is designed primarily for use by staff members. The better the policy is, the more frequently it will be consulted. Copies should be available for all library personnel, not just those with selection responsibilities.

A collection policy statement can serve a wider audience as well. It can be designed to be meaningful to library users and external funding and governing bodies. If well written, the policy tells administrators what the library is doing with its allocated funds and makes clear the library materials budget is not a "black hole" without definition or dimension. In the same way, a collection development policy defines the library for its external governing body. Other libraries can be part of the policy's audience. If the policy is intended to identify and develop cooperative collection building and use initiatives, then it must be shared with actual and potential partners.

Writing the Collection Development Policy Statement

A policy should be considered in terms of format, content, and style.[10] Authors, whether individuals or committees, should keep in mind their primary purpose and audience while writing the policy and tailor the document appropriately. For example, a policy that will be shared within a consortium and used for cooperative collection development planning should match the style of others in the consortia. A policy statement intended to inform teaching faculties or the parents of K–12 students might incorporate terminology from the curriculum. Format, content, and style can be crafted to meet specific ends and speak to specific audiences. Well-researched and well-written policy statements can address multiple purposes and audiences effectively.

Collection development policies usually are prepared according to one of three formats or models: classed analysis, narrative, or a combination of elements of these two models. Other policies include the e-resources format and supplemental policies, which deal with specific issues.

CLASSED MODEL

The classed analysis model describes the collection, current collecting levels, and future collecting levels in abbreviated language and numerical codes, most typically according to the Library of Congress classification scheme. Though often extensive, this model allows one to see the collection as a whole, displayed on charts. This format grew out of libraries' need to develop an effective, consistent way of defining subjects and levels of collecting.

The Research Libraries Group (RLG) was a leader in developing the classed analysis format as the conspectus. The conspectus is examined in detail in chapter 9. Complemented by verification studies and supplemental guidelines, the RLG Conspectus has done much to define concepts, standardize procedures and terminology, and offer consistent techniques for describing and managing collections.[11] WLN also uses the conspectus to describe collections and collecting levels in detail. The conspectus approach to assessing collections and defining both present collecting practice and future goals, though challenged by some as too dependent on individual perceptions, has become accepted as a tool that is both adaptable and widely applicable.

A library using the classed analysis model should use the same classification system for its collection development policy that is used to organize the library's collection. This allows the library to use title counts to verify existing levels and measure changes over time as described in the policy. The library can select the appropriate level of specificity to be used. The RLG Conspectus uses some 3,400 subject classifications; these can be simplified to describe collections for which less fine distinctions between subjects are more appropriate.

Subject categories are defined by classification range and subject descriptors. Each category is assigned a series of numbers for existing collection strength, current collecting intensity, and desired collecting intensity. The numbers, often called collection depth indicators, range from 0 (out of scope—nothing is collected in this subject) to 5 (comprehensive—collecting is exhaustive, inclusive, and intensive). Language codes can be assigned to each category. Scope notes can be used to describe special features or parts of the collection. Librarians should not become too preoccupied with levels. Levels do not imply value. Reporting a level of 4 or 5 does not mean a library is better. The most important part of using collection depth indicators is to understand how the library's selectors are collecting and to reconcile practice with the library's mission, goals, objectives, and available funding.

NARRATIVE MODEL

The narrative model is text-based. It includes a series of narrative descriptions, one for each subject, discipline, or subcollection. The sections may be defined broadly (for example, Social Sciences, Humanities, and Sciences; or Adult Fiction, Children's Fiction, and Reference) or each section may have a narrower focus (for example, subdividing Agriculture into Animal Science, Agronomy, Soil Science, and so on; or Adult Fiction into Mysteries, Romances, Science Fiction, and so on). The purpose is to give a focused view of subjects or subdivisions and of collection management as practiced in the library preparing the policy. An advantage of the narrative model is use of terms to describe local programs and collections that are local and immediately familiar.

Many libraries use both classed analysis and narrative policies. Though both are subjective, the formal classed analysis, through the use of standardized divisions and terminology, provides a vehicle for verification, comparisons and cooperation between libraries, clear division and coordination among selecting responsibilities, measurement of progress, and information for developing and modifying approval plan profiles and can define the context in which selection and collection management occurs. Even libraries that do not prepare narrative policy statements for each subject usually write a general narrative policy statement. Narrative policies provide guidelines and the context in which selection and collection management occurs.

CONTENT OF A NARRATIVE POLICY

A narrative collection development policy statement has several standard elements. The introduction serves to set the stage for the policies and guidelines that follow. It begins by stating the purpose of the policy and the audience to whom it is directed. If the library has a mission statement, this often is included in the introduction. Guidelines governing the appropriateness of materials, subjects, formats, and language must be coherent with the library's mission.

The introduction usually describes the community, including numbers and types of users served and these users' needs. Types of users mentioned in an academic library may include undergraduates, graduate and special students, faculty, distance education students, and the general public. The policy for an academic library will describes academic programs, degrees granted, and research centers. The policy of a public library will describe the citizens and their needs. Types of users might include K–12 students, students at local higher education institutions and community colleges, ethnic communities, care facilities' residents, local businesses, elderly, visually impaired, and prison inmates. Description of the user community is followed by a general statement of library priorities related to primary and secondary users.

Limitations affecting collection development and management are an important part of the policy's introduction. This is the point at which to note any factors that may limit the library in achieving its goals. New academic programs may have been added without additional library funding, meaning reduced support for all collection areas. The school enrollment or city's population may be increasing rapidly or changing significantly in ethnic composition. The impact of new technologies for information delivery, escalating monograph and serial prices, and reduced or steady state budgets may be addressed in this section.

A brief overview of the library and its collections follows. This includes a history of the collection or collections, broad subject areas emphasized or de-emphasized, and collection locations. The quality and character of existing collections are evaluated in broad terms, as is current collecting practice. A general statement about criteria guiding selection decisions usually appears in the introduction. The policy introduction lists any cooperative collection development and resource-sharing agreements. Finally, the introduction describes the library's collection development organization. It locates responsibility for collection building and management. The specific tasks of evaluation, selection, collection maintenance, budget management, user community liaison, and so forth are identified and assigned.

An overview of systemwide polices and guidelines follows the introduction. Collection development policy statements will vary greatly in what they cover, though some areas are addressed more consistently. Policies usually enumerate types of materials that are selected and not selected, referencing those that apply only to certain subjects. A typical list might include statements about books, periodicals, newspapers, textbooks, juvenile materials, reprints, maps, dissertations and theses, paperbacks, microforms, pamphlets, popular magazines, artworks, musical scores, video and audio recordings, software, and access to external electronic resources. Other issues addressed in general policies might be special collections and archives, reference materials, and government documents. Policy statements dealing with languages and translations, popular and trade materials, handling of superseded materials, duplicate copies, and expensive purchases are common.

Detailed analyses of each subject collection follow the introduction and overview of systemwide policies. Libraries may use either the classed or narrative approach or a combination for each subject. If narrative, these policy statements generally follow the outline and content of the overview. Each will discuss the specific user community, specific limitations or emphasis, types of materials collected or excluded, library unit or selector responsible for this collection, interdisciplinary relationships, additional resources, and other local factors.

A collection development policy should be well organized, consistent from section to section in use of terminology and elements addressed, detailed, and literate without being wordy. A collection development policy is a formal, official, documented policy of the library, but it should be crafted in such a way that is easy to understand and practical to use. A policy that is well written will be used; one that is not will be put in a file and left there. For an example of a narrative policy, *see* figure 3-1.

E-RESOURCES POLICY

Because of the complexities of selecting and managing e-resources, a library may develop a more detailed policy to address them.[12] This separate document or component of a larger policy will address both the acquisition of digital information and the purchase of rights to access remote digital resources. By making clear how the library's "materials" budget is used for acquiring and accessing electronic resources and if it is

Figure 3-1   Collection Development Policy: Geography

PROGRAMMATIC INFORMATION

Geography is both a social-behavioral and an environmental science. Selection of materials tends to be broad in scope because of its physical and cultural nature. The selection policy is based on the following:

- The research needs of the faculty, graduate, and undergraduate students in Geography and related disciplines. Areas of research include the following:

  Cultural Geography—demography, environmental perception, urban and regional planning, political geography, cultural landscapes, and geographic nomenclature

  Mathematical Geography—cartography (traditional and computer), remote sensing, and geographic information systems

  Regional Geography—traditional and applied with emphasis in Russia, China, Latin America, South Asia, and Africa

  Economic Geography—industrial geography

  Physical Geography—climatology and geomorphology

- Instructional needs of the department's graduate and undergraduate programs.

COORDINATION AND COOPERATIVE INFORMATION

The selection of materials is coordinated by the Geography's fund administrator and the Library's liaison person (Map Librarian). Coordinated efforts should include, on occasion, the appropriate liaison people in the Earth and Mineral Science and the Life Science Librarian.

Materials ordered through the Geography fund are deposited in Pattee Library or the Earth and Mineral Science Library. Geoscience materials (monographs and serials) and publications on cartography, remote sensing, and geographic information systems are located in the E&MS [Earth and Mineral Science] Library. Maps and satellite imagery ordered through the Geography fund are housed within the Maps Collection (Pattee) or in the E&MS Library (Deike Building).

SUBJECT AND LANGUAGE MODIFIERS

Geographical. There is a global interest with emphasis on North America, Europe, regions of the former Soviet Union, and the developing countries in Latin America, Africa, and South Asia. Attempt is made to acquire up-to-date publications for other regions and countries in order to provide adequate graduate and undergraduate instruction.

Chronology. Up-to-date publications are emphasized. Historical materials (original or facsimile) may be acquired to fill in gaps in such fields as Historical Geography and the History of Geography.

(continued)

Figure 3-1 (continued)

Language. Although English is preferred, language should not be a detriment in selection.

DESCRIPTION OF MATERIALS COLLECTED
Monographs
Conference proceedings
Dissertations and theses
Government publications
Bibliographies
Maps and atlases (thematic)
Dictionaries and handbooks
Satellite images
Computer software
Journals and yearbooks

CONSPECTUS OF FIELDS AND LEVELS OF COLLECTIONS

G1-922	Geography, General	4
G1001-3122	Atlases (see Map Collection Policy Statement)	N/A
G3180999	Remote Sensing	N/A
GA40.7	Maps (see Map Collection Policy Statement)	5
GA70.2	Geographic Information Systems	5
GA51-87	Mathematical Geography	4
GA100-1999	Cartography	5
GB40-5070	Physical Geography	4
BG400-629	Geomorphology	5
GC63-1580	Oceanography	4
GF51-895	Human Ecology	4-5
HF1024	Economic Geography	4

Reprinted with the permission of Pennsylvania State University Library.

used for materials, equipment, and software in support of electronic information use and access, the library protects its budget by clarifying its responsibilities. The policy may protect by relating the responsibilities of the library to those of the computing center and campus automated network in acquiring and providing electronic information.

The Collection Development and Evaluation Section of ALA's Reference and User Services Association has assembled a set of standard elements found in electronic information collection policies.[13] E-resources policies typically address all the elements found in a standard policy statement, highlighting areas that require special attention. In describing the user community, the library may address the needs and expectations of distance learners along with the needs of the local community for remote access. It will identify any special e-resources collections (such as an electronic text center in the library) or special user groups (for example, students studying abroad who expect access to e-resources). It may repeat the criteria that guide selection decisions and note those considerations that are unique for e-resources. The policy statement lists the types of materials that are selected and excluded. The library's stance on preservation of e-resources and how this is handled may be detailed. It serves to coordinate the development of print, nonprint, and electronic collections.

The policy explains how the library handles contracts and licenses for e-resources, including who is responsible for their review and negotiation, and the role of individual selectors in the process. If the selector works with an e-resources committee or coordinating group or consults individually with staff members in other library units, this is specified. If legally binding documents are to be reviewed outside the library, the individual or unit with this authority and responsibility is identified. Library requirements that must be guaranteed in a contract will be identified. The library may require that all e-resources must provide a certain level of use statistics, that use by unaffiliated walk-in library users must be permitted, or that archival access to the resource is ensured. If the library will not accept certain contractual obligations, these are specified. For example, the library or its parent body may forbid indemnities that obligate the library.

SUPPLEMENTAL POLICIES

Other policies may be written that deal with specific issues. They may address procedures for donor relations and other considerations in accepting and declining gifts and large purchases opportunities. A preservation policy will discuss policies and procedures for maintaining the physical condition of the collections. These will cover criteria for making decisions about binding, conservation, reformatting, and other treatment options. Priorities for allocating preservation resources are covered here. A separate statement about weeding and deselection policy is useful. This will define the policy for review of materials for transfer between collections, transfer to remote storage, and withdrawal. It may include guidelines for canceling periodical subscriptions and disposing of unneeded materials. If appropriate, this section addresses the library's responsibilities as a library of record or resource for the region, district, state, or within a consortium.

Budgeting and Finance

Once a library's goals and objectives are understood through the planning process, its budget serves both to document those decisions through allocations and to coordinate achieving those goals and objectives. Allocations are a measure of the financial commitment to support activities necessary to reach the goals outlined in a plan. A well-crafted budget becomes an internal control that can measure operating effectiveness and performance. The materials budget, also called the acquisitions budget, collections budget, or the resources budget, is one portion of a library's total budget. Eugene L. Wiemers Jr. wrote that "the materials budget is both the plan and the framework that sets the boundaries within which choice will be allowed to operate. The 'correct' budget will produce the optimal set of limits on choice that will reflect the library's collection goals and priorities, and provide a mechanism to track the library's efforts to reach those goals."[14]

The word *budget* is used in two ways. In the planning sense, the library's budget is its plan for the use of money available during a fiscal year and reflects allocations, expected revenues, and projected expenditures. A proposed budget is presented to funding authorities as both a request for funding and a plan for what the library will do with the money it receives. Allocations are the dollar amounts that are distributed to various fund lines in the budget. This budget also is called a "budget document." Such a budget may include, in addition to allocations and other sources of revenue, fund balances and encumbrances brought forward from the previous year, if permitted by the parent agency. A fund balance consists of the dollars allocated but unexpended at the end of a fiscal year. Encumbrances represent the cost of orders that have been placed but not yet received. An encumbrance is recorded as soon as the obligation for payment is incurred, that is, when the order is placed. If encumbrances are present at the end of the fiscal year, unexpended funds must be held in escrow until payments for outstanding orders are made.

Budget also can mean the total amount of funds available to meet a library's expenditures over a fixed period of time. The budget will vary from year to year. This use of *budget* is at play when a librarian reports that he or she received an increase or decrease in the current year's budget, compared to the previous year. Most libraries manage their budgets on a fiscal year, which may or may not parallel the calendar year. Parent institutions determine the fiscal year. Most colleges, universities, schools, public libraries, and many companies run on a July-to-June fiscal year, while the U.S. government's fiscal year begins October 1 and ends September 30.

The materials budget is one part of the overall library budget. A library also has an operating budget, which covers ongoing expenses necessary to operate the library. The personnel budget may be managed within the operating budget, or it may be a third separate budget within the total budget. For many libraries, the split will be 30 percent for collections, 50 percent for personnel, and 20 percent for operating expenses. In some libraries, once funds are appropriated to the library and allocated to the library's materials budget, operating budget, and personnel budget, they cannot be moved from one budget section to another. However, as libraries purchase an increasing amount of access to computerized resources, the line between the operating and materials budgets becomes less and less distinct.

The planning process should make clear which budget will cover which types of expenses. The materials budget may be intended to cover the purchase of equipment to house collections, costs to support the technological infrastructure that provides access to electronic resources, binding and other preservation and conservation treatments, vendor service charges, and shipping and handling fees. Some libraries fund document delivery through the materials budget.

A materials budget should be consistent with both the library's long-range and its short-range plans. Budgets are most effective and most realistic if their preparation occurs within the context of organizational planning. Both the overall mission of the library and the goals and objectives of library departments should be considered. Because budgets so often parallel the accounting period, they often focus on short-range planning at the expense of the long-range view. Long-range fiscal planning is difficult because the library's future and that of its environment are so volatile. Libraries face problems in predicting materials costs and the effect of inflation, publication patterns, international currency fluctuations, and the funds that will be available. In addition, the parent agency may make unanticipated changes that affect the user community and user demands and expectations. Nevertheless, including long-range projections in the total budgeting process is important.

Materials budgets, both the request for funding and the allocations once funds are received, are usually prepared by the librarian with administrative responsibility for collections. In a smaller library, the head librarian may prepare the total budget, of which the materials budget is one portion. In larger libraries, the individual with administrative responsibility for collection development and management usually prepares the materials budget, generally in consultation with individual selectors or, perhaps, with a coordinating committee. Individual selectors usually are asked to present annual requests for the level of funding they wish to receive in their fund lines in the next fiscal year. The administrator with responsibility for the entire materials budget rolls these individual requests into the total requested for the library.

Approaches to the budgeting process vary from library to library. The parent institution may mandate the approach, and in some organizations, this may change from year to year. Zero-based budgets require a fresh start each year. The library is asked to begin with a blank page and determine how much to spend in each category of the budget. Each funding request is proposed and defended without reference to past practice. Few government and nonprofit organizations take this approach because of the amount of work involved. A program or performance budgeting approach looks at allocations for specific activities or programs and provides a very clear connection with planning documents and the objectives set each year. Most organizations use a historical or incremental budget approach, which determines the needed incremental changes in various categories. Combining incremental budgeting with program budgeting is a common practice. The library begins with the previous year's base budget and identifies programmatic priorities that should be funded at a higher level. The librarian should approach budget preparation in the manner required by his or her parent institution. An effective budget system provides the tools for making reasonable decisions about allocation or reallocation of resources.

Types of Funding Sources

For most libraries, the largest part of the budget is funded through an appropriation from the parent organization. Prior to the end of the fiscal year, the library prepares a funding request and, just prior to or soon after the beginning of the fiscal year, receives an appropriation. In many organizations, the budget for library materials is treated as a protected category and may receive extra scrutiny and interest in how it is allocated and spent. This scrutiny underlines the need for linking the budget to a well-crafted and widely supported plan. Sources of funding, in addition to an appropriation, include gifts, endowment income, grants, fees and charges, and fines.

Development Activities and Grant Proposal Writing

Supplemental funds are of increasing importance in most libraries. In the broadest sense, fund-raising is the process of seeking additional monies from sources other than the parent organization and covers seeking gifts, bequests, and grants. Collections librarians are becoming more involved in fund-raising. They may be called upon to write or present proposals to donors to solicit collections, obtain funds to purchase collections, and create endowments that will generate income to maintain collections. As institutions become more dependent on these sources of funds, they have found that the librarians closest to the collection and its users often can make the most convincing cases to the donor. Their enthusiasm and commitment can be infectious. A successful fund-raiser knows one's job, one's institution, and one's donor.[15] Selectors also play a critical role in the stewardship process by ensuring that gifts, whether dollars or collections, are managed well. Donors often mandate how the money is to be spent and expect that their gifts will be an addition to the amount currently allocated to that specific purpose. Most donors want to know that their gifts are being used to further the goals of the institution. Selectors are called upon to write letters or meet with donors to thank them, to let them know how their gifts are being used, and to encourage their continued involvement with the library.

Grants can provide additional funding for library collections. Collections librarians may be expected to seek grant funding from private and government agencies. Grant proposals draw upon the selector's knowledge of the collection and its users and require special writing skills. Once a library receives a grant, tracking mechanisms and reporting procedures will be specified in the grant guidelines. The reporting dates for the grant may be different from the library's fiscal year. Projects funded through grants should be consistent with the library's planning and reflect its goals.

Material Budget Requests

Prior to the beginning of the fiscal year, the library will be asked to submit a budget request. This is usually part of the overall planning process of the parent organization. The library can use this process for two purposes: to request funds and to inform. A well-crafted proposal begins by explaining a library's financial needs in reference to internal and external forces. Ideally, an environmental scan has assembled this information and informed the library's planning document. Through this explanation, the funding body or parent institution learns about pressures, constraints, and expectations the library faces. An initial summary of external and internal conditions sets the stage for a convincing proposal. This information must be presented clearly and succinctly but with enough detail to make a case.

Internal conditions are those factors in the library's immediate environment. Among these are changes in the population to be served. Many libraries are serving user communities that are becoming more diverse, and they are called upon to provide new resources to meet the needs of these changing populations. Special libraries may support new product research and development or other new corporate foci. School library media centers may have increasing or declining enrollments or new graduation standards. An academic institution may be expected to serve new graduate programs, undergraduate degrees, or research centers. Changing ways of teaching can affect how a collection is used and increase demand on secondary resources or access to online indexes and resources. Another internal influence on the budget is the collection mix, that is, the kinds of materials in the collection. A library with a higher ratio of serials to monographs can predict greater financial need. Libraries with a higher proportion of foreign acquisitions will be more vulnerable to fluctuations in foreign currency. Budgeting is forecasting future funding needs based on internal and external factors.

Some of the external conditions to which a budget proposal might draw attention are changes in pricing trends in library materials and services, volume of materials published, impact of electronic information, consumer price index, and value of the dollar on the international market. Over the last fifteen years, serials and book prices have increased at significantly greater rates than either the consumer price index or annual increases to most library's base allocations. An added pressure is the increase in the volume of materials to be considered for purchase. Attention also should be drawn to the extensive new resources available in electronic formats. Librarians, seeking to support user community needs and interest through access to these resources, should ensure that funding agencies are aware of the many pressures on materials budgets.

Indexing the materials budget to market prices has been a successful strategy for some libraries.[16] The underlying premise is that supporting a library is part of the operating costs of the parent institution or agency and that increases in materials costs should be covered in the same way that increases in heating and telecommunication are covered. Indexing monitors the levels of book and serial production, fluctuations in exchange rates, and inflation in materials costs and produces a target funding level that will maintain a specified rate of acquisitions and access.

Some libraries use the budgets of an agreed-upon set of peer institutions as benchmarks to support their own budget requests. In many cases, the parent institution may have determined a set of peers, and comparing the resources of the library to those held by the other members of the peer group can be useful. No matter the strategy used, a materials budget proposal should make clear the consequences of various funding levels. Using statistical data and meaningful information will strengthen the budget proposal and provide an opportunity to inform the parent institution of the library's short- and long-term plans. In the process, the library should take care to present consequences not as threats but as reality.

Several reliable sources provide statistical information. These include professional library publications, trade publications, and library service vendors. Possible sources are

"Periodical Price Survey," which appeared previously in *Library Journal* and *American Libraries* and is now published annually in *Library Resources and Technical Services;*

Bowker Annual Library and Book Trade Almanac;

Statistical Abstract of the United States, issued by the U.S. Department of Commerce and Bureau of the Census;

Publisher's Weekly;

Book Industry Trends, published by the Industry Study Group; and reports and projections prepared by serials and monograph service vendors, which can be found on their web sites.

Allocation of Funds

The allocation of funds within the collection development budget may absorb much of a head librarian's or a collection development officer's time. The annual allocation process is an opportunity to create "a successful budget [that] translates competing demands into real levels of financial support."[17] The goal of the allocation process is to reflect the goals and priorities set out in the library's planning process and to create a mechanism to track the library's efforts to reach those goals. The method used to make allocations should be understood clearly by both those within the library and by external parties.

Most materials budgets are line-item budgets, with subdivisions or subaccounts within the larger budget. A line-item budget allows easy comparisons from year to year. Large libraries may have 100 or more lines. In academic libraries, budgets typically are allocated first by subject or discipline. Academic libraries and other types of libraries may allocate by one or more of the following: location (main library, a branch library, children's department, remote research site); type of user (children and adult); and format or genre (monographs, serials, reference materials, fiction, microforms, online resources, newspapers). Very large libraries may further subdivide allocations. For example, funds allocated to purchase materials for children in a large public library may be subdivided to fund lines for nonfiction, fiction, picture books, and videos. In this way, allocations mirror the organizational structure of the library, the community served, and the collection development policy. Selectors are responsible for one or more fund lines. This division provides for accountability and convenience of reporting. It simplifies the process of aligning the library's goals with those of the parent institution, but it may heighten the political sensitivity of the process. Citizens or faculty members may question why the library spends more money in one area than another when the funding is allocated into readily identifiable budget lines. These allocations should be supported by a good plan and collection policy, which will help respond to concerns of this nature.

Libraries, even those that do not use multiple fund lines, typically divide the annual budget between discretionary and nondiscretionary allocations. Discretionary purchases are individual orders for items. Nondiscretionary purchases are those materials that arrive routinely and automatically without creating individual purchase orders. Recent rapid increases in the prices of serials have made keeping track of the balance between expenditures for serials and monographs especially critical. As serials have inflated in cost, many libraries have reduced the amount they allocate to monographs and other discretionary purchases to maintain current serial subscriptions or to contain the number of serials canceled. Establishing a ratio between serials and monographs can be useful. Although the collecting goals of each library will affect this ratio, a common practice in academic libraries is to maintain a ratio of no less than 30 percent of the budget spent on monographs and no more than 70 percent on serials. Public and school libraries generally aim for something closer to a 50/50 ratio. Special libraries may set a target that accepts spending 80 percent of the budget on serials. Libraries also use ratios to help guide their shift to purchasing electronic resources. One academic library has signaled its commitment to providing comprehensive electronic delivery of information by setting an initial goal of committing 8 percent of the materials budget to electronic resources by 2002 and projecting that this would grow to 40 percent by 2010.[18]

Various methods of allocating the budget to fund lines are used. These range from using an allocation formula to following a strict historical division of the budget. Allocation formulas are usually built on supply and demand factors.[19] The supply factors take into account the amount of material published in the subject area and the cost of those materials. Demand factors include number of students, faculty, courses offered, circulation, registered borrowers, or interlibrary rates. Often, factors are weighted to reflect institutional priorities or other factors. For example, the number of doctoral students may be weighted three times the number of undergraduates in the formula to accommodate the specialized resources needs of doctoral candidates. A public library may look at demographic data to determine a formula for allocating funds to different user communities. A formula provides an easily understandable explanation for allocations and is most useful in a setting where the budget is open to a wide and highly interested constituency of library users. Formulas may shift funds dramatically in response to changes in user demand. This might be the creation or elimination of an academic program or a new community emphasis, such as supporting small businesses.

Another method of allocation is more incremental and based on historical allocation. A senior collection development officer or the director of the library gathers information from selectors and from the parent organization and makes adjustments and changes in the historical allocations based on this information. The collection development officer often takes into account the same factors used in the allocation formula but brings to bear his or her knowledge of the parent institution and the library's longer-term goals in a less rigid manner. One advantage of this method is that the effects of unexpected and short-term shifts in the parent body are diminished.

Most libraries hold some money aside in a contingency fund, which may be managed by the collection development officer, the library director, or a library committee. This fund can be used to meet unexpected needs, to purchase large and expensive items, and to balance unexpected fluctuations in user demand. Holding between 5 and 10 percent of the total materials budget in a contingency fund is a common strategy.

Expending the Budget

Once the collections budget is allocated, it must be spent. Expenditures are tracked to inform the planning process and to allow the library to report on its progress to the parent institution or governing body. Many libraries use this information to assess the performance of selectors and of the library as a whole. For example, the parent institution may have a goal of supporting diversity. The library may set a goal of purchasing a certain number of items that support multicultural or diverse populations. The library will use the reports of funds expended to show progress toward this goal. In addition, reports of expenditures are useful when preparing stewardship reports and thanking donors.

Most libraries set targets for expenditures and encumbrances during and at the end of the fiscal year. Institutions that operate on a cash accounting system require that the funds be fully expended by the end of the fiscal year and do not permit the carry forward of unexpended funds. Some organizations using a cash accounting system do permit carrying forward of encumbrances and the funds held in escrow to cover payment when the ordered item is receipted. The accrual system of accounting allows one to carry over unexpended funds in addition to encumbered dollars, which are added to the new year's allocation. Some libraries and their parent organizations discourage developing large cash balances, often called reserves, which can suggest that the library or a particular budget line is overfunded. *See* figure 3-2.

Figure 3-2 Budget Planning Cycle

July	**Fiscal Year Closeout/New Year Start-up** • Open and partial orders and funds rolled over for new fiscal year cycle. • Preliminary allocations made and selectors advised to begin ordering, assuming they have 60% of previous year's allocation (all funds and endowments) and carryover and unexpended gift funds from previous year. • Administration notifies libraries about new general funds available for collections. • First half-year payment made to vendor to ensure approval plan discount.
August	**New Fiscal Year Allocation Planning** • Library Budget Advisory Group meets to determine distribution of general funds. • Selectors advised if serials cancellation required. • Assistant dean, collections, in consultation with Collection Development Advisory Group, determines subject and collection allocations.

September	• End-of-fiscal-year documentation prepared for selectors, including
	    summaries of allocations,
	    outstanding encumbrances, and
	    expenditures by category.
	• Balance of current FY funds (new general funds and endowment funds) is allocated to subject and collection fund lines.
	• Serial title cancellations due to Serials Department.
	• Selectors submit special purchase requests to the assistant dean, collections.

November	• General monographic funds should be 66% committed.
January	• General monographic funds should be 85% committed. • All non-U.S. source orders should be submitted by January 31. • Second half-year payment made to vendor to ensure approval plan discount.
March	• March 15th: Deadline for submitting monographic orders (should be 100% committed). • March 31st: Uncommitted general funds pooled for special purchases.
April	• Research purchase requests solicited, final decisions made, and orders placed.
June	• June 30th: Endowment funds should be fully committed.

In general, libraries experience a significant lag between the date an order is placed and the date the item is received and the invoice is paid. For large libraries, this lag can average as long as ninety days. The period between order placement and item receipt of highly specialized materials can be years. Selectors usually have encumbrance target dates that are based on the library's experience with receiving material and paying bills. The simplest way to accomplish this is to count backward from the end of the fiscal year and end the collection development year on the last day one can expect to receive and pay for the material. Setting interim dates to check the progress of the library toward its goal of fully expending the budget is important. The amount of material published can vary widely from year to year, and there may be a need for midyear adjustments to accommodate these changes to ensure all funds are spent by the end of the fiscal year.

Most institutions require some separation of selection, acquisition, and payment responsibilities. Depending on the size of the library, it may have three people or three departments. Within a large acquisitions department, separate units may order and receive materials. In very small libraries, the same person may handle all functions. However, the three functions should be clearly defined and distinguished to guard against fraud and malfeasance. Proper handling of these functions is necessary for a successful audit. Audits are reviews of financial records, usually conducted at regular intervals by parties external to the library. They serve to verify that financial records are accurate and orderly, that the library is in compliance with organizational and generally accepted accounting policies and procedures, and that units are operating effectively.

Monitoring the Materials Budget

Several individuals have responsibilities for monitoring the materials budget. The selector has a responsibility to monitor his or her allocations and to ensure that funds are being expended over the fiscal year in accordance with individual objectives and library goals. The collection development officer, or other librarian with overall responsibility for the materials budget, monitors the total budget to track that balances are being spent down and, when necessary, to reallocate unspent funds. He or she is charged with ensuring that the budget is being spent in a manner consistent with the library's planning documents. The library financial officer oversees procedures to determine that encumbrances and payments are correctly recorded. If any funds are to be carried forward into the next year, either as encumbered or cash balances, the financial officer negotiates and monitors this process. Usually, the financial officer prepares year-end reports. These show balances by fund line and report expenditures and encumbrances. The collection development officer uses this report to see if goals were met and to prepare the next year's budget request and to adjust allocations.

Summary

Formal, systematic planning is both an organizational and individual responsibility in libraries. Plans, by analyzing the library's environment and mission, improve the quality of all decisions. In other words, the library has a better understanding of its desired future and how to apply available resources to obtain that future. Systematic planning may follow one or more models, depending on the particular situation and the methods endorsed by its parent organization. Strategic planning, with its specific focus on understanding and responding to a changing environment through continual revision, is a commonly applied planning model. The process of planning brings librarians to a better understanding of their library's mission and goals. A plan, which includes desired goals and objectives toward reaching these goals, shares this information with constituents. Both library users and parent agencies are provided benchmarks against which to measure the library's effective use of financial resources. Planning, though time-consuming, is justified by its importance to future success.

The purpose of a library collection development policy, a central planning document, is to inform and protect. It defines the scope of existing collections, relates the library's collecting goals to the resources available to meet them, incorporates the parent institution's mission, and recognizes current and future user needs. A policy protects the library against external pressures, particularly in the areas of intellectual freedom and censorship. The policy's audience is the library's staff, its users, and its governing or administrative body.

Format, content, and style must be selected in response to the audience. Classed analysis, narrative, or a combination of the two are the most frequently used formats. Most policies contain information on the user community, limitations in meeting the needs of that community, an overview of the library and its collections, descriptions of cooperative arrangements, an overview of how collection development and management decisions are handled, and general policies, guidelines, and criteria. Policies in larger or more complex libraries will include detailed policy statements of particular formats, genre, subjects, and disciplines. All policies should be written clearly and succinctly. A collection policy statement describes—in a public voice—where the collections budget is going and how collections decisions are being made. The most effective policy statements are realistic documents, built on a theoretical base. The importance and value of a collection development policy lies in the context it provides for every decision made in a library.

Collections budgets are an important part of the planning process and also a mechanism for tracking effectiveness. A good collections budget is one that reflects the goals of the parent institution. It provides a mechanism to show the library's commitment to its goals in concrete fiscal terms and to monitor progress toward those goals. Good budgeting does not replace good selecting. They are complementary processes. Collections policies and budgeting are part of the planning process that informs collection development and management.

| CASE STUDY |

Plymouth Public Library is located in a small midwestern town of 6,000. It is a member of a regional public library network of twelve public libraries, each serving towns of similar size. The libraries share a union online catalog and have a twice-weekly delivery service between the libraries. The Plymouth Public Library has a collection of 22,500 volumes and 110 current subscriptions. The library has a small special collection focusing on Iowa authors and local history. Two public terminals provide access to the union catalog and the Internet. Through the regional library system, on-site patrons can access OCLC's WorldCat and Infotrac SearchBank. A full-time professional librarian, Sharon Vernon, who reports to the town's library board, manages the library. She has 2.5 full-time staff members, none of whom has a graduate library degree. One assistant, Nancy Anderson, has primary responsibility for children's programming and materials selection. Sharon selects all other materials. The annual materials budget is $25,000, of which $12,000 is spent on serials. The library has limited space and little hope of expansion or a new building. Plymouth has a consolidated elementary and high school, which draws students from farms and the nearby Native American reservation. The schools share a small media center, which contains basic reference materials, fifteen current magazines, and approximately 5,000 volumes of juvenile and young adult fiction and nonfiction. The school's English teachers regularly give the public library a list of novels that are being read in the high school. Students depend on the public library for most of their school research projects. Farming is the primary source of income, along with allied businesses. Plymouth is the county seat and the location of the county courthouse and jail. Approximately seventy-five people live in the Plymouth nursing home and rehabilitation center.

Activity

Prepare an outline for a collection policy statement and identify any supplemental policies that should be included. Identify stakeholders who might be consulted in writing the policy. Suggest the fund lines and subaccounts for a budget, which will parallel the policy and support the purposes of budgets to plan, coordinate, and control library activities through expenditures.

REFERENCES

1. Peter Drucker, *Management: Tasks, Responsibilities, Practices* (New York: Harper & Row, 1974), 125.
2. George Keller, *Academic Strategy: The Management Revolution in American Higher Education* (Baltimore, Md.: Johns Hopkins Univ. Pr., 1983), 140–41.
3. John D. Stoffels, "Environmental Scanning for Future Success," *Managerial Planning* 31, no. 3 (Nov./Dec. 1982): 4–12.
4. C. Davis Fogg, *Team-Based Strategic Planning: A Complete Guide to Structuring, Facilitating, and Implementing the Process* (New York: American Management Assn., 1994).
5. Not all librarians are convinced of the necessity of collection development policies. *See*, for example, Richard Snow, "Wasted Words: The Written Collection Development Policy and the Academic Library," *Journal of Academic Librarianship* 22 (May 1996): 191–94, which challenges this assumption.
6. Paul H. Mosher, "Fighting Back: From Growth to Management in Library Collection Development" (unpublished paper delivered at the Pilot Collection Management and Development Institute at Stanford University, July 6–10, 1981), 4.
7. Joanne S. Anderson, ed., *Guide for Written Collection Policy Statements*, 2d ed., Collection Management and Development Guides, no. 7 (Chicago: American Library Assn., 1996), 1.

8. American Library Assn., Coordinating Committee on Revision of Public Library Standards, *Public Library Service to America: A Guide to Evaluation, with Minimum Standards* (Chicago: American Library Assn., 1956); and American Assn. of School Librarians, *Policies and Procedures for the Selection of School Library Materials* (Chicago: American Library Assn., 1961).

9. The "Library Bill of Rights" and other resources on censorship, intellectual freedom, and the law and American Library Association's Free to Read initiative can be found in the *Intellectual Freedom Manual* (Chicago: American Library Assn., 2002).

10. Several resources on format, content, and style are available. Among these are Anderson's *Guide for Written Collection Policy Statements* and Elizabeth Futas, ed., *Collection Development Policies and Procedures,* 3d ed. (Phoenix, Ariz.: Oryx, 1995); Richard J. Wood and Frank Hoffmann, *Library Collection Development Policies: A Reference and Writers' Handbook* (Lanham, Md.: Scarecrow, 1996); and Beth Mazin, ed., *AcqWeb's Directory of Collection Development Policies on the Web,* available at http://acqweb.library. vanderbilt.edu/acqweb/cd_policy.html.

11. Dora Biblarz, "The Conspectus as a Blueprint for Creating Collection Development Policy Statements," in *Collection Assessment: A Look at the RLG Conspectus,* ed. Richard J. Wood and Katina P. Strauch, 169–76 (New York: Haworth, 1992).

12. Representative policies can be found at a site compiled by Ann Okerson, *Electronic Collection Development,* available at http://www.library.yale. edu/~okerson/ecd.html.

13. Reference and User Services Assn., Collection Development Policies Committee, *Core Elements of Electronic Collection Policy Statements,* available at the RUSA web site (http://www.ala.org/rusa); click "CODES" on the top navigation bar.

14. Eugene L. Wiemers Jr., "Budget," in *Collection Management: A New Treatise,* ed. Charles B. Osburn and Ross Atkinson, Foundations in Library and Information Science, v. 26 (Greenwich, Conn.: JAI Pr., 1991), 67.

15. David Farrell, "Fundraising for Collection Development Librarians," in *Collection Management and Development: Issues in an Electronic Era,* ed. Peggy Johnson and Bonnie MacEwan (Chicago: American Library Assn., 1994), 138.

16. Gay N. Dannelly, "Indexing Material Budgets at Ohio State University," in *Collection Management and Development: Issues in an Electronic Era,* ed. Peggy Johnson and Bonnie MacEwan (Chicago: American Library Assn., 1994), 126–32.

17. Wiemers Jr., "Budget," 68–69.

18. Colorado State University Libraries, "Vision for the Library," 2001, available at http://manta.library.colostate.edu/taskforce.pdf.

19. Charles B. Lowry, in "Reconciling Pragmatism, Equity, and Need in the Formula Allocation of Book and Serial Funds," *College and Research Libraries* 53, no. 2 (March 1992): 121–38, offers an overview of formulas, including the limits they have as allocation tools.

SUGGESTED READINGS

Birdsall, Douglas. "Strategic Planning in Academic Libraries: A Political Perspective." In *Restructuring Academic Libraries: Organizational Development in the Wake of Technological Change*, edited by Charles A. Schwartz, 253–61. ACRL Publications in Librarianship, no. 49. Chicago: American Library Assn., 1997.

Bryant, Bonita. "Collection Development Policies in Medium-Sized Academic Libraries." In *The Collection Building Reader*, edited by Betty-Carol Sellen and Arthur Curley, 45–56. New York: Neal-Schuman, 1992.

Bryson, John M. *Strategic Planning for Public and Nonprofit Organizations: A Guide to Strengthening and Sustaining Organizational Achievement*. Rev. ed. San Francisco: Jossey-Bass, 1995.

Curriculum Materials Center Collection Development Policy. 2d ed. Compiled by Beth G. Anderson et al. Chicago: Education and Behavioral Sciences Section, Assn. of College and Research Libraries, American Library Assn., 1993.

Daubert, Madeline J. *Financial Management for Small and Medium-Sized Libraries*. Chicago: American Library Assn., 1993.

Evans, G. Edward, Patricia Layzell Ward, and Bendik Rugaas. "The Planning Process." Chapter 7 in *Management Basics for Information Professionals*, 161–90. New York: Neal-Schuman, 2000.

Fisher, William, and Barbara G. Leonard. "Budgeting for Information Resources: Current Trends and Future Directions." In *Collection Management for the Twenty-first Century: A Handbook for Librarians*, edited by G. E. Gorman and Ruth H. Miller, 207–17. Westport, Conn.: Greenwood, 1997.

Friend, Frederick J. "Policy: Politics, Powers and People." In *Collection Management*, edited by G. E. Gorman, 45–58. International Yearbook of Library and Information Management, 2000/2001. London: Library Assn. Pub., 2000.

German, Lisa, et al., editors. *Guide to the Management of the Information Resources Budget*. Collection Management and Development Guides, no. 9. Lanham, Md.: Scarecrow and the Assn. for Library Collections and Technical Services, 2001.

Gieseck, Joan, ed. *Scenario Planning for Libraries*. Chicago: American Library Assn., 1998.

Hall-Ellis, Sylvia D., and Frank W. Hoffmann. *Grantsmanship for Small Libraries and School Library Media Centers*. Englewood, Colo.: Libraries Unlimited, 1999.

Hopkins, Diane M. "Put It in Writing: What You Should Know about Challenges to School Library Materials." *School Library Journal* 39 (Jan. 1993): 26–30.

Johnson, Peggy. "Collection Management Policies and Electronic Resources." In *Collection Management for the Twenty-first Century: A Handbook for Librarians*, edited by G. E. Gorman and Ruth H. Miller, 83–104. Westport, Conn.: Greenwood, 1997.

Kachel, Debra E. "The Written Collection Development Policy." In her *Collection Assessment and Management for School Libraries: Preparing for Cooperative Collection Development*, 53–76. Westport, Conn.: Greenwood, 1997.

Lynden, Frederick C. "Budgeting for Collection Development in the Electronic Environment." In *Collection Development in the Electronic Environment: Shifting Priorities,* edited by Sul H. Lee, 37–56. New York: Haworth, 1999. Also published in *Journal of Library Administration* 28, no. 4.

Maple, Amanda, and Jean Morrow. *Guide to Writing Collection Development Policies for Music.* Music Library Assn. Technical Reports Series, no. 26. Lanham, Md.: Scarecrow and the Music Library Assn., 2001.

Martin, Murray S. *Collection Development and Finance: A Guide to Strategic Library-Materials Budgeting.* Frontiers of Access to Library Materials, no. 2. Chicago: American Library Assn., 1995.

Packer, Donna. "Acquisitions Allocations: Equity, Politics, and Bundled Pricing." *Portal: Libraries and the Academy* 1, no. 3 (July 2001): 209–24.

Prentice, Ann E. *Financial Planning for Libraries.* 2d ed. Lanham, Md.: Scarecrow, 1996.

Public Library Assn. Policy Manual Committee. *PLA Handbook for Writers of Public Library Policies.* Chicago: American Library Assn., 1993.

Rounds, Richard S., and Margo C. Trumpeter. *Basic Budgeting Practices for Librarians.* 2d ed. Chicago: American Library Assn., 1994.

Scholtz, James C. "Developing Video Collection Development Policies to Accommodate Existing and New Technologies." In *Video Collection Development in Multi-Type Libraries,* 2d ed., edited by Gary P. Handman, 245–76. New York: Greenwood, 2002.

Smith, G. Stevenson. *Accounting for Libraries and Other Not-for-Profit Organizations.* 2d ed. Chicago: American Library Assn., 2002.

Smyth, Elaine B. "A Practical Approach to Writing a Collection Development Policy." *Rare Book and Manuscripts Librarianship* 14, no. 1 (1999): 27–31.

"Spending Smart: How to Budget and Finance." [Special section] *Book Report* 21, no. 1 (May/June 2002): 6–24.

Steele, Victoria, and Stephen D. Elder. *Becoming a Fundraiser: The Principles and Practice of Library Development.* Chicago: American Library Assn., 2000.

Stephens, Annabel K. "The Public Library Planning Process: Its Impact on Collection Development Policies and Practices." In *Public Library Collection Development in the Information Age,* edited by Annabel K. Stephens, 15–23. New York: Haworth, 1998. Also published in *The Acquisitions Librarian,* no. 20.

Strong, Rob. "A Collection Development Policy Incorporating Electronic Resources." *Journal of Interlibrary Loan, Document Delivery and Information Supply* 9, no. 4 (1999): 53–64.

Wilder, Stanley J., with the assistance of Mary Katherine Brannon and Tonya H. Chustz. "Materials Budget Management: Good Practice, Good Politics." In *Technical Services Today and Tomorrow,* 2d ed., edited by Michael Gorman, 53–65. Englewood, Colo.: Libraries Unlimited, 1998.

CHAPTER 4

▌ Developing Collections

Introduction

This chapter is titled "Developing Collections" because it covers the activities that develop collections both on-site and accessed remotely. It might have been called "Selection" in earlier times. Selecting between two or more options is part of nearly every decision collections librarians make as they seek to implement collection development and management goals. Dennis Carrigan has written that "the essence of collection development is choice."[1] This chapter introduces various typologies for defining types of materials and explores the selection process and selection criteria, sources for identifying titles, interaction with the acquisition process, acquisition options, diverse user communities and alternative literature, and censorship and intellectual freedom.

Selecting among the vast number of materials published each year can seem a daunting task. Book title output increases every year. The *UNESCO Statistical Yearbook* for 1999, the last year from which data are available, reported more than 900,000 hardbound, trade paper, and mass-market paperbound books published worldwide in 1996.[2] During 2001, more than 141,700 titles were published in the United States and more than 43,500 in Canada.[3] The forty-first edition of *Ulrich's Periodicals Directory* (2003) listed more than 164,000 periodical and irregular titles.[4]

Librarians are challenged by increasing materials costs as well as the vast number of publications. The costs of materials have been increasing far in excess of U.S. inflation for more than twenty years and usually in excess of most libraries' acquisition budgets. Between 2001 and 2002, the Consumer Price Index (CPI) increased by 2.4 percent, but the average price of U.S. periodicals journals increased by 7.9 percent.[5] The average unit cost of monographs acquired by Association of Research Libraries (ARL) members in 2002 increased from $48.09 to $50.17 (4.3 percent) over the previous year.[6] ARL statistics report that the cost of serials increased 227 percent and the cost of monographs increased 75 percent between 1986 and 2002.[7] No library can keep up with these increases. Among the ARL members during that same period, the number of serials purchased increased 9 percent and monographs decreased by 5 percent.[8] Selection becomes more challenging because collections librarians must be increasingly selective.

Types of Materials

A first step in selecting materials is to separate them into categories and assign responsibility for their selection and management. Several typologies have been and continue to be used. Many of these overlap. Format is a typical typology and distinguishes, for example, between print, microforms, video and audio recordings, and electronic resources. Format often guides how the material is handled in the library—who catalogs it and how it is marked, shelved or stored, and serviced or circulated. Other formats are maps, slides, pictures, globes, kits, models, games, manuscripts and archives, and realia.

Genre is often mingled incorrectly with format when discussing types of materials. Categories within genre include monographs, monographic series, dissertations, musical scores, newspapers, application software, numeric data sets, exhibition catalogs, pamphlets, novels, plays, manuals, web sites, encyclopedias, ephemera or gray literature, indexes and abstracts, directories, journals, magazines, textbooks, and government documents. A single genre may be presented in several formats. For example, serial publications can be acquired in print, microform, and various digital formats.

Resources may be categorized by subject. These may be broad divisions (humanities, social sciences, sciences), more narrow (literature, sociology, engineering) or very refined (American literature, family social science, chemical engineering). Often, the categories are described by divisions in a classification scheme, typically the Library of Congress or Dewey decimal systems. Some genres are more frequently found within subjects and disciplines. For example, the sciences rely heavily on proceedings and research reports. Tests and other measurement tools are part of the education and psychology literature.

Materials can be subdivided by language in which they are produced or geographic area in which they are published or which they cover. They may be considered by the age of the reader to whom they are directed—children, young adult, adult. These too can be subdivided (e.g., picture books, early readers, etc.). Some libraries employ categories that reflect their organizational structure. The staff members in the Reference Unit will select reference materials, librarians in the Children's Services Unit will select all materials for young readers, librarians in the Popular Reading collection select these materials, and so on. Academic and research libraries may distinguish between primary (source documents), secondary (reviews, state-of-the-art summaries, textbooks, interpretations of primary sources), and tertiary resources (repackaging of the primary literature in popular treatments, annuals, handbooks, and encyclopedias).

Typologies guide how reviews, publication lists, and introductions to the literature are organized or defined. These may reflect format, such as *CD-ROMs in Print*.[9] They may reflect subject areas *(Index to Social Sciences and Humanities Proceedings)*, reader groups *(Magazines for Kids and Teens)*, or genre *(Fiction Catalog)*.[10] An appendix at the end of this book suggests bibliographic tools, directories, and review resources to aid in selection.

Most libraries employ combinations of categorizations that merge various approaches. Academic libraries may use a combination of subject or discipline specialists, geographic area studies librarians, and a government documents librarian. Committees often are used to deal with a specific genre, for example, serials committees and electronic resources committees. Rigidly following typological distinctions in performing collections responsibilities can result in important resources being ignored because they are outside a selector's scope. The needs of the library and its clientele are best served when the entire collection is viewed as a coherent whole.

The Selection Process and Selection Criteria

Selection is both an art and a science. It results from a combination of knowledge, experience, and intuition. An experienced collections librarian is hard-pressed to explain exactly how he or she decides what to add and what to exclude. Jon Rutledge and Luke Swindler proposed a mental model that assigns a weighted value to each criterion considered. They suggested that a selector works through this mental model and reaches one of three conclusions: the title must be added, should be added, or could be added.[11] Lynn B. Williams explored how the mind works in the decision process, citing the role of recognition, "an automatic or deliberative decision-making process whereby a cue is subjected to some kind of familiarity test and an affirmative or negative response is given."[12] Recognition guides the selector to determine if the item is appropriate and helps answer questions about whether the content is relevant and whether the author, editor, publisher, or title is familiar. Williams noted that recognition capabilities are strengthened as a result of frequent, routine, and repeated collection building. Mastery comes through these activities.

Despite the central role that experience and intuition play in collection building, familiarity with the tools selectors use and understanding the techniques, processes, and potential problems are essential building blocks for success. The selector must know the appropriate resources for locating suitable materials. He or she needs skills in choosing between various materials and formats, evaluating materials' quality, and balancing costs with funds available.

All selection decisions begin with consideration of the user community and the long-term mission, goals, and priorities of the library and its parent body. Long ago, Francis K. W. Drury stated, "The high purpose of book selection is to provide the right book for the right reader at the right time."[13] In the ideal situation, a collections librarian has a written collection development policy that describes the library's mission and user community and provides guidance for developing and managing a collection and the subsection or category for which he or she is responsible. In the absence of a local policy, the librarian aims to understand the informal guidelines for collection building through a review of the collection and consultation with other librarians. Familiarity with the community and the collection guidelines or policy statement is part of the building blocks for good selection. To this is added knowledge of the literature for which the librarian is responsible. When the librarian has a firm grasp of these elements, he or she is equipped to begin selection.

Four Steps in Selection

The selection process can be thought of as a four-step process: (1) identification of the relevant, (2) assessment (is the item appropriate for the collection?) and evaluation (is the item worthy of selection?), (3) decision to purchase, and (4) order preparation. Identifying possible items requires basic, factual information about authors, titles, publishers, and topics. Many tools and resources exist to help librarians identify possible acquisitions.

SELECTION TOOLS AND RESOURCES

Bibliographies and lists may be issued by libraries, library publishers, school systems, professional societies, and commercial publishers. National bibliographies and trade lists have been standard tools in libraries for decades. Libraries often issue recent accession lists, prepared by other libraries. Recommended lists are prepared by library associations. Bibliographies published by commercial publishers are often updated frequently, either as a serial publication or in revised editions. Bibliographies and lists provide guidance for filling gaps in existing collections. For example, a librarian seeking to increase a collection of African American literature for children would consult *The Coretta Scott King Awards Book: 1970–1999*.[14] Indexing and abstracting resources provide a list of the titles indexed, which can be checked against library holdings. Some resources identify specific types of publications, such as *Proceedings in Print*.[15] Others focus on both a specific discipline and specific types, such as *Index to Social Sciences and Humanities Proceedings*.[16] Book dealers and jobbers frequently provide lists of books or individual title slips for items in stock. Bibliographies and lists, however, are not inclusive, not available in every field, and not always annotated.

Selectors in academic, large public, and research libraries can use *directories* to identify a discipline's professional associations. These tools include the *Encyclopedia of Associations, World of Learning,* and *Yearbook of International Organizations*.[17] Directory entries usually will list the association's periodical publications and contact information to request catalogs and other information on current imprints.

Reviews appear in the library-oriented press, popular media, and discipline-based journals. Public librarians should keep up with popular media reviews because these have a significant influence on reader interests. An Internet-based resource, Bookwire, indexes book review resources on the Internet, containing more than 5,000 links to book sites worldwide.[18] Many discipline-specific journals provide scholarly and critical reviews of high quality, but these often follow publication by several months or years. Finding reviews of Internet sites is becoming easier. *College and Research Libraries News* has a monthly feature reviewing selected Internet sites on a specific topic.[19] *Library Journal* has a similar feature series called "WebWatch."[20] The Argus Clearinghouse, described as "The Internet's Premier Research Library, A Selective Collection of Topical Guides," provides topical guides to Internet-based information resources.[21] *The Scout Report* offers a "selection of new and newly discovered high-quality online resources."[22] *Great Sites: Amazing, Spectacular, Mysterious, Colorful Web Sites for Kids and the Adults Who Care about Them* is maintained by the American Library Association (ALA).[23] The total number of titles reviewed is only a small portion of the world's publishing output.

Publisher announcements (brochures, advertisements, catalogs, web sites) provide detailed content descriptions, tables of contents, and biographical information about the author. Sample chapters may be found on publishers' web pages. Evaluative statements in publishers' announcements should be viewed with caution because most of these are solicited by the publisher as part of the promotional process. Announcements are timely—often appearing before or simultaneously with the publication—and are widely used by academic, special, and larger public libraries.

Review or approval copies are an ideal selection aid. Publishers often provide review copies at exhibits at librarians' conferences and will sometimes sell the item at the same time. Journal publishers often will provide a sample issue upon request. Many video suppliers provide a copy to preview before a final selection decision is made. Approval plans, by their nature, provide books "on approval." The approval plan vendor and library aim for a low return rate, but generally vendors will permit returning items if the library finds them unacceptable. Many electronic resources offer trial periods during which librarians and users can try the product.

Book fairs and bookstores provide an opportunity to examine materials before purchase. Book fairs bring together many publishers, who display and promote their publications. Book fairs may be local, regional, national, or international in scope. Among the most well known are the Frankfurt Book Fair and the Zimbabwe Book Fair. Many professional association conferences include publisher exhibitors. Though not book fairs in the true sense, they serve the same purpose of introducing new publications and, often, authors to attendees. Bookstores are particularly useful for locating alternative literature and materials from outside the predominant culture, which are less frequently reviewed in traditional sources.

Web-based tools provide several approaches to locating new and relevant older titles. Librarians can find reviews, out-of-print (OP) dealers willing to search for titles, vendor and publisher information, and online stores and catalogs covering all formats. Amazon.com is one of the more familiar online dealers and useful for subject-based searching, reviews, and speedy delivery of items. Publishers frequently provide the table of contents and sample chapters of new books on their web sites. Librarians can perform subject searches in national bibliographic utilities and in other libraries' catalogs. Electronic discussion groups and electronic newsletters directed toward collection development and acquisitions librarians can provide information about publishers and resources for specific subject areas and types of materials.

In-house information, such as interlibrary loan requests, can aid selection. Repeated requests from users for articles from a particular journal suggest that journal should be added to the collection. The same is true for interlibrary requests for a specific book title. Frequent recalls or a long waiting list for a book provide evidence that the title should be considered for duplication. Most libraries accept purchase requests from users. These suggest specific titles that should be considered for addition and may suggest formats, subject areas, or genre to which the library should add.

EVALUATION AND ASSESSMENT CRITERIA

Evaluation and assessment assist the collections librarian in deciding if the title should be added. Evaluation looks at item-intrinsic qualities. Each item is first considered on its own merits. These will vary from item to item and between categories of materials but generally include several of the following criteria:

- content or subject;
- language;
- currency;
- veracity;
- writing style (well written, easy to read, aesthetic aspects);
- completeness and scope of treatment;
- reputation, credentials, or authoritativeness of author, publisher, editor, reviewers;
- geographic coverage;
- quality of scholarship;
- frequency the title is referenced in bibliographies or citations;

- reading or user level to which content is directed;
- comprehensiveness and breadth;
- frequency of updates or revisions;
- access points (indexes, level of detail in the table of contents);
- ease of use;
- external resources that index the publication;
- physical quality—illustrations, paper and binding, format, typography; and
- uniqueness of content, capabilities, or features.

Assessment considers the item in relation to user needs, the existing collection, the mission of the library, and consortial obligations. Does the item support the curriculum, research interests, grants, faculty or teacher specialties, or specific community interests? Does it fall within the parameters of subjects or areas to be covered? Librarians need to consider if a title is being acquired to satisfy short-term needs and how it relates to long-term collection goals. Does the library need an additional work on this subject? Will the item fill a gap in the collection? Is a duplicate copy justified? Is it easily available from another library? Does the library have a consortial obligation to purchase the item?

Selection in school libraries is closely related to curricular trends in public schools. School librarians and media specialists often find themselves playing catch-up as the curriculum and its emphasis and philosophy shift. Lotsee P. Smith has identified three primary purposes of school library collections: supporting the curriculum, providing materials for recreational use, and providing professional aids for teachings, with primary emphasis on the first.[24] The current national emphasis on core competencies and meeting basic standards in order to be promoted to the next grade and to graduate are influencing selection activities. School library media specialists often seek to balance building collections that support curricular goals with building a core collection that meets more broad-based goals.

Two additional local considerations are part of selection: cost and ease of handling. Every selection decision must consider the cost of the item. Are the benefits this title brings to the library worth its cost? Are sufficient funds available to purchase the item? If the item is a journal, serial, multivolume series—can the library make a long-term financial commitment? The ability of the library to handle the title is a key element of any selection decision. Will it get prompt cataloging? Does the library have appropriate housing (shelf space, microform cabinets, server capacity), equipment (microform readers and printers, computer workstations, CD-ROM drives), and electrical and telecommunication infrastructure? Are staff members who work with the public prepared to support the title's use and service needs?

The elements that inform a selection decision are the same, with slight variations, for all formats and genre. Nevertheless, both librarians and the reviewing media tend to focus on print resources. Sheila S. Intner has called this a "bibliocentric" stance and recommends a nonbibliocentric approach that looks beyond print materials to include intellectual and artistic expressions in all formats.[25] Gary Handman, in the first edition of *Video Collection Development in Multi-Type Libraries,* cited a 1990 report that stated 70 percent of what contemporary children learn in their lives is through nonprint forms of communication.[26] Library users and nonusers like nonprint materials. Videos are immensely popular with library users, as are electronic resources. If libraries fail to respond effectively to the rapidly expanding media environment, patrons will go elsewhere. More important, failing to encompass all formats in collections ignores a tremendous wealth of information and artistic expression.

The process of selecting serials is similar to selecting other types of publications, except for consideration of the continuing financial commitment implicit in initiating a subscription. A serial, which can be in any medium, is "a publication issued over a period of time, usually on a regular basis (for example, weekly) with some sort of numbering used to identify issues (for example, volumes, issue numbers, dates). A serial does not have a foreseeable end."[27] Many librarians interchange the terms *serial* and *periodical.* Serials include general magazines, which are likely to appear on newsstands and provide recreational reading and popular sources of information on current social and political issues; scholarly and scientific journals, which are often specialized and directed to a narrow audience; annual reports and house organs of businesses; trade and technology-focused magazines; and "little magazines," which concentrate on literature, politics, or both and often fall within what is known as alternative literature.

When selecting a serial, the collections librarian pays particular attention to the purpose of the publication and to where it is indexed. Magazines, trade journals, scholarly periodicals, and so on each have an intended audience, and the evaluation criteria set out in this chapter are generally applicable. For example, part of evaluating a scholarly journal is considering the credentials of the editors and reviewers to determine the rigor with which submissions are analyzed. A public or school library will consider whether a popular magazine is indexed in *Readers' Guide to Periodical Literature*.[28]

The continuing financial commitment implicit in initiating a serial subscription is significant. The library pays, usually on an annual cycle, for periodicals before they are published. Most serials have ongoing costs for processing—receipting issues, claiming missing issues, shelving, binding, and storage. A librarian must consider the library budget's ability to accommodate annual periodical cost increases in excess of normal budget growth. He or she must be prepared to cancel serials as part of the selection process for new serials. Initiating a subscription, especially for electronic resources, raises user expectations that the title will continue to be available in future years.

Many libraries use selection committees to evaluate possible new serial titles. The committee can consider several titles at the same time, ranking them in priority order and seeking balanced coverage. Other libraries rely on selectors to balance monographs and serials within their own separate budgets. Academic libraries, school library media centers, and special libraries often seek serial evaluations from faculty members, teachers, and researchers. Most serials will supply a sample issue to aid in consideration.

DECISION TO PURCHASE

Once the selector has considered all relevant evaluation and assessment questions, he or she is ready to add or reject the item. Ross Atkinson has defined the universe of materials not locally owned as the anti-collection.[29] He holds that selection is, "to a great extent, a continuous series of decisions about which items in the anti-collection should be moved into the collection."[30] He goes on to suggest that the selection decision is relatively simple because the selector has only two options: buy or don't buy. Selectors employ a mental model that looks at the potential utility for current and future users. Atkinson believes that line between accepting and rejecting materials is primarily dependent on the financial resources available to the selector. Given the volume of materials being published and the finite nature of library budgets, librarians will always face choices about what not to add as they are choosing what to add.

ORDER PREPARATION

Acquisition refers to the processes and systems of ordering and obtaining library materials after they are selected. The acquisition of materials is closely related to collection development, though in most medium-sized and large libraries, selection and acquisition are handled by different individuals, who may be located in different library departments or units. Acquisitions responsibilities typically include placing orders, claiming, canceling, receipting, and invoice processing and may include payment processing. Selection and acquisitions may be handled separately in smaller libraries if the number of staff members makes this reasonable. The ease with which selectors can work directly with suppliers' online databases is blurring this traditional division of work. Selectors may place orders directly online as part of the item identification process.

Usually, the selector is expected to verify title, author or editor, publisher, publication date, and cost before an item is ordered. Ideally, the selector also provides series, ISBN or ISSN, and information about the source from which the publication is available. Many libraries request selectors to provide bibliographic information on forms that may be preprinted, completed online, or retrieved and printed from an online template (*see* figure 4-1). These forms usually require the selector to assign a fund or budget line, identify the collection to which the item will be added, request any special handling, and confirm, if appropriate, that a duplicate copy is desired. If the title being ordered is a serial, the selector will identify the volume with which the subscription should begin and any back files that are to be ordered.

The selection and acquisition of electronic resources add a complexity to the interaction of collections librarians and acquisitions staff because of contracts and license agreements, which must be signed or approved online by a designated signatory authority within the library or the library's parent agency to acquire or access the resource. In some libraries, the selector shepherds this approval process through the institution. In others, a specified collections librarian or library administrator may be charged with the responsibility, or it may be handled by acquisitions staff members.

Acquisition Options

Materials may be ordered from wholesale book vendors, who handle new imprints from a variety of publishers. Book jobbers may specialize

Figure 4-1 Online Order Request Form

Please order the following item for:

Account Name: [   ]

Account Number: [   ]

Fund Number: [   ]

Audiovisual: ○ Yes
                      ○ No

Electronic: ○ Yes
                      ○ No

Selector Name: [   ]

E-mail Address: [   ]

Location Code: [   ]

Rush?   ○ No   ○ Rush Order
                      ○ Rush Catalog   ○ Rush Order & Catalog

Author or Editor: [   ]

Title: [   ]

ISBN: [   ]

Publisher: [   ]

Place of Publication: [   ]

Date of Publication: [   ]

Edition: [   ]

Price $$: [   ]

No. of Copies: [   ]

Special Instructions: [   ]

Out of Print?   ○ Yes   ○ No   ○ Not Sure

Submit Request [   ]

in disciplines or subject areas, publishers, or materials for types of libraries (public, school, or academic). Research, jointly undertaken by the Association of American Publishers and Association for Library Collections and Technical Services (ALCTS) in 1999, reported that 77.3 percent of the 305 U.S. libraries surveyed were placing their orders through vendors.[31] Some types of materials, such as publications from small presses, may be available only by ordering directly from the publisher. Items that are ordered title by title are called discretionary purchases or firm orders. A firm order is an order for a specific title placed with a dealer or publisher that specifies a time limit for delivery and a price that must not be exceeded without the library's approval. Selecting individual titles is considered micro selection.

The alternative to micro selection is macro selection, which adds large quantities of materials to the library en bloc or en masse. Macro selection is managed through mass buying plans—standing orders, blanket orders, and approval plans—or the acquisition of large retrospective collections, either through purchase or as a gift. Order plans are used more commonly by larger public and academic libraries, in which firm orders account for a small percentage of annual budget expenditures. Several authors have argued convincingly that approval plans are desirable in smaller libraries for the same reasons they are used in larger libraries—efficiency and cost-effectiveness.[32] Access to many electronic publications, most commonly electronic journals, is through macro selection—that is, acquiring access to a extensive package of titles from a single publisher.

A large academic library will allocate anywhere from 65 to 90 percent of its acquisitions budget to nondiscretionary purchases. These include standing orders for monographic series and serials, blanket orders with publishers, and approval plans. Order plans provide speedier delivery, and some guarantee that titles in small publication runs will be acquired. They make it possible for libraries to expend large budgets effectively and efficiently and to focus selection attention on less mainstream resources. Blanket orders and approval plans provide a discounted price for the materials supplied, which are usually trade publications.

APPROVAL PLANS

Approval plans are business arrangements in which a wholesale dealer assumes responsibility for selecting and supplying, subject to return privileges, all new publications that match a library's collecting profile. Richard Abel is credited with the invention, in the early 1960s, of the approval plan as it is employed now.[33] An approval profile is defined by the library's collections librarians and specifies the subjects, collecting levels, formats, genre, prices, languages, publishers, and so on to be shipped. Most vendors and libraries aim for a 2 percent or less return rate. Some approval plans offer notification slips rather than the publications themselves (*see* figure 4-2). An approval plan may provide a combination of slips and books. Selectors refine and revise the profile as the library's goals and priorities change. Blanket order plans are an arrangement with an individual publisher or scholarly society, which will provide all its publications (or all publications below a specified price) each year, or with a vendor, who agrees to provide a copy of every book published in a particular country within certain parameters. A blanket order plan does not, in most cases, include return privileges.

The variety of services and enhancements provided by both approval plan vendors and firm order suppliers has grown to include machine-readable invoices, interactive access to the vendor or supplier database, upgraded CIP (Cataloging in Publication) records, and fully shelf-ready books. Shelf-ready books come to the library cataloged and processed with spine labels, bookplates, and anti-theft strips. Vendors are supplementing or replacing functions traditionally performed within libraries. Libraries that contract externally for services previously provided by inter-

Figure 4-2 Approval Plan Notification Slip

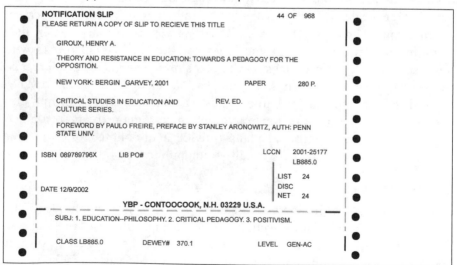

```
NOTIFICATION SLIP                                        44 OF  968
PLEASE RETURN A COPY OF SLIP TO RECIEVE THIS TITLE

   GIROUX, HENRY A.

   THEORY AND RESISTANCE IN EDUCATION: TOWARDS A PEDAGOGY FOR THE
   OPPOSITION.

   NEW YORK: BERGIN _GARVEY, 2001                 PAPER        280 P.

   CRITICAL STUDIES IN EDUCATION AND          REV. ED.
   CULTURE SERIES.

   FOREWORD BY PAULO FREIRE, PREFACE BY STANLEY ARONOWITZ, AUTH: PENN
   STATE UNIV.

ISBN 089789796X     LIB PO#                LCCN    2001-25177
                                                   LB885.0

                                           LIST   24
DATE 12/9/2002                             DISC
                                           NET    24
               YBP - CONTOOCOOK, N.H. 03229 U.S.A.

   SUBJ: 1. EDUCATION--PHILOSOPHY. 2. CRITICAL PEDAGOGY. 3. POSITIVISM.

   CLASS LB885.0        DEWEY#  370.1           LEVEL   GEN-AC
```

nal library staff members are outsourcing those services. Librarians have viewed outsourcing as a way to contain costs when library staffing has been reduced and as a way to release staff members for other responsibilities perceived as more important. Approval plans are widely employed because they can provide discounted prices, faster delivery of newly published books, reliable coverage, and reports that enable selectors to monitor plans. They can free selectors to look for more esoteric materials and to do other types of work.

Approval plans were the source of a major controversy in the library profession in the 1990s.[34] In 1996, the Hawaii State Public Library System took approval plans beyond their usual design and contracted with a vendor for purchasing, processing, cataloging, and 100 percent of selecting for its entire acquisitions budget and forty-nine branch libraries. Administrators saw this as a way to manage a 25 percent budget cut without laying off employees and to release technical services librarians for direct public service. Most of Hawaii's librarians felt unable to respond to users and that collections deteriorated under the plan. The librarians saw a challenge to the very heart of professional librarianship and moved the debate to a national forum. The Hawaii situation became an emotional issue for librarians across the United States, who resented the use of a vendor in a way that was perceived as causing "commodification, commercialization, and homogenization of books, information materials, and libraries."[35] Selection of materials was seen as an essential function of librarianship. The Hawaii contract with the vendor was terminated two years after it was begun, and selection returned to the librarians.

EXCHANGE AGREEMENTS

Many academic libraries use exchanges as a form of en bloc selection. Exchanges are most frequently with foreign exchange partners and can provide materials not available in other ways or more economically than direct purchase. The library supplies local institutional publications to a partner library or institution, which sends its own publications to the library. Partners may be libraries, scholarly societies and associations, university academic departments, and research academies and institutes. Exchanges should be established and monitored within the library's collections priorities. Some libraries are reducing their exchange programs, though many libraries continue exchange agreements because they serve as a cost-effective mechanism for obtaining publications, a cross-cultural activity, and a way of helping other libraries.

GIFTS AND OTHER FREE MATERIALS

Gifts may bring individual items or a collection of items to the library. A gift is transferred voluntarily without compensation. No payment to the donor does not mean the library has no costs associated with the gift. Costs arise when it is reviewed by the selector, cataloged and processed, shelved and reshelved, and repaired and preserved. Gift serial subscriptions have ongoing costs just as paid subscriptions do. Most selection decisions about gifts can be reduced to a trade-off between the cost of adding the item and its value to the library.

Gift materials are desirable because they can strengthen a library's holdings, fill gaps, supply replacements, and provide materials not available through purchase or that the library cannot afford to purchase. A collection of many items from a single donor often focuses on a particular area or discipline. It may contain OP items, serials runs in excellent condition, first editions, and other items of intrinsic value. Besides filling gaps, a gift collection can add both depth and breadth to a library's collection. Adding materials can strengthen institutional relations with individuals, who may make additional donations (both materials and funds) to the library and the institution over time. Gift materials can enter the library unsolicited, through direct negotiations with potential donors, or through requests to publishers. Special collections librarians or library development staff members may target individuals with known collections and negotiate a gift. A library may ask to receive all publications of a corporation, a research center, or an academic institution—in effect, a gift standing order.

The same criteria that guide selection of items for purchase should be considered when reviewing gifts. The first decision the selector must make is whether the material fits within the scope of the library's collecting policy or guidelines. The library may have policies about adding or not adding particular types of materials such as textbooks, laboratory manuals, duplicates, vanity press items, realia, reprints and preprints of individual articles, collections of reprinted journal articles, trade paperbacks, popular pamphlets, and commercial publications of a promotional nature.

Many librarians are selecting resources that are accessible without charge on the Internet. Selection of such items is an extension of a librarian's normal collection-building activities and presumes that intellectual access via catalog records and, perhaps, online subject-based finding aids is provided. In many library catalogs, the bibliographic record contains a live link to the web location of the item. The nature and complexity of free web resources suggests an important role for librarians in reviewing, evaluating, selecting, and cataloging web sites for library users.[36]

Donors must be considered as part of the selection process. Some gifts are not worth adding to the library precisely because of special conditions insisted upon by the potential donor. Donors may offer gifts with conditions about use, housing, and special treatment. Even a library that does not have guidelines for the selection of gift materials may have guidelines that address acceptable and unacceptable donor restrictions. The selector should weigh the value of the gift (and possible future gifts) to the library against any donor restrictions.

The library receiving gifts usually supplies the donor with a letter of acknowledgment. Under the U.S. Revenue Reconciliation Bill in 1993, which modified the 1984 Tax Reform Act slightly, donors are required to provide a written acknowledgment or formal deed-of-gift from the library for any noncash donation in which they are claiming a deduction of $250 or more. Libraries should not give appraisals or estimates of value to the donor. A letter provides the donor with a record that may be used to claim a tax deduction, creates a permanent record of gifts received for the library, and graciously acknowledges the donor's gift to the library. Such a deed eliminates any ambiguity regarding the library's right to use, retain, or dispose of materials received from donors.

If the donor's total deduction for all noncash contributions for the year is more than $500, the donor must file Internal Revenue Service (IRS) Form 8283 and attach the receiving organization's acknowledgment letter of receipt. The donor is responsible for determining the fair market value of the gift. If the property being contributed is worth $5,000 or more, the donor must retain a qualified appraiser to determine the gift's fair market value. U.S. tax law requires a recipient institution to retain any gift valued at $500 or above for two years. If the library disposes of the gift or portions of it and thereby reduces the value of the original gift, it must file an IRS Form 8282, which will affect the donor's original deduction.

Many U.S. libraries acquire federal government publications through their status as depository libraries. Approximately 1,400 public and academic libraries serve as depositories for U.S. government publications. Except for a limited number of regional libraries, which must select all depository items, depository libraries select by categories those publications that they wish to receive from the Government Printing Office (GPO). Selections are made by series and groups of publications in advance of printing, rather than title by title as they are published.

Libraries that are not depositories and depository libraries requiring more than one copy of a government publication may place purchase orders through the distribution center of the GPO.

Retrospective Selection

Retrospective selection is the process of selecting materials that are old, rare, antiquarian, used, and OP. It includes seeking replacements for missing or damaged materials and older materials not previously acquired. Many librarians develop desiderata files of titles to be purchased when funding is available or the item is located. These materials may be needed to fill gaps in the collection or to support new academic programs or community interests. Retrospective selection is more common in larger research libraries. The usual sources for materials are OP dealers' catalogs, auctions, and personal negotiations with a private owner.

OP titles are those that can no longer be obtained from the original publishers. This can happen rapidly as a result of the limited number of copies published in some fields. Many used and OP booksellers produce catalogs. These catalogs, either in print or online, usually list only single copies; therefore, the librarian must act quickly to ensure acquisition. Many OP dealers will accept lists of titles the library is seeking. Dealers can be located through the *American Book Trade Directory*.[37] Additional suppliers can be found through the Antiquarian Booksellers Association of America (ABAA) and the International League of Antiquarian Booksellers (ILAB).[38]

A specialized area within retrospective selection is filling gaps in serial runs and replacing missing issues. One source is the Duplicates Exchange Union (DEU), sponsored by the ALCTS.[39] Libraries prepare lists of periodical issues and books they are willing to supply to member libraries through a cooperative exchange of duplicate materials. Libraries then check these available issues against their needs. Sometimes a publisher can provide missing issues for a price. Many times, the library will be unable to locate replacement issues and will borrow and photocopy issues needed to complete a serials run.

Microforms, reprints, and digital collections are viable alternatives in retrospective selection. If the item is too costly to replace in print, the OP title or issues cannot be located, or the item will not see heavy use, microform is a reasonable solution. Some titles are available in reprint editions, which are usually photoreproductions of the original and satisfy most users' needs. Librarians can purchase extensive microform sets of retrospective titles on specific topics. Several publishers and vendors are providing CD-ROM collections as well as online access to important retrospective collections. Early English Books Online is one example.[40] The more than 125,000 titles published from 1475 to 1661 in this collection are also available in microfilm format.

Diverse Communities and Alternative Literatures

The United States is a multicultural society, reflecting diversity in race, religion, geographic origin, economic status, political affiliation, and personal preference. In 2000, 10 percent of U.S. residents were foreign born, up from 7.9 percent in 1990.[41] In 1999, 36 percent of schoolchildren were ethnic minorities.[42] This is projected to increase to 40 percent by 2010.[43] The librarian's professional obligation is to develop balanced collections that reflect and meet the educational and recreational needs of these diverse user communities and are not biased by his or her own cultural identity and personal experiences. In addition to meeting the needs of various populations, multicultural collections present opportunities to understand other people and cultures.

Publications that are not part of the dominant culture and do not share the perspective and beliefs of that culture are often considered alternative literature. Generally, these materials are published by small presses, independent publishers, the radical right and left, and other dissenting groups. Many topics that dominate alternative literature are the same topics that are challenged in library collections.[44] These include critiques of public life and the mass media, environmental activism, peace and antimilitarism, human rights (including right to life and free choice), freedom of speech and censorship, anarchism, situationist literature, critical education and free schools, sexual politics, paranormal and fortean phenomena, and literature of extremist groups. Alternative literature includes works of nonfiction, fiction, poetry, art, and music.

Librarians are generally comfortable selecting works that represent diverse cultural and ethnic groups, because this is perceived as the sensitive and politically correct stance. They are less at ease when making selection decisions that are inconsistent with their own social, moral, and political interests. Personal biases, concerns about accountability to governing bodies, and feelings of responsibility for collection users often result in a subtle conscious or unconscious self-censorship.

Censorship and Intellectual Freedom

Chapter 1 traced how the ideal of freedom to read came to replace a quite different ideology between 1876, when the ALA endorsed the librarian as moral censor, and the 1930s, when the first "Library Bill of Rights" was adopted by the ALA.[45] Librarians' attitudes toward censorship have changed in line with changing concepts of the public interest and of the library's democratic function. Intellectual freedom and free access to ideas are embodied in the First Amendment as a basic human right. The "Library Bill of Rights" continues to be an important statement for American librarians.

Library Bill of Rights

The American Library Association affirms that all libraries are forums for information and ideas, and that the following basic policies should guide their services.

I. Books and other library resources should be provided for the interest, information, and enlightenment of all people of the community the library serves. Materials should not be excluded because of the origin, background, or views of those contributing to their creation.

II. Libraries should provide materials and information presenting all points of view on current and historical issues. Materials should not be proscribed or removed because of partisan or doctrinal disapproval.

III. Libraries should challenge censorship in the fulfillment of their responsibility to provide information and enlightenment.

IV. Libraries should cooperate with all persons and groups concerned with resisting abridgment of free expression and free access to ideas.

V. A person's right to use a library should not be denied or abridged because of origin, age, background, or views.

VI. Libraries which make exhibit spaces and meeting rooms available to the public they serve should make such facilities available on an equitable basis, regardless of the beliefs or affiliations of individuals or groups requesting their use.[46]

Ensuring intellectual freedom is a major focus of ALA, which maintains an Office for Intellectual Freedom and publishes the *Intellectual Freedom Manual*.[47] The Freedom to Read Foundation, a sister organization to the ALA, was created to protect the freedoms of speech and press, with emphasis on First Amendment protection for libraries and library materials. The foundation provides support and legal counsel to libraries whose collections are challenged. An added challenge to intellectual freedom facing librarians is the public's concerns about ease of accessing questionable materials via the Internet.[48]

The ALA and many of its divisions have developed statements and various documents addressing intellectual freedom and free access to information, particularly in relation to electronic information. ALA has prepared "Access to Electronic Information, Services, and Networks: An Interpretation of the Library Bill of Rights."[49] Other examples include the Association of College and Research Libraries' expansion on the Library Bill of Rights in the academic setting, "Intellectual Freedom Principles for Academic Libraries," and the American Association of School Librarians' "Access to Resources and Services in the School Library Media Program: An Interpretation of the Library Bill of Rights."[50] ALA's "Freedom to Read" statement is a further iteration of librarians' commitment to free access to information and ideas.

Freedom to Read

1. It is in the public interest for publishers and librarians to make available the widest diversity of views and expressions, including those which are unorthodox or unpopular with the majority.

2. Publishers, librarians, and booksellers do not need to endorse every idea or presentation they make available. It would conflict with the public interest for them to establish their own political, moral, or aesthetic views as a standard for determining what should be published or circulated.

3. It is contrary to the public interest for publishers or librarians to bar access to writings on the basis of the personal history or political affiliations of the author.

4. There is no place in our society for efforts to coerce the taste of others, to confine adults to the reading matter deemed suitable for adolescents, or to inhibit the efforts of writers to achieve artistic expression.

5. It is not in the public interest to force a reader to accept with any expression the prejudgment of a label characterizing it or its author as subversive or dangerous.

6. It is the responsibility of publishers and librarians, as guardians of the people's freedom to read, to contest encroachments upon that freedom by individuals or groups seeking to impose their own standards or tastes upon the community at large.

7. It is the responsibility of publishers and librarians to give full meaning to the freedom to read by providing books that enrich the quality and diversity of thought and expression. By the exercise of this affirmative responsibility, they can demonstrate that the answer to a "bad" book is a good one, the answer to a "bad" idea is a good one.[51]

Librarians are charged with preventing censorship of collections and simultaneously ensuring freedom to read and access to diverse viewpoints within collections. Robert Hauptman has defined censorship as "the active suppression of books, journals, newspapers, theater pieces, lectures, discussions, radio and televisions programs, films, art works, etc.—either partially or in the entirety—that are deemed objectionable on moral, political, military, or other grounds."[52] In the name of intellectual freedom, librarians are encouraged to select, collect, and disseminate information without regard to race, sex, and other potential discriminators. The goal is a diverse collection, representing all points of view, including the extreme. A collection is not diverse if it includes only majority, noncontroversial, unoffensive opinions.

Herbert N. Foerstel wrote that the history of book censorship has consisted of the suppression of naughty stories.[53] Challenges on the grounds of immoral, obscene, or pornographic content are the most common, but other justifications, such as subversive political or social content, have been presented over the years. Challenges are most common in school and public libraries. Between 1990 and 2000, the ALA recorded 6,364 attempts by groups or individuals to have books removed from library shelves and from classrooms. Of these, 71 percent were in schools or school libraries.[54] In 2001, the ALA logged 448 challenges and estimated that four times that number of challenges are made, though not reported.[55] The following list, compiled by the ALA Office of Intellectual Freedom, identifies the ten most frequently challenged books in 2002:

1. Harry Potter series, by J. K. Rowling

2. Alice series, by Phyllis Reynolds Naylor
3. *The Chocolate War,* by Robert Cormier
4. *I Know Why the Caged Bird Sings,* by Maya Angelou
5. *Taming the Star Runner,* by S. E. Hinton
6. *Captain Underpants,* by Dav Pilkey
7. *The Adventures of Huckleberry Finn,* by Mark Twain
8. *Bridge to Terabithia,* by Katherine Paterson
9. *Roll of Thunder, Hear My Cry,* by Mildred D. Taylor
10. *Julie of the Wolves,* by Jean Craighead George[56]

Types of Censorship

Censorship comes in three varieties: mandated by the law, demanded by individuals or groups, and exercised by the librarian. Legal censorship occurs when national, state, or municipal legislation forbids access to materials deemed immoral or unacceptable (perhaps incendiary or subversive) under the law. Laws in the United States, notably the 1865 Mail Act and the Comstock Law of 1873, have sought to control access to "obscene," "lewd," or "lascivious" publications by controlling the mailing and receiving of such materials. The problem lies in defining these terms. Such Supreme Court cases as *United States v. One Book Called "Ulysses"* (1934), *Roth v. United States* (1957), and *Miller v. California* (1973) have considered obscenity in relation to contemporary community standards and whether a work may be seen to have serious literary, artistic, political, or social value.[57] The Supreme Court has ruled that the states may prohibit the printing and sale of works that portray sexual conduct in an offensive manner. The emphasis has shifted to local standards. When librarians are presented with legislation requiring the removal of materials, they are seldom in a position to contest the law in court. More often, organizations such as the American Civil Liberties Union and the ALA press a case.

Individuals and groups who challenge library materials may be parents, concerned citizens, school and library boards, religious and political organizations, and local police. They may seek to censor by banning books, severely limiting access, or labeling materials for special handling and restricted use. Most challenges revolve around sexual propriety, political views, religious beliefs, and the rights of minority groups (gays, lesbians, persons of color, atheists, etc.). Library publications such as *American Libraries, Library Journal,* and *Newsletter on Intellectual Freedom* regularly report on challenges to libraries around the United States. Censorship frequently becomes an emotional issue and can divide a community because it develops out of personal beliefs, convictions, and value systems. A report issued in 1993 stated that 41 percent of the attempts to remove or restrict access to materials in U.S. schools were successful.[58]

Some censorship is unintentional and results from failure to select materials representing a pluralistic society. Librarians can protect against unintentional self-censorship by being conscious of and sensitive to diverse communities and viewpoints. Monitoring bibliographic tools, selection sources, and reviews can improve the multicultural and comprehensive nature of collection building.

Intentional censorship by librarians is more troubling. Personal values and standards, fears about potential challenges, or user complaints can lead a librarian to decide not to purchase a title, to limit access to an item, or to remove an item from the collection. When one's employment and source of income is at risk, pragmatism has a way of modifying one's values. Research over the years has demonstrated that, although librarians support the concept of intellectual freedom, many do not stand by these principles in the face of censorship pressures.[59] Some scholars writing on this dilemma have sought to get around it by placing emphasis on the selection process instead of the rejection process.[60] The challenge for librarians is distinguishing between self-censorship and careful selection of materials consistent with appropriate selection criteria.

Censorship should not be confused with refusing to spend limited funds unwisely, to select materials inappropriate to the user community, or to provide illegal or socially detrimental information. One easily can insist that a librarian should never censor nor refuse to disseminate information. Nevertheless, all librarians are constrained by their budgets, their professional values, and legislation to exclude some materials. What is the judicious response when a high school student wants books on building pipe bombs, a white supremacist offers a free subscription of a racist newsletter to a public library, or those who deny the Holocaust insist the academic library purchase materials proving their point of view? When making decisions about material that is sexually explicit, racist, or dangerous to society, few librarians can take a neutral stance. They can only seek to exercise informed judgment. Free expression, intellectual freedom, and access to information must be protected, yet some materials are inappropriate and detrimental to certain user groups. The tension and the challenge arise in determining what falls within these categories.

Censorship and the Internet

The trend toward providing Internet access in libraries is presenting new concerns about censorship and debates over the responsibility of librarians to select what users can and cannot access. School and public libraries are receiving frequent demands that blocking or filtering software be installed on libraries' computers that access the Internet. One problem with filtering software is that useful sites can be blocked along with those that are objectionable. State and federal legislation has been passed and court cases have been filed on both sides of the issue. A significant judgment was made in 1997 in *Reno v. American Civil Liberties Union* (Reno I), when the U.S. Supreme Court unanimously declared that the federal Communications Decency Act (CDA) was unconstitutional.[61] That law made it a crime to send or display indecent material online in a way available to minors. The court held that the Internet is not comparable to broadcasting and instead, like books and newspapers, receives the highest level of First Amendment protection. Following Reno I, Congress passed the Child Online Protection Act (COPA), which sought to avoid the constitutional issues raised in the CDA. A federal district court in the case *American Civil Liberties Union v. Reno* (Reno II) has more recently determined that COPA is flawed in similar ways to the CDA.[62]

The Children's Internet Protection Act (CIPA) and the Neighborhood Children's Internet Protection Act (NCIPA) went into effect in 2001. CIPA requires libraries and schools to install filters on their Internet computers to retain federal funding and discounts for computers and Internet access. Because CIPA directly affected libraries and their ability to make legal information freely available to their patrons, the ALA and the Freedom to Read Foundation filed a lawsuit to overturn CIPA. In 2002, the Eastern District Court of Pennsylvania held CIPA to be unconstitutional and ruled Sections 1712(a)(2) and 1721(b) of CIPA to be facially invalid under the First Amendment. The lower court held the CIPA statute to be unconstitutional, because mandated filtering on all computers results in blocked access to substantial amounts of constitutionally protected speech. The Justice Department, acting on behalf of the Federal Communications Commission and the U.S. Institute of Museum and Library Sciences, appealed this ruling to the Supreme Court.

In June 2003, the Supreme Court reversed the district court's decision and rejected the plaintiffs' facial challenge to CIPA. Although six justices voted to uphold the law, there was no majority opinion for the Court. The plurality opinion, authored by Chief Justice William Hubbs Rehnquist, was joined by three other justices (Sandra Day O'Connor, Antonin Scalia, and Clarence Thomas). Because it did not have the support of five justices, the reasoning of the plurality opinion is not controlling. Justices Anthony M. Kennedy and Stephen Breyer each wrote concurring opinions upholding CIPA against the plaintiffs' facial challenge but on narrower grounds than those stated in the plurality opinion. In cases where no single opinion has the support of a majority of the justices, the narrower concurring opinions typically govern future interpretations and the precedential effect of the case.[63]

The dilemma is that filters can both overblock (block access to protected speech) and underblock (allow access to illegal or unconstitutional speech). The latter is of particular concern when libraries are perceived as violating obscenity, child pornography, and harmful-to-minors statutes, or permitting user activities that create a hostile work environment. Libraries can face potential liability for installing content-based filtering software or for failing to install it. When librarians specifically select and point to Internet resources, they apply the appropriate criteria for quality, authenticity, and so forth. However, "open" Internet access is a much more complex issue.[64] As the Internet expands and the number of public and school libraries with Internet access increases, this issue will continue to trouble librarians and their user communities.

The best defense against challenges to a library collection is prior preparation. This begins with a written collection development policy. Many libraries post the "Library Bill of Rights" in a public place and use additional methods to promote their commitment to intellectual freedom. The library should have a process for handling complaints, and staff members should be familiar with it. ALA's *Intellectual Freedom Manual* contains guidelines for developing a local process.[65] ALA's Office for Intellectual Freedom and many organizations provide advice and assistance in case of attempted censorship. These include National Council of Teachers of English, state educational and library associations, and the American Civil Liberties Union. Notifying the material's publisher may be helpful because the publisher may have assembled information in response to previous challenges.

Summary

Collection building is about making choices within parameters defined by the community being served and the funds available. Selection begins with knowing the types of materials for which one is responsible. Responsibility may be assigned according to format, genre, subject, language, geographic coverage, and reader or user group. In a small library, a librarian may be responsible for selection decisions crossing all these areas and types. Collection building consists of four steps: identifying the relevant items, assessing the item to decide if it is appropriate for the collection and evaluating its quality, deciding to purchase, and preparing an order. Identifying materials requires factual information about authors, titles, publishers, and topics. Many tools and resources help identify possible acquisitions. Items are appropriate if they meet the needs of current and future users, are consistent with collection development policies, and are fiscally responsible. Evaluating criteria can be extensive, ranging from literary merit to comprehensiveness and breadth to ease of access and use.

Collection building is intimately involved with the acquisition process. In some libraries, the individuals who select items also place the orders. Title-by-title selecting is selection at the micro level. Macro selection describes processes through which many items are added to the library without being selected individually. The most common of these are approval plans, through which vendors select items for a library based on a profile defined by that library. Other forms of macro selection are standing orders, blanket orders, exchange agreements, and government document depository agreements. Libraries add collections of materials that are donated. Gifts must be reviewed carefully and have legal, financial, and political implications. Retrospective selection is the process through which older materials are selected either to fill gaps or to develop new collection areas.

As society and libraries' specific user communities become more diverse, librarians have an obligation to develop collections that reflect the interests and meet the needs of various user groups. Numerous resources and tools are available to help identify titles that reflect ethnic, racial, political, religious, social, and cultural diversity. Selectors must take care that their personal experiences, perspectives, and biases do not consciously or unconsciously influence the materials they select or the materials they exclude. This constitutes self-censorship.

Censorship, whether self-imposed or external, restricts free access to ideas and intellectual freedom, rights embodied in the First Amendment. Librarians are encouraged to prevent censorship and ensure freedom to read and to access diverse viewpoints within their collections. Most attempts to remove or limit availability of materials are made on the grounds of immoral, obscene, or pornographic content. Other reasons to exclude materials are that they are inappropriate to some age groups, politically subversive, and socially offensive. Most challenges against materials are lodged in schools and school libraries. Many are the result of different viewpoints about what is dangerous, offensive, inappropriate, and illegal. Although librarians support the idea of freedom to read, they frequently moderate selection (self-censorship) to avoid possible confrontations. Many attempts to censor materials are successful, but more than half are not. Librarians who have a written collection development policy and formal procedures to handle calls for censoring materials are best positioned to handle them effectively.

| CASE STUDY |

The central library for the Dacatur County Library System is located in Milton, in a rural region of southern Minnesota. Milton has a population of 4,364. Three branch libraries are located in nearby smaller towns. The four sites serve a total population of 11,500. The library in Milton has an annual budget of $47,000 for acquisition of books, periodicals, and audiovisual materials. An additional $3,000 are expended on access to remote databases. The library has 80,000 print volumes, 178 active periodical subscriptions, 436 CD-ROMs, 630 audio CDs and tapes, and a small collection of slide sets and maps. The Dacatur County Library System is a member of a larger regional library system and shares an automated catalog with twelve other county systems comprising the regional system. Milton's population has changed dramatically in the last seven years. Hispanic immigrants, who have been attracted to food-processing jobs that pay near-minimum wages, now make up 20 percent of the residents. The Minnesota legislature has allocated $1 million to expand and renovate Milton's cramped library and increase acquisitions; the county and the town have each designated $250,000 to the project. A major aspect of the project is to turn the library into a "multicultural learning center" as a way to help immigrants merge into the community and teach job skills to all interested residents.

   The library in Milton has decided to expend $50,000 of the new money over the next two years to acquire materials specifically to serve the Hispanic population. Ten thousand dollars of these funds will be continuing and will be used in subsequent years for maintaining periodical subscriptions, access to electronic resources, and purchasing new monographs.

Activity

Identify appropriate sources for locating monographic titles, periodicals, and multimedia that will meet the needs and interests of all ages in the Hispanic community and provide guidance in fostering literacy and enhancing job skills. Suggest reasonable ways in which the $50,000 should be allocated between adult and young patrons; between books, periodicals, and multimedia; between electronic and traditional materials; and between fiction and nonfiction. You are not selecting resources. Your responsibility is to develop the guidelines and processes that will inform the selection of specific titles.

REFERENCES

1. Dennis P. Carrigan, "Librarians and the 'Dismal Science,'" *Library Journal* 113 (June 15, 1988): 22.
2. *UNESCO Statistical Yearbook* (Paris: UNESCO, 1999).
3. Andrew Grabois, comp., "U.S. Book Production Statistics: All Hard and Paper," (Bowker), available at http://www.bookwire.com/bookwire/BookProduction/ decadebookproduction.html; and his "Canadian Book Production, 1999–2001 (All Hard and Paper)," (Bowker), available at http://www.bookwire.com/ bookwire/canadianbookproduction.htm.
4. *Ulrich's Periodicals Directory,* 41st ed. (Medford, N.J.: Bowker, 2003).
5. Sharon G. Sullivan, "Prices of U.S. and Foreign Published Materials," in *The Bowker Annual: Library and Book Trade Almanac,* 48th ed. (Medford, N.J.: Information Today, 2003): 491.
6. *Monographs and Serials Costs in ARL Libraries, 1986–2002* (Washington, D.C.: Assn. of Research Libraries, 2002), available at http://www.arl.org/ stats/arlstat/graphs/2002/2002t2.html.
7. Ibid.
8. Ibid.
9. *CD-ROMs in Print* (Detroit: Gale, 1987–).
10. *Index to Social Sciences and Humanities Proceedings* (Philadelphia: Institute for Scientific Information, published quarterly); *Magazines for Kids and Teens: A Resource for Parents, Teachers, Librarians, and Kids!* rev. ed. (Glassboro, N.J.: Education Press Assn. of America; International Reading Assn., 1997); and *Fiction Catalog,* 14th ed. (New York: Wilson, 2001).
11. John Rutledge and Luke Swindler, "The Selection Decision: Defining Criteria and Establishing Priorities," *College and Research Libraries* 48 (March 1987): 128.

12. Lynn B. Williams, "Subject Knowledge for Subject Specialists: What the Novice Bibliographer Needs to Know," *Collection Management* 14, no. 3/4 (1991): 39.
13. Francis K. W. Drury, *Book Selection* (Chicago: American Library Assn., 1930), 1.
14. Henrietta M. Smith, *The Coretta Scott King Awards Book: 1970–1999* (Chicago: American Library Assn., 1999).
15. *Proceedings in Print* (Halifax, Mass.: Proceedings in Print, 1964–).
16. *Index to Social Sciences and Humanities Proceedings* (Philadelphia: Institute for Scientific Information, 1979–).
17. *Encyclopedia of Associations* (Detroit: Gale, 1961–); *World of Learning* (London: Allen & Unwin, 1947–); and *Yearbook of International Organizations* (Brussels: Union of International Associations, 1967–).
18. Bookwire [WWW home page of Bookwire, Bowker]. Available [Online]: http://www.bookwire.com.
19. *College and Research Libraries News* (Chicago: Assn. of College and Research Libraries, 1967–); C&RL NewsNet [WWW home page of C&RL NewsNet, which archives reviews of Internet resources that appear in *C&RL News.*] Available [Online]: http://www.bowdoin.edu/~samato/IRA/.
20. *Library Journal* (New York: Bowker, 1876–).
21. Argus Clearinghouse [WWW home page of Argus Clearinghouse, University of Michigan School of Information, Ann Arbor, Mich.]. Available [Online]: http://www.clearinghouse.net/.
22. *The Scout Report* is published by the Internet Scout Project, located in the Department of Computer Sciences at the University of Wisconsin–Madison, available at http://www.scout.cs.wisc.edu/.
23. *Great Sites: Amazing, Spectacular, Mysterious, Colorful Web Sites for Kids and the Adults Who Care about Them* [WWW home page of Great Sites, Great Web Sites Committee, American Library Assn.]. Available at the Association for Library Service to Children web site (http://www.ala.org/alsc); click "Great Web Sites for Kids" on the left column.
24. Lotsee P. Smith, "The Curriculum and Materials Selection: Requisite for Collection Development," *Collection Management* 7, no. 3/4 (fall 1985/winter 1985–86): 39.
25. Sheila S. Intner, "Recruiting Non-Bibliocentric Collection Builders," in *Recruiting, Educating, and Training Librarians for Collection Development*, ed. Peggy Johnson and Sheila S. Intner (Westport, Conn.: Greenwood, 1994), 69–84.
26. Gary P. Handman, ed., *Video Collection Development in Multi-Type Libraries: A Handbook* (Westport, Conn.: Greenwood, 1994), xiv.
27. Serials Section Education Committee, Assn. for Library Collections and Technical Services, American Library Assn., "Unraveling the Mysteries of Serials," 1996, available at the ALCTS web site (http://www.ala.org/alcts); click "Publications" on the left column; click "Web Publication."
28. *Readers' Guide to Periodical Literature* (New York: Wilson, 1901–).
29. Ross Atkinson, "Access, Ownership, and the Future of Collection Development," in *Collection Management and Development: Issues in an Electronic Era*, ed. Peggy Johnson and Bonnie MacEwan (Chicago: American Library Assn., 1994), 92–109.
30. Ibid., 97.

31. Preliminary information reported at "Marketing to Libraries for the Millennium: Librarians, Vendors, and Publishers Review the Landmark Third Industry-Wide Survey of Library Marketing Practices and Trends," an all-day program held June 27, 1999, at the American Library Association Conference in New Orleans.

32. *See,* for example, Wanda V. Dole, "The Feasibility of Approval Plans for Small College Libraries," in *Collection Development in College Libraries,* ed. Joanne Schneider Hill, William E. Hannaford Jr., and Ronald H. Epp (Chicago: American Library Assn., 1991), 154–62; and L. Hunter Kevil, "The Approval Plan of Smaller Scope," *Library Acquisitions: Practice and Theory* 9 (1985): 13–20.

33. Ann L. O'Neill, "How the Richard Abel Co., Inc. Changed the Way We Work," *Library Acquisitions: Practice and Theory* 17 (1993): 41–46.

34. *See* Carol Reid, "Down and Outsourced in Hawaii," *American Libraries* 28 (June/July 1997): 56-58; Rebecca Knuth and Donna G. Bair-Mundy, "Revolt over Outsourcing: Hawaii's Librarians Speak Out about Contracted Selection," *Collection Management* 23, no. 12 (1998): 81–112.

35. Knuth and Bair-Mundy, "Revolt over Outsourcing," 109.

36. Louis A. Pitschmann, *Building Sustainable Collections of Free Third-Party Web Resources* (Washington, D.C.: Digital Library Federation and Council on Library and Information Resources, 2001), 6, available at http://www.clir.org/pubs/reports/pub98/contents.html

37. *American Book Trade Directory* (New Providence, R.I.: Bowker, 1925–).

38. Antiquarian Booksellers Assn. of America [WWW home page of the Antiquarian Booksellers Assn. of America]. Available [Online]: http://abaa.org/; and International League of Antiquarian Booksellers [WWW home page of the International League of Antiquarian Booksellers]. Available [Online]: http://www.ilab-lila.com/.

39. Duplicates Exchange Union [WWW home page of the Duplicates Exchange Union, Assn. for Library Collections and Technical Services, American Library Assn.]. Available at the ALCTS web site (http://www.ala.org/alcts); click "Publications" on the left column; click "Duplicates Exchange Union."

40. Early English Books [WWW home page of Early English Books Online]. Available [Online]: http://wwwlib.umi.com/eebo.

41. *Coming to America: A Profile of the Nation's Foreign-Born (2000 Update),* Census Brief, Current Population Survey CENBR/01-1 (Washington, D.C.: U.S. Census Bureau, Feb. 2002), available at http://www.census.gov/prod/www/abs/briefs.html.

42. "School Enrollment—Social and Economic Characteristics of Students," Current Population Reports P20-533 (Washington, D.C.: U.S. Census Bureau, March 2001), available at http://www.census.gov/population/www/socdemo/school.html.

43. "(NP-D1-A) Annual Projections of the Resident Population by Age, Sex, Race, and Hispanic Origin: Lowest, Middle, Highest Series and Zero International Migration Series, 1999 to 2100" (Washington, D.C.: U.S. Census Bureau, Jan. 13, 2000), available at http://www.census.gov/population/projections/nation/detail/d2001_10.pdf.

44. Chris Atton, "The Subjects of Alternative Literature—A General Guide," in his *Alternative Literature: A Practical Guide for Librarians* (Aldershot, Hampshire, England: Gower, 1996), 39–64.

45. American Library Assn., "Library Bill of Rights," adopted June 18, 1948; amended Feb. 2, 1961, and Jan. 23, 1980, inclusion of "age" reaffirmed Jan. 23, 1996, by the ALA Council, available at the ALA web site (http://www. ala.org); click "Our Association" on the top navigation menu, click "Offices" on the left column, click "Intellectual Freedom," and click "Statements and Policies."

46. Ibid.

47. American Library Assn., Office for Intellectual Freedom, *Intellectual Freedom Manual,* 6th ed. (Chicago: American Library Assn., 2002).

48. Barbara A. Jones, *Libraries, Access, and Intellectual Freedom: Developing Policies for Public and Academic Libraries* (Chicago: American Library Assn., 2000).

49. American Library Assn., "Access to Electronic Information, Services, and Networks: An Interpretation of the Library Bill of Rights," adopted by the ALA Council Jan. 24, 1996, available at the ALA web site (http://www.ala.org); click "Our Association" on the top navigation menu, click "Offices" on the left column, click "Intellectual Freedom," click "Statements and Policies," click "Library Bill of Rights," and click "Interpretations."

50. Assn. of College and Research Libraries, "Intellectual Freedom Principles for Academic Libraries," approved by ACRL Board of Directors June 29, 1999, available at the ACRL web site (http://www.ala.org/acrl); click "Publications" on the top navigation bar; click "White Papers and Reports" on the left column; and American Assn. of School Librarians, "Access to Resources and Services in the School Library Media Program: An Interpretation of the Library Bill of Rights," adopted July 2, 1986; amended Jan. 10, 1990, July 12, 2000, by the ALA Council, available at the AASL web site (http://www.ala.org/aasl); click "Professional Tools" on the top navigation bar; click "Position Statements" on the left column.

51. American Library Assn., "Freedom to Read," adopted June 25, 1953; revised Jan. 28, 1972, Jan. 16, 1991, July 12, 2000, by the ALA Council and the AAP Freedom to Read Committee, available at the ALA web site (http://www. ala.org); click "Our Association" on the top navigation menu, click "Offices" on the left column, click "Intellectual Freedom," and click "Statements and Policies."

52. Robert Hauptman, *Ethical Challenges in Librarianship* (Phoenix, Ariz.: Oryx, 1988), 66.

53. Herbert N. Foerstel, *Banned in the Media: A Reference Guide to Censorship in the Press, Motion Pictures, Broadcasting, and the Internet* (Westport, Conn.: Greenwood, 1998), 2.

54. "The 100 Most Frequently Challenged Books of 1990–2000: Challenges by Initiator, Institution, Type, and Year," available at the ALA web site (http:// www.ala.org); click "Our Association" on the top navigation bar, click "Office" on the left column, click "Intellectual Freedom," and click "Banned Books Week."

55. News release from the American Library Assn., Jan. 2002.

56. This list can be found on ALA's web site (http://www.ala.org); click "Our Association" on the top navigation bar, click "Offices" on the left navigation bar, click "Intellectual Freedom," and click "Banned Books Week."

57. *United States v. One Book Called "Ulysses,"* 5 F. Supp. 182 (S.D.N.Y. 1933), affirmed 72 F. 2d 705 (2d Cir. 1934); *Roth v. United States,* 354 U.S. 476 (1957); and *Miller v. California,* 413 U.S. 15 (1973).

58. People for the American Way, "Censors Succeed in 41% of School Cases," *Library Hotline* 22 (Sept. 27, 1993): 2.

59. *See* L. B. Woods and Claudia Perry-Holmes, "Libraries Practice Prior Censorship to Avoid the Flack if We Had *The Joy of Sex* Here," *Library Journal* 107 (Sept. 15, 1982): 1711–15; Frances B. MacDonald, *Censorship and Intellectual Freedom: A Survey of School Librarians, Attitudes, and Moral Reasoning* (Metuchen, N.J.: Scarecrow, 1993); and Andrea E. Niosi, "An Investigation of Censorship and Selection in Southern California Public Libraries," *Public Libraries* 37, no. 5 (Sept./Oct. 1998): 310–15.

60. Lester E. Asheim, "The Librarian's Responsibility: Not Censorship, but Selection," in *Freedom of Book Selection: Proceedings of the Second Conference on Intellectual Freedom, Whittier, California, June 20–21, 1953,* 90–99 (Chicago: American Library Assn., 1954).

61. *Reno v. American Civil Liberties Union,* 521 U.S. 844 (1997).

62. *American Civil Liberties Union v. Reno,* 31 F. Supp. 2d 473 (E. D. Pa. 1999).

63. Information on CIPA can be found at the ALA web site (http://www.ala.org).

64. For in-depth analyses of censorship and Internet access, *see* Elizabeth Werby, "The Cyber- Library: Legal and Policy Issues Facing Public Libraries in the High-Tech Era," National Coalition Against Censorship, 1999, available at http://www.ncac.org/cyberlibrary.html; and "Internet Filtering in Public Libraries," memorandum to the American Library Assn. from Jenner & Block, Feb. 4, 2000, available at the ALA web site (http://www.ala.org); click "Our Association" on the top navigation bar, click "Offices" on the left column, click "Intellectual Freedom," and click "Intellectual Freedom Issues."

65. ALA, *Intellectual Freedom Manual,* 6th ed.

SUGGESTED READINGS

Alabaster, Carol. *Developing an Outstanding Core Collection: A Guide for Libraries.* Chicago: American Library Assn., 2002.

Allison, DeeAnn, Beth McNeil, and Signe Swanson. "Database Selection: One Size Does Not Fit All." *College and Research Libraries* 61, no. 1 (Jan. 2000): 56–63.

Auger, C. P. *Information Sources in Grey Literature.* 4th ed. London: Bowker-Saur, 1998.

Barreau, Deborah. "Information Systems and Collection Development in Public Libraries." *Library Collections, Acquisitions, and Technical Services* 25, no. 3 (fall 2001): 263–79.

Bobkoff, Miriam. "A Bookworm's Eye-View of Collection Development: Making Use of Gift Books." *Public Libraries* 38, no. 6 (Nov./Dec. 1999): 364–70.

Carrico, Steven. "Gifts and Exchanges." In *Understanding the Business of Acquisitions,* 2d ed., edited by Karen A. Schmidt, 205–23. Chicago: American Library Assn., 1999.

Collections, Content, and the Web. Washington, D.C.: Council on Library and Information Resources, 2000. Also available at http://www.clir.org/pubs/reports/pub88/contents.html.

Diedrichs, Carol Pitts, and Trisha L. Davis. "Serials Exchanges: Streamlining and Elimination." *Serials Review* 23, no. 1 (spring 1997): 9–22.

Doll, Carol A. "School Library Media Center and Public Library Collections and the High School Curriculum." *Collection Management* 20, no. 1/2 (1995): 99–114.

Farmer, Lesley S. J. "Collection Development in Partnership with Youth: Uncovering Best Practices." *Collection Management* 26, no. 2 (2001): 67–78.

Flowers, Janet L. "Standing Orders: Considerations for Acquisitions Method." *Library Collections, Acquisitions, and Technical Services* 25, no. 3 (fall 2001): 323–28.

Gillespie, John T. *Guides to Collection Development for Children and Young Adults.* Englewood, Colo.: Libraries Unlimited, 1998.

Grant, Joan. "Approval Plans: Library-Vendor Partnerships for Acquisitions and Collection Development." In *Understanding the Business of Acquisitions,* 2d ed., edited by Karen A. Schmidt, 143–56. Chicago: American Library Assn., 1999.

Great Web Site for Kids Selection Criteria: How to Tell if You Are Looking at a Great Web Site. Chicago: American Library Assn. Assn. for Library Services to Children. Children and Technology Committee, 1997. Available at the ALSC web site (http://www.ala.org/alsc); click "Great Web Sites for Kids" on the left column.

Handman, Gary, ed. *Video Collection Development in Multi-Type Libraries: A Handbook.* 2d ed. Westport, Conn.: Greenwood, 2002.

Hearne, Betsy, and Deborah Stevenson. *Choosing Books for Children: A Common-sense Guide.* Urbana: Univ. of Illinois Pr., 1999.

Intner, Sheila S. "Impact of the Internet on Collection Development: Where Are We Now? Where Are We Headed? An Informal Study." *Library Collections, Acquisitions, and Technical Services* 25 (2001): 307–22.

Jewell, Timothy D. *Selection and Presentation of Commercially Available Electronic Resources: Issues and Practices.* Washington, D.C.: Digital Library Federation and Council on Library and Information Resources, 2001. Also available at http://www.clir.org/pubs/reports/pub99/contents.html.

Kilton, Thomas D. "Selecting and Acquiring Materials from Abroad." In *Understanding the Business of Acquisitions,* 2d ed., edited by Karen A. Schmidt, 100–142. Chicago: American Library Assn., 1999.

Kovacs, Diane. *Building Electronic Library Collections: The Essential Guide to Selection Criteria and Core Subject Collections.* New York: Neal-Schuman, 2000.

Landesman, Margaret. "Out-of-Print and Antiquarian Markets." In *Understanding the Business of Acquisitions,* 2d ed., edited by Karen A. Schmidt, 179–295. Chicago: American Library Assn., 1999.

Levitov, De, and Marilyn Sampson. *Guide for Developing and Evaluating School Library Media Programs.* Englewood, Colo.: Libraries Unlimited, 2000.

Metz, Paul. "Principles of Selection for Electronic Resources." Library Trends 48, no. 4 (spring 2000): 711–28.

Milnor, Nancy. "Cyberselection: The Impact of the Internet on Collection Development in Public Libraries." The Acquisitions Librarian, no. 20 (1998): 101–7.

Monroe, William S. "The Role of Selection in Collection Development: Past, Present, and Future." In Collection Management for the Twenty-first Century: A Handbook for Librarians, edited by G. E. Gorman and Ruth H. Miller, 105–18. Westport, Conn.: Greenwood, 1997.

Nisonger, Thomas E. "The Internet and Collection Management in Academic Libraries: Opportunities and Challenges." In The Role and Impact of the Internet on Library and Information Services, edited by Lewis-Guodo Lui, 59–83. Contributions in Librarianship and Information Science, no. 96. Westport, Conn.: Greenwood, 2001.

Schweinsburg, Jane D. "Professional Awareness of the Ethics of Selection." In Encyclopedia of Library and Information Science, edited by Allen Kent, 63, Supplement 26, 247–59. New York: Marcel Dekker, 1998.

Swindler, Luke. "Serials Collection Development." In Managing Serials, by Marcia Tuttle with chapters by Luke Swindler and Frieda R. Rosenberg, 65–100. Foundations in Library and Information Science, v. 35. Greenwich, Conn.: JAI Pr., 1996.

Van Orden, Phyllis J. Selecting Books for the Elementary School Library Media Center: A Complete Guide. New York: Neal-Schuman, 2000.

Van Orden, Phyllis J., and Kay Bishop. The Collection Program in Schools: Concepts, Practices, and Information Sources. 3d ed. Englewood, Colo.: Libraries Unlimited, 2001.

DIVERSE AND ALTERNATIVE LITERATURES AND COMMUNITIES

Anton, Chris. Alternative Literature: A Practical Guide for Librarians. Aldershot, Hampshire, England: Gower, 1996.

Clyde, Laurel A., and Majoria Lobban. "A Door Half Open: Young People's Access to Fiction Related to Homosexuality." School Libraries Worldwide 7, no. 2 (2001): 17–39.

Darby, Mary Ann. Hearing All the Voices: Multicultural Books for Adolescents. Lanham, Md.: Scarecrow, 2002.

Du Mont, Rosemary Ruhig, Lois Buttlar, and William Caynon. Multiculturalism in Libraries. Contributions in Librarianship and Information Science, no. 83. Westport, Conn.: Greenwood, 1994.

Gough, Cal, and Ellen Greenblatt. "Gay and Lesbian Library Materials: A Book Selector's Toolkit." In Public Library Collection Development in the Information Age, edited by Annabel K. Stephens, 151–70. New York: Haworth, 1998. Also published in The Acquisitions Librarian, no. 20 (1998).

Helbig, Alethea K., and Agnes Regan Perkins. Many Peoples, One Land: A Guide to New Multicultural Literature for Children and Young Adults. Westport, Conn.: Greenwood, 2001.

Kranich, Nancy. "A Question of Balance: The Role of Libraries in Providing Alternatives to the Mainstream Media." *Collection Building* 19, no. 1 (2000): 85–90.

Moore, Rachelle, and Harry Llull. "Cultural Diversity as a Collection Development Goal: A Return to Issues and Strategies." In *Issues in Collection Management: Librarians, Booksellers, Publishers,* edited by Murray S. Martin, 73–85. Foundations in Library and Information Science, v. 31. Greenwich, Conn.: JAI Pr., 1995.

Pride, Lula, and Lois Schultz. "Selection of Materials for Special Needs Students." In *Serving Special Needs Students in the School Library Media Center,* edited by Caren L. Wesson and Margaret J. Keefe, 81–96. Westport, Conn.: Greenwood, 1995.

Tjoumas, Renee. "Native American Literature for Young People: A Survey of Collection Development Methods in Public Libraries." *Library Trends* 41 (winter 1993): 493–523.

Totten, Herman L., and Risa W. Brown. *Culturally Diverse Library Collections for Children.* New York: Neal-Schuman, 1994.

Totten, Herman L., Risa W. Brown, and Carolyn Garner. *Culturally Diverse Library Collections for Youth.* New York: Neal-Schuman, 1996.

Warner, Jody Nyasha. "Moving beyond Whiteness in North American Academic Libraries." *Libri* 51, no. 3 (Sept. 2001): 167–72.

Watson, Dana. "Multicultural Children's Literature Selection and Evaluation: Incorporating the World Wide Web." In *Public Library Collection Development in the Information Age,* edited by Annabel K. Stephens, 171–83. Also published in *The Acquisitions Librarian,* no. 20 (1998).

Wesson, Caren, and Margaret J. Keefe, eds. *Serving Special Needs Students in the School Library Media Center.* Westport, Conn.: Greenwood, 1995.

Wood, Irene, ed. *Culturally Diverse Videos, Audios, and CD-ROMs for Children and Young Adults.* New York: Neal-Schuman, 1999.

CENSORSHIP AND INTELLECTUAL FREEDOM

American Library Assn., Office for Intellectual Freedom. *Intellectual Freedom Manual.* 6th ed. Chicago: American Library Assn., 2002.

Assn. for Library Service to Children. *Intellectual Freedom for Children: The Censor Is Coming.* Chicago: American Library Assn., 2000.

Bukoff, Ronald N. "Censorship and the American College Library." *College and Research Libraries* 56 (Sept. 1995): 395–407.

Buschman, John. "Librarians, Self-Censorship, and Information Technologies." *College and Research Libraries* 55, no. 3 (May 1994): 221–28.

Cline, Edward. "Censorship." In *Encyclopedia of Library and Information Science,* edited by Allen Kent, 62, Supplement 25, 65–82. New York: Marcel Dekker, 1998.

Foerstel, Herbert N. *Banned in the U.S.A.: A Reference Guide to Book Censorship in Schools and Public Libraries.* Westport, Conn.: Greenwood, 1994.

————. *Free Expression and Censorship in America: An Encyclopedia.* Westport, Conn.: Greenwood, 1997.

Higgins, Susan E. "Information, Technology, and Diversity: Censorship in the Twenty-first Century." In *Collection Management,* edited by G. E. Gorman, 99–117. International Yearbook of Library and Information Management, 2000/2001. London: Library Assn. Pub., 2000.

Hopkins, Dianne McAfee. "The Library Bill of Rights and School Library Media Programs." *Library Trends* 45, no. 1 (summer 1996): 61–74.

Karolides, Nicholas J. *Censored Books II: Critical Viewpoints, 1985–2000.* Lanham, Md.: Scarecrow, 2002.

Karolides, Nicholas J., Lee Burress, and John M. Kean. *Censored Books: Critical Viewpoints.* Metuchen, N.J.: Scarecrow, 1993.

Peace, A. Graham. "Academia, Censorship, and the Internet." *Journal of Information Ethics* 6, no. 2 (fall 1997): 35–47.

Peck, Robert S. *Libraries, the First Amendment, and Cyberspace: What You Need to Know.* Chicago: American Library Assn., 2000.

Reichman, Henry. *Censorship and Selection: Issues and Answers for Schools.* 3d ed. Chicago: American Library Assn.; Arlington, Va.: American Assn. of School Administrators, 2001.

CHAPTER 5 | Managing Collections

Introduction

Much of the education and training for collection development focuses on building collections. An equally important responsibility is collection management or collection maintenance. Collection management is an umbrella term covering all the decisions made after an item is part of the collection. These decisions often become critical tasks because of condition, budget or space limitations, or shifts in the library's user community and priorities. Collection management often is more politically charged than collection development. User communities, administrative agencies, and funding bodies may be suspicious about the disposition of materials for which "good money" has been spent. They may have an emotional investment in the library's collections. Some preservation reformatting products are less comfortable to use. Moving materials to remote storage sites delays access. Canceling journals will distress at least part of the user group. This chapter explores making decisions about withdrawal, transfer to storage, preservation, and serials cancellation and concludes with a section on protecting collections from theft, mutilation, and natural disasters.

Withdrawal

Withdrawal is the process of removing materials from the active collection. Other terms used for this activity are *weeding, pruning, thinning, deselection, deaccession, relegation, deacquisition, retirement, reverse selection, negative selection,* and *book stock control.* The extensive list of euphemisms suggests the degree to which librarians are uncomfortable getting rid of materials. Some authors make distinctions between these terms; other use them synonymously. As Paul Mosher has written, "It is a paradox that a process established to *improve* the utility and cost-benefit of collections for users creates so high a level of anxiety."[1]

Items withdrawn from the active collection may be offered for sale, given to other organizations, discarded, or transferred to a storage site or to a special collection. Materials in a noncirculating reference collection may be moved to a circulating collection. Though public and school libraries traditionally have been more comfortable with withdrawal, some have run into political problems when their communities have discovered withdrawn materials in dumpsters and landfills. Nicholson Baker attracted national attention with his 1996 *New Yorker* article on massive withdrawal and discard projects at the San Francisco Public Library.[2] The University of New Mexico Library made the news in 2001 when faculty members protested withdrawing back runs of several hundred math jour nals.[3] The library faced severe space constraints and was, at the time of the withdrawal, providing online access to the titles through JSTOR. As a result of the protest, the library reacquired or replaced all withdrawn volumes. Withdrawal is one of the most sensitive functions librarians perform.

Libraries did not give much attention to withdrawals until late in the 1800s. Library materials were so scarce and valuable that the emphasis was on building collections, not culling them. As the number of books in libraries increased and space grew more limited, withdrawing and discarding items in public and school libraries became more common. One early report from the Lunn Public Library in Massachusetts noted that 500 books were withdrawn in 1883 because they were superseded or no longer useful.[4] Large academic and research libraries, which value comprehensiveness and quantity, have been less likely to discard materials, looking instead to transfer volumes to remote storage. In 1893, in one of the earliest documented examples, Harvard Librarian Justin Winsor oversaw moving 15,000 volumes to storage because of space constraints.[5]

Reasons for Withdrawal

Reasons for withdrawal are usually related to saving money or improving services and collections. More effective use of the library's space and staff required to maintain the collection represents one justification for withdrawal. Libraries can dispose of materials that are no longer useful or appropriate. Little-used materials can be sent to a site less expensive to maintain or put into compact storage in a less accessible area of the main library building. These tactics can alleviate space problems and make servicing the active collection easier. A more important reason is to assure continued quality in the collection. When weeding is justified on the grounds that user service will be improved, the rationale is that borrowers can more easily find up-to-date materials, out-of-date and possibly inaccurate materials are no longer available, the general appearance of the library will be improved, and browsing capability is enhanced.

A library should have established criteria, documented in a written policy, guiding withdrawal decisions. The library then has a measure of protection in pointing to a systematic plan for not only building, but also managing its collection. Criteria will vary from library to library, depending on the library's mission, priorities, users, physical facilities, staffing, and age and type of collection. The important elements in successful weeding are a clear purpose (improving the collection, making materials more accessible, freeing space, etc.), sound planning, good communication, sufficient time to do it well, and careful consideration. The process should be conscientious, consistent with policy and institutional goals, attentive to consortial commitments, and sensitive to users.

Robert D. Stueart has described the process of selecting to acquire and selecting to withdraw as linear. He stated, "On the one hand, one must evaluate materials before purchasing them, and on the other hand, one must re-evaluate their usefulness to the collection and then remove them, if they have lost their value. This removal requires judgement just as selection does, and involves added pressures that the initial purchase did not."[6] Weeding is not simple. It is time-consuming, involves many library units, and has political implications.

Ideally, libraries review materials for withdrawal with the same regularity that they add them. One technique is the use of periodic collection inventories or reviews. An example of this approach is offered in Joseph P. Segal's *Evaluating and Weeding Collections in Small and Medium-Sized Public Libraries: The CREW Method.*[7] The CREW (Continuous Review, Evaluation, and Weeding) manual recommends establishing guidelines for weeding each part of the collection according to the classification into which it falls, building weeding into the year's work calendar, and combining inventory review with careful consideration of each item in the collection for discarding, binding, weeding, or replacement.

More frequently, a withdrawal project is a discrete project, forced upon the library by circumstances. The motivation may be a critical demand for more space, the need to review a portion of the collection prior to compacting, or a project to reclassify materials. Such a crash project can put pressure on several library units—circulation, cataloging, stack maintenance—as well as the collections librarians reviewing items. Planning a project should include comparing the costs of the effort with the costs of doing nothing. Costs associated with weeding include staff time to review materials, revise associated records, move materials, educate users, and retrieve materials or obtain them from elsewhere if later requested. Costs resulting from doing nothing include ongoing collection maintenance (reshelving, shifting collections, maintaining catalog records, etc.), unavailable shelf space, and provision of dated and possibly inaccurate information.

Weeding Criteria

Most weeding processes combine mechanical, objective approaches (such as analysis of circulation data and citation frequency) with more judgmental, subjective considerations (such as local program needs and knowledge of the subject literature). Reviewing en masse depends more on objective data because each item is not considered individually. Criteria for weeding are similar to those used in selecting items, remembering that all libraries are different and criteria are more or less relevant depending on the subject area, format, and user community. The three most frequently asked questions are, Has it been used? Is it worn? Is it outdated? Although these are valid, the following questions also should be considered.

Is the content still pertinent?

Is it in a language that current and future users can read?

Is it duplicated in the collection?

Is it available elsewhere?

Is it rare or valuable or both?

Has it been superseded by a new edition?

Was it selected originally in error?

Is it cited in standard abstracting or indexing tools?

Is it listed in a standard bibliography of important works?

Does it have local relevance?

Does it fill a consortial commitment or regional need?

If available in electronic format, is continued access to retrospective files ensured?

Stanley J. Slote recommends an objective, scientific approach to collection weeding.[8] He states that the amount and time of use should be the principal criteria for deciding what items to remove. Slote proposed a macro methodology in which library materials are divided into two groups: a core collection that will serve 90 to 95 percent of current use and a "weedable" collection consisting of a larger group of materials that provides the remaining 5 to 10 percent of use. Much of the literature on collection review has considered use as a primary criterion. A famous study by Allen Kent and colleagues at the University of Pittsburgh indicated that 40 percent of materials purchased never circulated.[9] Richard W. Trueswell's study, conducted in the 1960s, determined that 20 percent of a collection accounts for 80 percent of the circulation and that one-half of the collection meets 99 percent of its users' needs.[10] He noted that "the last circulation date may be an ideal statistic to define and measure circulation requirements and patterns."[11] Relying on past use data as a predictor of future use has its problems. Programs, interests, and priorities change. The energy crisis produced interest in peat and wind as sources of energy and sent researchers after publications that had not been requested in sixty years. Most circulation data do not reflect in-house use. Librarians have not been able to predict accurately the use of materials before purchase and cannot be confident that they will do much better after the item is in the collection. Predicted future use is seldom used as the single criterion for withdrawing items.

Shelf Scanning

The most frequently applied technique for weeding is shelf scanning, which involves direct examination of volumes. Title-by-title review provides information about the size, scope, depth, and currency of materials. It can, however, become a slow and tedious process if the selector seeks to answer all possible questions. Although success depends on the experience and knowledge of the selector, he or she must balance available time against the desired outcomes. Sometimes the selection works in consultation with teachers or faculty members. The selector makes a preliminary identification of items to withdraw, and teachers or faculty members review the decisions in a two-step process.

Decision forms can be simple, providing one or two treatment options, or quite detailed. Detailed forms may record all the information checked in reaching the decision or service to track the item through the review and treatment process. Figure 5-1 is an example of a simple form.

The simple form specifies the treatment the item is to receive. Figure 5-2 is more detailed and records answers to several questions that may be asked when reviewing items. It provides for approving the decisions by another person. The detailed form can provide additional data about the collection. For example, when a representative sample is in hand, several forms can be tallied to learn what percentage of the collection is in poor condition.

Because of the potential political consequences of disposing of materials, libraries should have a disposition policy. This will state the options and processes for disposing of materials and is consistent with the policies of the parent agency and legal considerations. Although the San Francisco Public Library acted within the governing laws in its massive weeding

Figure 5-1 Simple Treatment Decision Form

TREATMENT DECISION FORM

Title: _____

Call number: _____

☐   Rebind

☐   Repair

☐   Transfer to storage

☐   Withdraw

☐   Replace with print, microform, digital

☐   Replace with new edition

☐   Sell

☐   Donate to _____

☐   Destroy

Reviewer name: _____

Date: _____

Figure 5-2 Detailed Treatment Decision Form

TREATMENT DECISION FORM

Title: _____

Call number: _____

# of times circulated in last five years: _____

Duplicate?   ☐ Yes   ☐ No

Condition?   ☐ can no longer circulate
                     ☐ poor condition
                     ☐ acceptable condition

Out of scope?   ☐ Yes   ☐ No

Out of date?   ☐ Yes   ☐ No

Have later ed.?   ☐ Yes   ☐ No

Recommended Treatment

☐ Rebind

☐ Repair

☐ Transfer to storage

☐ Withdraw

☐ Replace with print, microform, digital

☐ Replace with new edition

☐ Sell

☐ Donate to _____

☐ Destroy

Reviewer name: _____

Date: _____

Treatment Approved By

Name: _____

Date: _____

Routing

☐ Cataloging Unit   Date: _____

☐ Binding Unit   Date: _____

☐ Circulation Unit   Date: _____

☐ Shipping Unit   Date: _____

project, city auditors have cited libraries for illegally disposing of city property.[12]

Variations in Library Types

School, public, and smaller academic libraries are more likely than large research libraries to withdraw and dispose of items. School library media centers need current nonfiction, attractive new items, and popular fiction, and they often have severe space limitations. Out-of-date information disadvantages students who should have the most recent and relevant information. A study conducted by Jacqueline C. Mancall and M. Carl Drott concluded that high school students paid little attention to the age of information resources when writing papers.[13] While this finding suggests that students need better education in selecting materials, it is also a warning to school library media centers to cull collections regularly.

Public libraries often have space limitations. In addition, much of their collection is recreational reading material and becomes dated within a few years. Multiple copies of popular novels do not need to be retained. Small and branch public libraries usually concentrate on high-demand materials and can rely on a central library or state or regional interlibrary loan system to supply items that have little demand. Small public libraries should routinely review popular fiction, children's and young adult books, and reference collections.

College libraries may be weeded regularly and carefully because of limited stack and storage space. Focusing on a working collection for undergraduates reduces the need to maintain a constantly growing collection of all materials acquired. Increased access to retrospective files of journals online along with improved bibliographic and physical access to collections elsewhere have reduced the pressures on small academic libraries to retain everything.

Reference collections in all types of libraries usually are weeded more regularly than other portions of collections. Some libraries have a policy that a title must be removed from the reference collection whenever a new volume is added. They may have a schedule for replacing reference books. Bibliographies and encyclopedias are of little use after ten years, with a few exceptions such as the famous *Britannica* eleventh edition. Almanacs and yearbooks should be withdrawn when they are superseded and a new edition is received.

Special libraries serve many different clientele groups, from hospitals to law firms to corporations. Weeding and withdrawal policies must pay special attention to the particular user community being served. Many special libraries are expected to provide up-to-date technical information and to withdraw obsolete materials. The emphasis tends to be on an efficient core collection, providing materials "just-in-time" instead of "just-in-case." Weeding is regular and constant.

Weeding with the intent to dispose of materials is not common in large academic and research libraries. Items considered outdated or less relevant are usually placed in storage instead of removed from the collection. A few circumstances, such as unneeded duplicates or materials in very poor condition (which are replaced or reformatted), will prompt removal.

Most of the literature on withdrawals focuses on print items, but all formats deserve consideration. Computer software becomes obsolete as new versions are released and new equipment is required for its use. Multimedia should be reviewed using the same criteria applied to print materials. Special attention should be given to visual and sound quality and physical condition. School library media specialists will consult with teachers to ensure that media continue to satisfy instructional needs.

Storage

Storing library materials has been called "a necessary evil for which there are no obvious alternatives."[14] It splits collections, limits browsability, and inconveniences users. Nevertheless, use of library storage facilities has a long history. It has been traced to the ancient library in Alexandria, which is reported to have placed duplicate scrolls in a separate location.[15] Whenever libraries run out of room, librarians face the choice of withdrawal or storage. Larger American research libraries were coping with this problem by the end of the nineteenth century. Charles W. Eliot, president of Harvard in 1891, wrote, "What, then, can keep the shelves from encumbrance? Only constant elimination, convenient storage, frequent rearrangement. The books less wanted must be stacked away . . . and the books most valued must be brought forward."[16]

Today, institutional and parent agency administrators often promote a simplistic solution to the problem of collections growing too large for facilities. They think space is no longer a problem for libraries because "everything is electronic." Although more new publications are being issued in electronic formats, international book trade statistics show the number of printed books continues to increase annually. For many parts of the world, publications are available only in print-on-paper formats.

Only a portion of materials, whether domestic or foreign, that libraries select and acquire every year is available in electronic format.

Administrators may assume that libraries can convert everything they own to digital format. High costs and federal law limit the feasibility of local conversion. Recent studies suggest digitizing a book of average size costs between $1,600 and $2,500, to which must be added the cost of refreshing the storage medium every ten years.[17] U.S. copyright law prohibits the large-scale transfer of copyrighted works from one medium to another. Permission to digitize many materials must be obtained from individual publishers and authors. Undertaking local retrospective digitizing of an entire collection is unrealistic and, for the present, impossible.

Journal Back Files

Digitally stored journal back files offer one area of electronic access through which libraries may gain space savings. The decision to store or remove print journal volumes remains complicated. A library may consider removing rather than storing older runs of journals when continued access to the older materials is assured, but this is not always certain. Many files remain available only from publishers or vendors. Access may be available only as long as the library pays an annual subscription fee. Access "in perpetuity" relies on the dependability of the provider. Two projects, JSTOR and Project MUSE, hold promise.[18]

JSTOR, the Scholarly Journal Archive, is intended to ease the problems faced by libraries seeking to provide stack space for long back files of scholarly journals. JSTOR titles are selected for digitization based on the number of institutional subscribers a journal has, citation analysis, recommendations from experts in the field, and the length of time that the journal has been published. JSTOR's agreements with publishers include an updating provision known as a "moving wall." The moving wall is a fixed period of time, ranging from two to five years, that defines the gap between the most recently published issue and the date of the most recent issues available in JSTOR.

Project MUSE, a collaborative effort by Johns Hopkins University Press and the Milton S. Eisenhower Library at Johns Hopkins, provides access to current and retrospective issues of scholarly journals in the humanities and social sciences. At the conclusion of each year during which a library subscribes to Project MUSE, it may request an archival digital file copy containing all of the articles published online during the previous subscription year. Libraries, therefore, own the material from the electronic files to which they subscribe. Project MUSE has made a commitment to providing permanent maintenance and preservation of all the digital files in the MUSE database. All MUSE partner publishers are contractually bound to allow journal content published in MUSE to remain permanently in the database, even if they should discontinue their relationship with MUSE. Finally, Project MUSE is working with other providers to arrange storage of backup copies of all digital files at their sites to ensure future availability. JSTOR and MUSE are making local decisions about withdrawal and storage easier by assuring archival access to digital files.

In 2002, Elsevier Science and the Koninklijke Bibliotheek (KB), the National Library of the Netherlands, announced an agreement through which the KB would become the official digital archive for Elsevier Science journals. The KB receives digital copies of all approximately 1,500 journals that Elsevier makes available on its web platform, ScienceDirect. Any new titles added to ScienceDirect will be added to the archive. As Elsevier digitizes older years of these journals, back files will be deposited with the KB. The KB provides access to the journals on a current basis to all who come to the library. If Elsevier ceases to make these journals available on a commercial basis, the KB will provide remote access to the entire archive.

Off-Site Storage

By the middle of the twentieth century, several academic and research libraries were coping with limited space by building off-site storage facilities. Many were shared by several institutions to gain further economies. The New England Depository opened in 1942 as a cooperative storage facility for seven academic libraries and four nonacademic libraries. The Midwest Inter-Library Center (now the Center for Research Libraries) opened in 1951 to provide storage for member academic libraries as part of several cooperative programs. In the 1980s, the University of California system opened the Northern and Southern Regional Library Facilities. The Elmer L. Andersen Library & the Minnesota Library Access Center, opened in 2000, provides a belowground storage cavern that is shared by libraries of all types in Minnesota. Most cooperative facilities have policies that address costs, criteria for placing materials in storage, retrieval procedures, whether on-site use is permitted, and requirements for bibliographic records.

Several institutions, including Cornell University, Penn State University, and Harvard, have their own storage facilities. Most storage facilities provide high-density shelving, in which items are arranged by size to maximize capacity. Items frequently are stored in trays or bins. Item bar codes are linked to tray bar codes, and the trays are linked to shelf and stack range numbers. Shelving areas normally are closed to users. Some storage facilities provide a reading room; others have no on-site users services.

Libraries place materials in storage because they do not have enough room in their main facility yet wish to retain the items. Lesser- or little-used materials, as well as materials that need special protection, are moved to storage. Many libraries face an economic necessity to find financially reasonable ways to retain materials. Yale has calculated off-site storage to be one-tenth as expensive as on-campus, open-stacks libraries.[19] The type of storage used depends on funds the library has to invest in storage facilities, the probable costs of moving materials back and forth, the difficulty of changing library records to show location of materials, and estimates of how much users will be inconvenienced by remote materials. Criteria for storing materials may be influenced by the provision of a reading room at the storage facility and the speed with which items are delivered to users at the main library. Placing materials in storage can serve as a conservation treatment if the storage facility has optimum temperature and humidity conditions. The reduction in handling that is a consequence of storage can benefit collections.

Selecting and processing materials for storage is labor-intensive. Staff members throughout the library are involved. Collection management librarians define the criteria and review materials. Even with the most logical and defensible criteria, informed judgment is necessary. Technical services staff change the location on bibliographic records and mark items for storage. Materials are pulled from stacks and transported to the new location. Physical control at the storage site requires a finding and retrieval system. This may involve creating a parallel catalog and putting additional markings on the items. Keeping users informed will help them accept the project and the need to store some items.

Either a separate policy or a section in the library's general collection management policy should address criteria and rationale for storing items. A policy should define the process through which materials are reviewed and evaluated, by whom, and how. Making clear the operating principles under which these decisions are made protects the library from charges of bias and irresponsible behavior. Academic librarians who have a policy that references institutional priorities and to which they can direct constituents will find it easier to explain that eliminating a degree program has led to transferring supporting materials to remote storage. By identifying the library's participation in cooperative collection-building, resource-sharing, and regional storage programs, the policy explains the library's obligations to its partners.

Criteria for Storage

The primary criterion for moving materials to storage has been use.[20] The simplest approach may be deciding to move to storage all materials that have not circulated after a specified date or that have circulated a certain number of times within a specified period. This ignores in-library use and variations between disciplines' use of their literatures. Projected use is a variation on historical use criteria and is, obviously, more subjective. This approach presupposes a clear understanding of institutional priorities and detailed knowledge of the collection. Because it is based on perceptions of future utility and cannot be documented, justification is difficult.

A simple approach is to move all inactive serials or all bound serial volumes published before a specified date. This has the advantage of freeing up the most space with the smallest number of bibliographic record changes. Again, variations between disciplines are ignored. Splitting serials runs can cause user confusion and frustration. Another straightforward approach is to apply the date of publication criteria to all formats. An advantage is that the "pain" of remote storage is spread across subjects. On the other hand, variations in literature use among disciplines are ignored. Date of publication criteria can serve a preservation function. All older materials are moved to a facility where they will have significantly less handling and usually benefit from environmental controls. Identifying blocks of materials for storage simplifies the review process and makes possible "global" changes to bibliographic records. This approach assumes knowledge of how the block of material is used—or not used. It also runs the risk of antagonizing an entire segment of users.

Refinements are added as required by users and as time and staffing permit. Typical additional criteria address superseded reference volumes, duplicates, print materials duplicated by microforms, condition, and value. Criteria can be modified within subjects or disciplines. For example, date of publication may be considered inappropriate in the humanities but appropriate in the sciences. However, exceptions are persistent. Older materials in botany are heavily used resources. Each exception requires a staff member to intervene and apply judgment. Review for transfer to storage typically follows procedures similar to those used for other collection review decisions, such as use of decision forms, consultation with other units in the library, and—as appropriate—consultation with teachers and faculty members.

Meeting the needs of collection users is a critical aspect of effective storage programs. Careful selection and good bibliographic control are meaningless without speedy and effective delivery of materials to users. A willingness to reverse storage decisions, sometimes called derelegation, can be desirable. Moving such items back to the main collection saves the library money and reduces user dissatisfaction. All criteria will be scrutinized and questioned by the collection users. Communicating with library users is a critical part of any storage initiative. Well-informed and well-prepared librarians can help defuse user anxieties and misconceptions.

Preservation

Preservation encompasses activities intended to prevent, retard, or stop deterioration of materials or to retain the intellectual content of materials no longer physically intact. Michael Gorman described preservation as part of librarians' stewardship responsibilities—"the preservation of the human record to ensure that future generations know what we know."[21] Preservation includes selecting replacement copies, moving items to a protected area, and selecting materials for reformatting. Binding, rebinding, repairing, using protective enclosures, controlling use, monitoring environmental conditions, and conserving are preservation activities intended to prolong the useful life of materials. An alternative to preservation is planned deterioration. The item is retained until it has deteriorated beyond use and then withdrawn or replaced. Preservation challenges all types of libraries. Federal funding, through the National Endowment for the Arts and, more recently, the Institute of Museum and Library Services, has provided millions of dollars for preservation activities across the country. Grants have funded conservation projects, reformatting projects, research, and education.

Heavy use may result in wear on even the newest materials, but many libraries face the added burden of an aging collection. The greatest source of deterioration in large academic and research collections is the acidic paper manufactured after 1840 and the binding, glues, and other components of printed objects. Before 1840, most paper was made from linen and cotton rags and is much more stable than the paper made from wood pulp that replaced it. Chemicals used during the papermaking process result in chemical processes that cause embrittlement.[22] Brittle paper breaks when page corners are folded one or two times. Books have been known to crumble when moved on shelves, leaving debris compared to cornflakes. Deterioration is compounded by poor housing conditions, in which temperature, excess light, and humidity extremes accelerate deterioration. Research conducted by Robert M. Hayes in the mid-1980s determined that 25 percent of the volumes held in Association of Research Libraries (ARL) member libraries was embrittled and the percentage was increasing annually.[23]

Librarians and publishers became increasingly aware of the brittle books problem in the 1970s and 1980s. Many scholarly publishers, government agencies, professional associations, and trade publishers now use alkaline papers and comply with the national standard for permanent paper, first issued in 1985.[24] Standards are concerned both with permanence (how long paper's shelf life is) and durability (how paper stands up to use). Several methods of deacidification have been developed, including processes that treat large numbers of items and techniques that can be applied individually.[25] The Wei T'o process, developed by Richard Smith, is one of the most common for treating collections of materials.

Before 1900, most techniques used to repair materials drew on traditional bookbinding practices and materials. As collections began to age and become worn, numerous detrimental treatments became common. Using Scotch brand cellophane tape, household glues and pastes, and flimsy, acidic pamphlet binders accelerated deterioration. Benign neglect has been more effective in preserving library materials. Librarians have become more conscious of the consequences of poor repair techniques and materials. Commercial suppliers now offer a variety of archivally sound and reversible materials for cleaning, repairing, and storing materials. Governmental and private agencies and organizations provide information, advice, and services.[26]

Preservation microfilming increased in popularity as a reformatting approach in the 1980s, though it has a long history. In the 1930s, the New York Public Library and Columbia University began microfilming fragile materials. As the library world became aware of the pervasive problem of embrittled paper and disintegrating collections, reformatting on a large scale became an attractive option. Many materials fell apart when handled, and reliable surrogates became desirable. Patricia Battin, president of the Commission on Preservation and Access, wrote, "We faced very painful and wrenching choices—we had to accept the fact that we couldn't save it all, that we had to accept the inevitability of triage, that we had to change our focus from single-item salvation to a mass production process, and we had to create a comprehensive cooperative strategy. We had to move from the cottage industries in our individual library back rooms to a coordinated nationwide mass-production effort."[27]

Several developments fostered cooperative preservation microfilming projects, which were seen as the best option for dealing with a critical situation. National standards for microfilm durability and permanence were developed, and 35-mm silver halide film was accepted as a reliable medium. National bibliographic utilities provided access to holdings and helped libraries avoid duplication of effort. The U.S. federal government began funding preservation microfilming projects. The Commission on Preservation and Access was created in 1986 to instigate and coordinate collaborative efforts, publicize the brittle books problem, and provide national leadership.[28] Cooperative microfilming projects through consortia and the United States Newspaper Program have coordinated national efforts to identify, describe, and preserve fragile resources.

Nicholson Baker focused the nation's attention on preservation microfilming.[29] He lamented the destruction and disposal of items that were microfilmed. Baker's book has been called a "journalistic jeremiad" because of his relentless attack on libraries, librarians, and preservation microfilming.[30] His critics maintain that the practices he described were in place for a limited period, and he misrepresented much of the history of library preservation.[31] Some statements he made regarding the durability of acidic paper remain under question. The routine disbanding and discarding of materials as part of microfilming is no longer done. In some cases, however, reformatting is the only option to preserve the content.

Preservation combines evaluating materials and selecting the appropriate action. Micro decisions often are made when an item in poor condition is discovered during circulation or when a staff member is working with materials on the shelves. Macro decisions treat large portions of a collection. The collections librarian reselects materials by selecting them for preservation. The questions to be answered are, Is treatment desirable? Suitable? Available? Affordable?

Nonprint collections also are in need of preservation. Libraries with digitally recorded videos and compact discs often replace the item, if it is still available, commercially. Digital files present different problems because of various formats and the speed with which standards, software, and hardware change. Libraries with digital collections may plan for refreshing and migrating the data if they wish to retain the content beyond the life of the medium. Jeff Rothenberg has suggested that one means of preserving digital information is to emulate obsolete software and hardware on future systems.[32] Collection development staff alone cannot address, much less resolve, the storage, access, and preservation issues associated with electronic formats.

The mutability of the Internet has led some scholars and librarians to ponder how to preserve collections in a medium that is constantly changing in content, location, and organization. The Internet Archive is building an Internet Library to offer free and permanent access to historical collections that exist in digital format.[33] Founded in 1996 by Brewster Kahle and John Gage, the Internet Archive is collaborating with institutions, such as the Library of Congress and the Smithsonian Institution, to collect and store web pages and to prevent Internet content and other born-digital materials from disappearing. By the summer of 2003, the Internet Library consisted of more than 100 terabytes of data and was growing at the rate of 12 terabytes per month. Part of this initiative is the Wayback Machine, which allows people to surf more than 10 billion web pages from 1996 to the present.

Repair and Conservation

School library media centers, small and medium-sized public libraries, and special libraries commonly focus on treatments that extend the physical life of items. They are unlikely to have full-time preservation staff. These libraries do not have a primary responsibility to retain materials or their intellectual content in perpetuity. They do have an obligation to extend the life of the items in their collections, to protect the investment reflected in their holdings, and to keep their collections as attractive as possible.[34] Many activities contribute to extending the useful life of materials. At the top of the list is good housekeeping—keeping materials dusted and the library free of food or other wastes that attract pests. Controlling temperature, humidity, pollution, and exposure to light protect collections. Educating staff members and users in proper handling of materials is important. Shelves should be the proper height for the items placed on them and should not be packed too tightly. Storage containers and protective enclosures should be archivally sound. Book drops should be padded and emptied frequently.

Library supply companies sell products that can be used for in-house cleaning and simple mending. Materials, procedures, and techniques should meet the latest standards and be acid-free, nondamaging, and safe for workers. Cleaning supplies can remove ballpoint pen ink and crayon marks from book pages, residue from compact discs, and mold and mildew. Assorted types of tape can mend pages or reinforce book spines. Libraries can reglue endpapers, headbands, and spines. Many of these supplies are appropriate for extending the life of the item but are not true conservation techniques. If, however, the library plans to retain the item in perpetuity, specialized cleaning and repair should be done by a trained conservator. Individual items may be encapsulated between sheets of Mylar or polyester. Deacidification can neutralize the acidity and stabilize paper but cannot restore lost physical properties or reverse the damage done.

Some materials may be appropriate for reconstructive binding, such as reference titles or other heavily used materials. Rebinding can be cost-effective if the volume has adequate margins, is not brittle, and if the original binding is not of value as an artifact. Libraries may have some soft-cover items bound on receipt if they expect heavy use. Most research libraries bind all the periodical titles they retain. Libraries rely on commercial binderies. Binding should follow the *Library Binding Institute Standard for Library Binding*.[35] Other options are to retain unbound periodical issues, to replace some or all periodicals with commercial microform, or to rely on centrally archived collections in digital format or held in larger libraries.

Any library may have some materials that require conservation. If the physical entity or artifact is of value, the library may choose to conserve it. Conservation is the effort to save an item in its original condition. The first step is to take good care of materials. This usually means storing in special containers, not circulating valuable items, and permitting use only under supervision. Effective conservation treatment is costly, requiring specialized training and expensive supplies and equipment. In such cases, relying on professional conservators and regional conservation centers is the best option.

Replacement and Reformatting

If the item is worn beyond repair or the cost of repair is too high, a library may replace it. Options are a commercial paper reprint or microform copy, a used copy through an out-of-print (OP) dealer, or local reformatting. Commercial publishers reprint and provide microforms of high-demand titles. Local reformatting should not be pursued unless the librarian has exhausted other replacement options. A library may decide to photocopy the original when it expects moderate use and cannot locate a reprint. Microfilm and microfiche are less appealing to users but withstand more use. Reformatting is expensive. The collections librarian must decide if the intellectual content of an item has sufficient enduring value to justify reformatting and if the format selected will capture the content and support current and future use. The librarian should select a company to produce the photocopy or microform that follows accepted guidelines and standards for permanence, durability, and fidelity. Librarians should be aware of the copyright law and its amendments.

Copyright law has been described as "complicated, arcane, and counterintuitive."[36] Copyright law gives authors several broad rights and also subjects these rights to exceptions, such as "first sale doctrine" (the copyright owner has no right to control the distribution of a copy of a work after he or she has sold that copy) and "fair use" (the legal privilege to make unauthorized use of a copyrighted work for good reason). Section 108 of Title 17, *United States Code*, grants libraries and archives the right to create reproductions of their own holdings during the last twenty years of any term of copyright for purposes of preservation and replacing deteriorated materials if the item cannot be obtained at a reasonable price. An important restriction applies to digital copies, which must be used within the library.

Digitizing as a preservation treatment is becoming increasingly accepted in libraries.[37] A digitized surrogate can add value through enhanced description and searching capability. Digitization has the advantage of reducing handling of the original artifact and making it accessible to more people as a surrogate. The Digital Library Federation (DLF) has developed a "Benchmark for Digital Reproductions of Monographs and Serials."[38] It provides standards for optimally formatted digital content that address quality, persistence, and interoperability. Digitization often is combined with conservation of the original or with microfilm reformatting. Libraries that undertake digitization as a preservation medium must have a robust hardware and software infrastructure and the resources to carry out the project and provide continuing access. Libraries should strive not to duplicate work done at other libraries. One option to aid in locating digitized works is a "Registry of Digital Reproductions of Paper-Based Books and Serials," proposed by the DLF.[39]

The Library of Congress Preservation Directorate compared the costs of various preservation treatments for a single 300-page book.[40] The estimated costs are binding or boxing—$10, mass deacidification—$15, preservation photocopy—$65, microfilming—$185, conservation—$430, base level digitization—$1,600, and enhanced digitization—$2,500. The Library of Congress's base level digitization includes machine-readable, minimally encoded text generated by fully automated processes of optical character recognition and text markup and basic bibliographic description. Enhanced digitization offers improved access through the addition of enhancements, such as essays and finding aids.

Preservation Plans

Many libraries prepare a systematic preservation plan.[41] The plan will vary in scale and complexity depending on the size and nature of the library. A comprehensive preservation plan prepares the library to deal with complex preservation challenges on an ongoing basis. Initially, it increases knowledge among library staff members of existing condition and use issues, possible approaches, existing capabilities, and the financial and technical resources currently available. A preservation plan is also a political instrument. It can serve to raise awareness in the library and the parent organization about preservation problems and help develop a consensus on how to address them.

The first element of a preservation plan is a survey of the collection condition. This involves determining the extent to which all parts of the collection are at risk from acidic paper; embrittlement; loose or incomplete text blocks; deterioration of the text, image, or medium; damaged bindings; or lack of protective enclosures. A second component of a plan is gathering data on environmental conditions (temperature, relative humidity, cleanliness), disaster preparedness, and staff and user education. This will include information about fire prevention, detection, and suppression systems and security measures. Identifying the protective measures in place allows the library to assess the degree to which collections are exposed to future deterioration and sudden damage.

Once librarians have an understanding of collection and environmental conditions, they can begin establishing preservation priorities. Priorities balance the importance of materials with treatment capacities within the context of available and potential funds and staffing. Possible strategies for selecting materials for preservation might be to treat those materials at greatest risk, those that can be treated quickly and inexpensively, those that need a particular type of treatment, or those materials most important to the library.

A library looks at available and potential resources for preservation activities. This means reviewing available staff time, staff competencies, and on-site equipment and funding sources. Technical expertise and resources available locally and regionally are inventoried. Information about the condition of the collections, their environment, and potential risk is weighed against the resources and technical capabilities available to address the needs identified. The result is a systematic plan to meet preservation needs now and in the future.

Serials Cancellation

Serials and standing orders are considered nondiscretionary purchases because a decision, once made, becomes a continuing commitment until it is reversed. The process of serials cancellation begins with a review that parallels that for other collection maintenance functions. Ideally, active serial subscriptions are reviewed regularly as part of ensuring that the collection continues to meet user needs and library goals and objectives. In reality, identifying serials to cancel has become an annual activity in many—perhaps most—libraries for at least the last fifteen years because of constant and rapid increases in serials prices in excess of budget increases.

The ARL reported that the cost of serials increased 227 percent between 1986 and 2002.[42] During many years, increases averaged 10 to 12 percent. Expenditures for serials among ARL member libraries increased 227 percent during that same period, yet they bought only 9 percent more serial titles.[43] One documented consequence of canceling serials year after year is the reduction in unique titles held nationally.[44] Although ARL libraries have been hit hardest because of their large acquisitions budgets and heavy concentration of expensive scholarly journals, all libraries have experienced serials cost increases in excess of national inflation rates.

Other reasons lead libraries to cancel serials. A library may aim for a constant ratio between expenditures for serials and for monographs. Libraries may cancel titles because they seek to maintain expenditure ratios between disciplines or between user groups. For example, journals in the children's and young adult room do not cost as much nor increase in price as rapidly as titles provided in the business section. Therefore, the library may opt to cancel more titles and set a higher dollar target when reviewing the business section serials. The focus of the curriculum or the user community may make some titles less relevant. The library may have access to an online version and not perceive a need for a paper copy. A compelling reason to cancel a journal is declining quality or content that is no longer appropriate.

Librarians use many techniques to make the cancellation process as logical and defensible as possible. Every library needs policies and procedures to guide cancellations and to keep user communities informed and involved to the extent that is reasonable and practical. The same criteria (quality and appropriateness) that guide the selection of a journal or standing order are applied when considering it for cancellation. Use is a leading criterion. Use data may be available from circulation statistics, interlibrary loan requests, user surveys, and in-house use.[45] The difficulty with use studies is that many libraries do not circulate serials, and in-house use data are notoriously unreliable.

Use data often are combined with cost of the title to determine a cost-per-use figure. Very expensive titles that get little use do not provide the benefits to the library and its users that cheaper titles with heavy use do. Journals in some disciplines, typically in the humanities and social sciences, may be more cost-effective. They are so low in price that subscribing to them may be cheaper than requesting them through interlibrary loan or document delivery.[46] Cost data combined with the number of pages or frequency of a publication is another way of looking at cost and benefit. Cost may be the first criterion considered when a library faces a budget-driven cancellation project.

Availability of serial titles within a consortium and through interlibrary loan can influence decisions. Libraries need to honor commitments made to partner libraries to retain titles and protect specific disciplines. Libraries first may cancel titles to which convenient access is available regionally or through an established cooperative delivery service. In many cases, commercial document delivery services and full-text online pay-per-use services have proven a viable and cost-effective alternative to local subscriptions in libraries.[47] Access via an electronic format, when canceling the paper subscription does not increase the cost of the electronic version, may be an option.

Librarians in academic libraries usually work closely with faculty when canceling serials. Canceling journals, like placing materials in storage and withdrawing items, has significant political implications. Many journal users in academic libraries remain oblivious to the extreme price increases that have haunted librarians for years. Librarians need to bring this problem before their user communities repeatedly. Consultation can prevent serious cancellation mistakes, though it can open heated debates in academic libraries as faculty members defend the importance of serial titles in their particular speciality. Nevertheless, surveying constituents is important both because it solicits their input and informs them of the continuing need for cancellations to operate within available budgets.

Librarians have been seeking an ideal way to combine data assembled during the review and consultation process. Several approaches, including using weighted formulas, have been described in the literature.[48] Use data often are the most heavily weighted element. Paul Metz and John Cosgriff have recommended creating a serials decision database to track information collected.[49] An important benefit of having data readily at hand is being able to explain and justify cancellations to disgruntled users.

Collection Protection and Security

Collection protection is another collection management responsibility. This includes proper handling of items by staff members and users, appropriate environmental conditions, security against theft and mutilation, protection of electronic resources, and planning for and responding to disasters. Some libraries hold regular training for staff members, covering such topics as how to remove volumes from shelves, the importance of not shelving volumes too tightly, and the need to use approved supplies for simple mending. Libraries often run publicity campaigns to educate users in the proper care of library materials and to protect against food and drink near collections and computers.

A proper environment protects collections. This encompasses sound shelving and storage containers, moderate temperature and humidity with minimal fluctuations in each, cleanliness including pest control, and the avoidance of excessive light and ultraviolet radiation. Ideal temperatures for general collections should be between sixty-five and seventy degrees for general collections and between fifty-five and sixty-five degrees for special collections and archives. Libraries generally make accommodations for personal comfort and increase temperatures slightly for areas in which users and collections share the same space. Optimum relative humidity is between 25 and 50 percent.

Protection against theft is the issue that comes most frequently to mind when considering collection security. The most famous book thief is Stephen Carrie Blumberg, who, when apprehended in 1990, had amassed nearly 25,000 volumes stolen over more than twenty years from 327 libraries across the United States.[50] People steal for different reasons—to build their own collections, to sell the items, because they are angry. Both library patrons and staff members can be thieves. Theft and mutilation have legal implications under local and federal ordinances and laws. Libraries should work with their governing body and local law enforcement agencies when theft is suspected.

Several steps help protect libraries from theft. All holdings should be documented through a catalog or other means. All items should carry ownership markings, unless inappropriate to the items. The library should conduct regular inventories. The library should have limited entrances and exits with, ideally, some sort of monitoring. Book theft detection systems are common. Some libraries employ surveillance camera systems. Others hire security monitors. Some libraries require users to show identification and register when entering. Collections are reviewed to determine which materials should be transferred to special collections or to other more secure areas either because of value or vulnerability to mutilation. Rare book and special collections usually have more stringent security measures, such as excluding users from the stacks and prohibiting briefcases and bags in the reading room. Protecting against theft needs to be balanced with users' access to the collection and their privacy rights.

Mutilation is frequently not discovered until someone uses an item. Mutilation can result when patrons remove pages because they do not want to make a photocopy, they want a high-quality illustration, they are censoring the collection, or they are making another type of personal statement. Protecting collections from mutilation involves many of the same procedures as protecting it against theft. Libraries have found that having good, convenient, inexpensive photocopy machines reduces collection damage. School library media centers and academic libraries may want to reach agreements with instructors regarding illustrative matter in submitted reports and papers. Ideally, homework should not contain material cut from original books and journals. Only photocopies, digitally generated images, or illustrations created by the student should be acceptable.

Natural disasters encompass earthquakes, fires, floods, burst pipes and building leaks, hurricanes, tornados, volcanoes, vermin infestations, wind damage, chemical spills, and extended power failures. Natural disasters can be very costly. A 1997 flood at Colorado State University caused $100 million in damages.[51] All libraries should have an up-to-date, comprehensive disaster preparedness plan. This document, also called a disaster response plan, provides a policy and procedures for responding to emergencies and specifies priorities and techniques for salvaging different types of material if damaged by fire, flood, or other kinds of disasters. It lists who should be notified, what the chain of command is, who is responsible for which steps, where equipment and supplies (such as buckets, plastic sheeting, gloves, dust masks) are kept, and safety considerations. It will provide contact information for services, which may include collection transport and rapid freezing, needed to respond to different conditions.

Ensuring security for electronic files and systems adds another dimension to collection protection. Issues of concern are protecting against unauthorized access, theft of resources, damage by hackers, viruses, unintentional damage, confidentiality of patron information, and ensuring availability of electronic resources to legitimate users. Libraries may back up information resources and seek to negotiate replacement files from suppliers in the event of data destruction.

Several activities can help librarians protect their collections. A staff training program can address proper handling of library materials, monitoring security issues, and responding to emergencies. A security audit and risk assessment will detect problem areas where the library and its collections are vulnerable. The library should have a clear reporting procedure and designated leader for each situation. An individualized disaster preparedness plan provides specific procedures for dealing with different crises. Although librarians can do much to minimize risk to collections, equally important is knowing how to react when problems develop.

Summary

Collection maintenance or collection management encompasses the decisions made about materials already selected by librarians. The criteria applied when initially selecting an item are revisited, and additional factors, primarily condition and use, are considered. Withdrawals are made to maximize space and to improve the library's collection and services. Titles may be withdrawn because of poor condition, decreased use, and lack of relevance to a changing user community. Items may be withdrawn from one collection or location and moved to another. They may be sold, donated to another library or agency, or destroyed. Storage is an option for materials that are still important though less frequently used, that must be retained for institutional reasons, or that require protection from theft or excessive handling. Preservation decisions address how best to extend the useful life of materials as artifacts or to preserve their content for future users.

Libraries preserve collections through careful handling, appropriate shelving, and clean and environmentally sound facilities. Simple mending and cleaning can be done in-house and can extend the life of items. Acidic paper and bindings are a major cause of deterioration in aging collections. Deacidification can neutralize the pH but does not restore embrittled volumes. Conservation treatments preserve the item itself and should conform to best practices. Librarians turn to trained conservators to restore valuable, unique, and rare items. Replacement is an option if the item itself is not precious. Librarians can seek paper reprints and microfilm or digital surrogates from commercial publishers or look for a replacement on the OP market. If the item cannot be replaced commercially, the librarian can choose to reformat the item as a photocopy, microfilm, or a digital surrogate. All should conform to national standards for durability and permanence.

Cancellation of serials and standing orders has been a concern of librarians for more than twenty years. Rapid increases in prices that have been in excess of inflation and most library budgets have forced librarians to review and cancel subscriptions frequently and regularly. Academic and research libraries have faced the most difficulty because of their dependence on scholarly titles in scientific, technical, and medical fields. These areas have the most expensive titles and have seen the most extreme price increases, but all libraries are obligated to review subscriptions and standing orders within the context of priorities and available funds.

Reviewing materials for withdrawal, storage, preservation, and cancellation is an ongoing responsibility and best guided by library policies and specific criteria. Review can be conducted on the macro and the micro level. Although some types of review are mandated by a crisis and must be handled rapidly and efficiently, continuous attention to collection maintenance is recommended. Decisions should be made within the context of cooperative agreements and local and regional resources. Consultation with other library units and staff members is important because the consequences of any decisions affect others in the library. Consultation with user groups is equally important in order to make informed decisions sensitive to user priorities and to keep the user community informed.

Collection maintenance decisions, like selection decisions, require a combination of objective data and sound subjective judgment.

Protecting collections against theft and damage requires attention to library facilities and security measures. Monitoring users and the use they make of library materials should be continuous. Temperature, humidity, and light should be within recommended guidelines to preserve collections as long as possible. An important part of protecting collections is having a disaster response plan that outlines responsibilities and tasks in the event of a natural disaster.

Maintaining and managing a collection requires personal attention, just as does building a collection. It is equally time-consuming and integral to a quality collection. In a process similar to selecting materials to add to a collection, librarians consider materials and their continuing importance to the library's mission and user community. Collection management is expensive, both in staff time to make the decisions and implement them and in dollars spent to replace, repair, reformat, conserve, and store materials. It seeks to balance access to library resources with their protection. Collection management is a central part of the library's and its librarians' investment in the quality and responsiveness of its collections.

▌CASE STUDY ▌

The Alpha University library system is closing the smallest of its twelve branch libraries for financial reasons. University administration has mandated a 5 percent retrenchment in all units and has approved closing the Museum of Natural History (MNH) Library, which is located in the same building as the university's Museum of Natural History. It has a very small natural history collection with a focus on ornithology and herpetology plus some materials on museology and ecology. The collection contains 12,500 volumes and has 301 active serial subscriptions. The total serials budget is $15,000; $7,000 is allocated for monographs. The MNH Library is staffed by a professional, who is retiring at the end of the year and will not be replaced, and five hours of student help. The museum is a unit within the College of Biological Sciences (CBS). The library system has other libraries that are part of the equation in planning to close the MNH Library. The Entomology, Fisheries, and Wildlife (EFW) Library supports the research and teaching of the College of Natural Resources (CNR). The EFW Library has one professional, two paraprofessionals, and forty hours of student staff. The Biochemistry Library, staffed by one paraprofessional and twenty hours of student help, supports the work of the CBS and is narrowly focused on biochemistry and biotechnology with an emphasis on the submolecular level. Both facilities have space for collection growth.

Faculty members in each of these two colleges are fiercely loyal to their respective colleges and protective of "their" branch libraries. Faculty members in the CBS are insisting the MNH Library collection be moved to the Biochemistry Library. The curators in the Museum of Natural History have asked that monographs and journal runs published before 1962 be given to the museum. Their rationale is that the MNH Library was a departmental library until 1962, when it was administratively transferred to the library system. The library system estimates that approximately one-third of the collection in the MNH Library is duplicated in the EFW Library, including $8,500 in active journal subscriptions. The MNH Library has approximately fifty reference books, which are superseded editions from larger libraries in the Alpha University library system. The university library system has an automated, integrated system, which can generate reports by holding location. Today is July 1, and the MNH Library must be closed by December 30. Materials must be relocated over the three-week holiday break at the end of December. Location changes in the online catalog can be made in December, and withdrawals can occur at any time. Journal cancellations must be made by the end of September.

Activity

Devise a plan for closing the MNH Library and handling the collections. Identify the stakeholders inside and outside the library system and how they will be involved in planning and implementing the project. Think about the collection and the different ways it might be analyzed—subject areas, active journals, ceased journals, duplicates, reference materials, worn items—and make recommendations on how it should be handled, including disposition. Consider communication needs within and outside the library system. Prepare a time line showing the tasks, who will do them, and when. Identify and describe the three largest problems.

REFERENCES

1. Paul H. Mosher, "Reviewing for Preservation, Storage, Weeding," in *Collection Management: A New Treatise,* ed. Charles B. Osburn and Ross Atkinson (Greenwich, Conn.: JAI Pr., 1991), 374.
2. Nicholson Baker, "The Author vs. the Library," *The New Yorker* 72, no. 31 (Oct. 14, 1996): 50–62; and his "A Couple of Codicils about San Francisco," *American Libraries* 30, no. 33 (March 1999): 35–36.
3. Michael Rogers and Norman Odor, "Spectre of Baker Hangs over UNM?" *Library Journal* (June 15, 2001), available at http://libraryjournal.reviewsnews. com/.
4. "Abstracts of and Extracts from Reports," *Library Journal* 8 (1883): 257.
5. Kenneth J. Brough, *Scholar's Workshop: Evolving Conceptions of Library Service,* Illinois Contributions to Librarianship, no. 5 (Urbana: University of Illinois Press, 1953), 124.
6. Robert D. Stueart, "Weeding of Library Materials—Politics and Policies," *Collection Management* 7, no. 2 (summer 1985): 49.
7. Joseph P. Segal, *Evaluating and Weeding Collections in Small and Medium-Sized Public Libraries: The CREW Method* (Chicago: American Library Assn., 1980).
8. Stanley J. Slote, *Weeding Library Collections: Library Weeding Methods,* 4th ed. (Littleton, Colo.: Libraries Unlimited, 1997).
9. Allen Kent et al., *Use of Library Materials: The University of Pittsburgh Study* (New York: Marcel Dekker, 1979), 9.
10. Richard W. Trueswell, "A Quantitative Measure of User Circulation Requirements and Its Possible Effect on Stack Thinning and Multiple Copy Determination," *American Documentation* 16 (Jan. 1965): 20–25; and his "Some Behavioral Patterns of Library Users: The 80/20 Rule," *Wilson Library Bulletin* 43 (1969): 458–61.
11. Richard W. Trueswell, "Determining the Optimal Number of Volumes for a Library's Core Collection," *Libri* 16 (1966): 58–59.
12. Evan St. Lifer, "City Rebukes Philadelphia Library on Weeding Practices," *Library Journal* 121 (May 15, 1979): 12.
13. Jacqueline C. Mancall and M. Carl Drott, *Measuring Student Information Use* (Littleton, Colo.: Libraries Unlimited, 1983).
14. Dan C. Hazen, "Selecting for Storage: Local Problems, Local Responses, and an Emerging Common Challenge," *Library Resources and Technical Services* 44, no. 4 (Oct. 2000): 176.
15. David Block, "'Remote Storage in Research Libraries: A Microhistory," *Library Resources and Technical Services* 44, no. 4 (Oct. 2000): 184.
16. Quoted by Kenneth I. Brough, *Scholars Workshop: Evolving Conceptions of Libraries Services,* Illinois Contributions to Librarianship, no. 5 (Urbana: University of Illinois Press, 1953), 125.
17. Stephen G. Nichols and Abby Smith, *The Evidence in Hand: The Report of the Task Force on the Artifact in Library Collections* (Washington, D.C.: Council on Library and Information Resources, 2001), 100.
18. JSTOR, The Scholarly Journal Archive [WWW home page of JSTOR]. Available [Online]: http://www.jstor.org; and Project MUSE, Scholarly Journals Online [WWW home page of Project MUSE]. Available [Online]: http://muse.jhu.edu.

19. Yale University, *Final Report of the Working Group, Library Shelving Facility,* Oct. 1996, available at http://www.library.yale.edu/Administration/Shelving/historical.html.

20. *See* Robert M. Hayes, "Making Access Allocation Decisions," in his *Strategic Management for Academic Libraries: A Handbook* (Westport, Conn.: Greenwood, 1993), 169–87; Hur-Li Lee, "The Library Space Problem: Future Demand and Collection Control," *Library Resources and Technical Services* 37, no. 2 (April 1993): 147–66; and Wendy P. Lougee, "Remote Shelving Comes of Age: Storage Collection Management at the University of Michigan," *Collection Management* 16, no. 2 (1992): 91–107.

21. Michael Gorman, *Our Enduring Values: Librarianship in the Twenty-first Century* (Chicago: American Library Assn., 2000), 58.

22. Chandru J. Shahani and William K. Wilson, "Preservation of Libraries and Archives," *American Scientist* 75 (May/June 1987): 240–51.

23. Robert M. Hayes, "Analysis of the Magnitude, Costs, and Benefits of the Preservation of Research Library Books," working paper, Council on Library Resources, Washington, D.C., 1985.

24. *American National Standard for Information Sciences—Permanence of Paper for Printed Publications and Documents in Libraries and Archives,* ANSI Z39.48-1992 (Gaithersburg, Md.: National Institute of Standards and Technology, 1992).

25. Michele V. Cloonan, "Mass Deacidification in the 1990s," *Rare Books and Manuscripts Librarianship* 5, no. 2 (1990): 95–103.

26. Among these are: American Institute for Conservation of Historic and Artistic Works [WWW home page]. Available [Online]: http://aic.stanford.edu; Preservation and Reformatting Section of the Assn. for Library Collections and Technical Services [WWW home page]. Available at the ALCTS web site (http://www.ala.org/alcts); click "Preservation" on the top navigation bar; and several regional conservation centers, such as the Northeast Document Conservation Center in Massachusetts [WWW home page]. Available [Online]: http://www.nedcc.org/

27. Patricia Battin, "Substitution: The American Experience," typescript, lecture in Oxford Library Seminars, "Preserving Our Library Heritage," Feb. 25, 1992, 9.

28. Council on Library and Information Resources [WWW home page of CLIR]. Available [Online]: http://www.clir.org.

29. Nicholson Baker, "Deadline: The Author's Desperate Bid to Save America's Past," *The New Yorker* 76, no. 29 (July 24, 2000): 42–61; and his *Double Fold: Libraries and the Assault on Paper* (New York: Random House, 2001).

30. Robert Darnton, "The Great Book Massacre," review of *Double Fold: Libraries and the Assault on Paper,* by Nicholson Baker, *The New York Review of Books* 48, i7 (April 26, 2001): 16–19.

31. Richard J. Cox, *Vandals in the Stacks? A Response to Nicholson Baker's Assault on Libraries,* Contributions in Librarianship and Information Science, no. 98 (Westport, Conn.: Greenwood, 2002), offers one of many thoughtful responses to Nicholson Baker.

32. Jeff Rothenberg, *Avoiding Technological Quicksand: Finding a Viable Technical Foundation* (Washington, D.C.: Council on Library and Information Resources, 1999). Also available at http://www.clir.org/pubs/abstract/pub95abst.html.

33. Internet Archive [WWW home page of the Internet Archive]. Available [Online]: http://www.archive.org/.
34. Susan L. Tolbert, "Preservation in American Public Libraries: A Contradiction in Terms?" *Public Libraries* 36 (July/Aug. 1997): 236.
35. *Library Binding Institute Standard for Library Binding,* 8th ed. (Rochester, N.Y.: Library Binding Institute, 1986); *see also* Jan Merrill-Oldham and Paul A. Parisi, *Guide to the Library Binding Institute Standard for Library Binding* (Chicago: American Library Assn., 1990).
36. Jessica Litman, *Digital Copyright* (Amherst, N.Y.: Prometheus, 2001), 112.
37. Daniel Greenstein and Suzanne E. Thorin, *The Digital Library: A Biography* (Washington, D.C.: Council on Library and Information Resources, 2002), 56. Also available at http://www.clir.org/pubs/abstract/pub109abst.html.
38. Digital Library Federation, "Benchmark for Digital Reproductions of Monographs and Serials," as endorsed by the DLF, original prepared on July 30, 2001, revised on Jan. 25, 2002. Available at http://www.diglib.org/standards/bmarkfin.htm.
39. Registry of Digital Masters [WWW home page for the Digital Library Federation Initiative]. Available [Online]: http://www.diglib.org/collections/reg/reg.htm.
40. Stephen G. Nichols and Abby Smith, *The Evidence in Hand: The Report of the Task Force on the Artifact in Library Collections* (Washington, D.C.: Council on Library and Information Resources, 2001), 100. Also available at http://www.clir.org/pubs/abstract/pub103abst.html.
41. The following manual is a useful planning tool: *Preservation Planning Program: An Assisted Self-Study Manual for Libraries,* developed by Pamela W. Darling, with Duane E. Webster; revised by Jan Merrill-Oldham and Jutta Reed-Scott (Washington, D.C.: Assn. of Research Libraries, 1993).
42. *Monographs and Serials Costs in ARL Libraries, 1986–2002* (Washington, D.C.: Assn. of Research Libraries, 2002), available at http://www.arl.org/stats/arlstat/graphs/2002/2002t2.html.
43. Ibid.
44. Tina E. Chrzastowksi and Karen A. Schmidt, "Collections at Risk: Revisiting Serial Cancellations in Academic Libraries," *College and Research Libraries* 57, no. 4 (July 1996): 351–64; and their "Surveying the Damage: Academic Library Serial Cancellations, 1987–88 through 1989–90," *College and Research Libraries* 54, no. 2 (March 1993): 93–102.
45. *See* Margaret W. Maxfield, Rebecca DiCarlo, and Michael A. DiCarlo, "Decreasing Use of Monthly Serials after Publication Date," *Serials Librarian* 27, no. 4 (1995): 71–76; and Carol French and Eleanor Pollard, "Serials Usage Study in a Public Library," *Public Library Quarterly* 16, no. 4 (1997): 45–53.
46. Dorothy Milne and Bill Tiffany, "A Survey of the Cost-Effectiveness of Serials: A Cost-Per-Use Method and Its Results," *Serials Librarian* 19, no. 3/4 (1991): 137–49.
47. Richard P. Widdicombe, "Eliminating All Journal Subscriptions Has Freed Our Customers to Seek the Information They Really Want and Need: The Result—More Access, not Less," *Science and Technology Libraries* 14, no. 1 (fall 1993): 3–13.
48. *See* Betty E. Tucker, "The Journal Deselection Project: The LSUMC-S Experience," *Library Acquisitions: Practice and Theory* 19, no. 3 (fall 1995): 313–20; and

Managing Collections | 169

Paul Metz and John Cosgriff, "Building a Comprehensive Serials Decision Database at Virginia Tech," *College and Research Libraries* 61, no. 4 (July 2000): 324–34.

49. Metz and Cosgriff, "Building a Comprehensive Serials Decision Database at Virginia Tech," 324.

50. Susan M. Allen, "The Blumberg Case: A Costly Lesson for Librarians," *AB Bookman's Weekly* 88 (Sept. 2, 1991): 769–73; and Philip Weiss, "The Book Thief: A True Tale of Bibliomania," *Harper's Magazine* 288, no. 1724 (Jan. 1994): 37+.

51. "Flood Toll at Colorado State Could Reach $100 Million," *American Libraries* 28, no. 8 (Sept. 1997): 17.

SUGGESTED READINGS

Ackerson, Linda G. "Is Age an Appropriate Criterion for Moving Journals to Storage?" *Collection Management* 26, no. 3 (2001): 63–76.

Alire, Camila, ed. *Library Disaster Planning and Recovery Handbook.* New York: Neal-Schuman, 2000.

Allen, Susan M. "Preventing Theft in Academic Libraries and Special Collections." *Library and Archival Security* 14, no. 1 (1997): 29–43.

Banks, Paul, and Roberta Pilette, eds. *Preservation: Issues and Planning.* Chicago: American Library Assn., 2000.

Beagrie, Neil, and Maggie Jones. *Preservation Management of Digital Materials: A Handbook.* London: The British Library for Resource, the Council for Museums, Archives and Libraries, 2001. An online edition is maintained by the Digital Preservation Coalition and is available at http://www.dpconline.org/graphics/handbook/index.html.

Boon, Belina. *The CREW Method: Expanded Guidelines for Collection Evaluation and Weeding for Small and Medium-Sized Public Libraries.* Austin: Texas State Library, 1995.

Building a National Strategy for Digital Preservation: Issues in Digital Media Archiving. Washington D.C.: Council on Library and Information Resources and Library of Congress, 2002. Also available at http://www.clir.org/pubs/reports/pub106/contents.html.

Bushing, Mary, and Elaine Peterson. "Weeding Academic Libraries: Theory into Practice." *Advances in Collection Development and Resource Management* 1 (1995): 61–78.

Callison, Daniel. "Currentness." *School Library Media Activities Monthly* 15, no. 1 (Sept. 1998): 37–39.

The Complete Library Safety and Security Manual: A Comprehensive Resource Manual for Academic and Public Library Professionals and Law Enforcement Officers. Goshen, Ky.: Campus Crime Prevention Programs, 1998.

Curry, Ann, Susanna Flodin, and Kelly Matheson. "Theft and Mutilation of Library Materials: Coping with Biblio-Bandits." *Library and Archival Security* 15, no. 2 (2000): 9–26.

Davis, Vivian R. "Weeding the Library Media Center Collection." *School Library Media Activities Monthly* 17, no. 7 (March 2001): 26–28.

Drewes, Jeanne, and Julie A. Page, eds. *Promoting Preservation Awareness in Libraries: A Sourcebook for Academic, Public, School, and Special Collections.* Westport, Conn.: Greenwood, 1997.

French, Carol, and Eleanor Pollard. "Serials Usage Study in a Public Library." *Public Library Quarterly* 16, no. 4 (1997): 45–53.

Hazen, Dan C., Jeffrey L. Horrell, and Jan Merrill-Oldham. *Selecting Research Collections for Digitization.* Washington, D.C.: Council on Library and Information Resources, 1998. Also available at http://www.clir.org/pubs/reports/hazen/pub74.html.

Hickey, C. David. "Serials 'Derelegation' from Remote Storage." *Collection Building* 18, no. 4 (1999): 153–60.

Higginbotham, Barbra Buckner, and Judith W. Wild. *The Preservation Program Blueprint.* Frontiers of Access to Library Materials, no. 6. Chicago: American Library Assn., 2001.

Jaguszewski, Janice M., and Laura K. Probst. "The Impact of Electronic Resources on Serial Cancellations and Remote Storage Decisions in Academic Research Libraries." *Library Trends* 48, no. 4 (spring 2000): 799–820.

Johansson, David H. "Library Materials Theft, Mutilation, and Preventive Security Measures." *Public Library Quarterly* 15, no. 4 (1996): 51–66.

Lambert, Dennis K., et al. *Guide to Review of Library Collections: Preservation, Storage, and Withdrawal.* 2d ed. Collection Management and Development Guides, no. 9. Lanham, Md.: Assn. for Library Collections and Technical Services in cooperation with Scarecrow Press, 2001.

Matthews, Graham. "Surveying Collections: The Importance of Condition Assessment for Preservation Management." *Journal of Librarianship and Information Science* 27 (Dec. 1995): 227–36.

Metz, Paul. "Thirteen Steps to Avoiding Bad Luck in a Serials Cancellation Project." *Journal of Academic Librarianship* 18, no. 2 (May 1992): 76–82.

Nitecki, Danuta A., ed. *Library Off-Site Shelving: Guide for High-Density Facilities.* Englewood, Colo.: Libraries Unlimited, 2001.

Ogden, Sherelyn, ed. *Preservation of Library and Archival Materials: A Manual.* 3d ed. Andover, Mass.: Northeast Document Conservation Center, 1999.

Shuman, Bruce A. *Library Security and Safety Handbook: Prevention, Policies, and Procedures.* Chicago: American Library Assn., 1999.

Sitts, Maxine K., ed. *Handbook for Digital Projects: A Management Tool for Preservation and Access.* Andover, Mass.: Northeast Document Conservation Center, 2000.

Stack, Michael J. "Library Theft Detection Systems: Future Trends and Present Strategies." *Library and Archival Security* 14, no. 2 (1998): 25–37.

The State of Digital Preservation: An International Perspective. Washington, D.C.: Council on Library and Information Resources, 2002. Also available at http://www.clir.org/pubs/reports/pub107/contents.html.

Thomas, Charles F. "Preservation Management: Something Old, Something New." In *Collection Management,* edited by G. E. Gorman, 365–80. International Yearbook of Library and Information Management, 2000/2001. London: Library Assn. Publishing, 2000.

Wellheiser, Johanna, and Jude Scott. *An Ounce of Prevention: Integrated Disaster Planning for Archives, Libraries, and Record Centres.* 2d ed. Lanham, Md.: Scarecrow and Canadian Archives Foundation, 2002.

Williams, Roy. "Weeding Library Collections: Conundrums and Contradictions." In *Collection Management,* edited by G. E. Gorman, 339–61. International Yearbook of Library and Information Management, 2000/2001. London: Library Assn. Pub., 2000.

CHAPTER 6 | Marketing, Liaison, and Outreach Activities

Introduction

No library operates in a vacuum. Even an individual's private collection is crafted in response to that individual's needs and interests, within the resources available. Every library that serves a constituency seeks to build collections and develop services to match its service or user community. The challenge facing collection development librarians is learning about and keeping current with users' changing needs, wants, and demands in order to develop collections and services in response. To be truly effective, collection development must consider future needs, not simply those of today's most frequent or vocal users. Regular communication with clientele is essential for gathering the information needed both to perform routine collection development and management activities and to plan for the future. Regular communication, formal and informal, is equally fundamental for sharing information about the library—new acquisitions, new programs and services, successes, problems, and constraints. Regardless of library type, understanding the library's users, governing and funding bodies, community leaders, and administrators and consulting with these groups are fundamental responsibilities of librarians.

Liaison and outreach are terms that describe aspects of the same activity—communication with the library's community to share and gain information. Communication is a two-way enterprise. Librarians need to learn about and listen to their constituents' concerns and ideas as well as share information. Academic libraries tend to use *liaison* to refer to communication with their constituents. Liaison is communication for establishing and maintaining mutual understanding and cooperation. The "Guidelines for Liaison Work" developed by the American Library Association's Reference and Adult Services Division (RASD), now Reference and User Services Association (RUSA), explains liaison work as "the relationships, formal and informal, that librarians (in this instance, librarians with multiple responsibilities) develop with the library's clientele for the specific purpose of seeking input regarding the selection of materials. . . . This process also enables the library to communicate its collection building philosophy and activity to those it serves."[1]

Public and school librarians more commonly use the term *outreach* to describe the act of reaching out or extending services beyond current or usual limits. Part of outreach is informing constituents about the library's collections and services, especially those for special groups. Such targeted groups may be people who are homebound or visually impaired, preschool children, small business owners, and so forth. As librarians come in contact with users through the promotion and delivery of collections and services, they gain information that can translate user needs and suggestions into responsive collections.

Much of this outreach and liaison work includes the very tasks associated with marketing, and all librarians can benefit from knowing the basic marketing concepts.

What Is Marketing?

The vocabulary and concepts of marketing, more often used in the for-profit sector, can be applied to libraries' liaison and outreach activities. In a library context, the aim of marketing is to satisfy the library user and achieve a set of articulated goals, which may be increased use, community support, more patrons, a larger budget, or increased donations. For the collection development librarian, marketing means understanding the library's public (users, potential users, supporters, funding and administrative bodies) in order to develop a product (the collection). The success of that product is then measured or evaluated to ensure performance is responsive to the public and gains support. Library marketing always occurs within the context of the library's mission, goals, and objectives. Successful marketing helps position the library to plan for that future.

Marketing as part of collection development in libraries is not a new idea. In 1969, Martin Lopez wrote that marketing is one of the seven selector responsibilities comprising collection development.[2] The other responsibilities that Lopez identified are fiscal management, planning, evaluation, review, quality control, and resource sharing. The *Guide for Training Collection Development Librarians* contains a section on "Marketing, Outreach, and Communications with Constituencies," documenting the increasingly widespread acceptance of marketing as a core competency for selectors.[3] Marketing, as promotion, in libraries has an even longer history. O. Gene Norman identified 114 publications, published between 1981 and 1989 alone, on marketing in libraries.[4]

A common misconception is that marketing is the same as advertising or hard-sell promotion, which has had a negative connotation in the nonprofit sector. Although marketing does include promotion, this is only one aspect. The aim of marketing in collection development is to understand the library's present and future users in order to develop a collection that satisfies their needs, wants, and demands. Once the library understands its potential market, it formulates marketing strategies. These include developing overall plans to maximize impact on the market in both the short- and long-term, deciding which information resources and services to offer, and establishing standards and measures for performance. In other words, marketing is market analysis, planning, implementation, and control. These activities are increasingly important in the nonprofit sector. Social agencies, educational institutions, and charities are moving into marketing activities to learn the needs and wants of their target markets and to deliver the desired satisfaction more effectively and efficiently than their competitors. Many small private colleges have had active marketing offices for years. They have sought to identify and cultivate a target market—to develop programs that attract the best students, willing to pay to attend.

Marketing can challenge libraries because, without profit/loss figures found in the commercial sector, measuring the success of marketing efforts is often difficult. Yet performance measurement is an essential component of effective collection development and management, and various methodologies for evaluation and assessment have been developed over time. Librarians evaluate collections to determine how well they support the needs of users and the goals of the parent organization. They survey users to learn users' level of satisfaction. They assess collections by examining a collection in its own terms or relative to other collections and checklists.

The library's community, consisting of users, potential users, and its funding and governing bodies, is its market. Marketing is implicit in Charles B. Osburn's analysis of the relationship between libraries and their communities. He has written, "Since . . . libraries depend upon their communities for support, the future of libraries does hinge very definitely on the priority and importance assigned to them by their respective communities. . . . For this reason alone, each library will be better off for defining its community, trying to understand it, and demonstrating to it the value that can be expected of the library."[5] A library's marketing activities begin with knowing its public—its community.

Market Research

Librarians must undertake research to define and understand their user community or market. Market research establishes the overall size and structure of the community, identifies user characteristics, assesses needs of the users, and interprets trends. The terms *community analysis, needs assessment,* and *needs analysis* may be more familiar to librarians.[6] All are research or studies through which librarians seek as much information as possible about their community or constituencies—users, potential users, supporters, and funding bodies. Market research is conducted through analysis of secondary (existing) data and gathering and analysis of primary data. Primary data are obtained through observational research, qualitative research (individual interviews and focus groups), and formal research through surveys and experimental research. Marketing research can help the library be more effective but only if the process is purposeful and timely and the results are used.

One common strategy in market research is to divide the market into segments in order to understand each segment better. The library's user community can be understood in terms of its components or segments. Librarians can gather secondary and primary data about each market segment and then develop collections that respond to these various user groups. The community can be segmented in many ways. Common approaches consider demographic characteristics (age, sex, income level, ethnic background, occupation, and educational level), geographic characteristics (ability to travel to a library, the distance that must be traveled, and the residential or nonresidential status of the potential patron), behavioral characteristics (extent and type of a patron's use of the library in general or of specific collections and services within it), and sociological characteristics. The latter examines users on the basis of socioeconomic class, lifestyle, personality, interests, and opinions. A corporate library might segment its users into researchers, marketers, legal staff, and management, with the aim of satisfying the information needs of each.

George D'Elia divided public library users into six target markets: people who only borrow books, people who only use materials in the library, people who use the library lightly, heavy users, hard-core non-users, and potential users.[7] D'Elia's report predated remote online access to libraries. Another way to categorize public library users is suggested in the RASD/RUSA "Guidelines for Liaison Work." The categories or segments are

- recreational users;
- new adult readers, independent and lifelong learners;
- businesspersons;
- civic groups;
- local, state, and regional departments and agencies;
- nursery schools, elementary and secondary schools, colleges and universities;
- students ranging from preschool to graduate school;
- senior citizens;
- new immigrants and populations having English as a second language;
- people with disabilities; and
- institutionalized populations.[8]

Ulla De Stricker, writing about marketing in special libraries, stressed the need to identify the library's stakeholders.[9] Stakeholders can be active users of the special library or information center, its potential users, and managers and executives. Each group has different priorities and plans that should be understood in order to create library services and collections that match these priorities.

The academic library's community is often analyzed along the categories of faculty members, students, institutional staff members, administrators, and external users. The first four groups usually are considered primary or affiliated users. External users, who may be segmented into categories such as alumni and corporate researchers, are often called secondary or unaffiliated users. In many academic libraries, the same cat-egories are employed when developing outreach and liaison activities. Responsibilities for faculty liaison usually are divided between various selectors along subject or discipline lines. Outreach to students may be aligned according to subject foci or directed to undergraduate, graduate, and professional school student groups. In addition, librarians may have liaison responsibilities with student government bodies and student organ-izations (ethnic, social, service, etc.). Each targeted group can provide information that aids the selector in developing collections to meet that group's needs and interests.

School librarians usually think of their user community in terms of students, teachers, and—in some libraries—students' families. Students can be further segmented into, for example, age or grade groups, native English speakers and students for whom English is not their first language, or those with special needs or special abilities. Teachers can be categorized along similar lines. School librarians might consider parent advisory groups and site counsels, parent-teacher associations, school boards, and school administrators as part of the community for which their libraries are responsible and to whom they are accountable.

After a librarian chooses how he or she will define the components of the library's community, data are gathered. Secondary data can be ob-tained from various sources. Demographic information is found in census data, local government data, nonconfidential employee information from corporation personnel units, school enrollment statistics, and other pub-lished resources. Data on the ability of the existing collection to meet cur-rent needs can be found in reviews of interlibrary loan requests, circula-tion activity, reference questions (answered and unanswered), and purchase suggestions from users.

Library automation has the potential to produce a wealth of con-stituent use data that can guide collection development; however, not all systems live up to this promise, nor do selectors always make use of the available information. Of particular value are data reflecting circulation activity, interlibrary loan requests, and document delivery activity. Dennis P. Carrigan suggests that data can be used to guide decisions at the individ-ual title level or at the subject or call number range level.[10] If the auto-mated system is able to correlate use by various user categories (for example, activity by adult and juvenile users in a public library or by stu-dent, staff, faculty, or unaffiliated users in an academic library), the selec-tor will have hard data on market needs and wants that can help develop a responsive collection. Use statistics should be weighed against categories of materials for which such data are not collected, such as noncirculating materials and on-site use.

When selectors gather and analyze primary data through observation, interviews, and surveys, they seek specific answers that help guide collection development. Information collected in these ways must be analyzed cautiously because both user and researcher biases can skew results. User perceptions, memories, and understanding of collections and services may not always reflect reality. Researchers may have framed the questions in such a way that ambiguous responses result. Questions may address why an individual does or does not use a library resource, if a resource is easy to use or not, what the individual needed or wanted and was unable to obtain, how long he or she is willing to wait for the resource, and preferences for formats. Information gathered on these topics, in addition to guiding collection development, is useful in collection assessment.

Marketing Concepts in a Library Context

In *Strategic Marketing for Nonprofit Organizations,* Philip Kotler and Alan R. Andreasen define *marketing* as the effective management by an organization of its exchange relations with various markets and publics.[11] Marketing begins with an understanding of the market's needs, wants, and demands. A *need* is a state of felt deprivation of some basic satisfaction. Needs require solution. *Wants* are desires for specific satisfiers of these deeper needs. *Demands* are wants for specific products or services. Marketers can influence wants. For example, I need information. I want the library to help me find this information, by either giving it to me or directing me to a resource that will provide it. I demand, in the marketing sense of this word, to use an online resource. I have been influenced by marketing, either by the library or the commercial sector, to prefer electronic information resources instead of traditional printed information tools. Most people who enter the library or access it remotely seek information or entertainment. The individual may want a mystery novel. He or she may demand the newest John Grisham novel.

Selectors should be cautious about seeking to meet all their users' perceived needs and wants, which is usually too narrow an objective. Most libraries have long-range goals and objectives, articulated in a mission statement and mandated by a parent authority or agency. Kotler and Karen F. A.

Fox call keeping the bigger picture in mind a societal marketing orientation.[12] The selector's task is developing and managing collections to enhance the current users' level of satisfaction and to increase user support while preserving society's or the library's well-being and long-term interests.

Products and services are anything that can be offered to satisfy a need or want. Libraries provide products in the form of information, books, journals, multimedia, online resources, customized bibliographies, handouts, library web pages, and so on. Library services are reference, interlibrary loan, reader counseling, training, story hours, class visits, and any time a staff person comes in contact with a patron. Collection development librarians can see the collections they build and manage as the product. Every contact they make with their constituents is a service.

In addition to gathering information to better understand needs, the selector works with users to identify and solve problems that they have experienced with the library. These will include both inadequacies with the collection and problems with library services. Often, selectors will discover that a user's assessment of the collection is based on incomplete or inaccurate knowledge of resources held locally and of the means available to access remote resources either electronically or through interlibrary loans. The librarian gains information that will help develop outreach activities that more clearly and completely convey to users what the library has and does. When a user's dissatisfaction is based on real problems, not misunderstanding, the selector takes on the role of advocate in trying to solve these problems within the context of available library and institutional resources. The selector solicits advice from constituents regarding specific collection issues. This form of consultation is more common in academic and school libraries, in which faculty members and teachers make recommendations about purchasing expensive items, adding and canceling journal titles, replacing specific titles and materials in particular subject areas, placing materials in storage, and needing multiple copies of individual titles.

Value and satisfaction define how consumers choose between the products and services that might satisfy a given need. Value is a complicated concept with a long history in economic thought. Karl Marx thought that the value of an object depended on how much labor went into its production. Contemporary thought defines *value* as subjective and suggests that value depends on its capacity to satisfy wants. I value the library and its services to the extent my wants are met. Do I get the information I need? Does the library have the book I want? Did the selector order the book I recommended? How long do I have to wait? Even if I'm satisfied, I may not value the library. Recent research indicates that satisfaction does not necessarily translate into customer loyalty.[13]

Citizens may value the library, be satisfied with its collections and service, but be unwilling to approve a tax increase to support it. Faculty members may proclaim the library as essential for teaching and research but fail to protect its budget allocation. Parents and school boards value their school media centers but may reduce the number of media specialists before they will cut back on coaching staffing.

The term *exchange and transactions* describes the act of obtaining a desired product or service by offering something in return. Transactions consist of a trade of values between two parties. The commodity exchanged for the product or service may not be financial, though it often is. Academic libraries, frequently glibly called the heart of the university, are seldom funded to the financial level this "value" might suggest. Time and effort may be equally valuable commodities. The faculty member or teacher, valuing students who use the library, may give time in his or her classroom to the librarian, who provides an orientation to library resources and services. Many public libraries are finding that citizens are willing to pay for specialized reference service and document delivery if it is speedier and easier than doing the research and retrieval themselves.

The market consists of all the potential customers sharing a particular need or want and who might be willing and able to engage in exchange, which may be money, time, effort, or all three, to satisfy that need or want. A marketer is one who engages in marketing—who analyzes the market, develops a product or service for that market, and monitors satisfaction. Libraries typically deal with a complex community or potential customer base over which they have no authority and only indirect influence yet to which they must respond effectively in an anticipatory mode. Even when they do not seek direct cost recovery, libraries seek support and loyalty in exchange for user satisfaction. Sharon L. Baker and Karen L. Wallace have examined marketing in public libraries.[14] Much of what they write is relevant to all types of libraries. They state, "Mounting evidence documents that adopting thoughtful, cohesive marketing plans can help staff provide collections and services that satisfy patron and library objectives at reasonable costs while attracting public support for future endeavors."[15]

Kotler suggests that marketing can be understood in relation to what he calls the four Ps: product, price, place, and promotion.[16] Two additional factors can be added to Kotler's list to make it more applicable to libraries—performance measurement and the library's public. A collection development librarian can develop a marketing plan that organizes activities around each of these mutually dependent factors.

Product, Price, and Place

Product refers to both library collections (on-site and remote) and services. The library examines the needs, demands, and wants of all segments of its public and the long-term requirements of the communities it serves and designs a product—library services and resources—to meet those needs. Does the public library's community want more electronic resources, more copies of popular novels, more large-print materials, or fewer books and more journals? What services and types of contact do faculty members want from selectors? Can the library or the librarian modify current practices to satisfy the public better? Libraries face challenges building collections that balance formats, monographs and serials, and immediate needs and long-term mission. Developing and modifying the collections and services the librarian provides are what librarians do constantly, though they seldom think of this as marketing activities. The contact between librarian and community is an important product. The librarian should develop, monitor, and modify these liaison or outreach activities so that they become a valued service, for which the user community member is willing to exchange time, effort, and support.

Price and *place* are aspects of the product. Modifying either one modifies the product and influences demands. Librarians should understand these components and can adjust them, when appropriate, to increase the likelihood a patron will use and be satisfied with the library's collections and services. Price is what it costs the public (i.e., user community) to acquire and access the library's products and services. Price can be measured in financial cost or the time or effort needed to obtain the product. The librarian's goal is to set the price of using the collection and services as low as is feasible, given the constraints placed on the library by its budget and staffing. Generally, traditional or routine services have no financial cost for primary constituents. Fees are seldom charged to borrow books and audio recordings, read journals, consult reference materials and staff members, and use the library's electronic resources. Some libraries charge users fees for receiving interlibrary loans, borrowing videos and best-sellers, requesting recalls, being placed on a waiting list, and using reference services extending beyond a certain length of time. Most libraries charge for photocopy services, printing, and retrieval and delivery to a home or office, though special libraries may be budgeted to absorb these costs.

Collection development librarians have more influence on the time and effort cost to users than they do on prices. Librarians aim to lower users' perception of cost by saving their time and effort and assume that this will increase user satisfaction. In an ideal situation, everything that a user seeks is not only owned by his or her library, it is ready to use. Libraries' decreasing ability to develop collections that will meet most local user expectations directly affects the cost to users in time and effort. Waiting to use a computer workstation to access a single CD-ROM, waiting to access a remote electronic resource because the library has limited simultaneous users, initiating an interlibrary loan request and waiting for the item, and waiting on a list for a popular title all can decrease user satisfaction. Selectors are always seeking to satisfy users within the library's mission, priorities, and budget.

Place is the point at which the exchange of value for product and service occurs. It can be in the library, media center, or a bookmobile; via a web site; or closer to the user's office, home, or classroom. The librarian's goal is to design a place, point of contact, or distribution system that allows patrons to get what they want—which may be information, an item, the collection development librarian's attention—as quickly and conveniently as possible. The academic library may offer free or minimal-cost delivery of locally owned materials to on-campus offices. The selector, regardless of library type, may provide users with forms to use for recommending materials for purchase. Academic and special librarians may schedule office hours within the departments and divisions to facilitate contact with users. The goal is to make it as convenient as possible for selectors to provide services to their constituents. Selecting between print and electronic resources when making collection decisions has obvious place implications. Some users may find it extremely convenient to access electronic resources from home or office.

Promotion

All liaison and outreach activities are promotional in nature. Many users have very little idea of what librarians do or what they and the libraries in which they work offer. Liaison and outreach are the librarian's chance to inform and educate. The librarian should take every opportunity to promote the library's collections and services along with his or her availability. Information about the library should not focus only on collections and information resources. The selector keeps constituents aware of all relevant library services, programs, and policies. Some services may be offered by selectors. Others may be the responsibility of various library units. These might include current awareness services, routing of journals, document delivery services, preparation of library handouts tailored to specific class needs, workshops offered by the library, guest lectures by librarians, and library tours and demonstrations. Relevant policies may address collection development and management, gifts, Internet use, user privacy, course reserves, copyright, authorized access to electronic information resources, and borrowing privileges. Keeping constituents informed about all aspects of the library is an important part of outreach.

Promotional activities are both formal and informal. Formal activities are structured and planned interactions, such as scheduled presentations and meetings and the preparation of print and digital informational materials. Informal promotion can occur every time a librarian comes in contact with a member of the library's community. Advances in telecommunication options are expanding opportunities for library outreach and liaison activities. These include sending e-mail messages to individuals and groups and creating library web pages, with online opportunities for comments and questions and forms for suggesting materials for purchase.

Selectors in academic libraries can assemble a promotional packet of materials to give to each faculty member. This might include a collection development policy, budget information, relevant guides and bibliographies, and an information sheet about the selector. In addition, academic librarians can try some of the following activities:

Attend academic departmental meetings and special events and let people know they are representing the library.

Seek opportunities for collaborative teaching projects, research, and grants.

Participate in university orientation programs for new students, teaching assistants, research assistants, and international and graduate students.

Send notes of recognition when faculty members get grants and awards.

Audit classes.

Meet with new faculty members within their first academic term and tell them about the library collections and services.

Meet regularly with department chairs and library-faculty liaison groups.

Develop a mailing list and send regular announcements of library activities, acquisitions, and events of interest.

Librarians in public libraries, special libraries, and school libraries can apply similar approaches to promoting their collections and services. Regular contact with user community groups is essential. As appropriate, librarians can try some of the following activities:

Participate in teachers' meetings.

Be in the library during school open houses and parent-teacher meetings.

Schedule regular classroom visits.

Prepare bookmarks and handouts promoting specific collections, information resources, and services.

Publish library newsletters or new acquisitions lists, which can be targeted to specific user groups.

Prepare displays promoting new acquisitions and resources on a particular topic.

Give book talks in classes, in the library, to citizen's groups, and so forth.

Create a library web site that promotes collections and services.

Make book and journal request forms easily available.

Participate in company, business, and agency departmental meetings.

Participate in library friends group meetings.

Attend meetings of citizens' interest groups (e.g., Chamber of Commerce, Women Voters' League).

Mutual Information Sharing

Developing effective working relations with academic faculty members, K–12 teachers, and users of special libraries involves sharing information in both directions. It is a mutual effort, though it often feels as if the selector expends most of the energy in getting and giving information. The selector lets individuals and departments know about new acquisitions. This may be limited to information about expensive purchases and new journals or it may be in the form of regular "new acquisitions" lists. The librarian shares collection development policy statements, announcements about resource sharing and consortial partnerships, and information about collection analysis. He or she keeps the user community informed about library budgets, pricing trends, and other factors affecting purchasing ability.

Keeping those to whom the library is accountable, such as administrators, funding and governing bodies, and elected officials, informed about library successes, routine activities, and problems is an important aspect of outreach. These people want to know what the funding allocated to the library is purchasing and how it is being used. They want to know how the library is meeting and planning to meet community needs and interests. Sharing good news is important. Keeping these stakeholders informed about problems and potential problems is equally important. Regular and frequent news about pricing trends for materials, complexities of license agreements, and deteriorating collections means that no one will be blindsided when budget requests are presented.

Outreach in Academic Libraries

Liaison activities in academic libraries typically describe the official and assigned contacts between selectors and designated individuals, departments, units, committees, or organizations outside the library. Successful liaison provides a local context in which to apply all other collection development and management skills. Liaison activities can serve to promote the library's collections and services and provide improved visibility for the library. They provide a forum to gather data about the user community and enhance a selector's ability to build responsive collections.

Most liaison activities in academic libraries involve faculty members. A 1992 Association of Research Libraries survey reported that 77 percent of respondents identified the faculty as the primary liaison target; approximately 50 percent also considered students as part of the liaison's primary service group.[17] The specialist selector in an academic library cannot develop and manage a collection without knowing his or her user community. Faculty members are an important target or market segment because they depend on the library for research, give course assignments that use library resources, and can be important campus supporters of the library. Knowing and being known by faculty are important for success.

Each selector typically interacts with one or more groups of professors, usually defined by their affiliation with specific teaching departments or programs that parallel the subjects or disciplines for which the selector is responsible. Selectors assigned interdisciplinary responsibilities, including area studies, face a greater challenge in identifying whom their constituents are and in reaching them. No matter their subject assignment, selectors cannot depend solely on the knowledge they bring to the job. They must seek out their faculty user community and learn about them. By learning as much as possible about the specialities, needs, and interests of their assigned faculties, academic library selectors increase their ability to develop a collection that serves these specialities, needs, and interests. Besides following individual faculty member's requirements and expectations, the selector needs a collective understanding of the department's needs in order to balance collection development activities within this larger view.

Some academic libraries view outreach to faculty members as so important that they have created a separate position charged with developing systematic programs to reach all faculty and target university administrators as a special user group.[18] The understanding behind such an approach is that the faculty members and, especially, higher education administrators play a significant role in supporting the library when university budgets are allocated. Having informed advocates in decision-making positions in the university is certainly beneficial.

Various mechanisms provide information about their faculty constituents for librarians. Some facts about a department or program can be learned through secondary source research—reading course catalogs and departmental promotion and descriptive materials, such as academic departmental web pages. The selector should try to get on academic mailing lists in order to receive departmental newsletters and reports, which may list new hires, faculty publications, and research grants. Receiving notices of departmental meetings and their agendas is useful. The selector should try to attend these meetings and occasionally speak at them, using this as an opportunity to share news about collection development issues and library services.

Other information can be gained only through contact with faculty members. This may be through meeting with individual faculty members and attending departmental meetings. The lucky selector has an established vehicle for communication—a departmental library committee or a designated departmental liaison—through whom information and requests for advice on general issues can be funneled. Less formal meetings, such as getting together with one or two faculty members over coffee or lunch, foster communication as well. The following list identifies information that is helpful in understanding academic user communities.

- Faculty research interests and areas of concentration
- Faculty language abilities
- Grants and research centers
- Number of faculty members and their ranks
- Number of students and research assistants
- Courses being taught and being planned
- Special collection and resource needs
- Requests for particular library services
- Areas of crossover with other disciplines
- Plans for future programs and degrees
- National standing of the department or program
- The department's or program's priority in the institution

The academic library selector can begin by creating a list of faculty members in the subject areas for which he or she has collection management responsibilities. This list can be enhanced through the creation of faculty profiles and soliciting vitae. Monitor the teaching and research activities of each faculty member and track dissertation topics of graduate students. Many selectors regularly survey their constituents to learn their interests, needs, problems, and perceptions about library collections and services. An example of a survey instrument, used at Virginia Polytechnic Institute and State University in Blacksburg, is offered by Roger E. Stelk, Paul Metz, and Lane Rasmussen.[19] Catherine E. Pasterczyk provides a checklist that could be used to develop a questionnaire.[20]

Figure 6-1 provides one example of a faculty questionnaire. This instrument, in addition to collecting information for the selector's file on faculty members' interests, surveys individual perceptions about collections and services, both existing and desired. A selector could choose to limit the initial questionnaire to information about the faculty member

Figure 6-1   Faculty Profile

Name: _____

Office address: _____

E-mail address:_____

Phone: _____

Field(s) and geographical area(s) of interest:

_____

_____

Current research projects:

_____

_____

Course(s) you are currently teaching or have under development:

_____

_____

Library Collections

On a scale of 1 to 5 (1=poor; 3=satisfactory; 5=good), what is your perception of:

1. Adequacy of the library's book collection for

   a. your undergraduate students' needs   1   2   3   4   5
   b. your graduate students' needs   1   2   3   4   5
   c. your teaching needs   1   2   3   4   5
   d. your research needs   1   2   3   4   5

2. Adequacy of the library's journal collection for

   a. your undergraduate students' needs   1   2   3   4   5
   b. your graduate students' needs   1   2   3   4   5
   c. your teaching needs   1   2   3   4   5
   d. your research needs   1   2   3   4   5

3. Adequacy of the library's electronic resources for

   a. your undergraduate students' needs   1   2   3   4   5
   b. your graduate students' needs   1   2   3   4   5
   c. your teaching needs   1   2   3   4   5
   d. your research needs   1   2   3   4   5

Please make any comments you wish about your answers above:

_____

_____

Please comment on the library's collections (e.g., government documents, micro-form collections, newspapers, overall strengths and weaknesses):

_____
_____

Which publishers do you consider the most important to your field(s)?

_____
_____

List any journals to which the library does not subscribe and that you consider important:

_____
_____

Library Services

On a scale of 1 to 5 (1=poor; 3=some importance; 5=very important), rate the value you place (or would place if offered) on the following library activities or services.

General reference service	1 2 3 4 5
Individualized consultative reference or research service	1 2 3 4 5
Updates about new library policies, procedures, services, and activities	1 2 3 4 5
Lists of new acquisitions related to your field(s)	1 2 3 4 5
Course-related class instruction in library use	1 2 3 4 5
Non-course-related instruction sessions	1 2 3 4 5
Library orientation for new graduate students	1 2 3 4 5
Printed library guides about the collections	1 2 3 4 5

Additional comments about library collections and services:

_____
_____
_____
_____

Thank you!

Please return to: Mary Jones, 101 Central Library
                    641-2312, mjones@anyuniv.edu

and his or her interests, using subsequent surveys for more in-depth queries. A briefer first contact may be more likely to elicit responses. A single survey is never sufficient. Faculty members and their interests change, and selectors need to resurvey their constituents periodically. The selector's success in making and maintaining good user community contacts depends on both enthusiasm and initiative. Only through constant attention can the selector gain and supply the information needed to make liaison work meaningful. The approaches selectors use to learn about their constituents and their needs and interests will vary with the situation. Even the most aggressive selector may run into a brick wall with some departments and some faculty members, who fail to respond to any library initiative. In these situations, the selector should continue promotional activities, even if the communication remains one direction.

Using some form of user profiles is beneficial in all types of libraries. In public libraries, profiles can help identify the needs and interests of specific library and information center users. School librarians may maintain profiles for each teacher and his or her curriculum support needs. Special libraries may maintain profiles describing the research and development activities of individuals. In addition, larger group or market segment profiles can be useful. These are created through research in secondary sources, interaction at service points and other less formal contacts with user communities, and market segment surveys.

Liaison activities and community outreach are not only essential to successful collection development and management, they are both satisfying and fun. This part of collection development work places the selector at the heart of the community. The selector has the chance to satisfy needs, respond to requests, answer questions, and solve problems. Leading users, potential users, funding agencies, and governing bodies to an understanding of the library, its collections, services, and the constraints in which it operates benefits both the faculty and the library.

Performance Measurement

Performance measurement is the final *P* in marketing. This is monitoring and analyzing ongoing results and taking corrective actions where necessary. Developing a marketing program for the library or for an individual selector's services is pointless without a performance measurement component. Collections are evaluated to determine how well they support the needs of users and the goals of the parent organization. Collection assessment seeks to examine or describe collections in their own terms or relative to other collections and checklists. Measuring the community's response to collections is essential. Feedback should inform change. Performance measurement should occur as an integral part of working with the library's public. The selector seeks not only to learn the users' needs, wants, demands, and interests, but also the extent to which collection resources are meeting these preferences.

Performance measurement seeks to answer many questions. Are library users satisfied with the collection and information resources? Do teachers feel the school library media center is meeting their curriculum needs? Are faculty members happy with how they interact with selectors? Do users feel the library is responsive? Do they know what the library offers? The library or the selector needs to develop performance measures that are meaningful. Besides survey instruments and focus groups, selectors might track how frequently users contact them directly. Each library and selector will develop its own performance measures. The key issue is using performance measurement to improve and enhance collections and services and increase community satisfaction.

Successful marketing is a continuous cycle. The selector researches his or her user groups (public) to track their needs, wants, and demands. This is supplemented by information from secondary sources—demographic data, research foci, curricula standards, emerging programs, and so forth. The selector modifies the library collections and associated services (the products) to meet needs, wants, and demands while being mindful of the library's mission and financial resources. The selector promotes the product to the library's user community and monitors the users' perception of performance. The collection also is evaluated using external performance indicators. The library's collection will develop in response to its users, potential users, supporters, funding agencies, and governing bodies—always in the context of collection development policies, library mission, and available funding.

Benefits and Hazards of Liaison and Outreach Activities

The foremost benefit a selector gains through liaison work is the information necessary to develop a collection that meets the needs of constituents. Other benefits accrue over time. When an academic library selector has detailed knowledge about a department's programs, the research interests of faculty members, and the directions in which they are moving, he or she can make a case for appropriate support when library materials budgets are allocated. The same is true for other types of libraries. Knowing the particular foci of special library users positions the selector to respond appropriately and plan for the future. The selector has information at hand to explain need and justify the resources required to meet it.

Effective liaison work saves time. Knowledge about individuals' interests prepares the selector to contact the appropriate person for advice on particular topics. Knowing who specializes in decorative arts in the art department means that neither the librarian's nor other faculty members' time is wasted getting opinions on the value of a possible acquisition. Knowing and being known often mean less time spent in setting up appointments and making phone calls.

Ongoing liaison and outreach work give the selector the opportunity to establish credibility. He or she demonstrates subject knowledge, understanding of the literature, and expertise in library activities through consistent, frequent contact. Individuals come to trust the selector's judgment and to value his or her opinion. Good relationships with individual users and user groups are indispensable when undertaking serials cancellations. If the selector has kept the library's community informed about pricing trends and library budgets, the library's need to cancel serials or access to online resources will not come as a surprise. A productive relationship means that the selector is not seen simply as the bearer of bad news, but someone who understands user needs and will continue to work, despite constraints, to meet them. Decisions about canceling resources become just another part of the ongoing dialogue between the selector and the library's public.

Over time, the selector may come to personify the library to his or her constituents. Effectively handled, this relationship between selector and users can enhance the library's image and reputation. Public librarians become a felt presence in their communities because they attend community meetings, sponsor exhibits and programs, provide reading lists, and serve on the boards of community and governmental organizations. Library professionals are seen as peers and colleagues by faculty members throughout the academic institution. Departments call on the selector to represent the library on departmental committees, contribute to accreditation studies, and may ask the selector to participate in developing new courses, programs, and grant proposals. Teachers ask the selector to speak to their classes and help them with reference needs. Schools and community groups invite public librarians to give book talks. Users may begin to contact the selector for help in solving any problems they perceive with the library, its collections, and services.

Becoming a user's preferred contact with the library can lead to the most troubling pitfall. Selectors must be cautious not to become connected more to academic departments than the library. The solitary nature of collection development and the importance of working closely with the faculty can lead to isolation within the library. The selector must take care not to put department concerns before library priorities. The biggest dangers a selector faces are becoming alienated from the library and library colleagues and distanced from the library's mission.

A parallel hazard is unreasonable or inappropriate requests by users for services or information that the selector cannot or should not provide. Some individuals and constituent groups can become extremely demanding, pressuring the selector for personal services, special treatment, and purchase of out-of-scope materials. The selector becomes a personal or private librarian, caught between personal demands and library obligations. A fine line exists in liaison work between supporting user needs and demands and allegiance to the library.

At the heart of successful liaison work are good interpersonal and communication skills. Selectors need to work at building good working relationships with all members of their community. They must be skilled in dealing with demanding and unreasonable constituents as well as those who understand the selector's responsibilities to the library. Selectors need to make these responsibilities clear while emphasizing their role in supporting users' needs and interests.

Summary

Outreach and liaison are critical for libraries and for collection development librarians, in particular. In a climate in which explicit community support for libraries is increasingly important, effective techniques for understanding and reaching that community are essential. Marketing techniques equip the library and librarians to monitor changing needs, wants, and demands and to adjust services and collection development practices as needs and wants evolve. A societal marketing orientation ensures that current needs and wants are balanced against the library's mission and long-term goals.

Market research describes how librarians come to understand various segments of their market—that is, their user community, stakeholders, or public. The library's public includes many types of users, potential and inactive users, library supporters, governing bodies, and funding agencies. Information about the market comes from existing published information and information collected and generated by the library over the course of routine activities. Information also is collected through primary research, which may involve individual interviews, surveys, and focus groups. The selector's goal in market research is to learn as much as possible about the library's public in order to develop responsive collections.

The product the selector develops is the library's collection, which includes on-site and remotely accessed resources, and the services he or she provides the users. Part of developing the collection is understanding what it costs the user in time and effort to use the collection and what the user is willing to expend to do so. These data inform selectors' decisions about what to acquire for on-site use and for remote access and which items can be borrowed from other collections. Equally integral to product is an understanding of place—what location of information resources means to the user and how the user wishes to interact with the selector.

Promotion is an important part of marketing. The intent is to bring a thorough understanding of the collections and allied services to the user and to provide the user with information about how to influence future collection development. Effective promotion involves two-way communication. The selector both shares information and gains information. Many vehicles exist for fostering formal and informal information sharing. The information gained through outreach and liaison activities becomes part of market research. It contributes toward performance measurement.

Performance measurement completes the marketing cycle, leading the selector back to responding to the public and modifying the collection to better meet public needs, wants, demands, and interests. Marketing is market analysis, planning, implementation, and control.

| CASE STUDY |

Karen Nichols is a new selector in a large academic library. Her collection responsibilities encompass sociology, social work, family social science, and rural sociology. She has regular reference desk hours in the main library, which houses the humanities and social sciences collections. The library provides numerous digital resources, including indexes and abstracting sources, online reference tools, full-text files, and numeric data files. The library has had an integrated, automated system for more than fifteen years and provides a multifaceted library web presence, though the page addressing the library's collections and services in Karen's subject areas is brief. Karen has an M.L.S. and a second master's in family social science. She has eleven years' experience as a subject specialist in the social sciences in two previous positions.

Karen's predecessor, Mark Jacobson, had held the position for twenty-two years. Mark had earned a second master's in sociology from one of the departments he supported and had developed personal friendships as well as professional credibility with many faculty members. Mark regularly attended various departmental meetings and socialized with faculty members. He was considered an excellent selector by faculty members and his library supervisors. He reviewed and revised his collection development policy annually. The files he left his successor included the policy statement, his approval plan profiles, and lists of active serials, standing orders, and blanket order plans. Karen also received library system–generated budget reports on annual allocations and expenditures for several years. She found no information about constituencies in Mark's files.

Activity

Karen needs to learn about her public and develop avenues for communication. Identify the activities that would comprise a marketing plan and a schedule for Karen to implement over the next six months. How will she

> research her market,
>
> segment the market,
>
> gather secondary and primary data,
>
> promote the collections for which she is responsible, and
>
> evaluate performance?

REFERENCES

1. "Guidelines for Liaison Work in Managing Collections and Services," prepared by American Library Assn.'s Reference and User Services Assn., Liaison with Users Committee, *Reference and User Services Quarterly* 41, no. 2 (winter 2001): 107–9.
2. Martin Lopez, "A Guide for Beginning Bibliographers," *Library Resources and Technical Services* 13 (fall 1969): 462–70.
3. Susan L. Fales, ed., *Guide for Training Collection Development Librarians,* Collection Management and Development Guides, no. 8 (Chicago: American Library Assn., 1996): 18–20.
4. O. Gene Norman, "Marketing Library and Information Services: An Annotated Guide to Recent Trends and Developments," *Reference Services Review* 17, no. 1 (spring 1989): 43–64.
5. Charles B. Osburn, "Toward a Reconceptualization of Collection Development," *Advances in Library Administration and Organization* 2 (1983): 188.
6. David Nicholas, *Assessing Information Needs: Tools and Techniques* (London: The Assn. for Information Management, 1996), provides a concise introduction to data collection methods for user studies.
7. George D'Elia, "A Descriptive Market Segmentation Model of the Adult Members of the Public Library's Community," in *Beyond PR: Marketing for Libraries: LJ Special Report 18,* ed. Joseph Eisner (New York: Library Journal, 1981): 37–42.
8. "Guidelines for Liaison Work," 199.
9. Ulla De Stricker, "Marketing with a Capital S: Strategic Planning for Knowledge-Based Services," *Information Outlook* 2 (Feb. 1998): 28–32.
10. Dennis P. Carrigan, "Data-Guided Collection Development: A Promise Unfilled," *College and Research Libraries* 57, no. 5 (Sept. 1996): 432.
11. Philip Kotler and Alan R. Andreasen, *Strategic Marketing for Nonprofit Organizations* (Upper Saddle River, N.J.: Prentice-Hall, 1996), 25.
12. Philip Kotler and Karen F. A. Fox, *Strategic Marketing for Educational Institutions,* 2d ed. (Englewood Cliffs, N.J.: Prentice-Hall, 1994), 10.
13. Ottar Olsen Svein, "Comparative Evaluation and the Relationship between Quality, Satisfaction, and Repurchase Loyalty," *Journal of the Academy of Marketing Science* 30 (summer 2002): 240–49.
14. Sharon L. Baker and Karen L. Wallace, *The Responsive Public Library Collection: How to Develop and Market a Winning Collection,* 2d ed. (Englewood, Colo.: Libraries Unlimited, 1993).
15. Ibid., 5.
16. Philip Kotler, *Principles of Marketing,* 8th ed. (Upper Saddle River, N.J.: Prentice-Hall, 1998).
17. Gail F. Latta, comp., *Liaison Services in ARL Libraries,* SPEC Kit, no. 189 (Washington, D.C.: Assn. of Research Libraries, 1992), i.
18. Scott Stebelman et al., "Improving Library Relations with the Faculty and University Administrators: The Role of the Faculty Outreach Librarian," *College and Research Libraries* 60, no. 2 (March 1999): 121–30.
19. Roger E. Stelk, Paul Metz, and Lane Rasmussen, "Departmental Profiles: A Collection Development Aid," *C&RL News* 54 (April 1993): 196–99. *See also User Surveys in College Libraries,* comp. Mignon S. Adams and Jeffrey A. Beck,

CLIP Note, no. 23 (Chicago: Assn. of College and Research Libraries, 1990), for a collection of survey instruments used by college libraries, including surveys of online services and user satisfaction.

20. Catherine E. Pasterczyk, "Checklist for the New Selector," *C&RL News* 49 (July/Aug. 1988): 434–35.

SUGGESTED READINGS

Adams, Kate E., and Mary E. Cassner. "Marketing Library Resources and Services to Distance Faculty." *Journal of Library Administration* 31, no. 3/4 (2001): 5–22.

Bell, Lori, Eileen Sheppard, and H. Neil Kelley. "Outreach Perspective." *Public Libraries* 34 (March/April 1995): 73–74.

Block, Marylaine. "The Secret of Library Marketing: Make Yourself Indispensable." *American Libraries* 32, no. 8 (Sept. 2001): 48–50.

Bordeianu, Sever. "Faculty Liaison Models: One Alternative." In *Issues in Collection Management: Librarians, Booksellers, Publishers*, edited by Murray S. Martin, 115–23. Foundations in Library and Information Science, v. 31. Greenwich, Conn.: JAI Pr., 1995.

Brown, Suzan A. "Marketing the Corporate Information Center for Success." *Online* 21, no. 4 (July/Aug. 1997): 74–79.

Callison, Daniel. "StudentTalk." *School Library Media Activities Monthly* 14, no. 10 (June 1998): 38–41.

Chu, Felix Tse-Hsiu. "Librarian-Faculty Relations in Collection Development." *The Journal of Academic Librarianship* 23 (Jan. 1997): 15–20.

Coffman, Steve. "What if You Ran Your Library Like a Bookstore?" *American Libraries* 29 (March 1998): 40–46.

Davis, Marta A., and M. Kathleen Cook. "Implementing a Library Liaison Program: Personnel, Budget, and Training." *Collection Management* 20, no. 3/4 (1996): 157–65.

De Saez, Eileen Elliott. *Marketing Concepts for Libraries and Information Services.* 2d ed. London: Facet, 2002.

Fleming, Helen R. "Library CPR: Marketing Can Save Your Library." *Library Journal* 118 (Sept. 15, 1993): 32–35.

Flowers, Helen F. *Public Relations for School Library Media Programs: 500 Ways to Influence People and Win Friends for Your School Library Media Center.* New York: Neal-Schuman, 1998.

Harrington, Deborah Lynn, and Xiaodong Li. "Spinning an Academic Web Community: Measuring Marketing Effectiveness." *The Journal of Academic Librarianship* 27, no. 3 (May 2001): 199–207.

Hart, Judith L., Vicki Coleman, and Hong Yu. "Marketing Electronic Resources and Services: Surveying Faculty Use as a First Step." *The Reference Librarian*, no. 67/68 (1999): 41–55.

Hartridge, Digby, Gill Baker, and Christiane Nicholson. "Implementing a Marketing Strategy." *Public Library Journal* 11, no. 3 (May/June 1996): 65–68.

Karp, Rashelle S. *Powerful Public Relations: A How-to Guide for Libraries.* Chicago: American Library Assn., 2002.

Lee, Tamera, and Claudine Jenda, comps. *The Role of ARL Libraries in Extension/Outreach.* SPEC Kit, no. 233. Washington, D.C.: Assn. of Research Libraries, 1998.

Mozenter, Frada L., Bridgette T. Sanders, and Jeanie M. Welch. "Restructuring a Liaison Program in an Academic Library." *College and Research Libraries* 61, no. 5 (Sept. 2000): 432–40.

Reed, Sally Gardner. *Making the Case for Your Library: A How-To-Do-It Manual.* How-To-Do-It Manuals for Librarians, no. 104. New York: Neal-Schuman, 2001.

Simmons, Elizabeth A., and Randall M. MacDonald. "Reference Services and Collection Development Faculty Outreach through the Campus Network." *The Reference Librarian,* no. 58 (1997): 101–6.

Smykla, Evelyn Ortiz, comp. *Marketing and Public Relations Activities in ARL Libraries.* SPEC Kit, no. 240. Washington, D.C.: Assn. of Research Libraries, 1999.

Soules, Aline. "The Principles of Marketing and Relationship Management." *Portal: Libraries and the Academy* 2, no. 3 (July 2001): 339–50.

Thorsen, Jeanne. "Community Studies: Raising the Roof and Other Recommendations." *Acquisitions Librarian* 20 (1998): 5–13.

Trotta, Marcia. *Managing Library Outreach Programs: A How-To-Do-It Manual for Librarians.* How-To-Do-It Manuals for Libraries, no. 33. New York: Neal-Schuman, 1993.

Wadley, Andrea L., Judith E. Broady-Preston, and Tim E. Hayward. "Marketing the Public Library Service to the Full-Time Employed: Future Directions?" *Library Management* 18, no. 5/6 (1997): 253–63.

Walters, Suzanne. *Marketing: A How-To-Do-It Manual for Librarians.* How-To-Do-It Manuals for Libraries, no. 20. New York: Neal-Schuman, 1992.

Weingand, Darlene E. *Future-Driven Library Marketing.* Chicago: American Library Assn., 1998.

———. *Marketing/Planning Library and Information Services.* 2d ed. Englewood, Colo.: Libraries Unlimited, 1999.

Westbrook, Lynn, and Robert Waldman. "Outreach in Academic Libraries: Principle into Practice." *Research Strategies* 11 (spring 1993): 60–65.

Wilson, Thomas D. "Tools for the Analysis of Business Information Needs." *Aslib Proceedings* 46 (Jan. 1994): 19–23.

Wolfe, Lisa A. *Library Public Relations, Promotions, and Communications: A How-To-Do-It Manual.* How-To-Do-It Manuals for Librarians, no. 75. New York: Neal-Schuman, 1997.

Wu, Connie, et al. "Effective Liaison Relationships in an Academic Library." *College and Research Libraries News* 55, no. 5 (1994): 254, 303.

CHAPTER 7

Electronic Resources

Introduction

Electronic resources are like other library materials in many ways. They are selected, acquired, cataloged, managed, explained and promoted to users, evaluated, preserved, withdrawn, and canceled. The same decision-making criteria should be applied to all resources. However, electronic resources are profoundly different from other types of library materials. This book has aimed to incorporate electronic resources in every chapter, yet their complexity necessitates a separate chapter. Issues, such as selecting between delivery formats, evaluating and assessing electronic resources, and licensing, are frequently different from other resources. This chapter addresses the history of electronic resources, selection criteria, budgeting, and legal issues. The chapter concludes with a look at the changing nature of scholarly communication. Throughout, definitions and concepts are introduced so that selectors will have the vocabulary and understanding to evaluate options and make informed decisions. The realm of electronic resources is expanding and evolving quickly. Consequently, some information in this chapter will become outdated rapidly, an unavoidable problem in a print-based medium.

What Are Electronic Resources?

This chapter uses the phrase *electronic resources* (e-resources) as an umbrella term for all digital resources. Digital information exists in a format (numeric digits) that a computer can store, organize, transmit, and display without any intervening conversion process. Some digital information is created in that format, often described as "born digital." Digitized information has been transformed from an analog source. The printed page is analog. Digitization projects can make print materials more easily accessible to users, create surrogates that are less vulnerable to theft and wear, and serve as a preservation medium.

Electronic resources encompass many genre, format, and storage and delivery mediums. Genre includes newspapers, reference books, journals, nonfiction books, novels, indexes, and abstracts. Tools such as applications software, educational software, and systems for electronic document delivery can be considered part of the digital library. Formats, in the broad sense, include numeric and geospatial data, images, text, video, and audio. More narrowly, file formats are used to encode information in a file. Digital content is created in native format—that is, the file format that an application uses internally. Native format may be standards-based or proprietary. The medium that is used to store and deliver content sometimes is called the container. This may be a CD-ROM, magnetic tape, or a server accessed through a network. The delivery format is often different from the native format. The content is not materially altered when it is rendered from native format to the delivery format.

Librarians and their governing boards, funding agencies, and user communities often use the phrase *digital library*. A digital library may refer only to electronic resources or mean a combination of electronic resources, services that support using those resources, and services that are provided via a network. For some, "going digital" is seen as the salvation of library budgets, the end of space problems, and a way to provide the ultimate in easy access to collections. Librarians try to promote a better understanding of what a digital library is so that constituent expectations will be realistic. The Digital Library Federation, a group of research libraries, offers the following definition: "Digital libraries are organizations that provide the resources, including the specialized staff, to select, structure, offer intellectual access to, interpret, distribute, preserve the integrity of, and ensure the persistence over time of collections of digital works so that they are readily and economically available for use by a defined community or set of communities."[1] Few libraries are solely digital. Most libraries exist in dual environments: analog and digital, traditional formats and electronic.

Electronic resources offer libraries and their users many advantages.

Potential benefits include the following:

- Ease of searching and powerful search and retrieval capabilities
- Remote access to resources from outside a single physical library
- Consolidation of many volumes and years into one searchable file
- Inclusion of video and sound
- Reduction in theft and mutilation
- Content, including formulae and graphics, that can be extracted and manipulated
- Use by several people simultaneously
- Easy export of information to a personal database
- Reduced costs for binding, storage, and stack maintenance
- Hyperlinks, which move beyond the linearity of print within documents and link citations with full-text documents
- Access outside the library's normal hours of service

The challenges associated with e-resources include technical issues, costs for equipment and connectivity, equity of access, copyright, security, bibliographic control, indexing, archiving, licensing, user instruction, and—in the case of the Internet—questions of authority, quality, accuracy, instability and mutability, and mobility of information. Slow response time can be much more frustrating for users than waiting for another patron to return a print index to the shelf. Remote users trying to connect from outside the library may experience technical problems with no assistance available. Searching success depends on the quality of indexing, keywords, and text markup and the effectiveness of the search engine. The duration and amount of work required in negotiating license agreements can be significant. Authorization and authentication issues may be complex. Libraries typically lose access to back files at the termination of a contract for an e-resource. E-resources can be extremely expensive. Librarians who seek to identify, monitor, and direct users to free web-based resources face particular challenges tracking, organizing, and maintaining access to such online materials.

Standards and best practices for e-resources are still in the development stage in many areas. This includes the ability to handle exchange of materials between systems, that is, the compatibility of systems and data types used for transfer of information. Work continues on such areas as model license agreements for electronic resources, standard format and content for vendor-supplied use statistics for e-resources, requirements for digitally reformatted books and serials, standards to support interoperability, and a data-encoding and transmission scheme to convey information about structural, administrative, and technical characteristics of digital objects (e.g., metadata).

The first chapter in this book introduced the concept of contact zones and the position of the library at the center of significant changes in society. Clifford A. Lynch has written that "the impact of the transition to electronic information, and particularly to networked electronic information and communication, goes far beyond the library and promises major changes in a wide range of social, institutional, economic, legal and political structures."[2] Libraries exist within this broader context and do not fully control their own destinies. Libraries face not a single adaptation to the digital world, but several decades of constant change.

History and Terminology

Electronic resources located in and remotely accessed by libraries have been characterized by continuous, incremental growth in products and services. This section includes several definitions to help understand the context in which electronic resources are selected and managed.

Much of the discussion of electronic resources in a library involves how they are managed and accessed. An initial distinction is made between resources accessible through a stand-alone or nonnetworked computer (e.g., one that is not connected to a network) and computers that are networked. A stand-alone computer may have the electronic resource stored on the hard drive or use CD-ROMs. Only one person can use the e-resource via a stand-alone computer at a time. A local area network (LAN) includes a local server and two or more computers that can handle many users using (potentially) several e-resources simultaneously. The resource is loaded on the local server, and the library is responsible for maintenance and network connectivity. Remotely accessed resources are accessed via wide area networks (WANs), which span large geographic distances. The Internet is the largest WAN.

Medical Literature Analysis and Retrieval System (MEDLARS) was the first on-demand computer-based information retrieval service, becoming operational in 1964. MEDLINE, the online version of MEDLARS, became the first major remote database search service in 1971. Dialog offered the first public online commercial database in 1972. This and other similar services provided online access, through a dial-up modem, to the digital version of print indexes and abstracting services. Libraries established searching accounts with the early online database providers, conducted mediated searching, and were charged for connect time.

Librarians began to select e-resources in the mid-1980s, when CD-ROMs were introduced and offered on a subscription basis. Many early CD-ROMs were versions of paper products and the online indexing and abstracting databases accessed via modems. They were supplied on a subscription basis, with quarterly updates. From the beginning, the publisher retained ownership of the data. Subscribers, who were leasing the CD-ROMs, were required to return superceded disks. Some publishers began selling CD-ROMs that offered the complete version of a print publication, such as an encyclopedia or dictionary. The unit price was high and use was limited to one individual at a time. In the 1990s, CD-ROM prices began to drop, and personal computers became cheaper and widely available. Hardware and software solutions now allowed several library patrons to access the same CD-ROM database simultaneously via a LAN.

The Internet

The Advanced Research Projects Agency Network (ARPANet) was an initial step toward the Internet. ARPANet was created in the 1960s and 1970s by the U.S. Department of Defense to link military, research, and academic computer centers. As other networks connected internationally, the Internet, a worldwide network, evolved. Use of the Internet for electronic mail became more common in the early 1990s. With the development of the World Wide Web (WWW or, simply, the Web) in the mid-1990s and easy access to large remote files through graphical user interfaces such as Netscape, access to and, therefore, selection of electronic resources changed dramatically in libraries.

Various methods are used to prepare and deliver documents in digital format. PDF (Portable Document Format) and PostScript are two page-description languages that allow the appearance of a printed page to be described in a high-level, device-independent way. These languages store and deliver printable documents as bitmapped images. Their primary application is to describe the appearance of text, graphical shapes, and images on printed or displayed pages. They do not permit navigation within articles, live links to other documents, or smooth flow of information on a screen. Native format (such as XML) may be rendered to PDF for ease of delivery.

Markup or encoding makes the features of a text document that are implicit for the reader explicit for computer processing. It identifies the different elements of the referencing scheme, distinguishes among features that would otherwise be ambiguous, and marks features of interest. Encoding a text involves cataloging its parts. A text document without markup can only be used for very simple applications. SGML (Standard Generalized Markup Language) is a markup language with the potential of richly tagged files that facilitate complex searching. SGML is not in itself an encoding scheme. It describes the structure of a text and provides a framework within which the descriptive information about an electronic text can be encoded. SGML identifies document elements such as titles, paragraphs, and tables as separate objects. Once a document is converted into SGML and the information has been "tagged," it can be searched, printed, or programmatically manipulated by SGML-aware applications.

The Web is a system of Internet servers that support specially formatted documents. It is based on a technology called hypertext. The documents are formatted in a script called HTML (Hypertext Markup Language) that supports links to other documents, graphics, audio, and video files and linking within articles. The Web merges hypertext with techniques of information retrieval. The development of the graphical user interface (GUI) resulted in rapid growth of the Web in a short time. Stuart Moulthrop has written that hypertext is about "promiscuous, pervasive, and polymorphously perverse connection."[3]

HTML documents and the Web are nonlinear. They create a different kind of reading and spatial reference with the potential to overwhelm and confuse users. Many users of library-supplied Internet-based resources lose track of where they are and even if they are consulting a resource identified and made available by the library. Students often say, "I found it on the Internet" without any point of reference. Marlene Manoff stated that "hypertext, with its surfeit of narrative possibilities, becomes the fulfillment of the postmodern dream of multiplicity. It signals an end to linear narrative as it consistently seduces the reader into clicking on yet another link and interrupting the narrative flow. Reading thus becomes a process of continually detouring and refocusing as each new link introduces a new path or option."[4]

Electronic Journals

Electronic journals (e-journals) are serial publications available in digital format. Serials include magazines, newsletters, newspapers, annual publications, journals, memoirs, proceedings, transactions of societies, 'zines, and numbered series. Some e-journals are distributed via e-mail or on CD-ROMs; most now are available through the Internet. Some are free, and some are available only by subscription. Increasingly, publishers are using standards-based native formats, such as XML, in the creating of products but rendering the content in multiple formats (e.g., HTML and PDF) for delivery. This ensures easy delivery of content and increases options for consumers.

The growth of electronic journals parallels the growth of the Web. E-journals can be an electronic version of an established journal, an "electronic only" journal, or a journal that is issued in both electronic and print format. Some e-journals are digitally reformatted versions of print journals and may contain all or only portions of the print version. The first peer-reviewed journal distributed on the Internet, *New Horizons in Adult Education,* appeared in 1987.[5] It was in ASCII text, free, and distributed via an electronic mailing list, with printed copies mailed to those who had no e-mail. ASCII text was the common format in early electronic journals, but it cannot represent complex mathematical formulae or symbols.

The 1991 edition of the *Directory of Electronic Journals, Newsletters and Academic Discussion Lists* listed 27 e-journals, of which 7 were peer-reviewed.[6] In 2000, the directory listed only peer-reviewed e-journals, of which there were 3,915.[7] This is an astounding 560 percent increase. Most of this growth is the result of traditional commercial publishers, such as Academic Press, Elsevier, and Springer-Verlag, moving into Internet publishing in the second half of the 1990s. With the entry of commercial publishers into the realm of e-journals, the issues that still trouble libraries came to the fore. These include pricing, access (how, who, and limitations) and authentication, archiving of paper and electronic versions, and licensing. Digital versions of established, respected print titles continue to dominate the e-journal market.

Another development of the last few years has been the appearance of e-publication aggregators, which Project MUSE became in 1999, when it began to include titles from several publishers. Aggregators are intermediaries that assemble electronic journals from multiple publishers and offer the end user access to these journals through a common interface. Aggregate digital collections often use hypertext links between catalogs and indexes to full-text electronic documents. Some aggregators provide help with licensing and title-specific usage statistics. An example of an aggregator or intermediary is Ingenta Select, which hosts more than 5,550 journals for 230 publishers.[8] Ingenta Select provides access to content via major abstracting and indexing services, through subscription agent gateways, or directly from a library's own web site. Aggregators' collection of electronic subscriptions have been volatile, with publishers signing on with an aggregator and then withdrawing from the agreement. Sometimes an aggregator does not provide the full journal issue; instead, it provides selected articles and may not include book reviews, editorials, and advertisements.

Stanford University's HighWire Press, which began in early 1995 with the production and online distribution of the weekly *Journal of Biological Chemistry,* is a partnership of scientists, librarians, and publishers.[9] High Wire serves both as an aggregator and publisher. By the summer of 2003, HighWire produced 337 sites online for scientific society and academic publishers. From its inception, HighWire has sought to take advantage of the Internet by adding links among authors, articles, and citations and by using advanced searching capabilities, high-resolution images and multimedia, and interactivity. Working within the different subscription policies of the societies and publishers, HighWire manages subscriber access to the journals that it puts online. This ranges from individual subscriptions to institutional access to consortial packages.

Most large commercial publishers now offer bundled packages of their journals. For example, Elsevier and the American Chemical Society market their entire line of electronic journals as a complete package. Some of these publishers and some aggregators have sought to implement "all or none" site licensing of their entire list of journals. This has been called the "Big Deal" and been the source of considerable discussion among academic libraries.[10] The large commercial publishers and aggregators are being pressured by libraries to offer customized e-journal packages, which will match the libraries' collection priorities and help control costs.

E-Books

The Association of American Publishers has provided the following definition of an e-book: "An ebook is a Literary Work in the form of a Digital Object consisting of one or more Unique Identifiers, Metatdata, and a Monographic body of content, intended to be published and accessed electronically."[11] The core of this definition is that an e-book is content, a digital object containing an electronic representation of a book, most commonly thought of as the electronic analog of a printed book. This type of e-book has been delivered electronically on CD-ROMs, diskettes, and via networks to terminals and workstations since the early 1980s. An early noncommercial initiative is Project Gutenberg, which began in 1971 when Michael Hart and a group of volunteers began to convert what Hart called "the world's great literature" to electronic versions and make them widely and freely available.[12] Most of the more than 3,000 texts in Project Gutenberg are stored as ASCII text with little or no standard treatment of versions. All books in Project Gutenberg are in the public domain and are not considered authoritative.

The term *e-book* now most often is used to refer to digital objects specifically made to be read with reading applications operating on either a handheld device or a personal computer. An e-book is usually a collection of several digital objects or documents, consisting of content files, style sheets, metadata, digital rights, navigation, and other components. The content consists of text documents and image documents. Style sheets give typographic and layout directives on how to display the content of the book while other files organize the order of the book's content. Metadata provides a summary about the book (e.g., authors, publisher, ISBN, and price), while digital rights management (DRM) files specify the rights of the owner of the book. All of these different documents are collected in one publication in a proprietary format.

E-books as a commercial venture by trade publishers, such as Peanut Press and Questia Media, took off in the fall of 1998. The commercial e-book industry has focused on publishing and distribution technologies, profits, and rights management with little attention to archival and preservation issues. The impetus was the development of electronic book-reading devices or electronic book readers for individual users. Publishers and distributors have, for the most part, not considered libraries as part of their market. One problem with these initiatives is device-specific licensing, the current approach to DRM. DRM encompasses the technologies, tools, and processes that protect intellectual property during digital content commerce. If a library or individual downloads and pays for an electronic text for one of the devices, the text is exclusively licensed for that particular e-book device. An e-book is encrypted so that it can only be read on a single, specific reader. Publishers seek to ensure that e-books cannot be copied and are limited to use by a single individual. Most major U.S. publishing companies have launched extensive e-book production programs.

NetLibrary employs a more traditional service and marketing model. It delivers the full text of reference, scholarly, and professional books via the Internet. Now a division of OCLC, netLibrary works only with academic, K–12, public, corporate, and special libraries and does not market to the individual consumer. NetLibrary was providing more than 58,000 e-books by the summer of 2003. These could be purchased individually or in multiple copies by libraries for use by patrons, who have the option of either checking out an e-book, viewing it online, or viewing it offline by downloading the e-book onto their personal computers.

Two efforts are under way to address e-book standards and interoperability. Members of the Association of American Publishers are working with Andersen Consulting (now Accenture) on the Open Ebook (OEB) Standards Initiative.[13] Publishers participating in the project are seeking to make it easier and more comfortable for publishers and authors to get into the market. OEB presents standards in the areas of numbering and metadata and recommendations for standards in the area of digital rights management.

The second initiative is the Open eBook Forum, an international trade and standards organization.[14] Members are hardware and software companies, publishers, authors, users of electronic books, and related organizations working to establish specifications and standards for electronic publishing. They have developed the Open eBook Publication Structure, a specification for e-book file and format structure based on HTML and XML. A publisher can format a title once according to the specification, and the content will be compatible with a wide variety of reading devices. This agreement on a common set of file specifications will eliminate the need for publishers to reformat their titles for each machine. This specification is designed to be compatible with the development plans of the major e-book efforts already under way.

Another project, the Open Archives Initiative (OAI), is focusing on standards for the interoperability of digital resources of academic and scholarly interest. Supported by the Digital Library Federation, Coalition for Networked Information, and National Science Foundation, OAI is working to develop and promote standards to facilitate exchange of digital content and to support metadata harvesting for a wide range of digital resources.[15]

Because most commercial e-books are marketed to individuals, libraries have faced problems in incorporating them into collections. A study in 1999/2001 by six academic, public, and school libraries field-tested e-books.[16] The study concluded that users were often positive about using e-books. Users reported that the device screens do not seem to cause any eyestrain; rather, the combination of large font and backlight makes it easier on the eyes. Library patrons were eager to try e-books. Within two weeks of the trial's start, six months of holds were placed on all ten public library devices. When asked in what format the library patron would want to read his or her next book, 40 percent chose e-book over paper. Lighter weight was the most common suggestion for how the devices could be improved. Academic library patrons, who often wish to print portions of monographs for more careful reading, stated a preference for delivery via a multifunctional device, such as a laptop or a PDA (personal desk assistant), instead of one dedicated solely to e-book reading.

Lynch has written extensively on the future of e-books.[17] He observed, "Issues of preservation, continuity of access, and the integrity of our cultural and intellectual record are particularly critical in the context of e-book readers and the works designed for them. . . . Digital books, in all of their complexity and potential, are as yet only dimly defined, and will be a continued focus for the creativity and ingenuity of present and future generations of authors, teachers, and scholars."[18] Defining the role of libraries as managers of the intellectual archives of society will call on the creativity and ingenuity of librarians.

Selection

As with any selection decision, the most important criteria when considering an e-resource is whether it serves the mission, goals, and objectives of the library for which it is being contemplated. However, the complicated nature of e-resources can mitigate this first rule of good selection. In a 1999 study of the Association of Research Libraries (ARL), 76 percent of the respondents reported that acceptable licensing language was the single most important criteria, and only 46 percent said that supporting the library's strategic goals was most important.[19]

The selection criteria presented in chapter 4 are applicable to all formats but may have added aspects when applied to e-resources. For example, a selector evaluating the currency of an e-journal will ask whether issues are available as quickly as the paper version. Questions about authority and credibility will look at the organization or entity mounting a web site as well as the credentials of the author. Selecting and pointing to free third-party Internet resources should call forth the same rigor with which purchased content is reviewed and evaluated. Some aspects of e-resources suggest additional criteria. A selector may consider

- response time;
- local service implications;

- support for information transfer (output options);
- physical and logistical requirements within the library, including space, furniture, hardware, wiring, and telecommunication and data ports;
- effective use of technology;
- licensing and contractual terms, limitations, and obligations;
- pricing considerations, including discounts for retaining paper subscriptions and discounts for consortial purchase; and
- availability of data to measure use and effectiveness.

Comparing the same content delivered several ways can be a challenge. A product may be available in print, CD-ROM, remotely from several suppliers, and with different pricing packages. For example, *PsychINFO* can be acquired through EBSCO, Ovid, or FirstSearch. When possible, a library should arrange demonstrations and free trials and involve staffs in public services and the library's information technology unit in reviewing the e-resource. One approach to evaluating similar products is to create a decision matrix into which comparative information, including cost, is recorded for each product.[20] This facilitates comparing similarities, differences, advantages, and disadvantages of the options being considered.

E-Resources and the Role of Collections Librarians

Technology is accelerating the dissolution of the functional lines among collections work, reference, and technical services. Manoff wrote that "the demands of the digital environment—electronic reserves, Web resources, virtual collections, electronic journals, and digital preservation—require an integration of functions and expertise sometimes at odds with traditional library structures."[21] Selectors need to understand the universe with which they are dealing—file formats, methods of access and delivery, hardware, software, pricing options, licensing and contracts—so they can test, explore, and evaluate options and involve the right people in their library and parent institution in making choices.

Many libraries have separate policies or specific sections within their general collection development policy dealing with e-resources. Chapter 3 looks at collection development policies, including those for e-resources. Even libraries that do not have a formal electronic resources selection policy often have a document addressing who is involved in the decision-making process. Selection decisions are never made in isolation. More than any other format, electronic information requires broad communication and cooperation of staff across various units working toward common goals and applying common values. Typical consultations involve automation or systems staff, legal counsel, reference and cataloging staff, and, perhaps, senior library administrators. The final responsibility for evaluating the intellectual content and potential use of electronic products and services normally remains with collections librarians.

Libraries usually develop a formal mechanism for consultation, even if all decisions about electronic resources do not require systemwide or upper-level approval. Libraries may use a checklist of individuals who are consulted. The checklist may serve as a routing form that is to be reviewed and initialed by staff in the systems office, the business office, cataloging, acquisition, and collection development. However, the process likely will not be as linear as a form or checklist implies. Decisions require continuing interaction.

A standing committee, similar to a serials review committee, may have responsibility for reviewing e-resources, especially large, expensive electronic databases and especially those that are multidisciplinary in nature. Committees can bring together the expertise needed and might include selectors, catalogers, acquisitions staff, reference staff, and staff from the library's systems or information technology unit. Typical committee responsibilities might include one or more of the following:

Developing and maintaining policies and procedures for ordering, implementing, and evaluating electronic resources

Setting up and overseeing trials of electronic resources

Identifying and deliberating critical licensing issues

Making recommendations regarding purchase and renewal of multidisciplinary resources

Working with the technical service unit to assure effective acquisition of and intellectual access to electronic resources

Ensuring adequate technology infrastructure to support resource(s) under consideration,

Organizing staff and user training and user promotion

Seeking out and pursuing opportunities for institutional collaboration and potential funding opportunities related to electronic resources

This broader input may lead to better results, but can lead to bureaucratization of the selection process, which can become cumbersome because of the number of people and units that need to be consulted and involved in a decision. The input from individual selectors can become diluted, yet the traditional model in which collections decisions are made by individual selectors is often not valid with e-resources because decisions cannot be made in isolation. Consortial purchases further complicate this system.[22]

Large libraries are seeing an increased emphasis on the role of the collection development officer (CDO) in the acquisition of e-resource packages, primarily because of their high cost and multidisciplinary nature. The CDO may have the initial contact with the publisher or aggregator, arrange a trial, and negotiate the license or contract. In some cases, library directors are taking on this role. Other libraries are creating a new position—the electronic resources librarian (ERL), who, although not making the final decision, is charged with reviewing licenses, handling negotiations, and coordinating e-resources. This usually involves serving as the liaison between the library and legal counsel in the negotiation of contracts and licenses, collecting and maintaining copies of all contracts and licenses, and keeping track of billing and renewal cycles. The ERL may maintain a database or paper file that tracks the review and decision process for each title under consideration, manage an inventory file or database that records all information about each resource selected (vendor contact, date of renewal, type of authentication, unusual restrictions or obligations, etc.), monitor and disseminate use statistics, interpret the license agreement to library staff and users and educate them in their rights and responsibilities, and coordinate e-resources activities with consortial partners, branch libraries in a large system, or libraries on coordinate campuses in a large academic institution. See figure 7-1 for an example of an e-resources decision-making flowchart. The tasks assigned to the ERL in this example might be handled by the CDO in another library.

The emergence of aggregator packages and the "all or nothing" approach of some publishers are resulting in another significant change in collection development work. Selectors are losing the ability to make decisions about adding or canceling individual titles. Many selection decisions about e-resources are at the macro level when a complete package of titles is under consideration, and the selector cannot select or reject certain titles.

Nevertheless, the role of individual selectors in the e-resources arena remains critically important. They prepare and contribute to selection

Figure 7-1 E-Resources Decision-Making Flowchart

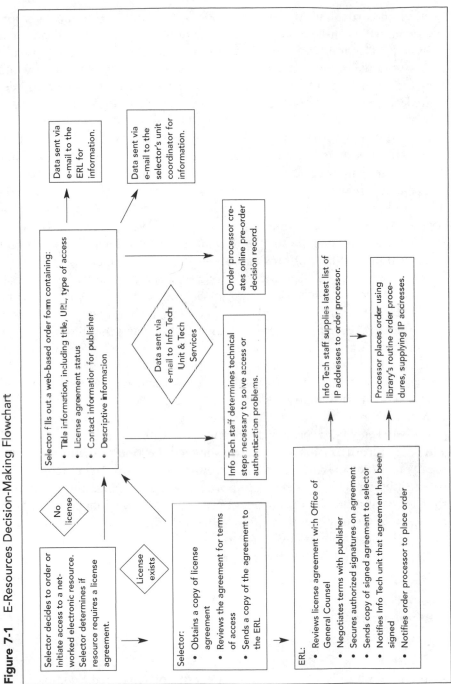

policies and articulate strategic approaches for handling e-resources, coordinate activities, and identify, select, and monitor e-resources within their assigned collection areas for acquisition or access. Many titles do not require broad review and consultation because their focus is narrow and they are ordered on a title-by-title basis. Selectors select free web resources and decide, within library policies, how to direct users to these sites. Selectors need to understand contracts and licenses and be ready to inform users about contractual obligations. They may identify local resources for digitization, both as a preservation medium and to enhance access. They provide user support and promote resources to their user community.

Selectors may perform the Internet-based version of bibliography, creating and maintaining a web site that is subject-based, age-appropriate, or focuses on the collection of a particular library. Web pages built by selectors can help compensate for the difficulties of traditional library subject classification and lack of browsability in the Internet and online catalogs by providing discipline-specific searching tips. Selectors describe local collections, offer discipline-related resources, and provide links to appropriate web resources, both free and those for which the library pays a fee. These tools for users are sometimes called online pathfinders or webliographies.

Libraries are turning to local databases and in-house programming to feed data to web pages that list the resources and services offered. Webliography can create paths to local collections and to resources provided elsewhere. Library resource users often lose the context for information they retrieve remotely. Boundaries are ambiguous, and users do not distinguish between what is provided by their library and what is "on the Web." The difficulty users have in determining where online material resides means that they may not know what connection, if any, such material has to the library. This context is important in determining the reliability, timeliness, and quality of information resources. Providing subject-based pointers from within a web page as well as creating individual title records in an online catalog with live links to the resources help the user retain his or her context and switch between titles in a logical manner.

Budget Issues

Budgeting for e-resources presents several challenges. These include the high cost of some access agreements and increases in percentage of budget spent on e-resources; a variety of payment options that make comparisons difficult; supplemental costs not associated with print and other traditional formats; difficulty in determining cost-benefit comparisons between options; shifting expenditures from acquiring capital assets to leasing access rights; and aggregator and publisher packages that make determining costs of individual titles nearly impossible. The latter suggests the need for a centralized e-resources fund because selectors may no longer manage all subject-specific titles and associated expenditures within their own fund lines.

Accountability and being able to report to library boards, funding agencies, institutional administrators, and constituents how dollars are being spent on e-resources is an important responsibility. Total dollars spent, including associated expenses, total e-resources provided, and use statistics, are meaningful data to maintain. Libraries may allocate a specific portion of the acquisitions budget to e-resources or they may make distinctions only in tracking expenditures. Sixty percent of the respondents to an ARL survey conducted in 1999 had a separate budget line for networked information resources.[23] By 2000/2001, the average percentage of the ARL member libraries' acquisitions budget spent on electronic materials was 16.25 percent, nearly five times as much as in 1992/1993, when it was 3.6 percent.[24]

The extremely high cost of some bundled e-resources and some individual products increases the impact of choosing the wrong product. The potential financial loss resulting from a poor choice is often significantly higher for e-resources. Obtaining a prorated refund is not always possible. Upper-level library administrators often negotiate and make the final decision in these cases because of the need for administrative accountability for such large expenditures.

A variety of payment options for the same product makes comparisons difficult and complicates the negotiation process. Options for pricing include the following:

Yearly flat fee for the e-resource, allowing unlimited use

Free with print subscription

Reduced price for electronic only, if print subscription is canceled

Augmented price, in which a library subscribes to a title's print version and pays a surcharge for the electronic format

Extra cost for print, in which the library subscribes to the electronic version and pays extra for the print

Pay per use, usually managed via a set number of simultaneous users or ports. The cost may drop per user when the library increases the number of simultaneous users.

Price based on number of physical sites or Internet Protocol (IP) addresses to which access is granted, passwords issued, size of acquisitions budget, or dollars spent with publisher

Price based on number of potential users (e.g., based on size of community served). This is most often used in academic and school libraries because counting students is straightforward. Sometimes a weighted full-time equivalent (FTE) total, in which each part-time student is counted as a fraction, is used. Some count total number of students, faculty, researchers, and staff—or employees in a company. A variation is to count the number of students in a specific program if they are the primary or only users of a specific e-resource.

Pay per connect time

Pay per article accessed or retrieved, sometimes called "acquisitions on demand" or "pay by the drink"

Bundling or packaging a group of titles, in which a group of e-journals are priced together at a discount price

Consortia pricing, for a group of libraries, with a discount based on the number of participating institutions

Discounts for multiyear contracts

An important part of the costs of e-resources is supplemental and not associated with print and other more traditional formats. These are initial and continuing expenses in addition to the direct cost of the resource. They include costs to acquire, maintain, and upgrade expensive equipment; educate and assist users; add telecommunication lines and ports; and negotiate and manage licenses and contracts. In addition, as with any selection decision, choosing an e-resource redirects funds from other possible purchases. These supplemental costs often continue for the duration of the e-resource, and their long-term impact on the library's budget must be considered.

Some library costs associated with print products disappear if the library moves away from print subscriptions. Among these are staffing costs to receipt issues and claim missing issues, circulate items, manage shelving, order replacements if needed, and bind into volumes—along with the cost of binding and repair of physical volumes. The user's time, an increasingly valuable commodity, is saved when he or she has direct and immediate access to indexes and full text online. Librarians have had difficulty in determining cost-benefit comparisons between options, because so many variables are involved. Research conducted by Carol Hansen Montgomery at Drexel University's library suggested that electronic journals are more cost-effective than paper on a per-use basis.[25] Montgomery noted the major expense of storing low-use bound journals. Ultimately, the library will make the most cost-effective investment it can that will provide the level of access and functionality needed by its users.

Until the mid-1990s, nearly everything libraries acquired was a physical entity and added to a tangible collection. These materials constitute a permanent capital expenditure; that is, the library collection is a fixed asset and—over time—can become the most valuable capital asset on a campus or in a town. Library collections, unlike most capital expenditures, appreciate in value rather than depreciate, especially if they are well maintained. The library's annual financial report shows a direct relationship between the allocations it receives, its expenditures, and growth of the collection's value as a long-term capital asset. Purchasing the right to access a remote resource or leasing a product on CD-ROM that must be returned at the termination of the lease are not capital expenditures. Thus, libraries and their parent bodies are experiencing a shift in return on investment. Money allocated to a library will not increase the net capital value of the library to the extent it has done in the past. Collections librarians should be aware of this trend and be able to explain why it is happening and articulate both cost savings and the less tangible value accruing in improved access to materials and user satisfaction.

Managing expenditures for e-resources in a manner that holds selectors, CDOs, and libraries accountable is a continuing challenge. Libraries may develop a formal policy or rely on generally understood principles to track sources of funds for e-resources and responsibility for expenditures. Libraries typically have a salaries budget, an operating budget, and a materials budget. Each library faces decisions about the sources of funding to cover costs associated with acquiring, servicing, managing, and accessing electronic information. Possible costs include initial purchase for separate items and back files; continuing annual lease or subscription costs; hardware, furniture, software, and search engines and their upgrades; loaders (if files are loaded locally); connect time to remote files; storage and file refreshing; initial wiring and telecommunication installation;

continuing technical support; staff and user training; and documentation. Even free electronic resources have financial consequences found in the preceding list. A library may opt to cover all, some, or none of these expenses with the materials budget. A selector should understand the funding sources for supplemental costs and, if outside the materials budget, ensure that the responsible parties are willing to absorb the cost.

Another aspect of budgeting for e-resources is allocation of funds and responsibility for expending these funds. Various models are in use. Some libraries have a single central fund line used for all electronic resources. This can be found in libraries that have a single selector and those that have several. A single separate fund can stress the priority of e-resources to the organization and make tracking expenditures easier, but it can also stress their separateness from other selection and management activities. At the other end of the continuum is the model in which all funds are allocated to subject lines, and individual selectors manage these fund lines as they manage fund lines for more traditional library materials. Selectors may make cooperative purchases with other selectors by pooling funds, but no resources are funded centrally. A middle ground retains some money in a central fund for resources (perhaps a general periodical index and associated full-text file, an encyclopedia, or an aggregator package) of systemwide interest and allocates to the individual subject line level for more narrowly focused titles. Ideally, responsibility for managing funds should be consistent with policies that assign responsibility for selection and collection management decisions.

Legal Issues

Gay N. Dannelly observed in 1994 that leases and licenses for electronic information "are anything but standard, except in the inclusion of legal terminology."[26] This remains the case, despite persistent efforts to develop model contracts that will be accepted by both librarians and publishers.[27] The contracts for e-resources presented to librarians have no standard format, order of content, or labeling of contract elements and clauses. Several professional organizations have developed licensing principles to guide librarians in negotiating contracts for e-resources and to inform publishers and vendors of preferred practices.[28] Classes and workshops have been offered and web resources developed to help with this very important and potentially confusing area. The most comprehensive of these web sites is

LibLicense, maintained by Yale University Library with support from the Council on Library and Information Resources.[29]

A discussion of legal issues begins with an understanding of terms. Many familiar words have different and distinct meanings when part of a legal agreement. A contract is a formal, legally binding written agreement between two or more parties. At its most basic, a contract consists of an offer, acceptance of the offer, and consideration, which is the exchange of something of value in the eyes of the law (e.g., a good, service, or money). The publisher or vendor (e.g., licensor) offers a product with terms and conditions set forth in the contract, the library accepts the offer, and the vendor provides access to the product for which the library pays a fee. The licensor is free to ask whatever price and set whatever conditions on use the market will bear. A license or license agreement is a legally binding form of a contract through which a library (the licensee) pays for the right to use or access a resource, usually for a fixed period of time in exchange. A lease is a contract by which one party grants access to another party to use a resource for a specified term and for a specified amount. Other legal terms are defined as they are used.

Contracts are based on contract law and come from the domain of private law. They take precedence over copyright law, which comes from the government's interest in fostering a free market while protecting its citizens' access to information. Once a contract is signed, fair use and other rights granted under copyright law are superseded by the terms of the contract. The publishing industry is substituting contract law for copyright because the ease of copying and transmitting digital data significantly increases the possibility for widespread theft of intellectual content. Jessica Litman has written that people "find it very hard to believe that there's really a law out there that says the stuff the copyright law says."[30] The Internet can create an illusion that everything on it is free and exempt from copyright protection, leading to content piracy. Appropriation of intellectual content and creative works, wherever located, violates copyright law and is punishable. The litigation involving Napster is an example of copyright infringement as determined by the courts. This successful effort by the entertainment industry to protect the rights of creators and publishers is bringing the ideals that originally motivated the passage of copyright law into question.

The intended purpose of copyright is to balance the rights of the public for access to information and creative expression with the rights of its creator and to provide incentives for the advancement of knowledge and creativity. Copyright law gives authors and the owners of copyrighted materials several broad rights and also subjects these rights to exceptions by granting certain rights to the public. Of most interest to librarians are "first sale doctrine" (the copyright owner has no right to control the distribution of a copy of a work after he or she has sold that copy), "fair use" (the legal privilege to make unauthorized use of a copyrighted work for good reason), and the right to make copies for archival and preservation purposes, for patrons, and for interlibrary loan (ILL). The 1978 Copyright Act, Section 107, codified fair use. Fair use permits reproduction of copyrighted works for research, teaching, journalism, commentary, criticism, and library use without the user having to pay or request permission from the copyright owner. Section 109, the doctrine of first sale, gives libraries the right to lend materials. Electronic content presents new challenges for fair use and the doctrine of first sale. Even the mass media *Time* magazine published an article about libraries and the ease with which the electronic content to which they provide access can be downloaded and shared.[31]

The Digital Millennium Copyright Act, which became effective in the United States in October 1998, is intended to protect intellectual property in the digital age. It prohibits unauthorized circumvention of the technological protection measures used to control access and to protect exclusive rights in copyright-protected works. The law includes several complex exceptions intended to benefit libraries and higher education. The law specifies that nothing in it will affect the right of fair use, and it allows libraries to circumvent technological protections if the library is making digital copies for preservation purposes. Much of this legislation has been controversial, and the library and education community lobbied for modifications before its passage and continue to monitor its interpretation in the courts.[32]

Licensing Terms and Conditions

Everything within a contract can be changed through negotiation. By its nature, a contract must be mutually acceptable before it is signed. The librarian's goal is a contract that allows the user community to pursue its usual activities, renders a fair exchange of money for product and service, and balances the rights, responsibilities, and legal liabilities of all parties. Librarians should be able to identify the issues that need to be addressed when negotiating a contract. The following list is an introduction to these important considerations. Readers are encouraged to explore this topic in more depth in the suggested readings for this chapter before negotiating and signing any contract.

Content. The contract should describe the product and make clear if the library is acquiring a product or content that it can keep forever, leasing content, or purchasing the rights to access the product. It should state whether or not the library has any permanent rights to the product, perhaps the files in existence at the time the contract is terminated.

Parties. The parties (the licensee and licensor) to the agreement are named or defined. If a library is part of a larger institution or organization, the licensee may be the firm or corporation, the college or the university, or the executive board, board of education, or board of regents.

Definitions. All potentially disputable terms should be defined. The most important of these are *authorized user* and *authorized site*. Authorized users are those individuals authorized under the contract to have access to the product. They may be the citizens of a state; currently enrolled student, faculty, and staff of an educational institution; or current employees of a specific office in a corporation. A college or university may wish to ensure that visiting lecturers, emeriti, and part-time students are also authorized users. Many academic libraries seek to permit insubstantial use by unaffiliated, walk-in users; these are part of the definition of *authorized users*. If the library expects to provide the resource to remote users, this should be addressed in the definition. The authorized site is the physical location where the licensee provides access to the e-resources. Libraries with several branches or located on several campuses or in several buildings will want to ensure that the authorized site(s) defines these.

Authentication. This is the process through which the identity of authorized users is verified before access is granted and often is specified in the agreement. Some common methods are passwords and user IDs, IP addresses, and public keys and digital certificates.

Grant of rights and restrictions. Rights are the permitted uses of the licensed digital information. By contract law, any rights not expressly granted in the license agreement are reserved to the licensor. Typical rights are user rights to search, browse, retrieve, view, display, download, and print the search results; store or save them to disk for a specific period; forward electronically to others or to oneself; fax to oneself and to others; and library rights to use the product in ILL transactions, distance education, and course reserves. Most contracts explicitly prohibit copying substantial portions of the database, downloading or printing issues of a journal, or modifying the search software or content. Type of use may be restricted to, for example, academic or noncommercial use. Some may grant the right to the library to make and save a copy of the e-resource and of the software during the duration of the contract.

Contractual obligations. Contracts typically assign obligations to both parties. Obligations of the licensor may include training staff, providing user support updates, replacing defective products, guaranteeing hours of access and service for a remote resource, and protecting the privacy of users.[33] The library may seek to obligate the licensor to provide use statistics. Library obligations most often have to do with the level and type of security provided. Care must be taken so that the library is not promising a level of control it cannot provide. A breach is the failure of a party to perform a contractual obligation.

Penalties. Penalties are applied when contractual obligations are not fulfilled. One example is a penalty fee charged a library for a late payment.

Warranties. Warranties are promises or assurances made by parties to the contract. The licensor may guarantee hours of access or server performance for a remote resource. Another typical warranty is the assurance that the licensor legally owns the copyright to or the content of the product.

Payment and cost. This section lays out the terms of payment—cost, how it is determined, and payment schedule.

Contract term and termination. The term of the contract is its duration, which may or may not match the term of the subscription. It may be automatically renewed unless the licensee notifies the licensor. The section dealing with termination will specify under what conditions the contract can be terminated—for failure to fulfill obligations or deception in the warranties. For example, the licensor may specify immediate termination of access in the case of a security breach. Libraries usually ask for a cure period in which to remedy the breach.

Indemnity and limitation of liability. Indemnification is one party's agreement to insure or otherwise defend another party against any claims by third parties resulting from performance under the agreement. It can, for example, provide for financial compensation should the warranties made in the contract prove false. A limit of liability clause sets out how much and what kind of damages will be paid for remedies. Many libraries have policies that forbid them from indemnifying a licensor or holding them harmless to other parties.

Force majeure. This clause excuses the licensor from poor performance or nondelivery in the case of conditions beyond the reasonable control of the vendor. Typical instances are war, postal strikes, and acts of terrorism.

Governing law. Governing law identifies the state's or country's law or courts under which a dispute relating to the contract will be adjudicated. Libraries usually negotiate for the laws of the state in which they are located; the licensor will prefer the state or country in which its primary office is located. A reasonable compromise is to agree to adjudicate the dispute in the state or country in which the grieving party is located.

Amendments. These are any modifications to the original contract. They should be dated and signed by all parties who signed the original agreement.

Authorized signature. The contract is signed by an individual authorized to represent the parties to the contract. Care should be taken in a library that signatory authority is carefully controlled; this helps ensure thoughtful review of contracts by focusing responsibility within the library. All parties to the contract should receive signed and countersigned copies.

Archives and perpetual access. Libraries signing contracts should consider the importance they are willing to place on access to archived materials, if such an archive exists. Most contracts provide access to or use of a product only during the duration of the agreement. Some may include a provision to provide files created during the term of the contract in a specified format (perhaps CD-ROM) or a format yet to be determined. A perpetual license guarantees access to those files after the contract is terminated.

Negotiating contracts and contract law is complex. Librarians should know when to call for expert opinion and advice. They should understand the policies of the library and its parent body regarding contracts, leases, purchasing, and accountability to ensure that all contracts and their signing are consistent in these policies.

Collection Management Issues

Most of the collection management issues associated with electronic resources are essentially the same as those found with other formats. Collection management covers what one does with collections after they are acquired—decisions about retention, cancellation, withdrawals, preservation, storage, and protection. Decisions about e-resources, after they have been selected and are in use, involve assessment of the e-resource's ability to meet user needs and evaluation of the product—both its inherent quality and in relation to other products. Earlier in this chapter, approaches for comparing products during selection were suggested. This comparison should continue as long as the library retains a product because alternatives in delivery mechanisms, content providers, and pricing packages are constantly being introduced into the market.

Decisions about preservation of and archives for e-resources, especially those digitized locally, can fall within the purview of collections librarians. Although the issue of perpetual access to the back files or archives of an e-resource is, ideally, addressed in the contract, a librarian should check periodically to see that the licensor is prepared to deliver. Locally digitized documents require an infrastructure that guarantees data permanence and data access when hardware and software are constantly changing. The librarian within whose area these documents fall should be attentive to these issues. Decisions about the retention of paper versions of materials now available electronically may require consideration. In some cases, libraries cooperate to have one central repository for the paper copies, thus reducing the need for each partner to duplicate paper holdings.

Collections librarians often participate in the preparation of library policies relating to the use of e-resources. One example is a privacy policy, which explains how user confidentiality is protected in the library and through contractual privacy clauses. Another policy may address appropriate and acceptable use of e-resources, explaining the rules and procedures that users are expected to follow when accessing the Internet from the library. This policy will explain limitations that contracts place on use of e-resources and what is permissible under copyright law. The policy may explain how the library seeks to balance the rights of intellectual freedom with inappropriate and potentially illegal use of e-resources and technology available in the library.

Scholarly Communication

The topic of scholarly communication has preoccupied academic librarians and others in the academy for more than a decade. A vast body of literature has explored the problems, how they developed, and what might be done. The relationship between scholarly communication and electronic publishing seems to garner much of the attention, because new technologies for distribution are seen as one way out of the dilemma.[34]

"Scholarly communication" describes the formal publication of research and continuing access to the scholarly record in print and digital format. More broadly, it includes informal discourse among colleagues, class discussions and lectures, and data retrieval through local and global networks. The "scholarly communication system" refers to the interactions of participants in the system who create, distribute, collect, preserve, make available, and use the research of scholars and scientists.

Formal scholarly communication serves as a means of conferring qualitative evaluation and judgment of the scholarship through peer review and of establishing the reputation of scholars. Scholarly books and journals provide an efficient way to disseminate scholarly findings, secure the final version of their work, and make it accessible by future generations. Publication is an essential component of current promotion and tenure decisions. The system of scholarly publishing is sometimes called a food chain. Universities and external funding agencies subsidize and pay the costs of research. Faculty members then give away this intellectual property, transferring copyright to publishers. Faculty serve on editorial boards and review papers submitted for publication for free. Publishers handle copyediting and typography, though some monograph publishers require camera-ready copy. The publisher is responsible for production and distribution. Value is added, but academic customers question whether the prices being charged exceed the cost of adding that value. Finally, college and university libraries buy back the final products to fulfill their role of organizing, providing, and archiving scholarly works.

Today's scholarly communication has its roots in the 1600s, when European scholarly societies first were established. Their purpose was to provide a forum in which independent scholars could share and discuss their research. Eventually, these societies began to publish their findings in serial publications with names like *Comptes rendus, Transactions,* and *Abhandlungen.* These periodicals were issued by the society, and their content was vetted by the society members or a small group selected to serve that role. In the United States, as in Europe, the original system of scholarly communication was the realm of the wealthy; the creators and the consumers of scholarship were the same people, with virtually no middlemen involved.

This began to change in America with the Morrill Act (1862), which established funding for land-grant universities and placed obligations on the faculties at these institutions to conduct research that would benefit society. A direct result was a tremendous increase in publication of journals and monographs. The next big change in scholarly communication came after World War II, when college and university enrollments swelled and the U.S. government began to direct large amounts of money to higher education for research. The volume of scholarly publications grew exponentially. Professional and scholarly societies could not keep pace, and many turned to the for-profit sector to take on their publishing activities, which quickly saw the profit potential. Commercial publishers have been merging over the last ten years, resulting in significantly fewer journal publishers. Conglomerates can hold near monopolies in some disciplines. Some librarians and scholars feel that the potential of electronic publishing to decrease costs and increase access has been thwarted by commercial publishers.

Scholarly monographs traditionally have been published by university presses. Many universities now expect these presses to generate a profit or, at a minimum, sustain no losses. The result is that university presses are more market-sensitive and publishing fewer economically marginal books. Financial pressures in libraries to keep up with increasing serial costs mean libraries are buying fewer books, which further decreases the market for scholarly monographs. Many presses have been shut down by their universities. The result is a significant decrease in opportunities for scholars to publish monographs.

Rapidly escalating prices and the library's difficulty in acquiring the materials needed to support the research and teaching missions of their educational institutions have been called "the library's problem." Academic libraries started by addressing increasing serial costs in the 1980s and began to talk about the "the serials crisis." Over time, librarians realized that they alone could not bring about the changes needed in a system driven largely by tenure considerations and profit-making concerns outside the control of libraries. They have sought to educate and involve faculty and college and university administrators in solving problems and to take advantage of new technologies.

In 2000, a group of librarians, academic administrators, and representatives from professional associations met in Tempe, Arizona, and agreed to a set of "Principles for Emerging Systems of Scholarly Publishing."[35] The meeting was held to facilitate discussion among the various academic stakeholders in the scholarly publishing process and to build consensus on a set of principles that could guide the transformation of the scholarly publishing system. These principles suggest three approaches to the current problems: increased use of electronic capabilities, review of promotion and tenure practices, and responsible copyright management.

Three initiatives demonstrate efforts to modify the present scholarly communication system. Paul Ginsparg, now at Cornell University, established the first electronic e-print service in 1991 while he worked at Los Alamos National Laboratories.[36] Serving as an online preprint archive and distribution server for research papers, this service has become a major forum for speedy dissemination of results in physics and related disciplines, mathematics, nonlinear sciences, computational linguistics, and neuroscience. The objectives of the archive—to provide functionality that was not otherwise available, speedy access to research, and a level playing field for researchers at different academic levels and different geographic locations—continue to be met.

The Scholarly Publishing and Academic Resources Coalition (SPARC) is another proactive approach.[37] SPARC is an international alliance of libraries, research institutions, and organizations from the academic and research community that encourages competition in the scholarly communication market through the support of high-quality, economical alternatives to high-priced scholarly journals. SPARC is underwriting the launch of journals aimed at competing with expensive titles and applying technology to improve the process of scholarly communication and reduce the costs of production and distribution.

The Open Archives Initiative (OAI) is supported by the Digital Library Federation, Coalition for Networked Information, and National Science Foundation. Its goal is to develop and promote interoperability standards to facilitate exchange of digital content and to support metadata harvesting for a wide range of digital resources of academic and scholarly interest.

Summary

Electronic resources offer many advantages to libraries and their users. They can increase speed and ease of access and the amount of information available. They can save library space and staff time. They are not yet, however, the solution to all of libraries' financial, space, access, and service problems. Most libraries continue to operate in a dual environment—print and electronic. E-resources, whether physically located within a library or accessed via a network, are part of the library's collection and should be evaluated and assessed with the same criteria and rigor applied to all collections decisions.

The challenges that come with e-resources include technical issues, costs, copyright, equity of access, security, bibliographic control, licensing, user instruction, and issues of authority, quality, accuracy, instability and mutability, and mobility of information. Understanding the issues, vocabulary, and options test librarians on a daily basis. Distinguishing between formats and storage and delivery media is a critical first step in making informed choices. Content is created in native format and rendered into a delivery format. Both of these may be proprietary and may or may not be standards-based. The storage and delivery medium is the temporary container that delivers the content to the users. The medium may be a CD-ROM, a magnetic tape, or a server that is accessed via the Internet.

Librarians began to select CD-ROMs for use in libraries in the mid-1980s, when publishers began using them to deliver indexes and abstracting tools. Options expanded in the 1990s with the development of graphical user interfaces and easy access to the Internet via the World Wide Web. Commercial journal publishers quickly saw the potential and expanded into the e-journal market in the last five years of the twentieth century. E-books are a more recent option for digital content delivery. Developing standards for interoperability between formats and between storage and delivery media, formalizing digital rights management, and adhering to associated copyright issues are important areas of concern for both producers and consumers (both libraries and individuals).

Although the same selection criteria apply to all items collections librarians consider, e-resources present unique considerations. These include comparing various access and delivery media for the same content, wide consultation with others in the library, large costs and complex pricing structures, access to retrospective files, and contractual and licensing issues. The appearance of aggregators and publishers' bundled serials packages have meant that some selection decisions are no longer made by individual selectors. Librarians should understand the legal obligations and service consequences found in contracts and licenses. Complicated legal issues often require involvement with legal experts outside the library.

The relationship between scholarly communication and electronic publishing is of great interest to librarians and scholars. Many see the potential to return publication of research and continuing access to the scholarly record to the academy and take it back from the commercial sector. Librarians, academics, researchers, and scholarly societies are collaborating in projects that explore this new arena for change.

| CASE STUDY |

Casey Connor is the art librarian at Metropolitan University, a private institution with 12,000 students, half of whom are graduate students. The school focuses on the arts and humanities and has a national reputation for high-quality academic programs. Metropolitan University offers undergraduate majors in both art history and fine arts and has two graduate programs: master's of art history and master's of fine arts. The school does not offer doctoral programs. Casey is responsible for selecting resources in all formats to support the students and faculty in these programs. A graduate of the M.F.A. program, who is a very successful commercial artist with a computer software firm, has given the library a $1 million endowment to support the acquisition of digital resources to support the arts programs. The only condition is that no funding currently allocated to the arts collections be redirected to other subject areas. Casey is interested in adding indexes, abstracting tools, and, perhaps, some full-text resources. For the purposes of this exercise, assume that Casey does not need to direct part of the new money to her serials budget and that cost is not a consideration.

Activity

Select two electronic reference resources that support instruction and research in art history and fine arts. Each product should be considered separately, but an analysis should compare various delivery media (CD-ROM, print, online) for the same content, and, where logical, the two products may be compared and contrasted. Using the selection criteria introduced in chapter 4 and in this chapter, evaluate each product. Consider such aspects as coverage, currency, content, output options, ease of use, search options, unique features, quality of graphics and images, training needs, and cost. Possible products to analyze are *Art Abstracts*, *Art Full Text*, *ART-Bibliographies Modern*, *Bibliography of the History of Art*, *Design and Applied Arts Index*, and *Grove Dictionary of Art*. Locate information through consulting product reviews and from the publishers' web sites.

REFERENCES

1. Daniel Greenstein, "DLF Draft Strategy and Business Plan," public version 2.0. Washington, D.C.: Digital Library Federation, Sept. 25, 2000, available at http://www.diglib.org/about/stratpv.htm.

2. Clifford A. Lynch, "Recomputerizing the Library: New Roles for Information Technology in a Time of Networked Information," in *Recreating the Academic Library: Breaking Virtual Ground,* ed. Cheryl LaGuardia (New York: Neal-Schuman, 1999), 5.

3. Stuart Moulthrop, "You Say You Want a Revolution: Hypertext and the Laws of Media." In *Essays in Postmodern Culture,* ed. Eyal Amiran and John Unsworth (New York: Oxford Univ. Pr., 1993), 84.

4. Marlene Manoff, "Hybridity, Mutability, Multiplicity: Theorizing Electronic Library Collections," *Library Trends* 49, no. 1 (summer 2000): 863.

5. *New Horizons in Adult Education,* Syracuse, N.Y.: Syracuse University Kellogg Project, available at http://www.nova.edu/~aed/newhorizons.html.

6. *Directory of Electronic Journals, Newsletters and Academic Discussion Lists* (Washington, D.C.: Assn. of Research Libraries, 1991–1997).

7. *Directory of Scholarly Electronic Journals and Academic Discussion Lists* (Washington, D.C.: Assn. of Research Libraries, Office of Scholarly Communication, 2000–).

8. Ingenta Select [WWW home page of Ingenta Select]. Available [Online]: http://www.ingentaselect.co.uk/.

9. HighWire [WWW home page of HighWire, Library of the Sciences and Medicine]. Available [Online]: http://highwire.stanford.edu.

10. Kenneth Frazier, "The Librarians' Dilemma: Contemplating the Costs of the 'Big Deal,'" *D-Lib Magazine* 7, no. 3 (March 2001), available at http://www.dlib.org/dlib/march01/frazier/03frazier.html; *see also* letters to the editor, written in response to Frazier's article, which appeared in the April 2001 issue of *D-Lib Magazine* 7, no. 4, available at http://www.dlib.org/dlib/april01/04letters.html.

11. *Number Standards for Ebooks* (New York: Assn. of American Publishers, 2000), 7.

12. Project Gutenberg [WWW page for Project Gutenberg]. Available [Online]: http://promo.net/pg/index.html.

13. Digital Policy/Ebook Project—Project Information [WWW home page of the Assn. of American Publishers Digital Policy/Ebook Project]. Available [Online]: http://www.publishers.org/digital/info.cfm.

14. Open eBook Forum [WWW home page of Open eBook Forum, the International Trade and Standards Organization for the eBook Industry]. Available [Online]: http://www.openebook.org.

15. Open Archives Initiative [WWW home page of OAI]. Available [Online]: http://www.openarchives.org/index.html.

16. Electronic Books in Libraries [WWW home page of Electronic Books in Libraries, Univ. of Rochester Libraries]. Available [Online]: http://www.lib.rochester.edu/main/ebooks/index.htm. *See* Susan Gibbons, "Ebooks: Some Concerns and Surprises," *Portal: Libraries and the Academy* 1, no. 2 (2001): 71–75, for a project report.

17. Clifford A. Lynch, "The Battle to Define the Future of the Book in the Digital World," *First Monday* 6, no. 6 (June 2001), available at http://firstmonday.org/

issues/issue6_6/lynch/index.html; "Electrifying the Book, Part I," *NetConnect,* Supplement to *Library Journal* 124, no. 17 (Oct. 1999): 3–6; "Electrifying the Book, Part II," *NetConnect,* Supplement to *Library Journal* 125, no. 1 (Jan. 2000): 24–27.

18. Clifford A. Lynch, "The Battle to Define the Future of the Book in the Digital World."

19. Richard Bleiler and Terry Plum, *Networked Information Resources,* SPEC Kit, no. 253 (Washington, D.C.: Assn. of Research Libraries, 1999), 11.

20. Peggy Johnson, "Selecting Electronic Resources: Developing a Local Decision-Making Matrix," in *Electronic Resources: Selection and Bibliographic Control,* ed. Ling-yuh W. Pattie and Bonnie Jean Cox (New York: Haworth, 1996), 9–24; also published in *Cataloging and Classification Quarterly,* v. 22, no. 3/4.

21. Manoff, "Hybridity, Mutability, Multiplicity: Theorizing Electronic Library Collections," 858.

22. Glenda A. Thornton, "Impact of Electronic Resources on Collection Development, the Roles of Librarians, and Library Consortia," *Library Trends* 48, no. 4 (spring 2000): 842.

23. Richard Bleiler and Terry Plum, *Networked Information Resources,* SPEC Kit, no. 253 (Washington, D.C.: Assn. of Research Libraries, 1999), 12.

24. Assn. of Research Libraries, *ARL Supplementary Statistics, 2000–2001,* available at http://www.arl.org/stats/sup/index.html.

25. Carol Hansen Montgomery, "Measuring the Impact of an Electronic Journal Collection on Library Costs: A Framework and Preliminary Observations," *D-Lib Magazine* 6, no. 10 (Oct. 2000). Available at http://www.dlib.org/dlib/october00/montgomery/10montgomery.html.

26. Gay N. Dannelly, "Strategic Issues in Planning for Electronic Resources," *Technicalities* 14, no. 5 (May 1994): 13.

27. *See,* for example, the model license developed by the Council on Library and Information Resources, the Digital Library Federation, and Yale University Library available at http://www.library.yale.edu/~llicense/modlic.shtml; and *Model Standard Licenses for Use by Publishers, Librarians and Subscription Agents for Electronic Resources,* available at http://www.licensingmodels.com.

28. International Federation of Library Assns., Committee on Copyright and other Legal Matters, *Licensing Principles* (May 1, 2001), available at http://ifla.org/V/ebpb/copy.htm; American Assn. of Law Libraries, American Library Assn., Assn. of Academic Health Sciences Libraries, Assn. of Research Libraries, Medical Library Assn., Special Libraries Assn., *Principles for Licensing Electronic Resources* (July 15, 1997), available at http://www.arl.org/scomm/licensing/principles.html; and Patricia Brennan, Karen Hersey, and Georgia Harper, *Strategic and Practical Considerations for Signing Electronic Information Delivery Agreements,* available at http://arl.cni.org/scomm/licensing/licbooklet.html.

29. LibLicense: Licensing Digital Information: A Resource for Librarians [WWW home page of LibLicense]. Available [Online]: http://www.library.yale.edu/~llicense/index.shtml.

30. Jessica Litman, *Digital Copyright* (Amherst, N.Y.: Prometheus, 2001), 112.

31. Katherine Bonamici, "Are Libraries the Next Napsters?" *Time.COM* (July 24, 2001), available at http://www.time.com/time/nation/article/0,8599,168798,00.html.

32. Information about the Digital Millennium Copyright Act is available on the ALA web site (http://www.ala.org); click "Our Association" on the top navigation bar, click "Offices" in the left column, and click "Washington Office."

33. International Coalition of Library Consortia, *Privacy Guidelines for Electronic Resources Vendors* (July 2002), available at http://www.library.yale.edu/consortia/2002privacyguidelines.html.

34. Charles W. Bailey Jr.'s *The Scholarly Electronic Publishing Bibliography*, available at http://info.lib.uh.edu/sepb/sepb.html, listed more than 1,900 articles, books, electronic documents, and other sources on scholarly electronic publishing when version 49 was announced in June 2003.

35. "Principles for Emerging Systems of Scholarly Publishing" [also known as the Tempe Principles] (March 2–4, 2000), available at http://www.arl.org/scomm/tempe.html.

36. arXiv.org ePrint archive [WWW home page of the electronic archive and distribution server for research papers in physics and related disciplines, mathematics, nonlinear sciences, computational linguistics, and neuroscience]. Available [Online]: http://arxiv.org.

37. SPARC [WWW home page of the Scholarly Publishing and Academic Resources Coalition]. Available [Online]: http://www.arl.org/sparc/.

SUGGESTED READINGS

Atkinson, Ross. "A Rationale for the Redesign of Scholarly Information Exchange." *Library Resources and Technical Services* 44, no. 2 (April 2000): 59–69.

Bebbington, Laurence W. "Managing Content: Licensing, Copyright and Privacy Issues in Managing Electronic Resources." *Legal Information Management* 1, no. 2 (summer 2001): 4–12.

Bielefied, Arlene, and Lawrence Cheeseman. *Interpreting and Negotiating Licensing Agreements: A Guidebook for the Library, Research, and Teaching Professions.* New York: Neal-Schuman, 1999.

Bluh, Pamela H., ed. *Managing Electronic Serials.* ALCTS Papers on Library Technical Services and Collection, no. 9. Chicago: American Library Assn., 2001.

Budd, John M., and Bart M. Harloe. "Collection Development and Scholarly Communication in the Twenty-first Century: From Collection Management to Content Management." In *Collection Management for the Twenty-first Century: A Handbook for Librarians,* edited by G. E. Gorman and Ruth H. Miller, 3–25. Westport, Conn.: Greenwood, 1997.

Crews, Kenneth D. "Licensing for Information Resources: Creative Contracts and the Library Mission." In *Virtually Yours: Models for Managing Electronic Resources and Services,* edited by Peggy Johnson and Bonnie MacEwan, 98–110. ALCTS Papers on Library Technical Services and Collections, no. 8. Chicago: American Library Assn., 1999.

Dorner, Daniel G. "The Blurring of Boundaries: Digital Information and Its Impact on Collection Management." In *Collection Management,* edited by G. E. Gorman, 15–44. International Yearbook of Library and Information Management, 2000/2001. London: Library Assn. Pub., 2000.

Duranceau, Ellen Finnie. "License Tracking." *Serials Review* 26, no. 3 (2000): 69–73.

Greenstein, Daniel, and Suzanne E. Thorin. *The Digital Library: A Biography.* Washington, D.C.: Council on Library and Information Resources, 2002. Also available at http://www.clir.org/pubs/abstract/pub109abst.html.

Gyeszly, Suzanne D. "Electronic or Paper Journals? Budgetary, Collection Development, and User Satisfaction Questions." *Collection Building* 20, no. 1 (2001): 5–10.

Hanson, Terry, and Joan Day, eds. *Managing the Electronic Library: A Practical Guide for Information Professionals.* London, New Providence, N.J.: Bowker-Saur, 1998.

Harris, Steven R. "Webliography: The Process of Building Internet Subject Access." In *Acquisitions and Collection Development in the Humanities,* edited by Irene Owens, 29–43. New York: Haworth, 1997. Also published in *The Acquisitions Librarian,* no. 17/18.

Hillesund, Terje. "Will E-books Change the World?" *First Monday* 6, no. 10 (Oct. 1, 2001). Available at http://www.firstmonday.dk/issues/issue6_10/hillesund/index.html.

Hoffmann, Gretchen McCord. *Copyright in Cyberspace: Questions and Answers for Librarians.* New York: Neal-Schuman, 2001.

Holleman, Curt. "Electronic Resources: Are Basic Criteria for the Selection of Materials Changing?" *Library Trends* 48, no. 4 (2000): 694–710.

Hughes, Carol Ann. "The Myth of 'Obsolescence': The Monograph in the Digital Library." *Portal: Libraries and the Academy* 1, no. 2. (April 2001): 113–99.

Jantz, Ronald. "E-books and New Library Service Models: An Analysis of the Impact of E-book Technology on Academic Libraries." *Information Technology and Libraries* 20, no. 2 (June 2001): 104–12.

Jewell, Timothy D. *Selection and Presentation of Commercially Available Electronic Resources: Issues and Practices.* Washington, D.C.: Digital Library Federation and Council on Library and Information Resources, 2001. Also available at http://www.clir.org/pubs/reports/pub99/contents.html.

Lee, Stuart D. *Building an Electronic Resource Collection: A Practical Guide.* New York: Neal-Schuman, 2002.

Lougee, Wendy P. *Diffuse Libraries: Emergent Roles for the Research Library in the Digital Age.* Washington, D.C.: Council on Library and Information Resources, 2002. Also available at http://www.clir.org/pubs/abstract/pub108abst.html.

Marcum, Deanna B., ed. *Development of Digital Libraries: An American Perspective.* Contributions in Librarianship and Information Science, no. 95. Westport, Conn.: Greenwood, 2001.

Mooney, Stephen. "Interoperability: Digital Rights Management and the Emerging E-book Environment." *D-Lib Magazine* 7, no. 1 (Jan. 2001). Available at: http://www.dlib.org/dlib/january01/mooney/01mooney.html.

Moyo, Lesley M. "Collections on the Web: Some Access and Navigation Issues." *Library Collections, Acquisitions, and Technical Services* 26, no. 1 (spring 2002): 47–59.

Odlyzko, Andrew M. "Competition and Cooperation: Libraries and Publishers in the Transition to Electronic Scholarly Journals." *Journal of Scholarly Publishing* 30, no. 4 (July 1999): 163–85.

Okerson, Ann Shumelda. "Are We There Yet? Online E-resources Ten Years After." In *Collection Development in an Electronic Environment,* edited by Thomas E. Nisonger, a special issue of *Library Trends* 48, no. 4 (spring 2000): 671–93.

Quinn, Brian. "The Impact of Aggregator Packages on Collection Management." *Collection Management* 25, no. 3 (2001): 53–74.

Tuete, Fredrika J. "To Publish and Perish: Who Are the Dinosaurs in Scholarly Publishing?" *Journal of Scholarly Publishing* 32, no. 2 (Jan. 2001): 102–12.

Valauskas, Edward J., and Monica Ertel, eds. *The Internet for Teachers and School Library Media Specialists: Today's Applications, Tomorrow's Prospects.* New York: Neal-Schuman, 1996.

Winston, Brian. *Media Technology and Society: A History from the Telegraph to the Internet.* London: Routledge, 1998.

| Cooperative Collection
Development
and Management

Introduction

David H. Stam has provided one of the more elegant descriptions of library cooperation. He wrote that "all libraries are linked in a great chain of access and what each has and does will have importance for the whole universe of libraries and their users."[1] He built on the ancient concept of creation known as the great chain of being—a theme that permeated science, literature, and philosophy beginning with the time of Plato and was refined in the eighteenth century by Gottfried Wilhelm von Leibnitz. This view held that all of existence is defined by plenitude, continuity, and gradation. These three elements can, as Stam implied, apply to libraries when *plenitude* is understood to mean abundance of the whole, *continuity* to mean uninterrupted connection, and *gradation* to mean variations between similar and related components.

Library cooperation is not a new idea. In 1886, Melvil Dewey listed one of the major needs of the modern library movement as "a practical means of bringing the enormous benefits of cooperation, which has been the watch word of the whole movement, into full play in the interests of the libraries."[2] Some have said that library cooperation is an unnatural act because of the difficulties it has presented libraries over the years, but most librarians believe, with Michael Gorman, that "Cooperation is as essential to a library as is water to a fish or air to a mammal."[3] This chapter presents an overview of cooperative collection development and management;

identifies types of cooperation, barriers to implementation, and elements that contribute to success; and concludes with an examination of the ownership access continuum.

Overview

A working definition of *cooperative collection development* is "the sharing of responsibilities among two or more libraries for the process of acquiring materials, developing collections, and managing the growth and maintenance of collections in a user-beneficial and cost-beneficial way."[4] The umbrella term used into the mid-1980s was *resource sharing* and applied to cooperative cataloging, shared storage facilities, shared preservation activities, interlibrary loan (ILL), and coordinated or cooperative collection development.[5] Today, *resource sharing* usually means the sharing of resources or materials through ILL.

ILL, the reciprocal lending and borrowing of materials between libraries, has a long history. One of the earliest references dates from 200 B.C., when the library in Alexandria is known to have lent materials to Pergamum.[6] Interlibrary lending did not become common in the United States until the last quarter of the nineteenth century. Ernest C. Richardson, librarian at Princeton University, promoted ILL and called for a national lending library in 1899. His rationale resonates in today's libraries. He wrote, "It is a matter of common observation that with the present limited facilities for our American libraries, students, whether dependent on college libraries or on general reference libraries, are constantly in lack of the books which they want. . . . We are duplicating, every year, a great many sets of periodicals, as we would not need to do under some system where all were free to borrow."[7] Although the United States did not develop a national lending library, a formal process for managing lending and borrowing between libraries was in place in the United States early in the twentieth century. The Library of Congress issued its first policy governing ILL in 1907, and the American Library Association published its first ILL code in 1916.[8] ILL is the most pervasive form of library cooperation and links most libraries across the United States and Canada and internationally as well. Association of Research Libraries (ARL) statistics for the year 2001/2002 show a 106 percent increase in borrowing by its member libraries between 1991 and 2002.[9]

Cooperative collection development is now understood to mean much more than resource sharing. Some authors have sought to distinguish between cooperative, collaborative, and coordinated collection development. The *Guide to Cooperative Collection Development* does not differentiate, and this book uses these terms interchangeably.[10] Cooperative collection development and management is an overarching planning strategy that libraries employ to provide materials and information for their users that a single library cannot afford to have on its own. The goal of cooperative collection development and management is improving access to information and resources through maximizing the use of those resources and leveraging available funding. Cooperative collection development and management have three interdependent components: resource sharing, bibliographic access, and coordinated collection development and management. *See* figure 8-1.

Resource sharing is a system for making requests and providing delivery of information, chiefly through the ILL process. ILL handles both returnables (items that must be returned to the lender) and nonreturnables (photocopies or digital transmissions). ILL may be strengthened by agreements among members of a consortium to expedite service to members and permit on-site use of collections by clientele of member libraries. ILL encompasses a protocol for making requests and acceptable methods of delivery. The second component in cooperative collection development is bibliographic access or knowing what is available from other sites through printed or microform catalogs, a shared or union catalog, or a regional, national, or international bibliographic utility. The third component,

Figure 8-1 The Three Components of Successful Cooperation

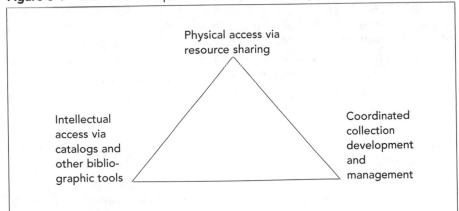

coordinated collection development and management, is, in its ideal manifestation, a coordinated scheme of purchasing and maintaining collections. Cooperative collection development's aim is the building of complementary collections on which the cooperating libraries can draw. Joseph J. Branin identified activities that are part of cooperative collection development: mutual notification of purchasing decisions, joint purchase, and assigned subject specialization in building collections.[11] In recent years, cooperative collection development has expanded to include consortial agreements to purchase group access to electronic resources at discounted prices.

None of these three components works without some degree of success in the other two areas. Christy Hightower and George J. Soete have written that "bibliographic access without physical access is an empty promise."[12] Effective delivery is central to the success of cooperative efforts. Improvements in telecommunications have had a significant impact on physical access, both in the transmission of requests and the delivery of articles. Both OCLC and the Research Libraries Group (RLG) support automated ILL subsystems that transmit requests to members. For example, the Ariel software, developed by the RLG, supports high-quality scanning of articles and transmits the electronic images to other Ariel-equipped workstations anywhere in the world, using either FTP (file transfer protocol) or e-mail. Some consortia, such as the CIC (Committee on Institutional Cooperation—the Big Ten, plus the University of Chicago and Pennsylvania State University), have contracted with a single courier service to expedite delivery, especially of returnables that are not suitable for electronic transmission. The CIC has also taken a leadership role in patron-initiated ILL via direct access to CIC member libraries' online catalogs.

Bibliographic access to the holdings of other libraries is a critical component of cooperation. For many years, libraries depended on printed holdings information—records in the *National Union Catalog*, individual libraries' printed book catalogs, and union serials holdings lists. The first regional union catalog was developed at the California State Library in 1901, and the Library of Congress established the *National Union Catalog* in 1902. Checking such resources was tedious. The development of bibliographic utilities, regional online shared catalogs, and web-based access to online catalogs has been a tremendous step forward in bibliographic access for both library patrons and library staffs. The dramatic increase in bibliographic access that has accompanied the proliferation of electronic databases and online library catalogs brings increased pressure for immediate physical access.

Neither speedy delivery nor bibliographic access has meaning unless the resource the user wishes can be located. If libraries have established partnerships to ensure coverage and collection gaps still exist, cooperation is not succeeding. A gap in one collection can be accommodated only if the same gap does not exist at a partner library. The ideal situation is equitable distribution of little-used titles. Collection overlaps (titles held by more than one library) are often justified because these materials will be used heavily in each library that owns them.

Cooperative collection development seldom saves money. Cooperative collection development leverages available funds by increasing access to a wider collection of information resources. It enlarges the universe of titles available to library users and, when properly supported, speeds the delivery of materials through interlibrary lending and borrowing systems. Cooperative collection development and management also can be viewed as cost containment through purchase avoidance. The libraries that participate in cooperative collection development reduce duplication in order to provide strengthened resources and increased user satisfaction.

Despite a few isolated cooperative collection development successes, libraries do not have a notable history of altering traditional collection development behaviors. Libraries have not, in general, developed policies and practices that acknowledge or take advantage of being linked in a great chain of being. The extent to which meaningful and practical cooperation has been implemented falls short of the enthusiasm with which it is proclaimed. Dan C. Hazen observed that the theory is compelling, but the results have been inconsequential.[13] Stella Bentley noted that, despite the popularity of cooperative collection development as a topic, libraries actually spend a small percentage of total budgets on cooperative purchases.[14]

Types of Cooperative Collection Development

Several varieties of cooperative collection development have evolved. For many years, libraries have practiced what Paul H. Mosher and Marcia Pankake called the "status quo approach" to cooperative collection development.[15] This approach presumes that libraries' total collecting activities will build, on a national scale, reasonable depth in every area of interest. In other words, every title that anyone might want now and in the future will be held somewhere in the United States simply as a result of serendipitous collection development and management. This is optimistic and increasingly unrealistic, given the financial constraints most libraries are experiencing.

Synergistic Cooperation

Ross Atkinson called a second approach the synergistic version, in which different libraries take responsibilities for collecting different publications, according to some coordinated and collaborative plan.[16] This also could be called distributed responsibility for collection development. Underlying all efforts at cooperation is, in the words of Edward Shreeves, a "widespread belief that cooperation in building collections can improve significantly the quality of library service by broadening and deepening the range of materials collectively available."[17] Formal coordinated and collaborative collection development and management programs are normally guided by written agreements, contracts, or other documents outlining the commitments and responsibilities of the participants.

The synergistic approach calls for dividing the information universe into core and peripheral materials and then dividing the periphery between the consortium members. An academic library has a responsibility to maintain a core collection on-site that serves immediate needs, especially those of its undergraduates. Librarians use the term *core* to mean two kinds of core collections: a collection representing the intellectual nucleus of each discipline (consisting of the classic, synoptic, and most influential text) and a nucleus of materials that is determined by heaviest use.[18] Core material, in this latter definition, is often considered the 20 percent of the collection that satisfies 80 percent of library users' needs. Simultaneously, the library will develop collections of peripheral materials that respond to local priorities but also serve consortial needs. This local collection, in turn, is backed up by the collections of consortial partners built through distributed responsibility for peripheral materials in complementary fields.

Defining what *core* and *peripheral* mean in terms of collecting behavior has been a stumbling block to successful synergistic collection development projects. Generally, materials in the periphery are considered to be research materials that will not be in heavy demand and will fall into conspectus levels 4 (research collections) and 5 (comprehensive collections). One problem is that any library's understanding of the core tends to shrink and expand in response to the funds available to that library during each budget cycle. Predicting what will constitute core materials is also a challenge. Ross Atkinson has written, "Our effort to . . . distinguish core from non-core materials has been so far singularly unsuccessful, except through such retrospective methods as citation analysis or the use of circulation records. For purposes of planning, budgeting, or coordination, the concept of the core, for all its use, is practically useless."[19]

The only application of synergistic cooperation that is both logical and practical is one in which a library accepts responsibility for collecting in areas that also meet local needs and reflect local strengths. At the same time, a commitment by one library to a particular area does not obligate the other consortial partners to give up supporting that area. Stam wrote "resource sharing does not remove in any way the obligation for any institution to fulfill its local mission."[20] Cooperative collection development cannot substitute for adequate local collections.

Two early examples of synergistic cooperative collection development are the agreement between the Research Triangle University Libraries in North Carolina and the Farmington Plan. The earliest is the Research Triangle, consisting of Duke University, North Carolina State University, and the University of North Carolina at Chapel Hill.[21] In 1933, the University of North Carolina at Chapel Hill and Duke University formed the Joint Committee on Intellectual Cooperation in an effort to leverage limited financial resources during the Great Depression. Library cooperation began in 1934 with a plan for systematic division of responsibility for publications in major disciplines. This evolved into the area studies concept of dividing responsibilities by geographic coverage or language or both. The Research Triangle has an enviable record of success in leveraging financial resources and making unique materials available to its membership. Patricia Buck Dominguez and Luke Swindler reported in 1993 that 76 percent of the titles in the shared union catalog were found on only one campus, and only 7 percent were held by all three universities.[22] Much of the success of the Research Triangle can be attributed to upper-level institutional support; geographic proximity, which has meant easy and speedy access; bibliographic access to titles held in each of the three member libraries; and a long history of realizing its goals.

The Farmington Plan was less successful.[23] Launched in 1948 under the sponsorship of the ARL, it was a voluntary agreement on the part of approximately sixty academic, special, and research libraries. The goal of the Farmington Plan was to increase the nation's total resources for research. The participating libraries agreed to collect, for specified countries and subjects, one copy of each new foreign publication in which a U.S. researcher could be presumed to be interested. The Farmington Plan designed blanket order profiles that were placed with foreign dealers. Libraries were expected to accept all materials within the scope of their commitments.

The Farmington Plan was not concerned with the financial situations of its participants and expected each library to provide the budgetary support needed to accomplish the comprehensive plan goals. The Farmington Plan ceased in 1972 primarily because it failed to recognize the first condition of every successful cooperative plan—libraries will always give priority to local needs and priorities. Ideally, each participating library should be able to combine self-interest with the overarching aims of the agreement. Each participant must be confident that it will receive benefits that outweigh its sacrifices. Successful cooperation depends on a high degree of altruism and a true sense of the common good. The tension between local needs and the needs of the consortium underlies all cooperative collection development ventures.

Most of the professional literature on synergistic or coordinated collection development and management focuses on academic and research libraries. Public libraries, unless they are large research and reference libraries like the New York Public Library and Boston Public Library, are less likely to be interested in the expensive scientific, technical, and medical journals; major retrospective microform sets; and academic indexes and abstracting tools that have been the focus of much cooperative collection development. This is changing as all libraries' budgets are constrained and as interest in cost-effective access to electronic resources increases. Statewide and regional consortia for libraries of all types are acquiring electronic resources for shared access at discounted prices.

Coordinated collection development and management can benefit school library media centers and public libraries. *Information Power,* published by the American Association of School Librarians and the Association for Educational Communications and Technology, recommends that school library media specialists "participate in networks that enhance access to resources located outside the school."[24] Many school library media centers are creating and joining consortia or networks, developing resource-sharing agreements, and implementing mechanisms to request and deliver materials. Formal networking between schools and public libraries is increasingly common as both face budget constraints. Such arrangements can expand the resources available to K–12 students, but school library media centers—perhaps even more than academic libraries—are constrained by the local imperative.

Cooperative collection building among schools is less likely to find diverse collections than in the past. The problem is a tendency of libraries and centers in the same region to develop very similar collections because all are aiming to collect resources that support equally similar curricula and graduation standards. However, automated and shared catalogs do make bibliographic access more feasible within school districts. Intellectual access is one important motivator for building complementary collections. Debra E. Kachel has suggested several steps that will better prepare school library media centers to engage in coordinated collection development.[25] These include individual collection assessment, individual collection development policies, and regional resource mapping. When these are in place, then school library media specialists can begin to meet and discuss options and levels of participation that are appropriate for their region and individual situations.

Cooperative Funding

A third approach to cooperative collection development relies on cooperative funding for shared purchases with agreed locations. This approach, sometimes called cooperative acquisition, depends on a pool of shared monies used to acquire less used expensive items. The items purchased are placed either in a central site or in the library with the highest anticipated local use. A still successful program in the shared purchase mode is the Center for Research Libraries (CRL).[26] Part of each library's annual membership fee goes to purchase materials that the membership agrees are important. The CRL serves as a library's library—a complementary collection to extend the resources available to the membership.

The CRL is considered the nation's oldest cooperative research library. It had nearly 200 academic and research library members in 2003.[27] The CRL facility in Chicago houses more than 5.6 million volumes of unique, rarely held, primary research materials. CRL members pool their resources to acquire, store, and preserve materials that would otherwise be too costly for a single institution. As a result of these efforts, the average CRL member has gained access to a million new volumes over the last decade for a cost of $.23 a volume.[28] The CRL has very clear objectives and a long history of leveraging investments to provide a collection of resources that no one library can afford on its own.

Coordinated Weeding and Retention

A fourth approach to cooperation is coordinated weeding and retention. These agreements seek to reduce the costs of maintaining collections by distributing responsibilities and sharing costs. Efforts to achieve space economies through cooperative storage facilities have the longest history. The New England Depository Library, founded in 1942, is the oldest cooperative storage facility in the United States. The CRL has a depository storage function as one of its major reasons for existence. In addition to housing cooperative purchases, member libraries place less used materials from their own collections in the central storage building.

Consortia and Electronic Resources

Collaborating in the acquisition of electronic resources, the most recent cooperative activity, has expanded rapidly among all types of libraries. Sometimes called consortial cost sharing or buying clubs, these are one of most successful areas of cooperation.[29] Barbara McFadden Allen reported that the CIC libraries realized more than $1 million in cost savings (paying less for resources they were already buying) and cost avoidance (mounting data at one site rather than at all member libraries) in their first two years of collaborative acquisitions of electronic resources.[30] By March 2002, the CIC reported savings in excess of $15.5 million through consortial licensing and purchasing of e-resources.[31] Libraries that have not previously engaged in formal cooperative agreements are joining multiple organizations to gain savings and greater power in contract negotiations with suppliers or electronic information resources. When assured of a certain number of purchasers, vendors frequently will offer discounted pricing. Libraries are leveraging investments through reductions in resource costs. This can be seen as cost avoidance because the library spends more than if it acquired nothing but less than if it paid the full price charged individual libraries. Some cost reductions also may accrue if a library decides to cancel print and microform resources that duplicate the electronic resource. Other savings gained by working through a consortia can result from having a centralized staff to manage the information and computer resources and to negotiate and administer the contracts. Another form of consortial sharing of electronic resources is to cooperate in the joint production, maintenance, and distribution of electronic texts.

The role of consortia in acquiring electronic resources and access continues to expand. A potent illustration of this is the International Coalition of Library Consortia (ICOLC), organized in 1997.[32] This informal group has a membership of more than 135 library consortia in several countries. Representatives from the various consortia, which primarily represent higher education institutions, meet twice a year with electronic resource providers and vendors to discuss new offerings, pricing practices, and contractual issues. Barbara McFadden Allen and Arnold Hirshon have called ICOLC "a reverse cartel because these independent consortia come together not to limit competition or fix prices, but to leverage their collection power to open up the market."[33] In 1998, ICOLC released its "Statement of Current Perspective and Preferred Practices for the Selection and Purchase of Electronic Information," which sought to establish an international perspective on consortial licensing and cooperative purchasing of electronic information by libraries.[34]

Libraries are cooperating to provide better access to free Internet resources. HealthWeb is a collaborative project of the health sciences libraries of the Greater Midwest Region of the National Network of Libraries of Medicine and those of the Committee for Institutional Cooperation.[35] The HealthWeb project, established in 1994, works cooperatively to provide organized access to evaluated noncommercial, health-related, Internet-accessible resources. Libraries contributing to the HealthWeb choose subject areas, identify and evaluate resources, and keep their respective areas up-to-date. Another example is maintained by sixteen public libraries in the Outagamie Waupaca Library system in northeastern Wisconsin.[36] Their goal is to create and maintain a selective list of quality Internet resources and guides in a format that extends beyond traditional indexes. "Cooler by the Lake: Northeast Wisconsin Librarians' Field Guide to the Web" was open for access in October 1999.[37] Both these projects avoid duplicating effort through cooperation in the selection and maintenance of Internet-based information resources.

Additional Areas of Cooperation

Other cooperative initiatives directly related to cooperative collection development and management are library automation, cataloging, and preservation. Many libraries, particularly smaller libraries, have joined together in shared library automation projects to save money through the implementation of a single system and to provide easy bibliographic access to holdings in all participating libraries. Some cooperative initiatives distribute responsibility for cataloging materials according to language or subject. This often goes along with distributed responsibility for acquiring those materials because intellectual access is an essential component of cooperative collection building. For example, a library that accepts an obligation for acquiring Korean materials also will agree to provide the specialized cataloging necessary to add those materials in a timely manner to an accessible catalog.

The costly process of preserving print publications through microfilming has led to several cooperative projects. Among ARL member libraries, preservation agreements are the second most common form of collaboration.[38] Primarily funded through National Endowment for the Humanities (NEH) grants, these projects seek to develop a national collection of preserved documents while meeting agreed-upon archival standards for quality and storage. Since the 1980s, both RLG and CIC have coordinated several projects that have filmed many thousands of volumes. The United States Agricultural Information Network and the National Agricultural Library have coordinated a project that began in the early 1990s and, through a series of NEH grants, is microfilming important agricultural publications on a state-by-state basis. The Library of Congress and the NEH are directing the United States Newspaper Program, a cooperative national effort to locate, catalog, preserve on microfilm, and make available to researchers newspapers published in the United States from the eighteenth century to the present.[39]

RLG, one of the most ambitious and energetic efforts to create a national cooperative library initiative, was formed in 1973 by Harvard University, Yale University, Columbia University, and the New York Public Library. RLG's goal was to provide the three components of resource sharing: physical access through a good delivery system and reciprocal borrowing privileges, a shared online catalog of bibliographic records to facilitate coordinated acquisitions and resource sharing, and a program of coordinated collection building. A statement issued by the original membership stated they had "formed a partnership to achieve planned, coordinated interdependence in response to the threat posed by a climate of increasing economic restraint and financial uncertainty."[40]

Though Harvard withdrew from the partnership, RLG membership has expanded to include many major academic and research libraries in the United States and abroad. Several RLG programs and projects have had significant success. Among these are RLIN (the Research Library Information Network, a union database of bibliographic records and holdings), the RLG ILL system, and cooperative preservation projects.

Cooperative collection development was the focus of RLG's Collection Management and Development Committee (CMDC). The CMDC began with the realization that knowing the strengths, depth, and breadth of each library's collection was a first step toward coordination. To this end, the CMDC developed the RLG Conspectus, a systematic analysis and assessment tool using the Library of Congress classification scheme and a common language to describe collections. The conspectus has been modified by other groups, such as WLN, and applied internationally to all types of libraries.

Consortia as Vehicles for Cooperative Collection Development

Several mechanisms exist through which libraries manage cooperative activities. The terms *networks* and *consortia* are often used interchangeably. The *Guide to Cooperative Collection Development* provides the following definitions.[41] A consortium is "a community of two or more libraries that have formally agreed to coordinate, cooperate in, or consolidate certain functions. Consortia may be formed on a geographic, function, type, format, or subject basis." A network is "the linking of libraries through shared bibliographic utilities or other formal arrangements." James J. Koop calls the large member-driven bibliographic utilities such as OCLC and the RLG "megaconsortia."[42] Factors that affect organizational patterns include characteristics of individual members, administration of the program, kinds of cooperative activity, and sources of funding. Funding may be through membership fees or contributions, grants, external funds (for example, via an annual allocation from state government), or a combination of these. Cooperating libraries may have a centralized or decentralized administrative structure. The source of funds often determines the kind of administrative structure. The common feature of both consortia and networks is the use of formal agreements that provide operating principles and, usually, define the goals of the organization.[43]

The number of library consortia has grown rapidly since the mid-1960s. A major impetus behind this growth was the spread of library automation and the resulting development of shared bibliographic databases. Ninety-six academic library consortia were established just between 1966 and 1970.[44] The *American Library Directory, 2002–2003* listed more than 480 networks, consortia, and other cooperative library organizations in the United States and Canada.[45] Formal cooperative collection management relationships with other libraries may be local, statewide, regional, national, or international. They may be limited by type of library or be multitype. Many libraries belong to more than one network and consortium. For example, the University of Minnesota/Twin Cities Libraries belong to the RLG, OCLC, the CIC, the CRL, and the regional MINITEX Library Information Network.

State Cooperative Programs

Several states have effective cooperative collection development programs; a representative sampling are described here. California is the site of a long-term collaborative collection management agreement among eight libraries of the University of California (UC) system and Stanford University. A shared acquisitions program, SCAP (Shared Collections and Access Program), began in the mid-1970s. SCAP has used a central pool of funds to acquire resources and avoid duplication. It began with the purchase of microform sets and now funds the last copy of selected journal titles.

The UC system has a shared catalog, MELVYL; a shared large purchase program; shared regional storage facilities; and one of the largest and most successful cooperative projects to address digital content. The California Digital Library, established in 1997, is a collaborative effort of the ten UC campuses and is housed at the UC Office of the President.[46] It is charged with licensing and acquiring shared electronic content, developing systems and technology to enhance shared collections, and transforming the process of scholarly communication. Several projects involve collaboration with other California universities and organizations.

ILLINET, in Illinois, is more broadly based than the California programs described above.[47] ILLINET links more than 2,500 member libraries in a statewide, multitype library resource-sharing network of public, academic, and special libraries. It has a shared circulation system, statewide delivery system, and statewide online public access catalog; collaborates in purchasing electronic resources; and uses grants to support acquisition of materials too costly or too esoteric for a single institution to purchase. Patrons can directly request monographic titles to be delivered to their home library from any other participating library in the system. Working with the Illinois State Library and the Illinois Board of Higher Education, the Cooperative Collection Management Coordinating Committee awards state funds in the form of grants for purchase of titles endorsed by the committee. The program fosters the concept of a statewide collection and has been successful in pursuing collection building in a cooperative environment.

OhioLINK is a statewide network of more than seventy Ohio college, technical school, and university libraries and the State Library of Ohio.[48] Participants use a single vendor-based, linked automated system and share their collections. The system supports the submission of unmediated patron borrowing requests; provides access to numerous indexes, abstracting sources, research databases, and full-text electronic journals; and has a forty-eight-hour document delivery system.

Overcoming Barriers to Cooperative Collection Development

The persistent problem thwarting formal cooperative collection development is a continuing tension between local priorities and the priorities of the larger group seeking to cooperate. This tension, which has defined the history of library cooperation, has several components. At its simplest, the library's obligation to provide materials to meet present and local needs is a more powerful force than any external agreement to acquire materials to meet the needs of unknown, remote users. One source of this tension is the reality that every library serves a local community, which may be a higher education institution, local citizens and governing body, school students, partners in a legal firm, hospital staff members, and so forth. Any cooperative program that requires a library to buy materials needed at another library at the expense of materials needed locally will fail. As entities accountable to their local communities and parent agencies and institutions, libraries must have a clear understanding of their institutional mission and be able to explain how resources are being used to meet the community's needs and desires. The challenge of balancing local priorities and group commitments plagues every cooperative development initiative, but it must be managed if the initiative is to succeed.

Desire for Local Autonomy

Librarians, since the beginning of collection building, have seen meeting current and future community needs rapidly and effectively as their goal. This has resulted in tremendous pride in being able to do so in a self-sufficient manner. This tradition of a strong local collection of resources has been a defining characteristic of librarianship for centuries. Martin Runkle suggested this is fueled by "the major role of property in our social and legal system."[49] The dominant culture in the United States places tremendous value on ownership. In a material culture, the size of the local collection is a persistent measure of success. Many organizations, such as the ARL, are seeking supplemental measures of library success, yet the need for local ownership with its implications of control and independence remains a potent force against cooperation.

The desire for independence and local autonomy is as powerful a force as the value associated with holding large collections. Branin suggested that cooperative collection development has had problems in the United States because of a long and deep-rooted tradition of local autonomy.[50] Although cooperation and collaboration are considered good in the abstract, individual libraries' desire to be self-sufficient creates resistance to what is perceived as losing control. Consortia often stumble over the organizational and administrative aspects of establishing themselves. Branin has stated that "cooperative collection development is at its most basic level a political, not a technical issue."[51]

Professional Pride

The culture of collection development and the feeling that the role of every selector is to build the most complete collection possible also pulls against cooperation. This form of turf professionalism leads subject specialists in research libraries to see themselves as developing competing collections rather than cooperating to build a shared resource. A major challenge facing cooperative collection development is to change these selection virtues of the past. Pride among all types of librarians continues to focus on the quality of the local collection rather than the quality of the consortial or regional collections. A spirit of interdependence and trust among collection development librarians is a key element in successful cooperative collection development.

Attitudes of faculty members at academic institutions are equally constrained by the belief that large local collections equal academic status and prestige. Faculty fear that reductions in local collection growth, regardless of the wealth of resources readily available, will reduce their own program's reputation and negatively affect decisions about accreditation, joining the department, and faculty retention, promotion, and tenure. Local ownership of extremely expensive, esoteric items is a point of pride and prestige—even when such items are infrequently used. Changing faculty perceptions and expectations about the benefits of cooperative collection development remains a challenge as long as extensive local collections continue to hold such symbolic status. Nevertheless, library users who appreciate and have confidence in the mutual benefits that can result from cooperation are essential for success.

Additional Barriers to Success

Money remains a major barrier to successful cooperation. When funds are limited, priorities tend to be internal. However, the serials crisis, resulting cancellations, and the inevitability of depending on others have increased interest in formal cooperation even while making it difficult. Libraries participating in cooperative initiatives are concerned about financial parity. Financial commitments must be fair to all participants. This may be represented in a sliding scale of membership fees and equitable distribution of local financial commitments.

Another potential cause of the failure of cooperative initiatives lies within the library's own organization. Librarians often are unable to transcend organizational divisions and overcome communication barriers within their own libraries. If selection activities are too decentralized, they occur in isolation, and efforts at cooperative policymaking will not succeed. If coordinating selection activities within a library is difficult, coordinating with external partners is more so. Technical services, reference services, preservation activities, and ILL operations all must be aware of and support cooperative commitments and endeavors. If the library does not have a supportive internal organizational structure and clear authority for collection development, cooperation with other libraries is nearly impossible.

Lack of support and commitment from governing boards and administrators both within and external to the library can be a large problem. Strong leadership and constant support throughout the organization are important. The CIC is an example of a consortia that benefits from strong institutional support. The members of the governing committee are the chief academic officers from each of the twelve member universities. CIC programs and activities extend to all aspects of university activity except intercollegiate athletics. The Center for Library Initiatives is one of several cooperating ventures under the CIC umbrella, all of which are strongly supported by university administrators.

Once libraries make a commitment to build collections collaboratively, they must have a clear understanding of what they hold locally and a common way to assess and compare collections. Lack of knowledge of and training in collection assessment and evaluation and the absence of shared tools can stymie cooperation. Two comparative assessment tools frequently used are shelf list measurements, the North American Title Count being the primary example, and the conspectus.

Failure in advancing cooperative collection development often results from problems with the consortial governance structure. Many programs lack an effective organization, formally recognized governing structure, clear goals, or sufficient authority to make decisions. A competent, strong consortia leader or administrator is equally important. All formal agreements and commitments must be flexible and permit modification. Lack of clarity and inadequate understanding among partners of the shared goals and intentions of the consortia cause difficulties. The consortia must have a reliable communication system to quickly and widely share decisions and alterations in policy that members make. E-mail, electronic discussion lists, and consortial web sites have lessened some of these communication barriers, especially between individual selectors.

Dissatisfaction with the results of cooperation among library staff members and users creates difficulties. The absence of significant, observable accomplishments leads to self-defeating behaviors. Without some successes, momentum for progress is lacking. Thus, participants in cooperative collection development programs need a process for quantifying the cost benefits of cooperation and of regularly comparing the benefits of cooperation with those of independence.[52] Everyone must understand the consequences of ignoring consortial commitments. Documenting the benefits of cooperation and the results of failing to cooperate are powerful incentives.

Any difficulties in providing physical access to remote materials are a barrier to cooperative collection development. Users want speedy delivery of high-quality resources. To succeed, a consortia needs dependable mechanisms for affordable, timely, efficient, and effective delivery of resources.

Intellectual access to items among cooperating libraries is essential. Once a primary barrier to cooperative collection development, it has been increased significantly by evolving technologies and the widespread adoption of online catalogs. The Internet often provides interconnectivity to library catalogs in a consortia for both users and selectors. Advances in technology are making it possible for users to take direct responsibility for locating and requesting both returnables and nonreturnables. Selectors can more easily check holdings at other institutions, increasing the potential for title-by-title cooperative collection development.

Enlightened self-interest of each institution in the consortia may be the most important element leading toward success. Inculcating cooperation as a core value within the library will foster a willingness to make sacrifices and a belief that benefits will accrue. Success depends on a high degree of altruism and respect for and recognition of the value of increased collaboration. Clear goals for cooperation, institutional and administrative commitment to it, recognition of its value, and trust among the partners must be understood by all. For cooperation to succeed, it must be considered a routine part of all work in the library.

Whither Cooperation?

Bentley wrote, "Whither collaborative collection development? We will continue to pay lip service to cooperation, and we will continue to cooperate at the rather modest levels we do now, but I doubt that its future is any brighter than its past."[53] More optimistic librarians say that formal library cooperation is moving toward a brighter future. Michael Gorman wrote that "Resource sharing has two bases: the effectiveness of technology and the need to cooperate. . . . I think that we are, like it or not, entering a Golden Age of Cooperation because (1) the technology to link libraries and to make the users of one library aware of the collections of others is available and getting better all the time, and (2) economics are forcing us to cooperation."[54]

One possible approach to understanding the development and future of consortia and networks is to apply Bruce W. Tuckman's theory of small group behavior.[55] Tuckman contends that groups move through four stages over their existence. The first stage, forming, is one of discovery and testing. The group members are seeking to orient themselves within the groups and to understand and establish the situation. Group members focus on testing the group and other members and focus on answering the question "Why are we here?" The second stage, storming, is characterized by conflict, emotionality, and anxiety. The members feel threatened and resist the group and individuals within it. Members exhibit hostility toward each other, dissatisfaction with the group's accomplishments, and frustration over its failures. They resist the group and struggle to be independent. The phrase typical of the storming stage is "I want to have my say." During the third stage, norming, the group develops a feeling of cohesiveness and resistance fades. New standards evolve and new roles are adopted. Group members exchange opinions and begin to trust each other. The group begins to focus on action, and the descriptive phrase is "Let's do it!" The final stage, performing, is the one in which functional roles, a solution, and positive interdependence emerge. The energy of the group is channeled into the task. Structural issues have been resolved, and the structure becomes supportive of task performance.

Library consortia are moving back and forth between the storming and norming stages, with some movement toward performing. Consortia members are both frustrated at their failures and beginning to see and celebrate some successes. They are beginning to trust each other, to sort through their roles, and to recognize and honor their obligations. Most consortia still struggle between the need to be independent and the need to depend on the consortia to help solve problems. External forces, beyond the long-held belief of librarians that cooperation is a good thing, are providing the primary push to move consortia toward the performing stage.

Movement toward Cooperation

The forces pushing toward increased cooperation are, in large part, economic. Administrators and funding bodies tend to perceive libraries as a "bottomless pit." Peter T. Flawn, a former university president, wrote, "The university library is a bottomless pit that can absorb all the funds there are: no institution has enough money to maintain and operate a library that is satisfactory to the faculty."[56] The view is shared by those responsible for the budgets of public libraries, school libraries, and special libraries. The consequences of insufficient collection funds are collections with a narrower range, less richness and depth, and a more homogenous nature. Only cooperation can make a broader range of materials available. In addition, libraries working together can often secure reduced group purchase prices for electronic information that are lower than that which a single institution can obtain.

Other forces pushing toward cooperation can be traced to changes in information access and delivery. These include rapid expansion of the Web, rapid growth in information technology capabilities, disaggregation of electronic resources, changes in pricing structures, changes in the scholarly communication chain, and direct marketing of information to end users. In addition, publisher efforts to change copyright and intellectual property laws in the electronic environment are affecting pricing and service practices. Libraries, working together, are better positioned to influence producers and providers of electronic information.

Social and political pressure for parity of access to library materials, especially in rural areas, are leading funding bodies to look favorably on cooperative ventures. Cooperative ventures in several states, such as Ohio, Minnesota, and Georgia, are being funded at the state level—either through statewide academic initiatives or through projects that provide electronic resources to libraries of all types. State legislatures are finding the appropriation of new funds for statewide access to electronic resources through a central provider a more attractive option than funding several smaller agencies. Providing a common good continues to resonate with public funding agencies.

Access and Ownership

Since the 1980s, the profession has given much attention to what is known as the "access versus ownership" debate. This phrase describes the choice between deciding what to own locally and what to access remotely. Gay Dannelly called access versus ownership the primary paradox facing the profession in 1995 and it remains a continuing concern.[57] Sheila S. Intner defines access as "the temporary availability of materials without permanent ownership."[58] It covers leases and licenses to access electronically transmitted materials, commercial document delivery services, and ILL. Ownership is "the permanent addition of materials to a library's collections."[59] Access continues to increase in importance. The 1993 National Interlibrary Loan Code recognized the increased use and important role of ILL by changing the statement "Interlibrary loan is an adjunct to, not a substitute for, collection development" to "Interlibrary borrowing is an integral element of collection development for all libraries, not an ancillary option."[60]

"Access versus ownership" is frequently paired with a business phrase describing a means of inventory control called "just-in-time." The goal of just-in-time inventory management is to reduce the use of buffer inventories and to synchronize the movement of materials through the production process so that materials are delivered only just before they are needed. "Just-in-case" is the opposite of just-in-time and means that large inventories of production materials are held on-site so they are always on hand whenever they are needed. Manufacturing businesses have found that reducing the size of inventories decreases costs by reducing the need for large warehouses and staff to manage the inventory and reducing the investment sunk into inventory waiting in warehouses until needed. To be successful, the just-in-case strategy depends on rapid delivery of the needed part. A library can be said to follow a just-in-time approach when it acquires either though purchase or loan materials its users need when they need them and does not invest all or large portions of its materials budget in acquiring collections just-in-case users will need them at some future time.

Quality of Access

Ross Atkinson explained the quality of access—how well access is provided or achieved—in terms of time.[61] Users want speedy access to library resources because the user's time is a valuable commodity. Atkinson wrote, "Access time always is at least partially a function of space. Because the transportation of paper publications requires considerable time, value can be added to paper publications (i.e., their utility can be enhanced) by increasing their proximity to the potential users. This goal of proximity is achieved mainly through ownership—the library buys the publication to reduce the space between the user and the medium of information."[62] Librarians choose, as best they can, between spending money now to save the users' time in the future, realizing that some items acquired now may never be used, or spending money to meet users' needs at the time of need, realizing that most materials obtained just-in-time do not become part of the collection. Though the current trend is to see access and ownership as opposites, they are points on the same continuum of resources and information provision.[63]

The driving force on the access-ownership continuum over the last twenty years has been escalating serials costs. Libraries have had no choice but to rely on holdings elsewhere for at least part of their users' needs.[64] Many libraries moving toward the access end of the continuum for portions of the journal collection have turned to commercial document delivery services for some of their needs and also to ensure the speediest possible delivery. Most commercial services are similar and deliver journal articles via mail, fax, or the Internet for a per-item fee, which includes copyright charges.

Commercial suppliers are attractive because they usually provide a faster delivery time than ILL, ease of ordering, choice of delivery methods, and convenient invoicing and handle payment of copyright fees automatically. A survey of ARL libraries published in 1994 found that 87 percent of the ninety responding libraries were using commercial document suppliers to supply some of the materials they did not own.[65] Commercial document delivery services are not without problems. They cannot supply everything requested. Mary Jackson reported in 1995 that document delivery suppliers were able to supply less than half of a typical ILL department's photocopy requests.[66] Additional problems cited are lack of responsiveness, failure to meet promised turnaround time, and sometimes hefty charges.

Despite the proliferation of commercial document delivery services, libraries continue to rely on ILL for returnables and for many journal articles. ILL partners seldom charge each other, and when they do, the costs are much less than those charged by commercial services. Technological advances, including access to online catalogs, online ILL requesting services through the bibliographic utilities, and direct patron requests, are increasing the amount of ILL activity.

Cost-Effectiveness

The challenge is deciding when it is more cost-effective to own a journal in print format or in electronic format, to borrow articles through ILL, or to purchase them from commercial document delivery sources. Much of the research since the early 1990s has focused on alternatives for print journal subscriptions. Louisiana State University, in a study reported in 1997, found that commercial document delivery was more economical for high-cost, low-use journals than local subscriptions and that users accepted the service when it met promised expectations, including twenty-four-hour turnaround.[67]

In 1991 and 1992, Columbia University libraries compared costs for ownership with what it would cost to borrow or use commercial document delivery.[68] The study analyzed more than 15,000 requests from users in the biology, physics, and electrical engineering departments. Most books and periodical titles were requested only once during the study. The study found that the costs of owning a monograph used only once far exceeded the costs for accessing it through ILL. The study also confirmed that it was less expensive to access an article on demand than to subscribe to the journal. However, when ten or more articles were requested from an individual title, the costs were almost equal. The importance to researchers of browsing new periodical issues was also noted as a nonmeasurable, yet significant issue.

A cost-benefit analysis, which will help a library determine what is fiscally responsible, must consider several factors, many of which present problems when assigning a dollar value. The fixed cost of a journal subscription includes processing, binding, storing, reshelving, and the annual subscription price. Staff costs in the borrowing library must account for the cost to process the request (whether via ILL or commercial document delivery) and to process the item when it is received. The library pays a fee to the commercial document delivery service and, in some instances, for ILL. Additional cost components, such as equipment and its depreciation and telecommunication charges, might logically be part of an analysis. Unmediated patron requests can reduce library staff processing costs, especially when the item is delivered directly to the patron. Some libraries pass the costs for both ILL and commercial services to the patron.

Even harder to determine is the value of the patron's time. If the item is held locally, the patron must locate it and then, usually, make a photocopy—with associated costs. Against this is weighed the time the patron would spend filling out a request form for either ILL or document delivery and waiting for the item. Patron satisfaction or utility cost is equally difficult to assess. Economists use *utility* as a measure or expression of an individual's expected or anticipated satisfaction. Ideally, one would contrast the utility of on-site patron access, in which the patron has speedy access and does the retrieval personally, and ILL or commercial document delivery, in which the work is transferred to staff, access takes longer, and fees may be charged. Determining the opportunity cost (the true cost of choosing one alternative over another) to patrons is nearly impossible.

The advent of full-text electronic journals has raised new questions about access. Resource sharing is restricted in ways not experienced in a print environment. Many licenses and contracts to access electronic resources prohibit ILL. Libraries that relied on partners for some journals may find they can no longer request articles via ILL if the lending library has moved to an electronic version. Shared responsibility for retrospective holdings may not be viable in the electronic environment. Many electronic sources are available only for lease, and the library retains no back files when the title is canceled. That library then must turn to others for older requests, which will likely become more difficult and more costly to fill.

Even when a library secures a contract that provides access to back files in perpetuity, questions remain about the extent to which these back files will be maintained. Other questions remain unanswered. Will local collections and cooperative collection development diminish in significance as networked electronic resources become more common? Will consortial purchases to the same electronic resources further diminish collection diversity? Will publishers move toward fewer, more costly articles and "pay as you go" pricing models and force libraries away from any form of resource sharing? Ross Atkinson has written, "It is impossible to determine with any precision how the availability of increasing quantities of information online ultimately will affect information services in general or collection development in particular."[69]

Summary

Cooperative collection development needs three components to succeed. These are efficient resource sharing, easy bibliographic access to collections elsewhere, and coordinated collection development and management. Resource sharing was the first form of library cooperation. Escalating materials costs combined with budget constraints and increasing volume in publication are leading libraries to depend more on others to meet user needs and expectations. Library automation and the resulting ease of searching other catalogs have facilitated awareness of holdings elsewhere. Cooperative, coordinated collection development and management remains the greatest stumbling block because of the tension between local priorities and those of the larger group with whom cooperation is sought.

Cooperative collection building and maintenance can take several forms. The status quo approach assumes coordination and comprehensive coverage will just happen. In the synergistic approach, different libraries take responsibility for collecting in different areas according to a coordinated and collaborative plan. Cooperative funding is used for shared purchases in agreed-upon locations.

Coordinated weeding and retention mean that different libraries take responsibility for continuing to hold materials in different subjects or in different formats. Many libraries are participating in cooperative ventures to secure acquisition of and access to electronic resources at group discounted prices. Library cooperation also can apply to shared automation, cataloging, and preservation activities.

Consortia and networks are the primary vehicles for cooperation and range from two or three libraries with geographic proximity to multitype state ventures to national and international networks with hundreds of members. The most successful networks share bibliographic access, some mechanism to facilitate sharing of resources, and some degree of coordinated collection development and management. Several forces foster a successful consortia. These include a belief in and commitment to cooperation by local administrators and library staffs, equitable fees, clear understanding of local holdings and local needs, and effective consortial governance. Flexibility and responsiveness to local collection development needs are key to success.

Cooperative ventures have grown as the ability to build on-site collections has declined. Libraries struggle with making cost-effective decisions about their position on the access-ownership continuum. Analyzing the costs and the benefits for various approaches for providing materials remains a challenge and is further complicated by the availability of electronic resources. Restrictive licenses and contracts that prohibit resource sharing and lack of confidence in the future access to retrospective files cloud the future of cooperative collection development and management.

Nevertheless, most libraries have little choice but to cooperate. As libraries reduce acquisitions, they must rely on other libraries for critical materials that they do not have. To ensure access, they must work together to ensure that those materials will be available in a timely manner. Librarians will be forced to coordinate local collection building with regional and national cooperative collection development programs to guarantee that access to comprehensive national collections is maintained. Libraries will increase their participation in consortia and partner with local, statewide, regional, and national groups of libraries both to assign collecting and preserving responsibilities and to obtain buying group discounts for electronic resources. Cooperative collection development will attain its promise.

❚ CASE STUDY ❚

Arcadia College, located in New England, is a four-year liberal arts college with 1,300 students and 135 faculty members, 85 percent of whom have doctorates. Students must meet distribution requirements in science and math, social science, humanities, and the arts. More than half the students major in a science, and 75 percent of the students go on to graduate school. All students are required to write a senior thesis, which they develop as a independent study project with their faculty advisors. The Arcadia College library participates in ColCon, a regional consortia of eight other small colleges, one of which—Profundia—is located in the same town as Arcadia. Until now, the consortia has focused its activities on a shared online catalog and a daily delivery system. Arcadia students may check materials out from any of the other eight college libraries. Residents of the town in which Arcadia is located may use the college library and borrow items with their local public library card. The state's public university supplies, via ILL, most items not held by one of the nine colleges. Kevin Bleaker is Arcadia's collections librarian. The Arcadia library continues to receive a 3 percent annual increase for its collections.

Activity

What should be Kevin's top priority for cooperative initiatives in the next year? Why is this important? What steps should Kevin undertake to move this forward? What resources are needed? What should be the top three issues addressed by the consortia in the next three to five years and why? What five factors will most affect this consortia in the next five years? Explain why. What external factors do you think will most affect consortia in the next five years? Explain why.

REFERENCES

1. David H. Stam, "Think Globally, Act Locally: Collection Development and Resource Sharing," *Collection Building* 5 (spring 1983): 21.
2. Melvil Dewey, *Library Notes* 1 (June 1886): 5.
3. Michael Gorman, "Laying Siege to the 'Fortress Library,'" *American Libraries* 17 (May 1986): 325.
4. Joseph J. Branin, "Cooperative Collection Development," in *Collection Management: A New Treatise,* ed. Charles B. Osburn and Ross Atkinson (Greenwich, Conn.: JAI Pr., 1991), 82.
5. John R. Kaiser, "Resource Sharing in Collection Development," in *Collection Development in Libraries: A Treatise,* ed. Robert D. Stueart and George B. Miller Jr. (Greenwich, Conn.: JAI Pr., 1980), 139–57.
6. John Fetterman, "Resource Sharing in Libraries—Why, How, When, Next Steps?" in *Resource Sharing in Libraries,* ed. Allen Kent (New York: Marcel Dekker, 1974), 3.
7. Ernest C. Richardson, "Co-operation in Lending among College and Reference Libraries," *Library Journal* 24, no. 7 (July 1999): 32–33.
8. Ibid.
9. Assn. of Research Libraries, "Services Trends in ARL Libraries, 1991–2002," available at http://www.arl.org/stats/arlstat/graphs/2002/2002t1.html.
10. Bart Harloe, ed., *Guide to Cooperative Collection Development,* Collection Management and Development Guides, no. 6 (Chicago: American Library Assn., 1994).
11. Branin, "Cooperative Collection Development," 81.
12. Christy Hightower and George J. Soete, "The Consortium as Learning Organization: Twelve Steps to Success in Collaborative Collections Projects," *Journal of Academic Librarianship* 21, no. 2 (1995): 87–91.
13. Dan C. Hazen, "Cooperative Collection Development: Compelling Theory, Inconsequential Results?" in *Collection Management for the Twenty-first Century: A Handbook for Librarians,* ed. G. E. Gorman and Ruth H. Miller, 263–83 (Westport, Conn.: Greenwood, 1997).
14. Stella Bentley, "New Collections for Old, " in *Recreating the Academic Library: Breaking Virtual Ground,* ed. Cheryl LaGuardia (New York: Neal-Schuman, 1998), 129.
15. Paul H. Mosher and Marcia Pankake, "A Guide to Coordinated and Cooperative Collection Development," *Library Resources and Technical Services* 27, no. 4 (1983): 425.
16. Ross Atkinson, "Crisis and Opportunity: Reevaluating Acquisitions Budgeting in an Age of Transition," *Journal of Library Administration* 19, no. 2 (1993): 38.
17. Edward Shreeves, "Is There a Future for Cooperative Collection Development in the Digital Age?" *Library Trends* 45, no. 3 (winter 1997): 376.
18. Charles B. Osburn, "Collection Development and Management," in *Academic Libraries: Research Perspectives,* ed. Mary Jo Lynch, ACRL Publications in Librarianship, no. 47 (Chicago: American Library Assn., 1990), 16.
19. Ross Atkinson, "Old Forms, New Forms: The Challenge of Collection Development," *College and Research Libraries* 50 (Sept. 1989): 508.
20. Stam, "Think Globally, Act Locally," 21.

21. Patricia Buck Dominguez and Luke Swindler, "Cooperative Collection Development at the Research Triangle University Libraries, a Model for the Nation," *College and Research Libraries* 54, no. 6 (Nov. 1993): 470–96.
22. Ibid., 470.
23. Hendrick Edelman, "The Death of the Farmington Plan," *Library Journal* 98, no. 9 (April 15, 1973): 1251–53. *See also A History of the Farmington Plan*, by Ralph D. Wagner (Lanham, Md.: Scarecrow, 2002).
24. American Assn. of School Librarians and Assn. for Educational Communications and Technology, *Information Power: Guidelines for School Library Media Programs* (Chicago: American Library Assn.; Washington, D.C.: Assn. for Educational Communications and Technology, 1988), 1.
25. Debra E. Kachel, "Look Inward before Looking Outward: Preparing the School Library Media Center for Cooperative Collection Development," *School Library Media Quarterly* 23 (winter 1995): 101–13.
26. *See* Donald B. Simpson, "Economics of Cooperative Collection Development and Management: The United States' Experience with Rarely Held Research Materials," *IFLA Journal* 24, no. 3 (1998): 161–65; and Gay N. Dannelly, "The Center for Research Libraries and Cooperative Collection Development: Partnerships in Progress," in *Cooperative Collection Development: Significant Trends and Issues,* ed. Donald B. Simpson (New York: Haworth, 1998), 37–45.
27. Center for Research Libraries [WWW home page of the Center for Research Libraries]. Available [Online]: http://wwwcrl.uchicago.edu.
28. Milton T. Wolf and Marjorie E. Bloss, "Without Walls Means Collaboration," *Information Technology and Libraries* 17, no. 4 (Dec. 1998): 214.
29. George J. Soete, comp., *Collaborative Collections Management Programs in ARL Libraries,* SPEC Kit, no. 235 (Washington, D.C.: Assn. of Research Libraries, 1998).
30. Barbara McFadden Allen, "Negotiating Digital Information System Licenses without Losing Your Shirt or Your Soul," in *Economics of Digital Information: Collection, Storage and Delivery,* ed. Sul H. Lee (New York: Hayworth, 1997), 17.
31. CLI Consortial Agreement Program [WWW home page for the Committee on Institutional Cooperation, Center for Library Initiatives Consortial Agreement Program]. Available [Online]: http://www.cic.uiuc.edu/programs/CLIConsortialAgreementProgram/index.shtml.
32. International Coalition of Library Consortia [WWW home page of ICOLC]. Available [Online]: http://www.library.yale.edu/consortia/.
33. Barbara McFadden Allen and Arnold Hirshon, "Hanging Together to Avoid Hanging Separately: Opportunities for Academic Libraries and Consortia," *Information Technology and Libraries* 17, no. 1 (March 1998): 40.
34. International Coalition of Library Consortia, "Statement of Current Perspective and Preferred Practices for the Selection and Purchase of Electronic Information" (1998), available at http://www.library.yale.edu/consortia/statement.html. This was updated in December 2001, with "Statement of Current Perspective and Preferred Practices for the Selection and Purchase of Electronic Information: Update No. 1: New Developments In E-Journal Licensing (December 2001 Update to March 1998 Statement), available at http://www.library.yale.edu/consortia/2001currentpractices.htm.

35. HealthWeb [WWW home page of HealthWeb] Available [Online]: http://www.healthweb.org. *See* Patricia M. Redman et al., "Common Ground: The HealthWeb Project as a Model for Internet Collaboration," *Bulletin of the Medical Library Association* 85, no. 4 (Oct. 1997): 325–30; and Patricia M. Redman et al., "HealthWeb: A Collaborative Interinstitutional Internet Project," *Library Hi Tech* 61, no. 1 (1998): 37–44.
36. Beth Carpenter, "A Field Guide for Collaborative Collection Development," *Computers in Libraries* 20, no. 6 (June 2000): 28–33.
37. Cooler by the Lake [WWW home page of Cooler by the Lake, Northeast Wisconsin Librarians' Field Guide to the Web]. Available [Online]: http://www.cbtl.org.
38. Soete, *Collaborative Collections Management Programs in ARL Libraries,* [i].
39. United States Newspaper Program [WWW home page of the United States Newspaper Program]. Available [Online]: http://lcweb.loc.gov/preserv/usnppr.html.
40. Nancy E. Gwinn and Paul H. Mosher, "Coordinating Collection Development: The RLG Conspectus," *College and Research Libraries* 44 (1983): 128–40; *see also* David H. Stam, "Collaborative Collection Development: Progress, Problems and Potential," *Collection Building* 7, no. 3 (1985): 3–9, for an analysis of the conspectus's role in cooperative collection development.
41. Harloe, *Guide to Cooperative Collection Development,* 22, 24.
42. James J. Koop, "Library Consortia and Information Technology: The Past, the Present, the Promise," *Information Technology and Libraries* 17, no. 8 (March 1998): 8.
43. Bernie Sloan has gathered bylaws, memoranda of understanding, resource-sharing agreements, and strategic plans that address the governance and administration of library consortia and cooperatives at his "Library Consortia Documents Online," available at http://www.lis.uiuc.edu/~bsloan/consort.htm.
44. Carlos A. Cuadra and Ruth J. Patrick, "Survey of Academic Library Consortia in the U.S.," *College and Research Libraries* 33 (July 1972): 271–83.
45. *American Library Directory, 2002–2003,* v. 2 (Providence, R.I.: Bowker, 2002).
46. California Digital Library [WWW home page of the California Digital Library, a Co-Library of the Campuses of the University of California]. Available [Online]: http://www.cdlib.org.
47. Nancy Chipman Shlaes, "Cooperative Collection Management Succeeds in Illinois," *Resource Sharing and Information Networks* 12, no. 1 (1996): 49–53.
48. Naomi J. Goodman and Carole L. Hinchcliff, "From Crisis to Cooperation and Beyond: OhioLINK's First Ten Years," *Resource Sharing and Information Networks* 13, no. 1 (1997): 21–38.
49. Martin Runkle, "What Was the Original Mission of the Center for Research Libraries and How Has It Changed?" in *CRL's Role in the Emerging Global Resources Program, 1997 Symposium, Chicago, Illinois, April 25, 1997* (Chicago: Center for Research Libraries, 1997), 1–4.
50. Branin, "Cooperative Collection Development," 85.
51. Ibid., 104.
52. Atkinson, "Crisis and Opportunity," 40.
53. Bentley, "New Collections for Old," 129.

54. Michael Gorman, "The Academic Library in the Year 2001: Dream or Nightmare or Something in Between," *Journal of Academic Librarianship* 17, no. 1 (1991): 7.

55. Bruce W. Tuckman, "Development Sequence in Small Groups," *Psychological Bulletin* 63, no. 6 (1965): 384–99; and Bruce W. Tuckman and Mary Ann C. Jensen, "Stages of Small-Group Development Revisited," *Group and Organization Studies* 2, no. 4 (1977): 419–27.

56. Peter T. Flawn, *A Primer for University Presidents: Managing the Modern University* (Austin: University of Texas Press, 1990), 120.

57. Gay Dannelly, "Resource Sharing in the Electronic Era: Potentials and Paradoxes," *Library Trends* 43 (1995): 665.

58. Sheila S. Intner, "Ownership or Access? A Study of Collection Development Decision Making in Libraries," *Advances in Library Administration and Organization* 12 (1994): 5.

59. Ibid.

60. "National Interlibrary Loan Code, 1980," (adopted by the Reference and Adult Services Division Board of Directors, New York, 1980) *RQ* 20 (1980): 29; and "National Interlibrary Loan Code for the United States, 1993" (approved by the Reference and Adult Services Board of Directors, Feb. 8, 1994), *RQ* 33 (1994): 477.

61. Ross Atkinson, "Access, Ownership, and the Future of Collection Development," in *Collection Management and Development: Issues in an Electronic Era*, ed. Peggy Johnson and Bonnie MacEwan (Chicago: American Library Assn., 1993), 95.

62. Ibid.

63. Murray Martin, "The Invasion of the Library Materials Budget by Technology Serials and Databases," *Serials Review* 18 (1992): 10.

64. *See,* for example, Barbara von Wahlde, "Access vs. Ownership: A SUNY University Center Libraries Study of the Economics of Document Delivery," *Resource Sharing and Information Networks* 12, no. 2 (1997): 19–30; and Jane P. Kleiner and Charles A. Hamaker, "Libraries 2000: Transforming Libraries Using Document Delivery, Needs Assessment, and Networked Resources," *College and Research Libraries* 58, no. 4 (July 1997): 355–74.

65. Mary E. Jackson and Karen Croneis, comps., *Uses of Document Delivery Services,* SPEC Kit, no. 204 (Washington, D.C.: Assn. of Research Libraries, 1994), 1.

66. Mary Jackson, "Redesigning Interlibrary Loan and Document Delivery Services," *Wilson Library Bulletin* 69 (May 1995): 68–69+.

67. Kleiner and Hamaker, "Libraries 2000," 369.

68. Anthony W. Ferguson and Kathleen Kehoe, "Access versus Ownership: What Is More Cost-Effective in the Sciences?" *Journal of Library Administration* 19, no. 2 (1993): 89–99.

69. Atkinson, "Access, Ownership, and the Future of Collection Development," 100.

SUGGESTED READINGS

Alexander, Adrian W. "Toward 'The Perfection of Work': Library Consortia in the Digital Age." *Journal of Library Administration* 28, no. 2 (1999): 1–14.

Allen, Barbara McFadden, and Georgine N. Olson, eds. *Cooperative Collection Management: The Conspectus Approach.* New York: Neal-Schuman, 1994.

Atkinson, Ross. "Toward a Redefinition of Library Services." In *Virtually Yours: Models for Managing Electronic Resources and Services,* edited by Peggy Johnson and Bonnie MacEwan, 1–12. Chicago: American Library Assn., 1999.

Ball, David, and Jo Pye. "Library Purchasing Consortia: Their Activity and Effect on the Marketplace." In *Collection Management,* edited by G. E. Gorman, 199–220. International Yearbook of Library and Information Management, 2000/2001. London: Library Assn. Pub., 2000.

Crowe, William J. "Collection Development in the Cooperative Environment." *Journal of Library Administration* 15, no. 3/4 (1992): 37–48.

Dannelly, Gay N. "Resource Sharing in the Electronic Era: Potentials and Paradoxes." *Library Trends* 43, no. 4 (1995): 663–78.

———. "'Uneasy Lies the Head': Selecting Resources in a Consortial Setting." *Journal of Library Administration* 28, no. 2 (1999): 57–67.

Doll, Carol Ann. "School Library Media Center and Public Library Collections and the High School Curriculum." *Collection Management* 20, no. 1 (1995): 99–114.

Etschmaier, Gale, and Marifran Bustian. "Document Delivery and Collection Development: An Evolving Relationship." *Serials Librarian* 3, no. 3 (1997): 13–27.

Gossen, Eleanor A., and Suzanne Irving. "Ownership versus Access and Low-Use Periodical Titles." *Library Resources and Technical Services* 39, no. 1 (Jan. 1995): 43–52.

Higginbotham, Barbra Buckner, and Sally Bowdoin. *Access versus Assets: A Comprehensive Guide to Resource Sharing for Academic Librarians.* Chicago: American Library Assn., 1993.

Hiremath, Uma. "Electronic Consortia: Resource Sharing in the Digital Age." *Collection Building* 20, no. 2 (2001): 80–87.

Hirshon, Arnold. "Libraries, Consortia, and Change Management." *Journal of Academic Librarianship* 25, no. 2 (March 1999): 124–26.

Kachel, Debra E. "Cooperative Collection Development." In her *Collection Assessment and Management for School Libraries: Preparing for Cooperative Collection Development,* 77–92. Westport, Conn.: Greenwood, 1997.

Kane, Laura Townsend. "Access versus Ownership." In *Encyclopedia of Library and Information Science,* edited by Allen Kent, 64, Supplement 27, 1–21. New York: Marcel Dekker, 1999.

Kingma, Bruce R. "Economic Issues in Document Delivery: Access versus Ownership and Library Consortia." In *Experimentation and Collaboration: Creating Serials for a New Millennium,* edited by Charlene N. Simser and Michael A. Somers, 201–11. New York: Haworth, 1998. Also published in *The Serials Librarian,* 34, no. 1/2.

————. *The Economics of Information: A Guide to Economic and Cost-Benefit Analysis for Information Professionals.* Englewood, Colo.: Libraries Unlimited, 2001.

Landesman, Margaret, and Johann Van Reenen. "Consortia vs. Reform: Creating Congruence." *Journal of Electronic Publishing* 6, no. 2 (Dec. 2000). Also available at http://www.press.umich.edu/jep/0602/landesman.html.

Meyer, Richard. "Consortial Access versus Ownership." In *Technology and Scholarly Communication,* edited by Richard Ekman and Richard E. Quandt, 223–49. Berkeley: Univ. of California Pr., 1999.

Oder, Norman. "Consortia Hit Critical Mass." *Library Journal* 125, no. 2 (Feb. 1, 2000): 48–51.

Prabha, Chandra, and Gay N. Dannelly, issue eds. "Resource Sharing in a Changing Environment." *Library Trends* 45, no. 3 (winter 1997).

Sauer, Cynthia K. "Doing the Best We Can? The Use of Collection Development Policies and Cooperative Collecting Activities at Manuscript Repositories." *The American Archivist* 64, no. 2 (fall/winter 2001): 308–49.

Shaughnessy, Thomas W. "Resource Sharing and the End of Innocence." *Journal of Library Administration* 20, no. 1 (1994): 3–17.

Simpson, Donald B., ed. *Cooperative Collection Development: Significant Trends and Issues.* New York: Haworth, 1998. Also published in *Collection Management* 23, no. 4.

Wood, Richard J. "The Axioms, Barriers, and Components of Cooperative Collection Development." In *Collection Management for the Twenty-first Century: A Handbook for Librarians,* edited by G. E. Gorman and Ruth H. Miller, 221–48. Westport, Conn.: Greenwood, 1997.

| Collection Analysis

Evaluation and Assessment

Introduction

Collection analysis encompasses analysis of both the library's collection and its use. Analysis provides information on various aspects of the collection—for example, the number of pieces and titles in a particular subject; formats represented; age and condition of materials; breadth and depth of coverage; language in which the resources are available; and patron use and nonuse of the collection. Although librarians tend to think of collection analysis as measuring the collection's quality (an amorphous concept, at best), the real intent is to measure the collection's utility or how well it is satisfying its purpose. The library's goals and purpose, therefore, must be clearly stated before any meaningful evaluation of a library's collection can take place. Once collecting goals have been assigned to subject areas, the library can evaluate if it has been collecting at the desired level.

Collection analysis is part of the effective and efficient management of resources. It can provide information that documents how fiscal resources are being used and investments are being maintained. Increasing calls for accountability require evidence that libraries are delivering the collections and services expected on investments. In addition, collection analysis can serve as an internal control mechanism to measure individual performance. Decisions about other areas such as cooperative agreements, space limitations and needs, and ownership and access are informed through collection analysis.

Paul Mosher traces the formal evaluation of American library collections to Charles C. Jewett's 1850 report to the Smithsonian Institution, which investigated the capabilities of U.S. libraries to provide the literature for two extensive scholarly histories and found the nation's libraries deficient.[1] According to Mosher, examining the inadequacy of U.S. libraries characterized evaluation into the 1930s and 1940s, while attention turned more toward the assessment of individual collections in terms of given needs in the 1950s and 1960s.[2]

Librarians often use the terms *evaluation* and *assessment* interchangeably. They can, however, be distinguished from each other according to the intent of the analysis. The aim of assessment is to determine how well the collection supports the goals, needs, and mission of the library or parent organization. The collection (both locally held and remotely accessed materials) is assessed in the local context. Evaluation seeks to examine or describe collections either in their own terms or in relation to other collections and checking mechanisms, such as lists. Both evaluation and assessment provide a better understanding of the collection and the user community. A librarian gains information that helps him or her decide if a collection is meeting its objectives, how well it is serving its users, in which ways or areas it is deficient, and what remains to be done to develop the collection. As librarians learn more about the collection and its utility, they are able to manage the collection—its growth, preservation and conservation, storage, withdrawal, and cancellation of serials—in relation to users' needs and the library's and parent institution's mission.

Knowing the collection is a selector's responsibility. Collection analysis leads to this knowledge. Collection analysis, therefore, is not a one-time project. Collection analysis is an ongoing process defined both by individual analysis projects and constant attention to collection quality and its responsiveness to the user community. Assessment and evaluation provide, through specific analysis methodologies and continuous monitoring, information about the current collection and about progress toward collection goals. Each analysis project provides a snapshot of or baseline information about the existing collection.

A common misconception is that collection assessment and evaluation determine how "good" a collection is. Earlier chapters have explored the debate over what defines a good book or other library resources. Contemporary theory advances the idea that a collection is considered good and appropriate to the extent that it matches the goals of the library and its parent institution. The collection developed to serve an elementary school is not an appropriate or good collection for a high school, a collection serving a two-year technical college is not a good collection for a university with many graduate programs and professional schools, and a collection developed to meet the needs of an electrical engineering firm is not a good collection for a teaching hospital. Even when evaluation techniques examine the collection in relation to an external measure, that measure must relate to the goals of the collection being considered. Deciding what not to collect is as important as deciding what to collect. Although analyses do identify collection areas that should be developed as well as strengths, intentional nonstrengths are equally valid.

Collection Analysis Techniques

Collection analysis techniques or methodologies range from impressionistic, descriptive assessments to complex statistical analysis. All seek to provide organized, pertinent, specific, and accurate information about the collection. Two typologies are used in discussing the various approaches to analysis. Techniques are either collection-based or use- and user-based and either quantitative or qualitative. Figure 9-1 represents these typologies as a matrix within which various techniques are organized.

Figure 9-1 Collection Analysis Methods

	Collection-Based	**Use- or User-Based**
Quantitative	Collection size/growth Materials budget size/growth Collection size standards and formulas	Interlibrary loan statistics Circulation statistics In-house use statistics Document delivery statistics Shelf availability statistics
Qualitative	List checking Verification studies Citation analysis Direct collection checking Collection mapping (assigning conspectus levels) Brief tests of collection strength	User opinion surveys User observation Focus groups

Collection-based techniques examine the size, growth, depth, breadth, variety, balance, and coverage of library materials—often in comparison with an external standard or the holdings of one or more libraries known to be comprehensive in the relevant subject area. Techniques include checking lists, catalogs, and bibliographies; looking at materials on the shelf; and compiling statistics. Collection-based techniques provide information that can guide selector decisions about preservation and conservation treatments, withdrawals, serials cancellations, duplication, and storage.

Use- and user-based approaches look at who is using the materials, how often, and what their expectations are. Emphasis may be on the use or on the user. A use study focuses on the materials and examines individual titles or groups of titles or subject areas to determine user success in identifying and locating what is needed and in using these items. User studies focus on the individuals or groups using the collection and how they are using its various components. Use- and user-based studies include research into users' failure to locate and obtain materials locally and how alternatives, such as interlibrary loan (ILL), are used. Use and user studies collect information about user expectations, how users approach the collections, and the materials that users select from those available.

Quantitative analysis counts things. It measures titles, circulation transactions, ILL requests, transactions with electronic resources, and dollars spent. Quantitative analysis compares and contrasts measurements over time within a library and with other libraries. It considers ratios such as expenditures for serials in relation to expenditures for monographs and expenditures for print resources in relation to those for electronic resources. An academic library may analyze total collection expenditures in relation to number of students, faculty members, and degree programs. A public library may consider annual expenditures or circulation transactions per user group or branch library. Quantitative methods demonstrate growth and use of collections by looking at collection and circulation statistics, ILL requests, and budget information. Once a baseline is established, the size, growth, and use of a collection can be measured. Automated systems have made the collection of use data much easier, though research suggests that libraries are not making significant use of these data.[3]

Qualitative analysis is more subjective than quantitative analysis because it depends on perception and opinion. The goal of qualitative analysis is to determine collection strengths, weaknesses, and nonstrengths, which reflect conscious decisions not to collect. It depends on the opinion of selectors and external experts and the perceptions of users. Even when collections are checked against external lists, these lists are themselves the result of informed opinion about what constitutes a "good" collection, characterizes a collection designated as a specific collecting level, or comprises an appropriate collection for a specific user group.

All collection analysis, whether qualitative or quantitative, should employ sound research practices. These require a clear understanding of what is being measured, how to measure it, and how to interpret the results. Well-done research projects produce information that is both reliable (the likelihood that a given measurement procedure will yield the same results if that measurement is repeated) and valid (the extent to which a specific measurement provides data that relate to commonly accepted meanings of a particular concept). In other words, the findings are repeatable, and the conclusions are true. Several sources provide guidance for conducting research in libraries.[4] In addition to understanding and practicing sound research, librarians who plan to use survey instruments should consult with experts in their development and application.

Functions of Collection Analysis

A primary goal of collection analysis is increasing selector knowledge about the collection and its use so he or she can measure its success and manage it effectively. Collection analysis also provides information that may be used for many purposes. Analysis can be used to demonstrate accountability by marking progress toward performance goals and showing how investments are being used effectively.[5] A collection analysis provides a detailed subject profile that can inform new library staff members and users about the nature of the collection. It can assist in the writing or revision of a collection development policy and provide a measure of an existing policy's effectiveness. Collection analysis can help explain decisions and expenditures. For example, documented high use of electronic resources during hours the library building is closed might be used to explain allocating an increasing percentage of the total acquisitions budget for this format.

Information collected through collection analysis can be used in the planning process, including justifications for budget requests and funding referendums. It can guide and inform decisions and policymaking throughout the library, including budget and staffing allocations. Analysis projects that focus on the condition of materials and their availability can be used for disaster preparedness, inventory purposes, and space planning.

Reports from collection analysis projects can be used in accreditation reports and other external purposes. Some academic libraries are involved in institutional planning for new degree programs. A specific and detailed collection analysis can demonstrate the degree to which a library can and cannot support a new program or major. Information about collection strengths can be used to recruit new faculty members and students. Corporate libraries will have the information in hand to document their ability to support new research and development programs. Information may be gathered through collection analysis that can be used in press releases, library reports and newsletters, and for grant proposals. Collection analysis positions a library to share information with other libraries with which it is involved through existing or proposed partnerships.

Historical Overview of Collection Analysis

Until the end of the nineteenth century, collection analysis focused on description rather than assessment and evaluation. This was, in large part, a function of the manner in which collections were developed—through donations and what was available for acquisition, rather than intentional collection building to meet specific needs and goals. Around 1900, librarians began using selected bibliographies or lists against which individual library holdings were checked. These lists were prepared by the American Library Association (ALA), authoritative librarians, and subject specialists. Another form of list checking involved collecting favorable reviews and then determining if the library held the titles. Libraries also checked references and bibliographies in scholarly works against library holdings. List checking was the primary method of collection analysis until the middle of the twentieth century.

Quantitative Studies

In the 1960s, librarians began to promote more diverse and scientific methods of collection analysis. These included studying citation patterns, collection overlap and uniqueness, comparative statistics, and classification and curriculum relationships; developing formulas for collection size and acquisitions budgets; and employing sociological tools in the design and application of use and user studies. Much of the emphasis in this period was on the objectivity of analysis results. College and university librarians, particularly, sought quantitative measures that were both easy to apply and objective. Many studies focused on collecting and comparing collection size and expenditure statistics, both seen as measures of excellence.

Since the 1970s, both quantitative and qualitative collection analysis methods have been developed and promoted. Much of the impetus has been a desire to facilitate cooperative collection development in consortia and large library systems. Academic and research libraries have initiated several cooperative projects. The Association of Research Libraries (ARL) Collection Analysis Project was begun in the 1970s to analyze collections within institutional contexts and with hopes for increasing cooperative collection development among large research libraries.[6]

The North American Title Count (NATC) project (formerly the National Shelf List Count), started in 1973, is sponsored by the Collection Management and Development Section within ALA's Association for Library Collections and Technical Services.[7] Most of the more than fifty participating libraries rely on automated systems to generate reports. The NATC provides objective, comparative information about subject collections and rates of growth by counting titles in more than 600 Library of Congress classifications. It lists both title counts and percentage of collection in the classifications. Though the NATC is conducted every four years, libraries that collect this information annually can examine and compare their own growth from year to year. The NATC can identify areas of numeric strength and nonstrength, changes in collecting patterns, and areas of growth not reflected in collection policies and help identify library collections with whom cooperative arrangements might be desirable. It cannot evaluate the quality of a collection.

Collection size formulas have been developed that use local variables to calculate the number of volumes required to meet local needs. The use of formulas depends on the notion of a minimum size for collections or budgets relative to the size of a library's user community or level of parent institution's programs. The Clapp-Jordan formula, which uses an acceptable core collection count plus volumes per student, per faculty, per undergraduate field, and per graduate field, is one model for this approach.[8] Others have been proposed over the years. Existing collections can be compared to the ideal specified by the formula. Some library standards provide formulas for deciding optimum collection size. Formulas have become less popular as libraries have moved away from relying solely on numbers as a measure of quality.

Collection analysis by studying collection use produced one of the more controversial statistical studies—that conducted by Allen Kent and others at the University of Pittsburgh in the 1970s.[9] This study found that much of the University of Pittsburgh Library's collection was not being used and led researchers to suggest implications for past and future collection management practices. The 80/20 ratio describes the phenomena that 20 percent of the collection accounted for 80 percent of circulation. Questions remain whether frequency of book and journal circulation is an appropriate measure of academic library effectiveness. Circulation studies can provide guidance about which parts of the collection can be put in storage or withdrawn as well as which areas need to be developed.

Other quantitative use studies examine in-library use, shelf availability, document delivery, and interlibrary lending and borrowing statistics. Budget-based quantitative studies—which measure growth of the materials budget, track changes in the ratio of expenditures for serials to those for monographs, and compare allocations between subject areas—are additional techniques for considering the relation of a library's operations to its goals and long-term mission.

Qualitative Studies

Qualitative studies seek to evaluate the intrinsic worth of the collection and are, by nature, subjective. They depend on the perceptions of librarians and library users. Qualitative studies were hampered initially by a lack of standard terminology. One of the first steps toward developing a shared vocabulary to describe collection strength or levels appeared in the 1979 *Guidelines for Collection Development*.[10] This work designated five collecting levels, which were applied to existing collections ("collection density") and current collecting activity ("collection intensity"), and was one of the first sources to espouse a standard terminology that could be used to share information about collecting levels. The levels were (A) Comprehensive Level, (B) Research Level, (C) Study Level, (D) Basic Level, and (E) Minimal Level. This stratified view sought to analyze each collection according to its intended use.

These levels (with one additional level—Out of Scope) were inverted to form the basis of the Research Libraries Group (RLG) Conspectus, initiated in 1980. The conspectus, now in several versions, is one of the most widely used qualitative methods.[11] *Conspectus* means a brief survey or summary of a subject. The conspectus is a comprehensive collection analysis tool intended to provide a summary of collecting intensities arranged by subjects, classification scheme, or a combination of both. The conspectus methodology also is called collection mapping and inventory profiling.[12] Ideally, the conspectus provides a standardized procedure and terminology for sharing detailed descriptions of collections among libraries. Librarians apply numeric codes to identify six levels of existing collection strengths, current collecting levels, and desired collection levels. Additional alphabetical codes can be applied that describe language coverage, intended approach for physical treatments of materials, and plans for archiving of the intellectual content of various formats.

Each level builds on the previous level. The six RLG Conspectus levels follow:

0 *Out of Scope* (library does not collect in this area),

1 *Minimal* (library collects resources that support minimal inquiries about this subject and include a very limited collection of general resources),

2 *Basic Information* (library collects resources that introduce and define a subject and can support the needs of general library users through the first two years of college instruction)

3 *Study or Instructional Support* (library collects resources that provide knowledge about a subject in a systematic way, but at a level of less than research intensity, and support the needs of general library users through college and beginning graduate instruction)

4 *Research* (library collects the major published source materials required for doctoral study and independent research and is very extensive)

5 *Comprehensive* (library strives to collect as exhaustively as is reasonably possible in all pertinent formats, in all applicable languages, in both published materials and manuscripts)

Additional subcodes of the conspectus levels 1, 2, and 3 have been added to the WLN Conspectus to meet the needs of smaller, nonresearch libraries.[13]

The conspectus grew out of RLG's interests in mapping the collection depths of its members. The RLG Conspectus uses subject fields based on the Library of Congress classification and subject heading systems, which parallel those used by the NATC. It was designed for use in research libraries.

Other groups around the world have adapted the conspectus for their own use, both for individual library collection analysis and to provide a synopsis of a consortium's or a network's coordinated collection development. The WLN Conspectus permits use of the Library of Congress classification, the Dewey decimal classification, and the National Library of Medicine classification systems and adapts the RLG Conspectus for use in all types of libraries.[14] The conspectus approach to collection analysis, though challenged by some as too dependent on individual perceptions, has become accepted as a tool that is both adaptable and widely applicable.[15]

Conspectus-level definitions were revised in the mid-1990s to reflect the emerging role of electronic resources. Electronic resources, both locally held and remotely accessed, are considered equivalent to print materials as long as the policies and procedures for their use permit at least an equivalent information-gathering experience. The revised definitions use the term *defined access* to refer to menu options on a library's web interface linking the user to owned or remotely accessed electronic resources selected by the library. Defined access means more than simply providing patrons with access to the Internet and one or more Internet browsers.

Electronic Resources and Collection Analysis

The increasing use of electronic resources in all types and sizes of libraries is presenting new challenges in analysis. The cost of these materials and the increasing percentage of library budgets going toward their acquisition and access mandate careful consideration of their value to users and role within a library collection. Although electronic resources always should be considered part of the collection being analyzed, many of the analysis methods described in detail in the following section do not include these formats easily. Most electronic resources do not circulate nor are they available through ILL. Not all are classified and represented in a shelf list. Shelf availability studies, direct collection checking, and document delivery studies do not apply to most electronic resources. The lists developed for checking holdings are only now beginning to include electronic resources. Citation analysis studies are equally sparse in representing electronic resources. Comparative collection statistics have focused on traditional formats.

Librarians are seeking ways to assess and evaluate electronic resources within the framework of existing methodologies and to develop new approaches.[16] Use- and user-based techniques are most easily applicable. User opinion surveys, user observation, and focus groups can be designed to gather perceptions of the breadth, scope, and depth of coverage of electronic resources and the ease of access and use. If all electronic resources are represented in the catalog, subject-based checking can be substituted for classification-based checking of collection coverage. Many libraries monitor the percentage of their materials budgets expended annually for electronic resources acquisition and access, tracking changes over time. Agencies, associations, and consortia are beginning to grapple with how to include electronic resources in annual comparative statistical compilations.[17] The conspectus-level definitions have been modified to recognize the importance of appropriate electronic resources in each level.

Users are increasingly accessing e-resources from outside the library. Unless a user comes into the library with questions or seeks help through an online reference service, librarians are missing qualitative information about the resource. Librarians have difficulty determining who is using which e-resource and the degree to which it meets the users' needs. Effectiveness, impact factors, and data about outcomes are missing. Questions remain about how to determine which resources are of the greatest value to users and, for that matter, what makes a resource of greater or lesser value.

An important aspect of collection analysis is collecting information to document accountability and effective use of financial resources. Recent work in the analysis of electronic resources has concentrated on their cost-effectiveness and success in meeting user needs.[18] Often, the electronic resources collection is considered a subset of the collection for analysis purposes with particular emphasis on cost-performance benefits. Electronic resources are assessed to learn how well they are satisfying the library's objectives and meeting the demands placed on them. Another aspect is examining how efficiently objectives are being satisfied. In other words, do the resources justify the cost of providing them? Libraries look at congruity between electronic resources and local collecting priorities.

Use statistics for electronic resources is an area receiving more attention. Librarians are increasing pressure on the publishers and providers of electronic information resources to deliver meaningful use statistics. Some publishers may be unwilling to provide such information or may project high costs to implement a data collection function. A more fundamental problem has been the absence of comparable data for analysis. The International Coalition of Library Consortia (ICOLC) has been a leader in identifying both the statistics that are desirable and the obligations of remote resources providers to supply these statistics. In *Guidelines for Statistical Measures of Usage of Web-Based Information Resources*, first issued in 1998 and revised in 2001, ICOLC sought to define and create a common set of basic use information requirements that any electronic product should provide.[19] These statistics permit libraries to analyze use within the individual library and in comparison with others. The ARL started an initiative, E-Metrics (Measures for Electronic Resources), to address the need for measures of electronic information resources.[20] COUNTER (Counting Online Usage of NeTworked Electronic Resources), an international initiative of librarians and publishers and their professional organizations, was established to develop an international "Code of Practice" governing the recording and exchange of online usage data and to develop a plan for the ongoing implementation, upgrading, and extension of this code.[21]

One form of electronic resources use statistics that can be collected locally is a transaction log, which measures use of information held locally and delivered via a local server. Transaction logs can determine the type of user actions, percentage of users accessing the site from a specific domain, the number of hits the server gets during specific hours, the number of hits every page receives within a site, and the path by which a user navigates through the site. Transaction log analysis can assist in studying user behavior and is an efficient technique for collecting longitudinal usage data. However, extracting data, interpreting the data, and detecting trends and patterns can be difficult.[22]

Interdisciplinary Fields

Interdisciplinary fields can present unique problems for collection analysis.[23] Such areas as ecology and the environment, bioethics, women's studies, biotechnology and genetic engineering, and diversity and multiculturalism are highly fluid and evolving fields of study. The nature of interdisciplinary study, teaching, and research requires crossing traditional discipline divisions. These divisions are reflected in a library's classification schemes and subject headings. Interdisciplinary fields may have a core of materials but expand out to broader, related areas. Call number–based analysis methods present difficulties because of the extensive range of classifications used in interdisciplinary research. Citation studies and user surveys can offer viable alternatives for analyzing interdisciplinary fields.

Collection-Based Analysis Methods

The following methods are collection-based. Some are quantitative, some are qualitative, and some have aspects of both approaches.

List Checking

The selector compares lists of titles against the library's holdings. The list may be another library's catalog, general list, specialized list or bibliography, publisher's or dealer's catalog, annual subject compilation, list prepared by a professional association or government authority, course syllabi or required or recommended reading list, list of frequently cited journals, list of journals covered by an abstracting and indexing service, recent acquisitions list from a specialized library, or a list prepared for a specific library, type of library, or specific objective. ALA's *Books for College Libraries* (1988) remained a popular tool for checking the holdings of college libraries for many years, though much of its content is now out-of-date.[24] A collection is studied by finding the percentage of the titles on the list that are owned by the library.

Verification studies are a variation on list checking, in which two or more libraries carry out a collection analysis by checking their collections against a specially prepared list of titles, designed to encompass the most important works within a specific area. These lists are designed to verify that the libraries understand their collections' strengths and that they have reported them correctly and consistently on a shared analysis instrument, often the conspectus. Any list selected for checking should match the library's programs and goals and be appropriate to the subjects collected.

List checking is a frequently used method because it is easy to apply and lists are available that meet many different libraries' needs. Librarians usually can find a list that has credibility because of the authority and competence of those who compiled it. Many published lists are updated frequently and can be used to check the collection at regular intervals. List checking not only increases knowledge of the collection being analyzed, but it also increases the selector's knowledge of the subject or discipline's literature. A selector also can use a list as a purchase guide to identify missing titles that should be acquired.

List checking combines both qualitative and quantitative techniques. The selection by the librarian of the list to be checked is a subjective decision, as was the development of the list, but the result is a statistical report of the number of titles on the list that the library owns. When analyzing the report, the librarian usually converts this percentage to a quality judgment about the collection.

List checking has disadvantages as well as advantages.[25] The library may have used the list as a selection tool in the past. Any list prepared by an individual or group reflects the biases and opinions of the compilers. Its validity rests on the assumption that those titles in the resource list are worthy and that the library needs them to satisfy patrons and support programs. A selector may have difficulty finding a list that matches the focus of the collection being analyzed and the mission of the library. Finding an up-to-date list also may present problems. Carol A. Doll has cautioned about relying too heavily on standard bibliographies when evaluating school library media collections because such lists are often seriously out-of-date.[26] The selector should recognize that a supplemental tool may be necessary to analyze the collection for materials published since the list was compiled.

Direct Collection Analysis

Direct collection analysis means that a person with extensive knowledge of the literature physically examines the collection. The person then draws conclusions about the size, scope, depth or type of materials (textbooks, documents, paperbacks, beginning level, advanced level, professional level), and significance of the collection; the range and distribution of publishing dates; and the physical condition of the materials. Preservation, conservation, restoration, or replacement of materials may be taken into consideration in this process. This method is most practical when the collection is small or the subject treated is narrowly defined. The evaluator's reputation must be sufficient to give credibility to the evaluation results.

One advantage of this approach is its appropriateness to any discipline or library collection. Assuming that the collection being reviewed is of a reasonable size, its strengths, weaknesses, and condition can be evaluated rapidly. It is appropriate for a large collection if time is not a major consideration and if the selector is interested in working through the collection one segment at a time. Direct collection checking can serve several objectives simultaneously, because the items are physically handled. It is particularly useful as a learning tool for new selectors, who can gain an intimate knowledge of the collection.

The problems with direct collection checking stem from its dependency on individuals and personal perspective and its reliance on physical items. Local selectors may be less than objective as they review the collections they have built. External evaluators, who know the subject and its literature, have time to devote to the project, and are affordable, may be difficult to locate. The subjective and impressionistic nature of this method does not provide comparable information. Only careful recording of findings will provide a quantitative report, and its accuracy may be suspect. Because this approach examines the materials on the shelves, those items not on the shelf cannot be examined. This excludes most electronic resources. The evaluator also should consult a shelf list, subject headings in the local catalog, and circulation records. Filling in information from these sources does not provide condition information. Collection checking is most appropriate for small and focused collections or when the librarian has no time constraints.

A variation on direct collection analysis involves working from the shelf list, which may be a paper or electronic file, rather than the physical items on the shelf. Although physical items are not handled, this approach has the advantage of making all other information about the items immediately available. Detailed information about imprints—age, language of publication, percentage of duplication, and subject coverage—can be collected easily. One approach uses a sample to construct a collection profile.[27] Qualitative information can be used to supplement the quantitative information collected in a shelf list title count. The primary drawback of this method is the potential absence of many items and formats from the classified shelf list. Portions of the collection, such as electronic resources and microforms, may not be classified or the collection may be split between two or more classification schedules.

Comparative Statistics Compilation

Libraries have used comparative figures on collection size and materials expenditures to determine relative strengths for many years. The assumption often is made that bigger is better. Although depth and breadth of a collection are partly a function of collection size, numerical counts do not measure quality. The ARL member libraries submit comparative statistics in many areas, including several collection measures.[28] The ARL annually calculates an index formula and index for its university library members. The index is a summary measure of relative size among these members of the association, using five quantitative data elements. Although member libraries frequently reference their annual ranking in this index, the ARL states explicitly that the index does not measure a library's services, quality of collections, or success in meeting the needs of users.

When libraries collect and compare a specific group of statistics, they must agree on the definition of each statistical component and implement identical measurement methods. Comparisons are meaningless without consistency. Libraries typically measure size of collections in volumes and titles and by format, rate of net growth, and expenditures for library materials by format and by total budget. Additional collection comparisons may include volumes bound and expenditures on preservation and conservation treatments. Another comparison frequently used is the degree of collection overlap and extent of unique holdings. Libraries seek to determine how many titles are held in common among two or more libraries and what percentage of a library's holdings are unique.

Statistics can be gathered in various ways. Libraries' automated systems may generate counts based on cumulative transactions or through specially prepared programs run periodically. These reports will count totals as well as activity (titles added and withdrawn, dollars expended, etc.) within a specified period. Estimates and sampling seldom produce accurate numbers that can be used for comparative purposes either within a library or with other institutions.

If the various measures are clearly defined, the statistics can be compared and have meaning to a wide audience. If the statistics are accurate, they can provide objective, quantifiable data. Statistical compilations are not without problems. Portions of many libraries' collections are not cataloged and not reflected in either online records or paper files. Manual collection of statistics can be very labor-intensive. Statistics may not be recorded accurately if their collection is manual or if the definitions of categories are not consistently understood or applied. This can lead to results that are not comparable between libraries. Finally, statistics cannot measure collection quality or, on their own, verify collection levels.

Application of Collection Standards

Collection and resources standards, which have been developed by professional associations, accrediting agencies, funding agencies, and library boards, may be used by those types of libraries for which standards have been developed. These standards have moved away from prescriptive volume counts, budget sizes, and the application of formulas to addressing adequacy, access, and availability. The ALA and its divisions have been a leader in developing standards and output measures for various types of libraries.[29]

Standards developed by the ALA and other professional associations and agencies usually are considered authoritative and widely accepted. Their credibility often means that they can be effective in securing library support. If a standard exists for the library type being studied, it generally relates closely to the library's goals. Standards provide a framework for comparing libraries of similar types. However, the application of externally developed standards can present problems. Some standards are very general and difficult to apply to specific collections. As with any externally developed measure, standards are the product of opinion, and not everyone will agree with the standard. In addition, individuals may not agree with or accept the results reported. Most standards set a minimum level of volumes, expenditures, or collection levels, and the tendency is to view this minimum as the goal. If, for example, a college library reports its volume count as slightly above the minimum standard, some may believe that the library collection is acceptable because it is interpreted as exceeding the target.

Use- and User-Centered Analysis Methods

The analysis methods described in the following section focus on studying collection use and users. They may be quantitative, qualitative, or a combination of the two. Collecting and analyzing use and user data must be handled in a manner that protects and respects users' privacy. A cardinal principle of librarianship is protecting the privacy of library users with respect to their information seeking. Most academic institutions have specific policies that must be followed when data are gathered from human subjects, ensuring that the privacy as well as the well-being of individuals are not at risk. Many states have statutes that protect the privacy of citizens. The electronic environment makes it much easier to collect information about individuals. The ICOLC endorsed and released *Privacy Guidelines for Electronic Resources Vendors* in July 2002.[30] It includes the statement, "Publisher respects the privacy of the users of its products. Accordingly, Publisher will not disclose information about any individual user of its products . . . to a third party without the permission of that individual user, except as required by law." Librarians conducting user and usage studies must protect the privacy of individuals while collecting data.

Citation Studies

Citation studies are a type of bibliometrics, which is the quantitative treatment of the properties that describe and predict the nature of scholarly literature use. Source publications are searched for bibliographic references, and these citations are used to analyze the collection. Citation studies assume that the more frequently cited publications are the more valuable, will continue to be heavily used, and, consequently, are more important to have in the library collections. Citation analysis is closely related to list checking. Used primarily in academic and research libraries, it consists of counting or ranking (or both) the number of times documents are cited in published works, such as footnote references, bibliographies, or indexing and abstracting tools, and comparing those figures to the collection. There are two basic approaches: published citation studies based on use of the literature by many scholars or citation studies conducted in a specific library based on use of the literature by the library's patrons. The emphasis is on how many times an item is cited to establish relative importance. Citation studies are particularly useful in collections where journals are important. They are most frequently used to develop core lists of primary journals and to identify candidates for cancellation or storage.

Data collected in citation studies can be arranged easily into categories for analysis. Citation studies can identify trends in the literature. Online databases can make assembling a citation list efficient and rapid, and several published citation indexes exist. However, externally prepared citation lists may not match the bibliographic formats of the library, and developing a list of source items that reflect the subject studied or user needs can be challenging. Subareas of one discipline may have different citation patterns from the general subject. Citation studies are not appropriate to all disciplines. The inherent time lag in citations will not reflect changes of emphasis in disciplines or the emergence of new journals. Citation analysis is time-consuming and labor intensive. Important materials for consultation or background work may not be cited frequently. Finally, a citation to a work is not an inherent guarantee of quality.

Circulation Studies

Circulation studies analyze local circulation transactions. Information can be collected for all or part of the circulating collection by user group, location, date of publication, subject classification, and type of transaction, such as loans, recalls, reserves, renewals. Circulation studies can identify those portions of the collections that are little used. These materials can be weeded, transferred, or placed in storage. Information indicating less used subject areas may suggest curtailing future acquisitions in these areas. The librarian may decide to duplicate those titles that are heavily used. Circulation statistics can be used to compare use patterns in selected subject areas or by types of materials against their representation in the total collection. This information may be used to modify collection development practices or fund allocations. Journal use statistics, if they combine circulation and in-house use, can be used to calculate cost per use and provide guidance in making journal cancellation decisions.

The circulation data can be arranged easily into categories for analysis, and these categories can be correlated in various ways. For example, a public library system can compare circulation of various categories of fiction in each of several branch libraries, leading to decisions about where to locate larger mystery, romance, and science fiction collections. The information can be collected easily and is objective. Automated circulation systems make data collection extremely efficient.

The major problem with circulation studies is that they record circulation and exclude in-house use, unless a mechanism is in place to capture in-house use. Without this step, noncirculating collections and any materials consulted in the library are not represented. Also, circulation studies reflect only user successes in identifying, locating, and borrowing items. They provide no information on user failure to find or the collection's failure to provide materials.

In-House Use Studies

Several techniques are available for recording the use of materials consulted by users in the library and reshelved by library staff. This type of study can focus on either materials used or the users of materials. It can focus on the entire collection or a part of the collection or on all users or a sample of users. In-house use studies are most often used for noncirculating periodical collections or to measure book usage in noncirculating collections. It can be used to correlate type of user with type of materials used. Combined with a circulation study, an in-house use study gives more accurate information on use of the collection.

Use studies of noncirculating materials depend on users' willingness to refrain from reshelving materials after use. Materials must be set aside so use can be tracked either manually or by scanning bar codes directly into an automated system. Because in-house use studies rely on users' cooperation, they may be less accurate. Most libraries use direct observation to correct for uncooperative users. If the study is conducted over a limited time, care must be taken to time the study appropriately so data do not reflect use in peak or slow periods. Studies of in-house use report only users' success in locating materials; thus, user failures are not reported.

User Surveys

User surveys seek to determine how well the library's collections meet users' needs and expectations and to identify those that are unmet. Surveys may be administered in various ways: verbally in person or on the phone, electronically by e-mail or pop-up screens on the library's catalog or web page, or as written questionnaires, which are handed to users in the library either as they enter or exit or mailed to them at offices and homes. Information from user surveys can be used to assess quantitatively and qualitatively the effectiveness of the collections in meeting users' needs, help solve specific problems, define the makeup of the actual community of library users, identify user groups that need to be better served, provide feedback on successes as well as on deficiencies, improve public relations and assist in the education of the user community, and identify changing trends and interests.

User surveys can improve the library's relations with its community and help educate users and nonusers. User surveys are not limited to existing data, such as circulation statistics, but permit the library to study new areas. They solicit direct responses from users and can collect opinions not normally shared with the library. The survey can range from short and simple to lengthy and complex.

However, designing even the shortest survey instrument can be difficult. Crafting questions that yield the results sought often requires the help of an experienced questionnaire designer. The parent agency of some libraries may require prior approval of any research that involves human subjects, even a brief library user survey. Analyzing and interpreting data from an opinion survey is challenging. Users are often passive about collections and so must be surveyed individually, increasing survey costs. Even with individual attention, some users may not cooperate in the survey, resulting in skewed results. Many users are uninformed or unaware of actual and possible library collections. They have difficulty in judging what is adequate or appropriate. User surveys may record perceptions, intentions, and recollections that do not reflect actual experiences or patterns of user behavior. Perceptions and opinions are not always quantifiable. By definition, surveys of user opinions will miss valuable statements from and about the nonuser.

LibQUAL+ is a recent research and development effort that seeks to measure users' perceptions of library service quality across institutions via a web-based survey.[31] It is a project undertaken by the ARL in collaboration with Texas A&M University. The LibQUAL+ survey instrument is a derivation of the SERVQUAL tool created to measure service quality in the private sector.[32] Sections of the survey measure quality in provision of physical collections and access to collections. Twelve libraries piloted the survey in 2000, and in 2003, more than 306 academic libraries of all sizes participated. LibQUAL+ has the potential to collect longitudinal data for a single library and comparative data that libraries can share.

Shelf Availability Studies

Shelf availability studies, also called retrieval studies, are intended to find out if an item that the library is supposed to own can be located and retrieved by the user. This approach has the advantage of studying users as they seek materials in the collection.[33] By monitoring user inquiries directly, availability studies measure how often the collection is deficient when a user cannot find an item and how often the user's error causes an item to be inaccessible. Problems in the collection may be caused by lost or misshelved items or items that are unavailable because they are circulating or in a course reserve readings collection. User problems may be caused by an incorrect or incomplete citation, inaccurate transcription of call number, or inability to find the location in the library.

Availability studies define a specific period during which users are asked to name the titles that they could not find in the library. In one approach, library staff members interview users or ask them to complete a brief written questionnaire as they leave the library. Another technique is to provide forms to users when they enter the library and ask them to record the titles of items they cannot locate. The survey may include all library users or can focus on a random sample. Availability studies report the failures of real users in finding materials. They can identify problems with services, such as signage, shelving accuracy, or user instruction, that should be addressed as well as collection problems. Availability studies provide clear performance benchmarks and can be repeated to measure changes over time. Shelf availability studies depend on the cooperation of users. Frustrated users who have failed to find the materials they seek are less likely to respond. Often, users cannot remember all items they were unable to find. Because this is a variation of the user survey, it can be difficult and time-consuming to design and execute. The needs of nonusers are not reflected.

Interlibrary Loan Analysis

Items requested through ILL represent a use of the collection because the requester has checked the collection, found the item lacking (either not owned or missing), and decided that he or she still needs it. ILL analysis can identify areas in which the collection is not satisfying patron needs and specific current or retrospective journal titles to be purchased and can monitor resource-sharing agreements. Statistical results often are readily available and can be analyzed by title, classification, date of imprints, or language. Analyses of subject classifications are best interpreted in conjunction with corresponding acquisitions and circulation data. Results must be interpreted in relation to the collection development policy and in relation to existing resource-sharing agreements that rely on ILL. Requests can serve as an indicator to the library of new research staff, new program needs, changes in the community, or a long-standing deficiency. One problem with the use of ILL statistics is that their significance may be difficult to interpret. Also, this type of study does not reflect users who go elsewhere instead of requesting resources through ILL.

Document Delivery Test

This technique is used to check the library's ability to provide users with items at the time they are needed. It is similar to the shelf availability study, but searching is done by library staff, who simulate users. Document delivery tests build on citation studies by determining first if the library owns a certain item and then if the item can be located and how long it takes to do so. The most frequent approach is to compile a list of citations that reflect the library users' information needs. Externally developed lists can also be used. The test determines both the number of items owned by the library and the time required to locate a specific item. Document delivery testing can provide objective measurements of a collection's ability to satisfy user needs. If identical lists are used by two or more libraries, data can be compared. As with shelf availability studies, this type of testing may identify service problems that can then be corrected. Benchmark data are gathered, and changes can be measured through subsequent testing. However, compiling a list of representative citations can be challenging. Because the testing is done by library staff members, it can underestimate the problems encountered by users, such as user error in locating materials. To be meaningful, results require repeated tests or comparisons with studies conducted in other libraries.

Each method described here has advantages and unique benefits for analyzing collections. Each also has disadvantages. Effective collection analysis requires a combination of techniques to gain a complete understanding of a collection and its users. Most methods provide data that can be compared against data collected in subsequent studies. Repeating studies at regular intervals permits the library to show progress toward meeting goals and identify areas that need attention.

Planning and Conducting a Collection Analysis Project

Although collection analysis should be an ongoing project, it tends to be defined by discrete analysis projects. Ideally, the projects can be repeated and are part of a long-range analysis plan. Each project should be planned carefully to ensure efficiency and effectiveness. An analysis plan can be developed by the individual selector or by a working group. The first step is to define the purposes of the study and the hypotheses that will be tested. What are the objectives of this project, why is the information being collected, and how will it be used? A plan identifies specific questions that will be answered.

The next step is to determine the data that will be gathered and the methodology that will be used to collect and analyze the data. Each measurement technique collects specific information, and each has drawbacks and advantages. In what format will the results be presented? What tables will be generated from these data? Subject the choice of data to the same rigorous standards used in defining purposes, because each data element adds to the expense and complexity of the study.

The librarian should decide the intended audience of the resulting report. This may be the chief collection development officer, the library director, school principal, or a funding agency or board. An analysis project may generate information that will be used for more than one audience or purpose. The librarian decides which part of the collection or representative sample will be studied. This will depend on the size of the collection and the time and resources available to conduct the analysis.

All steps in an analysis project should be documented so that it can be repeated easily. The librarian should consider whether comparability of results with those of other libraries is desirable and what commonly used classification divisions, statistical categories, terminology, output measures, or survey questions may facilitate comparisons. Before undertaking an analysis project, the librarian should estimate the resources in staff time and funding needed to conduct the analysis. Many methods are time-consuming or require external experts. The librarian should consult existing collection information. This may include a collection development policy, library mission or goal statement, and previously conducted analysis projects.

After the data are collected and analyzed, the report is prepared and disseminated. The report should follow generally accepted practices for reports. It should explain the purposes of the study, method(s) used, and problems encountered. It will provide general comments on the collection analyzed and the purposes it is intended to serve. As part of the findings, the report will summarize specific strengths, nonstrengths, and weaknesses. A good report will provide both prose and graphic representations of findings. It will draw relevant conclusions and suggest a plan to improve a collection in areas of undesirable weakness along with listing specific items or types of materials needed and cost estimates.

Summary

Collection assessment measures the extent to which the collection, both on-site and accessed remotely, meets the goals, needs, and mission of the library and its parent organization. Collection evaluation examines the collection in relation to other collections and comparative tools or considers the collection on its own terms. Analysis techniques may be quantitative or qualitative. They may focus on the collection or on the collection's use and users. Each technique has disadvantages and advantages. Using two or more approaches provides a more complete understanding of the collection and serves to validate findings. Some analyses, such as the conspectus and NATC project, facilitate comparisons and cooperation between libraries through the use of standardized definitions or classification ranges. To be effective, collection analysis projects should be repeatable and comparable.

Collection analysis serves many purposes. Through increased knowledge of the collection and its use, the selector can better understand the extent to which the collection meets the goals and mission of the library and can adjust collecting and managing activities to increase congruence between collection and mission. Demonstrating effective use of financial resources can document accountability and satisfy the requirements of funding bodies. Electronic information resources are creating new challenges for assessment and evaluation.

Collection analysis should be continuous and systematic. When specific analysis projects are undertaken, they should be planned carefully. The librarian or librarians conducting the research should have a clear understanding of the uses for which the resulting report is intended. Collection analysis is now an important part of collection development and management responsibilities, and every librarian should understand it, how to perform it, and the purposes it serves.

| CASE STUDY |

Claudia Evans is the new librarian at Webster Elementary School. She is the professional responsible for the school's library and media center. The school serves 900 students in kindergarten through sixth grade. Webster Elementary School, though part of a large city school system, has a separate library budget, supplemented by grants awarded by the school's parent-teacher organization through its fund-raising activities. The library collection totals 30,000 volumes, 500 videos and multimedia kits, and fifteen current magazine subscriptions. The library has had an automated circulation system for three years. The library has limited space, and the collection gets heavy use. Each class visits the library at least once a week. Additional visits are scheduled when classes are assigned research projects. Teachers often borrow 25 to 30 books on the same topic for classroom use. Claudia knows that her predecessor routinely withdrew 400 volumes each year, primarily because of condition. The library has a total budget of $7,500 for the year. Claudia has help with circulation and shelving from a school aid, who works in the library fifteen hours a week, and an additional ten hours per week of parent volunteer help.

Activity

Identify two or more collection-based and use- or user-based analysis methods that Claudia can employ to know her collection and its users. Develop a plan for applying each method, including an explanation of why each approach is being used, what information will be collected, how the information will be used, who the audience is, and a schedule for the projects. Balance Claudia's immediate need to get an overview of the collection, its use and users, and its success in satisfying its purposes while realizing that she has nine months to expend the annual budget allocation and expects to remain at this school for several years. Explain how the approaches proposed complement each other.

REFERENCES

1. Charles C. Jewett, *Appendix to the Report of Regents of the Smithsonian Institution Containing a Report on the Public Libraries of the United States of America. January 1, 1850* (Washington, D.C.: Smithsonian Institution, 1850).
2. Paul H. Mosher, "Quality and Library Collections: New Directions in Research and Practice in Collection Evaluation," *Advances in Librarianship* 13 (1984): 212–13.
3. Dennis P. Carrigan, "Data-Guided Collection Development: A Promise Unfulfilled," *College and Research Libraries* 57, no. 5 (Sept. 1996): 429–37.
4. See G. E. Gorman and Peter Crayton, *Qualitative Research for the Information Professional: A Practical Handbook* (London: Library Assn. Pub., 1997); Ronald R. Powell, *Basic Research Methods for Librarians*, 3d ed. (Greenwich, Conn.: Ablex, 1997); and F. W. Lancaster, *If You Want to Evaluate Your Library*, 2d ed. (Champaign: University of Illinois, Graduate School of Library and Information Science, 1993).
5. Sheila S. Intner and Elizabeth Futas, "Evaluating Public Library Collections: Why Do It, and How to Use the Results," *American Libraries* 25, no. 5 (May 1994): 410–12.
6. Jeffrey J. Gamer and Duane E. Webster, *The Collection Analysis Project: Operating Manual for the Review and Analysis of the Collection Development Function in Academic and Research Libraries: CAP Manual* (Washington, D.C.: Assn. of Research Libraries, 1978).
7. For an overview, *see* Gay N. Dannelly, "The National Shelflist Count: A Tool for Collection Management," *Library Acquisitions: Practice and Theory* 13, no. 3 (1989): 241–50.
8. Verner W. Clapp and Robert T. Jordan, "Quantitative Criteria for Adequacy of Academic Library Collections," *College and Research Libraries* 50, no. 3 (March 1989): 154–63. This article was originally published in 1965.
9. Allen Kent et al., *Use of Library Materials: The University of Pittsburgh Study* (New York: Marcel Dekker, 1979).

10. David L. Perkins, ed., *Guidelines for Collection Development* (Chicago: Collection Development Committee, Resources and Technical Services Division, American Library Assn., 1979).

11. The RLG Conspectus has been the subject of debate and numerous papers. The following offer a representative sample: Richard J. Wood, "The Conspectus: A Collection Analysis and Development Success," *Library Acquisitions: Practice and Theory* 20, no. 4 (1996): 429–53; Virgil L. P. Blake and Renee Tjoumas, "The Conspectus Approach to Collection Evaluation: Panacea or False Prophet?" *Collection Management* 18, no. 3/4 (1994): 1–31; and Frederick J. Stielow and Helen R. Tibbo, "Collection Analysis in Modern Librarianship: A Stratified, Multidimensional Model," *Collection Management* 11, no. 3/4 (1989): 73–91.

12. David V. Loertscher looked at collection mapping in a school library media center in his "Collection Mapping: An Evaluation Strategy for Collection Development," *Drexel Library Quarterly* 21 (1985): 9–21; and Debra E. Kachel applied the conspectus approach to school libraries in her *Collection Assessment and Management for School Libraries: Preparing for Cooperative Collection Development* (Westport, Conn.: Greenwood, 1997).

13. The WLN Conspectus is now part of the Automated Collection and Analysis Services offered by OCLC/WLN; more information is available at http://www.wln.org/products/aca/conspect.htm.

14. Mary Bushing, Burns Davis, and Nancy Powell, *Using the Conspectus Method: A Collection Assessment Handbook* (Lacey, Wash.: WLN, 1997).

15. Georgine N. Olson and Barbara McFadden Allen, eds., *Cooperative Collection Management: The Conspectus Approach* (New York: Neal-Schuman, 1994); also published in *Collection Building* 13, no. 2/3 (1994).

16. Charles McClure has done considerable work on the assessment of electronic services. *See* his early work on public library access to and use of the Internet in Charles McClure et al., *Public Libraries and the Internet: Study Results, Policy Issues, and Recommendations: Final Report* (Washington, D.C.: National Commission on Libraries and Information Science, 1994).

17. "EQUINOX: Library Performance Measurement and Quality Management System" is a project funded by the European Commission to develop methods for measuring performance in the electronic library environment. Information is available at http://equinox.dcu.ie/. The Association of Research Libraries is seeking to develop new performance measures that will supplement the statistical measures that ARL has collected for decades. *See* "ARL New Measures Initiative" [WWW home page for this project]. Available [Online]: http://www.arl.org/stats/newmeas/newmeas.html. Neither resource, however, directly addresses evaluating and assessing electronic resources.

18. *See* Gary W. White and Gregory A. Crawford, "Cost-Benefit Analysis of Electronic Information: A Case Study," *College and Research Libraries* 59, no. 6 (Nov. 1998): 503–10; A. Craig Hawbaker and Cynthia K. Wagner, "Periodical Ownership versus Fulltext Online Access: A Cost-Benefit Analysis," *Journal of Academic Librarianship* 22 (March 1996): 105–10; and Mark Smith and Gerry Rowland, "To Boldly Go: Searching for Output Measures for Electronic Services," *Public Libraries* 36 (May/June 1997): 168–72.

19. *Guidelines for Statistical Measures of Usage of Web-Based Information Resources* (Dec. 2001 revision of original Nov. 1998 *Guidelines*), issued by the

International Coalition of Library Consortia, available at http://www.library. yale.edu/consortia/2001webstats.htm.

20. Wonsik Shim, Charles R. McClure, and John Carol Bertot, *ARL E-Metrics Project: Developing Statistics and Performance Measures to Describe Electronic Information Services and Resources for ARL Libraries* (Washington, D.C.: Assn. of Research Libraries, 2000), available at http://www.arl.org/stats/newmeas/ emetrics/phaseone.pdf.

21. COUNTER [WWW home page of Counting Online Usage of NeTworked Electronic Resources]. Available [Online]: http://www.projectcounter.org.

22. An examination of transaction log analysis can be found in Denise Troll Covey, *Usage and Usability Assessment: Library Practices and Concerns* (Washington, D.C.: Digital Library Federation, Council on Library and Information Resources, 2002), also available at http://www.clir.org/pubs/reports/pub105/ contents.html.

23. Terese Heidenwolf, "Evaluating an Interdisciplinary Research Collection," *Collection Management* 18, no. 3/4 (1994): 33–48; and Cynthia Dobson, Jeffrey D. Kushkowski, and Kristin H. Gerhard, "Collection Evaluation for Interdisciplinary Fields: A Comprehensive Approach," *Journal of Academic Librarianship* 22 (July 1996): 279–84.

24. Virginia Clark, ed., *Books for College Libraries: A Core Collection of 50,000 Titles,* 3d ed., 6 vols. (Chicago: American Library Assn., 1988).

25. For studies on the utility of list checking, see Robert N. Bland, "The College Textbook as a Tool for Collection Evaluation, Analysis, and Retrospective Collection Development," *Library Acquisitions: Practice and Theory,* no. 3/4 (1980): 193–97; and Anne H. Lundin, "List-Checking in Collection Development: An Imprecise Art," *Collection Management* 11, no. 3/4 (1989): 305–14.

26. Carol A. Doll, "Quality and Elementary School Library Media Collections," *School Library Media Quarterly* 25 (winter 1997): 95–102.

27. Beth M. Paskoff and Anna H. Perrault, "A Tool for Comparative Collection Analysis: Conducting a Shelflist Sample to Construct a Collection Profile," *Library Resources and Technical Services* 34, no. 2 (April 1990): 179–214.

28. The Association of Research Libraries maintains member statistics on the ARL statistics web page. Available [Online]: http://www.arl.org/stats/.

29. Two recent examples are: "Standards for College Libraries: The Final Version, Approved January 2000," *College and Research Libraries News* 60, no. 5 (May 1999): 375–81; and Virginia A. Walter, *Output Measures and More: Planning and Evaluating Public Library Services for Young Adults: Part of the Public Library Development Program* (Chicago: American Library Assn., 1995).

30. International Coalition of Library Consortia, *Privacy Guidelines for Electronic Resources Vendors* (July 2002), available at http://www.library.yale.edu/ consortia/2002privacyguidelines.html.

31. For more information, *see* LibQUAL+ [WWW home page for the LibQUAL+ project, Assn. of Research Libraries]. Available [Online]: http://www. arl.org/libqual/index.html; and Yvonna S. Lincoln, "Insights into Library Services and Users from Qualitative Research: Designing the LibQUAL Survey Instrument," *Library and Information Science Research* 24, no. 1 (2002): 3–16.

32. A. Parasuraman, Valerie A. Zeitharnl, and Leonard L. Berry, "SERVQUAL: A Multiple-Item Scale for Measuring Consumer Perceptions of Service Quality," *Journal of Retailing* 64 (spring 1988): 12–40.

33. Anne Ciliberti et al., "Empty Handed? A Material Availability Study and Transaction Log Analysis Verification," *Journal of Academic Librarianship* 24, no. 4 (July 1998): 282–89, describe the results of a shelf availability study in which OPACs and CD-ROM journal indexes were the starting points for users seeking materials.

SUGGESTED READINGS

Baker, Sharon L., and F. Wilfrid Lancaster. *The Measurement and Evaluation of Library Services.* 2d ed. Arlington, Va.: Information Resources, 1991.

Bauer, Kathleen. "Indexes as a Tool for Measuring Usage of Print and Electronic Resources." *College and Research Libraries* 62, no. 1 (Jan. 2001): 36–43.

Biblarz, Dora, Stephen Bosch, and Chris Sugnet. *Guide to Library User Needs Assessment for Integrated Information Resource Collection Management and Development.* Collection Management and Development Guides, no. 11. Lanham, Md.: Scarecrow and the Assn. for Library Collections and Technical Services, 2001.

Blecic, Deborah D., Joan B. Fiscella, and Stephen E. Wiberley Jr. "The Measurement of Use of Web-Based Information Resources: An Early Look at Vendor-Supplied Data." *College & Research Libraries* 62, no. 5 (Sept. 2001): 434–53.

Bradburn, Frances Bryant. *Output Measures for School Library Media Programs.* New York: Neal-Schuman, 1999.

Calvert, Philip J. "Collection Development and Performance Measurement." In *Collection Management for the Twenty-first Century: A Handbook for Librarians,* edited by G. E. Gorman and Ruth H. Miller, 121–33. Westport, Conn.: Greenwood, 1997.

Davis, Burns. "How the WLN Conspectus Works for Small Libraries." In *Public Library Collection Development in the Information Age,* edited by Bill Katz, 53–72. New York: Haworth, 1998. Also published in *The Acquisitions Librarian,* no. 20.

Doll, Carol A. *Managing and Analyzing Your Collection: A Practical Guide for Small Libraries and School Media Centers.* Chicago: American Library Assn., 2002.

Gabriel, Michael. *Collection Development and Collection Evaluation: A Sourcebook.* Lanham Md.: Scarecrow, 1995.

Gorman, G. E., and Ruth H. Miller. "Changing Collections, Changing Evaluation." In *Collection Management,* edited by G. E. Gorman, 309–38. International Yearbook of Library and Information Management, 2000/2001. London: Library Assn. Pub., 2000.

Grover, Mark L. "Large Scale Collection Assessment." *Collection Building* 18, no. 2 (1999): 58–66.

Hernon, Peter, and Robert E. Dugan. *An Action Plan for Outcomes Assessment in Your Library.* Chicago: American Library Assn., 2002.

Kachel, Debra E. *Collection Assessment and Management for School Libraries: Preparing for Cooperative Collection Development.* Westport, Conn.: Greenwood, 1997.

Levitov, Deb, and Marilyn Sampson. *Guide for Developing and Evaluating School Library Media Programs*. Englewood, Colo.: Libraries Unlimited, 2000.

Lockett, Barbara, ed. *Guide to the Evaluation of Library Collections*. Collection Management and Development Guides, no. 2. Chicago: American Library Assn., 1989.

Luther, Judy. *White Paper on Electronic Journal Usage Statistics*. Washington, D.C.: Council on Library and Information Resources, 2000. Also available at http://www.clir.org/pubs/reports/pub94/contents.html.

Perrault, Anna H. "National Collecting Trends: Collection Analysis Methods and Findings." *Library and Information Science Research* 21, no. 1 (1999): 47–67.

Poll, Roswitha. "The House That Jack Built: The Consequences of Measuring." *Performance Measurement and Metrics* 1, no. 1 (Aug. 1999): 31–44.

Powell, Ronald R. "Measurement and Evaluation of Electronic Information Services." In *Information Services in an Electronic Environment,* edited by G. E. Gorman, 323–41. International Yearbook of Library and Information Management, 2001/2002. London: Library Assn. Pub., 2001.

Rosenblatt, Susan. "Developing Performance Measures for Library Collections and Services." In *The Mirage of Continuity: Reconfiguring Academic Information Resources for the Twenty-first Century,* edited by Brian L. Hawkins and Patricia Battin, 278–89. Washington, D.C.: Council on Library and Information Resources and Assn. of American Universities, 1998.

Shim, Wonsik, and Charles R. McClure. "Data Needs and Use of Electronic Resources and Services of Academic Research Libraries." *Portal: Libraries and the Academy* 2, no. 2 (April 2002): 217–36.

Smith, Mark. *Collecting and Using Public Library Statistics: A How-To-Do-It Manual for Librarians*. How-To-Do-It Manuals for Libraries, no. 56. New York: Neal-Schuman, 1995.

Tenopir, Carol. "Database and Online System Usage." *Library Journal* 126, no. 16 (Oct. 1, 2001): 41–45.

Twiss, Thomas M. "A Validation of Brief Tests of Collection Strength." *Collection Management* 25, no. 3 (2001): 23–37.

Walter, Virginia A. *Output Measures for Public Library Service to Children: A Manual of Standardized Procedures*. Chicago: Assn. for Library Service to Children, Public Library Assn., American Library Assn., 1992.

White, Howard D. *Brief Tests of Collection Strength: A Methodology for All Types of Libraries*. Contributions in Librarianship and Information Science, no. 88. Westport, Conn.: Greenwood, 1995.

APPENDIX
Selection Aids

Most of these tools are updated through new editions and supplements. Many are available in electronic format, either CD-ROMs or via the Internet. Selectors should consult the most recent resources available and be aware that publications cease and change names over time.

Bibliographical Tools and Directories

ALAN Review. Athens, Ga.: Assembly on Literature for Adolescents, National Council of Teachers of English. (three times per year)

The Alternative Press Center's Online Directory. Baltimore, Md.: The Alternative Press. Available at http://www.altpress.org/direct.html.

American Book Publishing Record. New Providence, N.J.: Bowker. (monthly)

Audiocassette and Compact Disc Finder: A Subject Guide to Educational and Literary Materials on Audiocassettes and Compact Discs. 3d ed. Medford, N.J.: Plexus-National Information Center for Educational Media, 1993.

AV Guide. Des Plains, Ill.: Educational Screen. (monthly)

Best Free Reference Web Sites. Chicago: American Library Assn., Reference and User Services Assn., Machine-Assisted Reference Section (MARS). Available on the RUSA web site (www.ala.org/rusa). Click "MARS" on the top navigation bar; click "Publications."

Bibliographic Guide to Conference Publications. Boston: Hall. (annual)

Book Report. Worthington, Ohio: Linworth. (bimonthly)

Books for College Libraries. 3d ed. Chicago: American Library Assn., 1988.

Books in Print. New Providence, N.J.: Bowker. (annual)

Bowker's Complete Video Directory. New Providence, N.J.: Bowker. (annual)

C&RL NewsNet: Internet Reviews. Available at http://www.bowdoin.edu/~samato/IRA/.

CD Guide. Peterborough, N.H.: Connell Communications. (semiannual)

CD-ROMs in Print. Detroit: Gale. (annual)

Children's Books in Print. New Providence, N.J.: Bowker. (annual)

Children's Catalog. 18th ed. New York: Wilson, 2001. (annual supplements)

Children's Magazine Guide, with subject and multimedia index. New Providence, N.J.: Bowker. (nine times per year)

CultureWatch: A Monthly Annotated Bibliography on Culture, Art and Political Affairs. Oakland, Calif.: The DataCenter. (monthly)

Cumulative Book Index. New York: Wilson. (quarterly)

Directory of Published Proceedings, issued in three sections: *SMET—Science/Medicine/Engineering/Technology; SSH—Social Sciences/Humanities; MLS—Medical/Life Sciences.* Harrison, N.Y.: InterDok Corp. (ten times per year with quarterly and annual cumulations)

Directory of Scholarly and Professional E-Conferences, maintained by Diane K. Kovacs. Available at http://www.kovacs.com/directory/.

Directory of Scholarly Electronic Journals and Academic Discussion Lists, compiled by Dru Mogge, Diane K. Kovacs, et al. Washington, D.C.: Assn. of Research Libraries, Office of Scientific and Academic Publishing. (annual)

Elementary School Library Collection: A Guide to Books and Other Media, Phases 123. Williamsport, Pa.: BroDart. (biennial)

Fiction Catalog. 14th ed. New York: Wilson, 2001. (quinquennial with annual supplements)

Film and Video Finder. 5th ed. Medford, N.J.: Plexus-National Information Center for Educational Media, 1997.

Filmstrip and Slide Set Finder. Medford, N.J.: Plexus-National Information Center for Educational Media, 1990.

Forthcoming Books. New Providence, N.J.: Bowker. (bimonthly)

Fulltext Sources Online: For Periodicals, Newspapers, Newsletters, Newswires and TV/Radio Transcripts. Medford, N.J.: Information Today. (annual)

Gale Directory of Databases. [available in two parts: "Online Databases," and "CD-ROM, Diskette, Magnetic Tape, Handheld and Batch Access Database Products"] Detroit: Gale. (annual with semiannual updates)

Gale Directory of Publications and Broadcast Media: An Annual Guide to Publications and Broadcasting Stations. Detroit: Gale. (annual)

Gale International Directory of Publications. Detroit: Gale. (irregular)

Government Information Quarterly. Greenwich, Conn.: JAI Pr. (quarterly)

Government Reports Announcement and Index. Springfield, Va.: U.S. National Technical Information Service. (semimonthly)

Great Sites: Amazing, Spectacular, Mysterious, Colorful Web Sites for Kids and the Adults Who Care about Them. Chicago: American Library Assn., Great Web Sites Committee. Available on the ALSC web site (www.ala.org/alsc). Click "Great Web Sites for Kids" on the left navigation bar.

Guide to Microforms in Print. New Providence, N.J.: Bowker. (annual)

Guide to Official Publications of Foreign Countries. 2d ed. Chicago: American Library Assn., Government Documents Roundtable, 1997.

Guide to Reference Books. 11th ed. Chicago: American Library Assn., 1996. [A revised edition is forthcoming.]

Guide to Reference Books for School Media Centers. Englewood, Colo.: Libraries Unlimited. (irregular)

Guide to Reprints. Munich: Saur. (annual)

Guide to the American Left: Directory and Bibliography. Olathe, Kans.: Laird Wilcox. (annual)

Guide to the American Right: Directory and Bibliography. Olathe, Kans.: Laird Wilcox. (annual)

Guide to U.S. Government Publications. McLean, Va.: Documents Index. (annual)

Index to Social Sciences and Humanities Proceedings. Philadelphia: Institute for Scientific Information. (quarterly)

International Books in Print. Munich: Saur. (annual)

International Directory of Little Magazines and Small Presses. Paradise, Calif.: Dustbooks. (annual)

The Internet Scout. Madison: University of Wisconsin, Dept. of Computer Sciences. Available at http://scout.cs.wisc.edu/report/sr/current/. (updated weekly)

Magazines for Kids and Teens: A Resource for Parents, Teachers, Librarians, and Kids! Rev. ed. Glassboro, N.J.: Education Press Assn. of America; International Reading Assn., 1997.

Magazines for Libraries. 10th ed. New Providence, N.J.: Bowker, 2000.

Magazines for Young People. 2d ed. New Providence, N.J.: Bowker, 1991.

Middle and Junior High School Library Catalog. 8th ed. New York: Wilson, 2000. (quinquennial)

Monthly Catalog of United States Government Publications. Washington, D.C.: Govt. Print. Off. (monthly)

New Products from the U.S. Government. Washington, D.C.: Govt. Print. Off. (bimonthly)

NewJour: Electronic Journals and Newsletters. [Announcement list for new serials on the Internet.] Available at http://gort.ucsd.edu/newjour/ NewJourWel.html. (updated frequently)

Newsletters in Print. Detroit: Gale. (annual)

NICEM Audiovisual Database. Albuquerque, N.Mex.: National Information Center for Educational Media. (An online subscription-based resource; updated frequently; also available as a CD-ROM subscription, titled *NICEM Reference*)

Oxbridge Directory of Newsletters. New York: Oxbridge Communications. (annual)

Proceedings in Print. Halifax, Mass.: Proceedings in Print. (bimonthly)

Public Library Catalog. 11th ed. New York: Wilson, 1999. (quinquennial, with annual supplements)

Schwann CD Review Digest—Classical. Woodland, Calif.: Schwann. (irregular)

Schwann CD Review Digest—Jazz, Popular, etc. Woodland, Calif.: Schwann. (irregular)

Schwann Opus. Woodland, Calif.: Schwann. (quarterly)

Schwann Spectrum. Woodland, Calif.: Schwann. (quarterly)

Senior High School Library Catalog. 16th ed. New York: Wilson, 2002. (quinquennial, with annual supplements)

Serials Directory: An International Reference Book. Birmingham, Ala.: EBSCO. (annual)

Software Encyclopedia. New Providence, N.J.: Bowker. (annual)

Spectrum: A Guide to the Independent Press and Informative Organizations. Olathe, Kans.: Laird Wilson. (annual)

Standard Periodical Directory. New York: Oxbridge Communications. (annual)

Ulrich's International Periodicals Directory, Including Irregular Serials and Annuals. New Providence, N.J.: Bowker. (annual, with triennial supplements)

Variety's Video Directory on Disc. New Providence, N.J.: Bowker. (annual)

The Video Sourcebook. Detroit: Gale. (annual with semiannual supplements)

Words on Cassette. New Providence, N.J.: Bowker. (annual)

Review Sources and Guides to Reviews
(Many with Associated Online Sites with Indexed Reviews)

American Reference Books Annual. Littleton, Colo.: Libraries Unlimited. (annual)

Argus Clearinghouse: The Internet's Premier Research Library, a Selective Collection of Topical Guides. Ann Arbor: Univ. of Michigan School of Information. Available at http://www.clearinghouse.net/. (updated frequently)

Billboard: The International Newsweekly of Music and Home Entertainment. New York: BPI Communications. (weekly)

Book Links: Connecting Books, Libraries, and Classrooms. Chicago: American Library Assn. (bimonthly)

Book Report: The Journal for Junior and Senior High School Librarians. Worthington, Ohio: Linworth. (five times per year)

Book Review Digest. New York: Wilson. (monthly except Feb. and July; annual cumulation)

Book Review Index. Detroit: Gale. (quarterly with annual cumulations)

Booklist. Chicago: American Library Assn. (semimonthly)

Bookwire. New York: Bowker. Available at http://www.bookwire.com.

Bulletin of the Center for Children's Books. Champaign: Univ. of Illinois Press. (monthly except Aug.)

Children's Software Revue. Flemington, N.J.: Active Learning Assn. (six issues per year)

Children's Video Report. Brooklyn, N.Y.: Great Mountain Proeditions. (eight issues per year)

Choice: Current Reviews of Academic Books. Middleton, Conn.: Assn. of College and Research Libraries. (monthly, except bimonthly in July/Aug.)

Chronicle of Higher Education. Washington, D.C.: The Chronicle. (forty-nine issues per year)

Counterpoise: For Social Responsibilities, Liberty and Dissent. Gainesville, Fla.: Task Force on Alternatives in Print, Social Responsibilities Round Table, American Library Assn. (quarterly)

Database: The Magazine of Database Reference and Review. Wilton, Conn.: Online. (six issues per year)

Down Beat. Elmhurst, Ill.: Maher Production. (monthly)

Factsheet 5. San Francisco: F5. (six issues per year)

Government Publications Review. Oxford, England: Pergamon. (bimonthly)

Harvard Gay and Lesbian Review: A Quarterly Journal of Arts, Letters, and Sciences. Boston: Harvard Gay and Lesbian Review. (quarterly)

Horn Book Magazine. Boston: Horn Book. (bimonthly)

Independent Film and Video Monthly. New York: Foundation for Independent Video and Film. (monthly)

Interracial Books for Children Bulletin. New York: Council on Interracial Books for Children. (four double issues)

Kirkus Reviews. New York: Kirkus. (semimonthly)

Lambda Book Review. Washington, D.C.: Lambda Literary Foundation. (monthly)

Library Journal. New Providence, N.J.: Bowker. (twenty issues per year)

Library Software Review. Thousand Oaks, Calif.: Sage. (quarterly)

Literature Film Quarterly. Salisbury, Md.: Salisbury State College. (quarterly)

Magazines for Libraries. New Providence, N.J.: Bowker. (irregular)

Media and Methods. Philadelphia: American Society of Educators. (five issues per year)

Media Review Digest. Ann Arbor, Mich.: Pierian. (annual)

Microform and Imaging Review. Munich: Saur. (quarterly)

Multicultural Review: Dedicated to a Better Understanding of Ethnic, Racial, and Religious Diversity. Westport, Conn.: Greenwood. (quarterly)

New Technical Books. New York: New York Public Library. (bimonthly)

New York Review of Books. New York: New York Review. (twenty issues per year)

New York Times Book Review. New York: New York Times Company. (weekly)

Notes. Canton, Mass.: Music Library Assn. (quarterly)

Online and CD-ROM Review. Oxford, England: Learned Information. (bimonthly)

Publishers' Weekly: The Journal of the Book Industry. New Providence, N.J.: Bowker. (weekly)

Quarterly Review of Film and Video. Chur, Switzerland: Harwood Academic. (quarterly)

Rolling Stone. New York: Wenner Media. (biweekly)

School Library Journal. New Providence, N.J.: Bowker. (monthly)

Science Books and Films. Washington, D.C.: American Assn. for the Advancement of Science. (nine issues per year)

Serials Review. Greenwich, Conn.: JAI Pr. (quarterly)

Sing Out. Bethlehem, Pa.: Sing Out Corp. (quarterly)

Small Press Book Review. Southport, Conn.: Greenfield. (quarterly)

Small Press Review. Paradise, Calif.: Dustbooks. (bimonthly)

Software Encyclopedia. New Providence, N.J.: Bowker. (quarterly)

Stereo Review's Sound and Vision Magazine. New York: Hachette Filipacchi Magazines. (ten issues per year)

Technology and Learning. Dayton, Ohio: Peter Li. (eight issues per year)

TLS Weekly [Times Literary Supplement]. London: Primary Source Media. (Times Newspapers of Great Britain)

Video Choice. Peterborough, N.H.: Connell Communications. (monthly)

Video Librarian. Seabeck, Calif.: Randy Pitman. (bimonthly)

VOYA: Voice of Youth Advocates. Lanham, Md.: Scarecrow. (bimonthly)

GLOSSARY

Terms in **boldface** are defined in the glossary.

Accrual method. An accounting method that focuses on the passage of time (usually a fiscal year) to recognize revenues and expenses.

Acid-free. Materials with a pH value of 7.0 (neutral) or greater (alkaline).

Acidic. Having a pH value less than 7.0 (neutral).

Acquisition. (1) The process of obtaining and receiving library materials for collections. (2) The organizational unit within a library that handles the acquisition function.

Agent. An individual or company that acts as an intermediary between a library and a **publisher** in the purchase of materials, e.g., a **subscription** service that manages **periodical** subscriptions.

Aggregator. A service or intermediary that provides access to a large number of **e-journals** and, perhaps, other electronic resources from different **publishers** and offers the end user access to these journals through a single interface.

Agreement. An understanding between two or more parties. *See also* **contract.**

Allocation. (1) The amount distributed to **fund lines** in the **budget.** (2) The process of distributing financial resources.

Alternative literature. Publications not part of the dominant culture and not sharing the perspectives and beliefs of that culture.

Alternative press. A small, independent **publisher.** Alternative press publications often address social issues and the interests of minority and diverse populations and publish innovative and experimental works.

Analog. Representations of information or data by some physically measurable quantity. Analog data cannot be processed by computers unless they are first translated into **digital** format.

ANSI (American National Standards Institute). A private, nonprofit organization that administers and coordinates the U.S. voluntary standardization and conformity assessment system.

Appropriation. Funds granted through formal action by a controlling or funding authority.

Approval plan. Method of acquiring library materials, usually books. The **vendor** supplies books automatically, according to a **profile** from the library, which may keep or return the books to the vendor. Some plans provide advance **notification slips** instead of sending the physical item. *See also* **blanket order.**

Approval profile. *See* **profile.**

Archivally sound. A nontechnical term describing a material or product that is permanent, durable, free of contaminates, and chemically stable. No formal standards exist that describe how long "archivally sound" material will last.

Artifact. A physical object made or modified by a person.

ASCII (American Standard Code for Information Interchange). (1) A binary code for representing English characters as numbers. Most computers use ASCII codes to represent text, which makes it possible to transfer data from one computer to another. (2) Text that has been converted to ASCII code; also known as "plain vanilla text."

Assessment. *See* **collection assessment.**

Association for Library Collections and Technical Services (ALCTS). A division of the American Library Association that serves the needs of those who are responsible for the following activities: **selection, evaluation** and **assessment, acquisition,** cataloging, classification, management, and **preservation** of library materials.

Association of American Publishers (AAP). The principal trade association of the book publishing industry.

Association of Research Libraries (ARL). An organization of approximately 120 leading university and research libraries in the United States and Canada.

Audit. The systematic evaluation of procedures, operations, and cash records to establish whether they conform to established financial criteria.

Authentication. A process that verifies the identity of a person or process, usually through a user name and password. In security systems, authentication is distinct from **authorization.** Authentication confirms that the individual is who he or she claims to be but does not address authorization.

Authorization. A process that gives or denies an individual access rights to a **network** resource based on his or her identity, which often is matched against a directory with various profiles granting various types of access. Most computer security systems are based on a two-step process: **authentication,** followed by authorization.

Authorized signature. The signature of a person legally empowered to represent a party to a **contract.**

Authorized user. A person having permission, under a **contract,** to access or use an electronic resource.

Back file or **back run.** Issues of a periodical that precede the current issue.

Banned book. A book that has been prohibited or suppressed by a governing or religious authority because its content is considered objectionable or dangerous, usually for moral, political, or cultural reasons. *See also* **censorship** and **intellectual freedom.**

Bibliographer. Usually a **subject specialist** in a larger library, whose primary or sole responsibility is selecting for and managing a collection. May be used interchangeably with **selector.**

Bibliographic utility. An online service that provides a shared **database** of cataloging records created by member libraries. The database may be used for copy cataloging, **interlibrary loan, selection,** and bibliographic verification.

Bibliography. (1) A systematic list of works by an individual author, on a given subject, or that share one or more characteristics. (2) A list of references to sources cited in the text of an article or book, or for further reading.

Bibliometrics. The use of mathematical and statistical methods to study the usage of materials and services within a library or to analyze the historical development of a specific body of literature. *See also* **citation analysis.**

Bitmapped image. A representation, consisting of rows and columns of dots, of a graphic image in computer memory. The value of each dot is stored in one or more bits of data.

Blanket order. An order placed with a **publisher, vendor,** or distributor to supply automatically all publications that match a **profile.** Blanket orders can be for a single publisher's series, all publications of an individual publisher, or all materials of a particular type or subject. Most blanket orders do not allow returns.

Bookseller. A person in the business of selling new or used books and related materials to the retail trade. *See also* **dealer** and **jobber.**

Breach. Failure to perform an obligation set forth in a **contract.**

Brittleness. Fragility of paper because of acid-caused deterioration. The standard test for brittleness in paper is whether a corner can withstand folding in each direction twice.

Budget. (1) A plan for the use of money available during a **fiscal year,** reflecting **allocations,** expected revenues, and projected **expenditures.** (2) The total amount of funds available to meet a library's expenditures over a fixed period of time. *See also* **fund** and **materials budget.**

Capital expenditure or **capital expense.** An **expenditure** made on a one-time basis, expected to benefit more than the current period, and recorded as an asset.

Library materials expenditures are usually capitalized, except in the case of expenditures for the rights to access a remote resource.

Cash method. A method of accounting that records transactions when a cash exchange has taken place.

Censorship. Suppression or prohibition of the production, distribution, circulation, or display of a work on grounds that it contains objectionable or dangerous material. Censored materials may be deemed objectionable on moral, political, military, or other grounds. *See also* **banned book.**

Center for Research Libraries (CRL). A cooperative, nonprofit organization of research institutions, located in Chicago, intended to increase research resources available for scholarly use. Members can deposit little-used publications at CRL, which also acquires some esoteric and little-used materials to lend to members.

Circulation analysis. Examination of statistics compiled on the circulation of library materials, usually broken down by classification, material type, category of borrower, time of year, and so on to determine patterns of usage.

Citation analysis. A **bibliometrics** technique that examines the works cited in publications to determine patterns. Two methods are counting the number of times a **journal** title appears in footnotes and bibliographies and counting the number of times a title is cited by local faculty.

Clapp-Jordan formula. A quantitative method, developed by Verner W. Clapp and Robert T. Jordan, to calculate the total number of volumes required for minimum-level collection adequacy in an academic library.

Classed analysis. A format for collection analysis that describes the collection and, perhaps, current collecting levels and desired future collecting levels in abbreviated language and numerical codes, according to a classification scheme.

Client-centered. *See* **user-centered.**

Closed stacks. A shelving area in a library to which only members of the library staff have access.

Collection. A group of materials assembled by a library or a previous owner. A collection consists of both physical items held by the library and digital resources currently selected and organized by the library and accessed by library users and staff members.

Collection assessment. Systematic quantitative and qualitative measurement of the degree to which a library's collections meet the library's goals and objectives and the needs of its users. *See also* **collection evaluation.**

Collection-centered analysis. An analysis method that focuses on the collection itself, not on its users.

Collection condition survey. A detailed survey of the physical nature and condition of the collection.

Collection development. Originally used to mean activities involved in developing a library collection in response to institutional priorities and user needs and interests—that is, the **selection** of materials to build a collection. Collection development was understood to cover several activities related to the development of library collections, including selection, determination and coordination of policies, needs assessment, collection use studies, collection analysis, **budget** management, community and user **outreach** and **liaison,** and planning for **resource sharing.** Now often used interchangeably with or in combination with **collection management.**

Collection development officer (CDO). The individual within a library charged with managing or overseeing collections-related activities. This person may also have an organizational title, such as assistant university librarian for collection development, deputy librarian for collections, or collections coordinator.

Collection development policy, collection development and management policy, or collection policy. A formal written statement of the principles guiding a library's **selection** of books and other materials, including the criteria used in selection, **deselection,** and acceptance of gifts. It may also address **intellectual freedom,** future goals, and special areas of attention.

Collection evaluation. Systematic consideration of a collection to determine its intrinsic merit or its "goodness." Evaluation seeks to examine or describe collections either in their own terms or in relation to other collections and checking mechanisms (lists, standards, etc.). *See also* **collection assessment.**

Collection management. Proposed in the 1980s as a term under which **collection development** was to be subsumed. In this construct, collection management includes collection development and an expanded suite of decisions about **withdrawal,** canceling **serials, storage,** and **preservation.** Collection development and collection management tend to be used synonymously or in tandem.

Collection mapping. *See* **conspectus.**

Collections librarian. *See* **selector.**

Committee on Institutional Cooperation (CIC). An academic consortium of twelve major teaching and research universities in the Midwest, with programs and activities in all aspects of university activity except intercollegiate athletics. The Center for Library Initiatives, a unit of the CIC, focuses on the activities of the libraries at CIC member institutions.

Compact storage or **compact shelving.** A storage area for lesser-used materials employing stacks that are either designed with narrower aisles and higher-than-normal shelves or that are mobile and compact by moving together. Compact storage accommodates more materials than conventional stack arrangements.

Conservation. Noninvasive physical or chemical methods employed to ensure the survival of manuscripts, books, and other **documents**. *See also* **preservation** and **restoration**.

Consortium. Two or more libraries that have formally agreed to coordinate, cooperate in, or consolidate certain functions. Consortia may be formed on a geographic, function, type, format, or subject basis.

Conspectus. A comprehensive collection survey instrument, first developed by the **Research Libraries Group**, to record existing collection strengths, current collecting intensities, and intended future intensities. It is arranged by subject, classification, or a combination of these two, and it contains standardized codes for languages of materials collected and for collection or collecting levels. Sometimes called collection mapping or inventory profiling.

Constituency. The users and potential users of a library.

Contingency fund. An amount set aside, usually at the beginning of the allocation process, in a **budget** to cover unexpected or unplanned **expenditures** and emergencies.

Contingency planning. The process of preparing a plan of action to be put into effect when prior arrangements become impossible or certain preestablished conditions arise.

Continuation order. *See* **standing order**.

Contract. A formal, legally binding written agreement between two or more parties. *See also* **license**.

Cooperative collection development. Sharing responsibilities among two or more libraries for the process of acquiring materials, developing collections, and managing the growth and maintenance of collections in a user- and cost-beneficial way.

Copyright. A set of exclusive **rights** to permit or forbid particular uses of a work for a specified period of time. In the United States, copyright is defined by statute. Copyright gives the author, the author's employer, or anyone to whom the author transfers his or her right the legal ability to control who may copy, adapt, distribute, publicly perform, or publicly display his or her work, subject to certain legal exceptions.

Copyright Term Extension Act (CTEA). Passed in 1998, it extends the duration of **copyright** an additional twenty years. Also called the Sonny Bono Copyright Term Extension Act.

Core collection. (1) A collection intended to meet the basic information needs of a library's primary user group. (2) A collection that represents the intellectual nucleus of a discipline.

Council on Library and Information Resources (CLIR). Formed by a merger of the Council on Library Resources (CLR) and the Commission on Preservation and Access in 1997, CLIR is an independent foundation that supports initiatives in **preservation** awareness, **digital** libraries, information economics, resources for scholarship, and international developments in library and information science.

Cure period. The time within which a party to a contract has to fix a contractual breach.

Data port. *See* **port.**

Database. A large store of digitized information, consisting of records of uniform format organized for ease and speed of search and retrieval and managed by a database management system.

Deaccession. *See* **withdrawal.**

Deacidification. Processes that chemically reduce the acid content of paper to a pH of 7.0 (neutral) or higher. Deacidification may also deposit an alkaline buffer intended to neutralize any acids that develop in the future.

Dealer. A individual or commercial company in the business of buying and selling new books, used books, and rare books for resale to libraries, collectors, and other booksellers. *See also* **bookseller** and **jobber.**

Deed of gift. A signed **document** stating the terms of agreement under which legal title to property, such as a gift to a library or archives, is transferred, voluntarily and without remuneration, by the donor to the recipient institution, with or without conditions.

Democratic planning. A cyclic planning process in which all units are requested to formulate their plans for program development on a regular schedule. The source of ideas rests with individuals and individual units, and these ideas are assembled into a coherent plan for the larger organization.

Depository library. A U.S. library legally designated to receive, without charge, all or a portion of the government documents provided by the U.S. Government Printing Office and other federal agencies to the Superintendent of Documents for distribution under the Federal Depository Library Program.

Deselection. Usually applied to the process of identifying serial **subscriptions** for cancellation. *See also* **withdrawal.**

Desiderata file. A list of materials needed and wanted by a library, to be purchased when money is available or when the item is located.

Digital. Of, pertaining to, or using digits, that is, numbers. Computers are digital machines because, at their most basic level, they distinguish between two values, 0 and 1, or off and on. *See also* **analog.**

Digital certificate. An attachment to an electronic message used for security purposes. A digital certificate serves to authenticate the user sending a message and to provide the receiver with the means to encode a reply.

Digital Library Federation (DLF). A **consortium** of major libraries and library-related agencies dedicated to establishing, maintaining, expanding, and preserving a distributed collection of **digital materials** accessible to scholars, students, and a wider public.

Digital materials. Both digital **surrogates** created by converting **analog** materials to digital format and "born digital" materials for which there is no analog equivalent.

Digital Millennium Copyright Act (DMCA). A law updating U.S. copyright law, passed in 1998, intended to protect **rights** to intellectual property in **digital** form.

Digital rights management (DRM). The technologies, tools, and process that protect intellectual property during **digital** content commerce.

Digitization. The process of converting **analog** materials to **digital** format.

Disaster preparedness plan or **disaster response plan.** Procedures prepared in advance by a library to deal with an unexpected occurrence (flood, fire, earthquake, etc.) that has the potential to cause injury to personnel or damage to equipment, collections, and facilities. *See also* **contingency planning.**

Discretionary purchase. An individual order for an item or items placed by a library that is outside of any existing **approval plan, blanket order** plan, serial **subscription,** or other **nondiscretionary purchase.** *See also* **firm order.**

Document. An object that comprises intellectual or artistic content or both and is conceived, produced, and issued as an entity.

Document delivery. The provision of documents upon request. Commercial document delivery services charge a fee to provide libraries or individuals with the requested item. The commercial service usually manages payments to **publishers** for copying **rights.**

E-journal or electronic journal. A **serial** publication available in **digital** format.

Electronic book or **e-book.** A book created in **digital** format, or converted from print to digital format, for electronic distribution.

Emergency plan. *See* **contingency planning** and **disaster preparedness plan.**

Emulation. Techniques for imitating obsolete computer systems on future generations of computers and thus providing continued access to **digital** content.

En masse and **en bloc.** A large collection of materials acquired at one time or through a single purchase decision.

Encumbrance. A recorded commitment of monies for an anticipated purchase. An encumbrance at the end of a **fiscal year** is carried forward into the next fiscal year as an outstanding commitment.

Endowment. A permanent fund consisting of gifts and bequests invested to earn interest. The interest can be spent, sometimes for purposes specified by the donor(s), leaving the principal intact to generate further income. *See also* **fund-raising.**

Entrepreneurial planning. A laissez-faire, individual approach to planning that relies on individuals to come forward whenever they have an idea for altering or expanding programs. Sometimes called opportunistic planning.

Environmental scanning. A methodology used to gather information and enhance understanding of the organization's environment and constituents. Its purpose is to detect, monitor, and analyze trends and issues in the environment, both internal and external, in which an organization operates.

Ephemera. Materials of everyday life not normally retained because they are perceived to have little or no permanent value. Pamphlets, leaflets, fliers, performance programs, and comic books often are considered ephemera. Sometimes called fugitive material. *See also* **gray literature.**

Ethics. Principles of conduct or standards of behavior governing an individual or a profession. These standards may be legal, moral, personal, or institutional.

Evaluation. *See* **collection evaluation.**

Exchange. (1) An arrangement in which a library sends items it owns to another library and receives in return items owned by the other library or sends duplicate copies to another library and receives duplicate materials in return. (2) Any publication given or received in this manner.

Expenditure. A payment made during the current fiscal period.

Fair use. A legal privilege, codified in Section 107 of the 1987 U.S. Copyright Act, which permits unauthorized use of copyrighted work for education, scholarship, research, news reporting, commentary, and research purposes.

Farmington Plan. A federally funded program (1948–1972) intended to ensure that at least one copy of every book important for research, regardless of place of publication, would be available in at least one U.S. library.

Firm order. A purchase order for an item submitted to a **publisher** or **vendor.** Money is encumbered for these orders, and the materials cannot normally be returned unless defective or damaged. Firm orders normally are placed for materials requested by individual selectors. *See also* **discretionary purchase.**

Fiscal year. A **budget** or accounting twelve-month cycle.

Fixed assets. Items with a determined and continuing value owned by the organization.

Focus group. A technique for gathering opinions and perspective on a specific topic. A small group of people, with common interests or characteristics, is led by a moderator, who asks questions and facilitates group interaction on the topic being investigated.

Force majeure. A clause that protects a party to a **contract** against failures to perform contractual obligations caused by unavoidable events beyond the party's control, that is, a greater force.

Free balance. Money available for purchasing. The free balance is the **allocation** minus payments made and any **encumbrances.**

Fund or **fund line.** A self-balancing account in a **budget** with monies set aside for a specific purpose.

Fund balance. The amount remaining in a **fund** that is the difference between assets (**allocations** or revenue or both) and liabilities (expenses and **encumbrances**). For most funds, a fund balance is available for additional **allocation** or spending.

Fund-raising. Programs and activities intended to encourage benefactors to contribute to a library or library system.

Gift. Items or money donated to a library, usually by an individual but sometimes by a group, organization, estate, or other library.

Governing law. The jurisdiction under which a dispute relating to a **contract** will be adjudicated.

Graphical user interface (GUI). A computer interface that allows the user to provide input and receive output interactively by manipulating menu bars, icons, and movable windows.

Gray (grey) literature. Printed works such as reports, internal documents, Ph.D. dissertations, and conference proceedings, not usually available through regular market channels because they were never commercially published, listed, or priced. *See also* **ephemera.**

Historical budgeting. *See* **incremental budgeting.**

Holdings. The entire **collection** of materials, print and nonprint, owned by a library or library system, usually listed in a catalog.

HTML (Hypertext Markup Language). A tagging scheme used to create **hypertext** documents accessible via the Web. Tags imbedded in the text control formatting.

Hypertext. A method of presenting **digital** information that allows related files and elements of data to be dynamically interlinked rather than viewed in linear sequence.

Incentive planning. A planning model that views the organization in economic terms and has an incentive structure that rewards particular types of activities. Incentives are frequently financial—increased budget **allocations** or the opportunity to retain funds generated through various activities or operations.

Incremental budgeting. A process by which historical **allocations** are added to or subtracted from a standard amount or percentage.

Indemnity. One party's agreement to insure or otherwise defend another party against any claims by third parties resulting from performance or nonperformance under the **contract**.

Inflation rate. The percentage the level of prices rises, usually in one year.

Intellectual freedom. The **right** granted in the First Amendment to the U.S. Constitution that permits a person to read or express views that may be unpopular or offensive to some people, within certain limitations. *See also* **banned book** and **censorship**.

Intellectual Freedom Round Table (IFRT). A round table in the American Library Association that advocates freedom of access and expression in libraries, provides support to librarians and other library employees who may be facing **censorship**, and monitors legal and other developments in **intellectual freedom** that affect libraries.

Intellectual property. Products of the human mind, creativity, and intelligence that are entitled to the legal status of personal property, especially works protected by **copyright**, inventions that have been patented, and registered trademarks.

Interlibrary loan (ILL). Transaction in which one library requests and another library lends an item from its collections (a returnable) or furnishes a copy, either paper or **digital**, of the item (a nonreturnable) to another library.

Interoperability. The condition achieved when two or more technical systems can exchange information directly.

Inventory profiling. *See* **conspectus**.

Invoice. A report sent to a purchaser by a **vendor** or other supplier indicating the total amount owed for items sold and services rendered. An invoice includes sufficient descriptive information to clearly identify the item or service.

IP (Internet Protocol) address. The physical address of a computer attached to a **network** governed by the **TCP/IP** protocol.

ISO (International Organization for Standardization). A network of national standards institutes from 140 countries working in partnership with international organizations, governments, industry, and business and consumer representatives.

Jobber. A wholesale **dealer** who stocks new books and nonprint materials issued by various **publishers** and supplies them to bookstores or libraries on order, usually at a discount. Some jobbers offer customized services such as **continuation orders**, **approval plans**, cataloging, technical processing, and so on.

Journal. A **serial** that disseminates original research and commentary on current developments within a specific subject area, discipline, or field of study. Librarians distinguish between journals and magazines, but **publishers** and users often use the terms interchangeably, for example—*Ladies Home Journal* is considered a **magazine** by librarians.

JSTOR. A nonprofit organization that provides searchable bibliographic **databases** containing the complete full-text **back files** of core scholarly journals in a wide range of disciplines, current to within two to five years.

Lease. A **contract** by which one party grants access to or the use of real estate, equipment, or a resource for a specified term and for a specified amount to another party.

Liability. Legal responsibility for an act or failure to act.

Liaison. Communication for establishing and maintaining mutual understanding and cooperation. The term is used in academic libraries to describe librarians' responsibilities to work with and reach out to academic departments to better meet their needs. *See also* **outreach.**

Library binding. An especially strong and durable binding, usually conforming to the **ANSI** standard for library binding.

Library cooperation. Methods by which libraries and library systems work together for mutual benefit, including **cooperative collection development,** cooperative cataloging, exchange of bibliographic information, **resource sharing,** union catalogs, and so on.

Library network. A mechanism that links libraries through shared bibliographic utilities or other formal arrangements.

Library survey. A written or oral question-and-answer instrument designed to elicit feedback from library users.

License or licensing agreement. Permission to do something that, without such permission, would be illegal. A license is a **contract** that presents the terms under which a **vendor** grants a license to a library, granting the **rights** to use one or more proprietary bibliographic **databases** or online resources, usually for a fixed period of time in exchange for payment.

Licensee. The party to a **contract** receiving permission or the **rights** to access or use an electronic resource.

Licensor. The party to a **contract** granting permission or the **rights** to use or access an electronic resource.

Local area network (LAN). Two or more **servers** connected to a local server.

Macro selection. Adding large quantities of materials to the library or access to numerous resources through a single decision. *See also* **micro selection.**

Magazine. A popular interest **serial** usually containing articles on a variety of topics, written by various authors in a nonscholarly style. *See also* **journal.**

Marketing. An umbrella term describing several activities: understanding an entity's market (in the case of a library—its present and future users), planning how best to serve that market, implementing the plan, and assessing its effectiveness.

Master planning. Top-down planning that begins in the administrative offices of an organization.

Materials budget. The portion of a library's budget allocated for the purchase of books, media, **serials,** and other information resources. Some libraries include electronic resources, postage and service charges associated with acquiring materials, and **conservation** and **preservation** in the materials budget; others make separate **allocations.** Also may be called the acquisition budget, access budget, or collections budget.

Mending. Minor **restoration** of a book's condition, not requiring replacement of material or removal of the bound sections from the cover. *See also* **rebinding** and **repairing.**

Metadata. Literally, data about data. Metadata are used for different purposes. (1) *Resource description* or *resource discovery* metadata serves to identify and locate a piece of information. Library cataloging is one specific use of a subset of resource discovery metadata; Dublin Core is an example of this descriptive metadata. The Dublin Core contains a **rights** element as well as descriptive elements. (2) *Rendering* is the process of realizing a specific information object on the user's computer. To do this, the receiving computer needs technical information, transmitted by metadata, about the characteristics of the object. For example, the need to open Adobe Acrobat to access a Web-based **document** is conveyed in metadata imbedded in that document in the file extension. (3) *Rights management* refers to the ownership of content and the right of a user to carry out any operation on that information object. This may involve making a payment to the owner of the right, or the operation (viewing, downloading, printing) may be carried out free of charge under an existing license agreement.

Micro selection. Selecting titles individually, one title at a time, to acquire or to which a library will provide access. *See also* **macro selection.**

Migration. (1) Transferring **digital** resources from one hardware or software (or both) generation to another. (2) Moving from one hardware platform or software system to another.

Monograph. Any nonserial publication, either complete in one volume or intended to be completed in a finite number of successive parts issued at regular or irregular intervals, consisting of a single work or collection of works.

Monographic series. A group of individual **monographs** that have a collective title applying to the group as a whole. Monographic series may be numbered or unnumbered; publication is expected to continue indefinitely.

Monographic set. A multipart title with a predetermined last volume; the date of the last volume may or may not be specified. Examples include encyclopedias and collected letters of historical or literary figures.

Mutilation. Intentional damage of library materials, either out of malicious intent or to mark or obtain parts of the items for personal use.

Narrative collection policy. A prose-based collection policy.

National Endowment for the Humanities (NEH). An independent grant-making agency of the U.S. government that supports research, education, **preservation,** and public programs in the humanities.

Native format. An original file format. Native format is the default format of a data file created by its associated software program. Many applications can work with files in a variety of formats, but an application's native file format is the one it uses internally. For all other formats, the application must first convert the file to its native format.

Needs analysis or **needs assessment.** A systematic process that gathers information about a user community and then analyzes that data for planning.

Network. Two or more computers connected through a server. *See also* **library network.**

Nondiscretionary purchase. Any purchase that happens automatically. Examples are serial **subscriptions, approval plans,** and **blanket orders.** Nondiscretionary purchases imply a continuing annual commitment against the acquisitions **budget.**

North American Title Count (NATC). An initiative through which academic and national libraries produce counts of their collections in approximately 600 Library of Congress classification areas. Used for internal and external comparative analysis.

Notification slip. Printed form provided by the library's **approval plan** vendor announcing a new book that meets the library's **profile.** In most cases, items are supplied only if the notification slip is returned to the **vendor** or the vendor is notified in some other way to supply the item.

Obscenity. Speech, writing, or artistic expression considered indecent by conventional standards of behavior because it offends ordinary people. *See also* **pornography.**

OCLC or **Online Computer Library Center.** The largest **bibliographic utility** in the world, providing cataloging and acquisitions services, **serials** and circulation control, **interlibrary loan** support, and access to online databases. OCLC maintains OCLC **WorldCat,** an online bibliographic database of member records and holdings.

OPAC (Online Public Access Catalog). A computer catalog of the books and other materials owned by a library; also called an online catalog.

Open Archives Initiative (OAI). OAI develops and promotes interoperability standards to facilitate the exchange of information content in **digital** formats.

Operating budget. A **budget** allocated to meet the ongoing expenses incurred in running a library or library system.

Opportunity cost. In economics, the true cost of choosing one alternative over another.

Out of print (OP). A publication no longer obtainable through regular market channels because the **publisher** has no more copies and does not plan another printing.

Outreach. The act of reaching out or extending services beyond current or usual limits; usually applied to activities in public and school libraries. *See also* **liaison.**

Outsourcing. The contracting of library services formerly performed in-house to an outside service **provider.** Examples of outsourcing are **conservation** and **preservation** (particularly binding and reformatting), purchasing catalog records in machine-readable form, purchasing cataloging for foreign-language materials, and acquisitions plans (**approval plans, blanket orders,** subscription **agents,** etc.).

PDF (Portable Document Format). A proprietary file format developed by Adobe Systems that renders documents formatted by a variety of desktop publishing applications into PDF for ease of delivery.

Peer review. (1) The process in which the job performance and professional contributions of a librarian or other library staff member are reviewed and evaluated by the individual's colleagues, who make recommendations about contract renewal, promotion, and tenure decisions. (2) The process in which experts critically evaluate the work of an author prior to publication.

Periodical. *See* **serial.**

Perpetual license. The continuing **rights** to access an electronic resource after the termination of a license.

Pittsburgh Study. A major study of the usage of library materials, conducted at the University of Pittsburgh by Allen Kent during the 1970s. It reported that approximately 40 percent of the materials purchased never circulated.

Pornography. Works of no artistic value in which sexuality is depicted with the conscious intention to arouse sexual desire. *See also* **obscenity.**

Port. A physical connection on a computer through which data are transmitted and received, usually to and from a **network.**

Preservation. A broad range of activities intended to prevent, retard, or stop deterioration of materials or to retain the intellectual content of materials no longer physically intact. *See also* **conservation.**

Preservation needs assessment. Analysis of the condition of a library collection and the environmental conditions in which it is housed to determine what **preservation** treatments are needed.

Price index. A method of calculating and describing the **inflation rate.** It shows the effects of price change on a fixed group of items over a period of time.

Profile. (1) Description prepared by a library for a **publisher** or **agent** who supplies materials on an **approval plan** or through a **blanket order.** The profile usually describes subject areas, levels of specialization and difficulty, languages, series, formats, price ranges, and so on. (2) A demographic study of the community served by a library or library system that measures economic, social, and educational variables.

Programmatic or program budgeting. A **budget** in which categories of funding relate to organizational goals or programs.

Project MUSE. A joint project of Johns Hopkins University Press and the Milton S. Eisenhower Library at Johns Hopkins that offers online access to the full text of more than 100 scholarly journals by **subscription.**

Providers. Individuals and entities providing access to information and delivery of services; includes traditional print and electronic scholarly **publishers,** trade publishers, information **aggregators, vendors,** and other electronic-only information disseminators.

Public key. Part of an encryption scheme to provide secure access to digital information. Each person gets a pair of keys, called the public key and the private key. Each person's public key is published while the private key is kept secret. Transmissions are encrypted using the intended recipient's public key and can only be decrypted using his or her private key.

Publisher. A person, commercial venture, university, or society that prepares and issues materials for public sale or distribution, normally on the basis of a legal **contract** in which the publisher is granted certain exclusive **rights** in exchange for assuming the financial risk of publication.

Purchase order (PO). An order placed by a library, authorizing a **publisher, jobber, dealer,** or **vendor** to deliver materials or services at a fixed price. A PO becomes a **contract** once it is accepted by the seller.

Qualitative methods. Analysis techniques that measure perceived success or goodness.

Quantitative methods. Analysis techniques that count things (volumes, circulation transactions, etc.).

Rebinding. The complete rehabilitation of a book too worn to be **mended** or **repaired.** Rebinding usually entails removing the case or cover, resewing the sections or regluing the text block, and applying a new cover.

Recasing. The process of regluing a book that has come loose from its cover.

Reference and User Services Association (RUSA). A division of the American Library Association responsible for stimulating and supporting the delivery of reference and information services. The Collection Development and Evaluation Section (CODES) of RUSA addresses the collection development interests of reference and user services librarians in libraries of all types.

Reformat. To copy information content from one storage medium to a different storage medium or to convert from one file format to a different file format.

Refresh. To copy **digital** information to a new storage medium without changing the data's content or structure.

Repairing. The partial rehabilitation of a worn book or other item, including **restoration** of the cover and reinforcement of the hinges or joints. More extensive than **mending** but less extensive than **recasing** or **rebinding.**

Reprint. A new printing of an existing edition, with no changes in the text except the correction of typographical errors.

Research Libraries Group (RLG). A not-for-profit membership corporation of more than 160 universities, national libraries, archives, historical societies, and other institutions. RLG develops and operates information resources, including **RLIN,** used by members and nonmembers around the world. *See also* **conspectus.**

Resource sharing. Sharing of resources among a group of libraries. Resource sharing traditionally has referred to the sharing of materials through **interlibrary loan.**

Restoration. Returning a book, **document,** or other archival material as nearly as possible to its original condition. Restoration can include **mending, repairing, rebinding,** and **deacidification.** *See also* **conservation** and **preservation.**

Retrospective selection. The process of selecting materials, which may be old, rare, antiquarian, used, and out of print, to fill in gaps in the collection or to replace missing or damaged items.

Rights. Powers or privileges granted by a **contract** or law.

RLG Conspectus. *See* **conspectus.**

RLIN (Research Library Information Network). A union **database** of member bibliographic records and **holdings** created by the **Research Libraries Group.**

Scenario planning. The process of developing scenarios describing alternative futures and formulating plans or strategies for the library in those various futures.

Scholarly communication. The means by which individuals engaged in academic research and creative endeavors inform their peers, formally or informally, of the work they have accomplished. *See also* **peer review.**

Scholarly Publishing and Academic Resources Coalition (SPARC). An international alliance of approximately 200 universities, research libraries, and library associations that seeks to educate faculty on academic **serials** issues, fosters competition in the **scholarly communication** market, and advocates changes in the system and culture of scholarly communication. *See also* **Open Archives Initiative.**

Search engine. Software that searches a file, **database,** or a **network** for a specific character string typed as input by the user.

Selection. The process of deciding which materials should be added to a library collection.

Selection criteria. The set of guidelines used by librarians in deciding whether an item should be added to the **collection.** *See also* **collection development policy.**

Selector. One who selects materials for a library and, usually, makes decisions about collection management (e.g., what will be withdrawn, preserved, stored, transferred, etc.). *See also* **bibliographer** and **subject specialist.**

Serial. A publication issued over a period of time, usually on a regular basis with some sort of numbering used to identify issues, without a foreseeable ending date. Serials may be popular **magazines,** scholarly **journals, electronic journals,** and annual reports. *Serial* is often used interchangeably with the term *periodical* to reflect the periodic nature of its publication.

Server. A computer that provides some service for other computers connected to it via a **network.**

Shelf-ready book. Book supplied by a **vendor** and received ready to go to the stacks. Shelf-ready books usually are cataloged and processed (with spine labels, book plates, anti-theft strips, etc.).

Site. As used in a **license,** a site is a physical location affiliated with the licensee where the licensee may permit access to digital information to authorized users.

Site license. A **license** granting official permission from the producer or **vendor** of an e-resource to use it, under specified conditions, on all the computers located at a specific location, a specific **IP (Internet Protocol) address,** or range of IP addresses.

Small press. A small independent **publisher.**

Standard Generalized Markup Language (SGML). An **ISO** standard governing the rules for defining tag sets that determine how machine-readable text **documents** are formatted. Not dependent on a specific computer system or type of software, SGML is widely used in preparing machine-readable text archives. The **HTML** code used to create web pages is an SGML language that uses a fixed set of predefined tags. *See also* **XML.**

Standing order. An order placed by a library with an **agent** or **publisher** to automatically supply until further notice each succeeding issue, volume, or part of a **serial** or series as published. Standing orders usually do not permit returns. *See also* **approval plan.**

Stewardship. Careful management of gifts; may include regular reports to the donor.

Storage. The transfer of little-used materials or rare, valuable, and fragile materials to restricted access areas within a library building or to a remote facility. *See also* **compact storage.**

Strategic planning. The systematic, broadly participative process by which an organization formulates policy objectives for future growth and development over a period of years. A strategic plan has an external focus and usually involves an **environmental scan.**

Subject or **area specialist.** A librarian responsible for selecting materials, managing a collection, and providing bibliographic instruction and reference services to users in a specific academic discipline or field of study. *See also* **bibliographer** and **selector.**

Subscription. The agreement or arrangement through which a library (or individual) receives a **periodical** or the **rights** to access a remote e-resource for a designated period of time or number of issues upon paying a fee to the **publisher,** subscription **agent,** or **vendor.**

Surrogate. A substitute for an original item. In preservation, a surrogate is usually made in another medium that is more durable.

Survey. *See* **library survey.**

TCP (Transmission Control Protocol). TCP is the most common protocol and enables two hosts on a **network** to connect and exchange data. TCP is pronounced as separate letters and nearly always used in the combination TCP/IP. *See also* **IP (Internet Protocol) address.**

Transfer. To physically move library materials from one location in a library to another.

Trial. A limited period during which a library may test a new electronic product or resource without paying a fee.

Trueswell's 80/20 Rule. A circulation pattern, first reported by Richard W. Trueswell in the 1960s, that determined that 20 percent of a library's collection accounts for 80 percent of its circulation.

User-centered. An assessment method that focuses on how the collection is being used and how well it meets user needs.

Utility. In economics, utility is a measure or expression of an individual's expected or anticipated satisfaction.

Vendor. (1) A distributor through which the library obtains books, **serials,** and so on instead of dealing directly with a **publisher.** (2) A company in the business of providing access to one or more electronic resources.

Verification list. An extensive subject-based list of important monographs and serials against which a library's holdings are checked to evaluate the quality of a collection.

Warranty. A promise or guarantee, such as assurances about ownership, quality, and hours of performance.

Weeding. The process of selecting items in a library collection for **withdrawal** or relocation to **storage**.

Wide area network (WAN). A computer **network** that spans a relatively large geographical area. The largest WAN in existence is the Internet.

Withdrawal. Removing an item from a library's active collection and removing the bibliographic record from the library's catalog.

WLN. Originally the Western Library Network, now part of **OCLC** and formally named the OCLC/WLN Pacific Northwest Service Center.

World Wide Web (WWW). A global **network** of Internet **servers** that provides access to **documents** written in Hypertext Markup Language (**HTML**) that allows content to be interlinked, locally and remotely.

WorldCat. The bibliographic **database** of materials cataloged and held by **OCLC** member libraries and institutions.

XML (Extensible Markup Language). A subset of **Standard Generalized Markup Language** (SGML) in which tags are unlimited and not predefined.

Zero-based budgeting. A budgeting process in which all **allocations** start at zero, and funding needs and requirements are estimated as if no previous allocation had been made.

'zine. A small circulation, narrowly focused, often irregular, noncommercial **magazine,** newsletter, or newspaper, self-published by one person or a small group and usually not available by **subscription.**

INDEX

80/20 ratio, 275

A

AASL. *See* American Association of
  School Librarians (AASL)
Abel, Richard, inventor of approval plans,
  113–14
academic libraries
  e-books in, 209
  faculty relations. *See* Faculty relations
  history, 4–6
  incentive planning in, 68–69
  marketing of place, 182
  mutilation of materials, 161
  new degree programs, 273
  nondiscretionary purchases, 113
  performance evaluations, 56–57
  promotion in, 183–84
  serials cancellations, 159–60
  serials ratio, 91
  subject specialists, 35–37
  user community, 79, 176–77
  value of, 180
  withdrawals, 146
access to information
  and cooperation, 254–55
  and user expectations, 19
access vs. ownership, 255–59
accountability
  and collection analysis, 272
  communication with stakeholders,
    184–85
  and electronic resources, 215, 217–18,
    278
  and formal planning, 72

accreditation reports and collection
  analysis, 273
accrual accounting system, 92
acidic paper, 151–52
acquisitions budget. *See* Materials
  budget
acquisitions process, 111–18
AcqWeb web site, 49–50
ACRL. *See* Association of College and
  Research Libraries (ACRL)
administrators as barrier to cooperative
  collection development, 251
Advanced Research Projects Agency
  Network (ARPANet), 203
aggregators, 205, 212
aggregators of electronic resources, 21
aging populations, trends in, 20
ALA. *See* American Library Association
  (ALA)
ALCTS. *See* Association for Library
  Collections and Technical Services
  (ALCTS)
"all or nothing" offerings by publishers,
  206, 212
Allen, Barbara McFadden, on consortia,
  244, 245
allocation formulas
  construction of, 91
  electronic resources, 218
allocation of budget, 85, 90–92
alternative literatures, acquisition of,
  119–20
amendments to licensing agreements,
  223

American Association of School
Librarians (AASL)
"Access to Resources and Services in
the School Library Media
Program," 121
on collection development policies, 73
on networks, 242
American Chemical Society, 206
American Civil Liberties Union, 126
American Civil Liberties Union v. Reno
(Reno II), 125
American Library Association (ALA)
bibliographies, 273
code of ethics, 46–47
collection development policies, 73
and intellectual freedom, 120–23,
125
interlibrary loan code, 236
standards for libraries, 283–84
Andreason, Alan R., on marketing, 178
appraisal of gifts, 75–76, 117
approval plans
in acquisitions process, 113–15
as selection tool, 106
archives. *See also* Back files of electronic
resources
electronic resources, 201, 224
in licensing agreements, 223
Ariel software, 238
ARL. *See* Association of Research
Libraries (ARL)
ARPANet (Advanced Research Projects
Agency Network), 203
Asheim, Lester, 13
assessment of collections
vs. evaluation, 269
tools for, 252
trends, 23
Association for Educational
Communications and Technology,
241
Association for Library Collections and
Technical Services (ALCTS)
Collection Management and
Development Section, 15
Duplicates Exchange Union, 118
supplement to ALA code of ethics
(text), 47

Association of College and Research
Libraries (ACRL)
collection development, 15
"Intellectual Freedom Principles for
Academic Libraries," 121
Association of Research Libraries (ARL)
Collection Analysis Project, 274
Collection Development Committee,
15
E-Metrics, 279
LibQual+ survey instrument, 288
Atkinson, Ross
on cooperation, 240
on core collections, 241
on electronic access, 259
on purchase decision, 110
on quality of access, 256
audience
for collection analysis reports, 290–91
for collection development policies, 76
audits of financial records, 94
authentication of users in licensing agreements, 221
authority of information in electronic
resources, 201, 209
authorization and authentication of users
as challenge for electronic resources,
201
in licensing agreements, 221
authorized signatures to licensing agreements, 223
automation librarians, 23
autonomy, local, as barrier to cooperative
collection development, 249–50
availability studies, 288–89

B

back files of electronic resources, 201,
258–59. *See also* Archives
Baker, Nicholson
on preservation microfilming, 153
on withdrawal of materials, 139
Baker, Sharon L., on marketing, 180
balanced coverage, 13–14, 119
Battin, Patricia
on academic libraries, 9
on microfilming projects, 153
benchmarks for materials budget, 89

Bentley, Stella, on cooperative collection development, 239, 253
bias, personal, and selection, 119–20
bibliographic access
  in cooperative collection development, 237, 238
  and success of consortia, 252–53
bibliographic control of electronic resources, 201
bibliographic tools and directories, 299–302
bibliographic utilities
  and bibliographic access, 238
  as consortia, 247
bibliographies and lists
  library web sites, 214
  preparation of, 33–34
  as selection tools, 105
"Big Deal" of all-or-none site licensing, 206
binding of materials, 155
blanket orders, 113, 114
Blumberg, Stephen Carrie, book thief, 161
Bolman, Lee G., on professional ethics, 46
book fairs, as selection tool, 106
book theft detection systems, 161
Books for College Libraries, 280
bookstores as selection tool, 106
Boston Public Library, 7
Bostwick, Arthur E., on censorship, 10
Branin, Joseph J., on cooperative collection development, 238
Braugh, Kenneth J., on Harvard, 8
Braverman, Harry, on deskilling, 40–41
Brill, Patricia L., on competencies, 51–52
brittle paper, 152
browsing and access vs. ownership debate, 258
Bryant, Bonita
  on measuring collection development, 39
  on organizational structure, 42
Budd, John M., on competencies, 51–52
budget planning cycle, 93
budget responsibility, 86
budgeting and finance, 84–95
  allocation of funds, 90–92
  and collection development policy, 74

development activities, 87–88
electronic resources, 214–18
expenditures, 92–94
materials budget, 85–86, 88–90, 94–95
responsibilities for, 33
types of budgets, 84–86
bundled serials packages, 113, 205

C
California Digital Library, 248
California State Library, regional union catalog, 238
capital expenditures, and e-resources, 217
caring in ethical relationships, 46
Carnovsky, Leon, on censorship, 13
Carrigan, Dennis P., on circulation data, 177
case studies
  closing a library, 164–65
  collection analysis, 292–93
  collection policy statement, 96–97
  competencies and training, 59
  consortia, 261
  diversity, selection for, 128–29
  electronic resources, 229
  marketing plan, 195
cash accounting system, 92
cataloging, cooperative, 245–46
CDA (Communications Decency Act), 125
CDO. See Collection development officer (CDO)
CD-ROMs, history, 203
censorship, 120–26
  internal, 13, 124
  and the Internet, 125–26
Center for Library Initiatives, 251
Center for Research Libraries (CRL)
  history, 148
  as cooperative storage facility, 244
  shared purchase model, 243
centralized selection, in public libraries, 37–38
challenges to library materials
  and collection development policies, 75
  history, 122–23
  reasons, 123–24
Child Online Protection Act (COPA), 125

Children's Internet Protection Act (CIPA), 125–26
children's materials
    competencies required, 51
    and environmental scanning, 70–71
CIC (Committee on Institutional Cooperation)
    cost savings, 244
    on document delivery, 238
    HealthWeb project, 245
    strong institutional support for, 251
CIPA (Children's Internet Protection Act), 125–26
circulation studies
    in collection analysis, 285–86
    in market research, 177
    and weeding, 142
citation studies, 285
Clapp-Jordan formula for collection size, 274
classed analysis model for collection development policies, 77–78
Cline, Nancy M., on competencies, 52–53
collaborative collection development. See Cooperative collection development
collection analysis, 268–97
    functions, 272–73
    history, 273–79
    planning, 290–91
    techniques, 270–72, 280–90
collection analysis projects, 290–91
collection depth indicators, in collection development policy, 78
collection development
    definitions, 1–3
    history, 3–10
Collection Development Committee (RTSD), 1977 preconference, 14
collection development officer (CDO)
    and electronic resources, 212
    and monitoring of budget, 94–95
    in public libraries, 37
    responsibilities of, 44–46, 58
    in school districts, 38
collection development policy, 72–84
    and challenges to materials, 126
    classed model, 77–78
    and collection analysis, 272

electronic resources, 210–11, 224
    history of, 8
    narrative model, 78–80
    supplemental policies, 80–84
    uses of, 73–76
    withdrawals, 140
    writing of, 76–84
collection management, 138–71
    definitions, 1–3
    electronic resources, 223–24
    preservation. See Preservation
    security, 160–62
    serials cancellations. See Serials cancellations
    storage. See Storage of materials
    trends, 16–25
    withdrawal. See Withdrawal of materials
Collection Management and Development Institute, 1977, 14–15
collection management policy, storage, 149–50
collection mapping. See Conspectus method
collection protection, 160–62
collection size formulas, 274
collection-based analysis, definition, 270–71
collections budget. See Materials budget
college libraries, withdrawals, 145
Columbia University libraries, document delivery services, 257–58
Committee on Institutional Cooperation. See CIC (Committee on Institutional Cooperation)
committees in collection work
    electronic resources, 43, 211–12
    function of, 43–44
    serials, 43, 110
communication. See also Scholarly communication
    collection development policies, 74
    planning as, 66
    responsibilities for, 33
Communications Decency Act (CDA), 125
community analysis. See Market research
comparative statistics compilation, 282–83

complaints, procedures for, 75. *See also*
    Challenges to library materials
conceptual learning, 50–53
confidentiality. *See* Privacy
conservation of materials, 154–55. *See
    also* Preservation
consortia
    and collection development policy, 77
    and cooperative collection develop-
        ment, 247–49
    definition, 247
    electronic resources, 238, 244–45
    governance structure, 252
    in serials cancellations, 159
    trends, 23–24
conspectus method, 275–76. *See also*
    Classed analysis model for collection
    development policies
    in assessment of collections, 252
    peripheral materials, 240
    RLG model, 77–78, 247
container for digital resources, definition,
    200
content in licensing agreements, 221
contingency funds, 92
contingency planning model, 67
continuity, 235
Continuous Review, Evaluation, and
    Weeding (CREW) method, 140
contracts and license agreements. *See*
    License agreements and contracts
cooperative acquisition, 243
cooperative collection development,
    235–67
    access vs. ownership, 255–59
    barriers to, 249–53
    and collection development policies,
        75, 76, 77
    history, 241
    overview, 236–39
    trends, 23–24, 253–55
    types of, 239–49
cooperative funding, 243
cooperative microfilming projects, 153
cooperative preservation programs, 24
coordinated collection development. *See*
    Cooperative collection development
coordination function of CDO, 45–46

COPA (Child Online Protection Act), 125
copyright law
    and cooperation, 255
    and digitization, 147
    purposes of, 219–20
    and reformatting, 156
    trends, 21
core collections vs. peripheral materials,
    240
corporate libraries. *See* Special and
    corporate libraries
Cosgriff, John, on serials cancellations,
    160
cost savings, in consortia, 244–45
costs
    and consortia, 254–55
    cooperative collection development,
        239
    of document delivery, 257–59
    electronic resources, 201, 278
    materials, 108
    of preservation treatments, 157
    and serials cancellations, 159
    storage, 149
    trends, 22–23
    of weeding projects, 141
Cotton des Houssayes, Jean-Baptiste, on
    libraries, 4
COUNTER (Counting Online Usage of
    NeTworked Electronic Resources),
    279
CREW (Continuous Review, Evaluation,
    and Weeding) method, 140
CRL. *See* Center for Research Libraries
    (CRL)
culture, libraries as transmitters of, 19
currency of information with electronic
    resources, 209
current awareness, 183. *See also*
    Environmental scanning
customer service, measurement of, 287–88
Cutter, Charles, on popular materials, 11

D

Dana, John Cotton, on book selection, 7
Dannelly, Gay N.
    on access vs. ownership, 255
    on licenses, 218

De Stricker, Ulla, marketing in special libraries, 176

Deal, Terrence E., on professional ethics, 46

decision matrix, 210

decision-making flow charts, 212–13

defined access, definition, 277

D'Elia, George, on public library users, 176

delivery format, definition, 200

delivery services
and cooperative collection development, 238, 254–55
and success of consortia, 252

demand vs. value, 13–14

depository libraries, 117–18

deselection. See Withdrawal of materials

deskilling, 40–41

deterioration, planned, 151

DEU (Duplicates Exchange Union), ALCTS, 118

development activities, 87–88, 116. See also Fund-raising

Dewey, Melvil, on cooperation, 235

Dialog, 202

digital divide, 17–18

digital libraries, definition, 200

Digital Library Federation (DLF)
"Benchmarks for Digital Reproductions of Monographs and Serials," 156
definition of digital libraries, 200

Digital Millennium Copyright Act (DMCA), 220

digital resources. See also Electronic resources
definition, 199–200
mediation by librarians, 20
preservation of, 24

digital rights management (DRM) files, 207

digitization
advantages, 200
as alternative to storage, 147
as preservation technique, 156

direct collection analysis, 281–82

disaster plans, 67, 161–62

discretionary and nondiscretionary allocations, 90–91

discretionary purchases, in acquisitions process, 113

discussion lists, as selection tool, 107

distance education
in e-resource collection development policies, 83
in licensing agreements, 221
trends in, 20

diversity
selection for, 119–20
trends in, 20

DLF (Digital Library Federation), 156, 200

DMCA (Digital Millennium Copyright Act), 220

Doares, Juanita, RTSD Collection Development Committee, 14

document delivery services
commercial services, 256–57
as promotion, 182, 183
and serials cancellations, 159

document delivery testing method, 289–90

Doll, Carol A., on standard bibliographies, 280

Dominguez, Patricia Buck, on library cooperation, 241

donor relations
importance of, 87
in selection process, 117

Dowd, Sheila, RTSD Collection Development Committee, 14

DRM (digital rights management) files, 207

Drott, M. Carl, on research habits, 145

Drucker, Peter, on planning, 66

Drury, Francis K. W.
on selection, 12–13, 104

dual responsibilities
training for, 55–56
as trend, 35–37
workload balance, 39

Duke University, 241

Duplicates Exchange Union (DEU), ALCTS, 118

duplication
and circulation studies, 286
and collection-based analysis, 271

E

ease of handling, in selection decisions, 108
e-books, 206–9
economic considerations and consortia, 254–55
Edelman, Hendrik, RTSD Collection Development Committee, 14
Education rate (Erate) program, 17–18
80/20 ratio, 275
e-journals. *See* Electronic journals
electronic book readers, 207
electronic information. *See also* Electronic resources
  growth of, 21
  skills required, 49–50, 58
electronic journals
  and access, 258–59
  as alternative to paper subscriptions, 159
  history, 204–6
electronic resources, 199–224. *See also* Digital resources
  acquisition of, 111
  advantages, 201
  budgeting, 91, 214–18
  bundled purchases, 113, 205
  and collection analysis, 277–79
  collection development policies, 80, 83
  collection management, 223–24
  committees, 43, 211–12
  and consortia, 244–45
  and conspectus levels, 277, 278
  contracts and licensing agreements, 218–19, 220–23
  copyright issues, 219–20
  definitions, 199–202
  e-books, 206–9
  electronic journals. *See* Electronic journals
  history of, 9–10, 202–3
  planning for, 66
  preservation of, 154
  and privacy of users, 284
  roles of collections librarians, 210–14
  security of, 162
  selection, 209–10
electronic resources librarian (ERL), 212

Elsevier Science journals, 148, 206
E-Metrics (Measures for Electronic Resources), 279
encumbrance policy, 94
entrepreneurial planning, 68
environmental controls, for protection of materials, 160
environmental scanning, 69–71
Erate (Education rate) program, 17–18
e-resources. *See* Electronic resources
ERL (electronic resources librarian), 212
ethics, 46–49, 58
evaluation of materials
  vs. assessment, 269
  criteria for, 107–10
exchange agreements, as acquisition method, 115
expending the budget, 92–94

F

faculty relations
  and barriers to cooperative collection development, 250–51
  on collection issues, 179
  liaison activities, 173, 185–90
  promotion to, 176, 183–84
  role in selection, 35, 39
  in serials cancellations, 159–60
  in withdrawal process, 142
"fair use" principle, 156, 220
Farmington Plan, 241–42
fee-based services, 22–23. *See also* "Price" in marketing
fiction, role of, 11–12
file formats, definition, 200
filtering of Internet content, 126
firm orders. *See* Discretionary purchases
"first sale doctrine," 220
fiscal year, 85
Flawn, Peter T., on libraries, 254
focus groups, 191, 278
Foerstel, Herbert N., on censorship, 122
Fogg, C. Davis, on environmental scanning, 70
force majeure in licensing agreements, 222–23
formal democratic planning, 67–68

formats of materials
  electronic resources, 200
  types of, 102
forms
  Faculty Profile, 188–89
  Online Order Request Form, 112
  Treatment Decision Form, 143–44
formulas for collection size, 274
four Ps theory of marketing, 180–84
Franklin, Benjamin, as library founder, 7
fraud in budgeting process, 94
free electronic resources
  cooperative access to, 245
  selection of, 214
  sources of, 116–17
  and supplemental costs, 218
Freedom to Read Foundation, 121
"Freedom to Read" statement (text),
    121–22
full-time vs. part-time collection responsi-
    bilities. See Dual responsibilities
functional model of organization, 42
funding
  budgeting in, 85
  in consortia, 247
  and cooperative collection develop-
    ment, 243, 251
  sources for, 87–88
fund-raising, 74, 87–88. See also
    Development activities

G
Gage, John, Internet Archive, 154
generality in ethical relationships, 46
genre, types of, 102
geographic model of organization, 43
Gibson, Catherine, on centralized selec-
    tion, 37
gifts
  as acquisition method, 116–18
  in collection development policy,
    75–76, 83
  management of, 87
Ginsparg, Paul, e-print service, 227
glossary, 307–26
Gorman, Michael
  on cooperation, 235, 253
  on preservation, 151

governing law in licensing agreements, 223
government publications, acquisition of,
    117–18
gradation, 235
grant of rights and restrictions in licensing
    agreements, 221–22
grant proposal writing, 87–88
Gray, Asa, as book selector, 6
Greater Midwest Region of the National
    Network of Libraries of Medicine,
    245
Guide for Training Collection
    Development Librarians, 55, 174
Guide to the Study and Use of Reference
    Books, history, 11
Guidelines for Collection Development,
    14, 275
Guidelines for Statistical Measures of
    Usage of Web-Based Information
    Resources, 279

H
Haines, Helen, on book selection, 12
handling of materials, 160
Handman, Gary, on nonprint materials,
    109
handouts as promotion, 183
hardware requirements. See also
    Technology
  for e-resources, 216
  and preservation of electronic
    resources, 224
  as selection criterion, 23, 210
Hart, Michael, Project Gutenberg, 207
Harvard University
  history, 5, 8
  storage, 146
  withdrawal of materials, 139
Hauptman, Robert, on censorship, 122
Hawaii State Public Library, outsourcing
    acquisitions, 115
Hayes, Robert M., on deterioration of
    materials, 152
Hazen, Dan C., on cooperative collection
    development, 239
HealthWeb, 245
Heyne, Christian Gottlob, on librarians as
    selectors, 6

Hightower, Christy, on cooperative collection development, 238
HighWire Press, 206
Hirshon, Arnold, on consortia, 245
hours of access, in licensing agreements, 222
HTML (Hypertext Markup Language), 204

I

ICOLC (International Coalition of Library Consortia), 244–45, 278–79, 284
ILLINET and Illinois libraries, 248–49
IMLS (Institute of Museum and Library Services), 151
incentive planning, 68–69
incremental budgeting, 86
indemnity in licensing agreements, 222
indexing and selection decisions
  electronic resources, 201
  serials, 109–10
indexing of materials budget, 89
Ingenta Select, 205–6
in-house use studies, 286–87
instability of information in electronic resources, 201
Institute of Museum and Library Services (IMLS), 151
intellectual freedom, 13, 75–76
intellectual property rights, 21, 51. See also Copyright law
interdisciplinary research
  and collection analysis, 279
  effect of technology on, 16–17
  and faculty relations, 186
  response of librarians to, 22
interlibrary loan
  and access vs. ownership debate, 255
  automation of, 238
  and electronic journals, 258–59
  history of, 9, 236
  in licensing agreements, 221
  as market research, 177
  as measure of collection quality, 289
  as selection tool, 107
  and serials cancellations, 159
  and user-based analysis, 271
Internal Revenue Service, and gift materials, 117

International Coalition of Library Consortia (ICOLC)
  history, 244–45
  privacy guidelines, 284
  statistics, 278–79
Internet. See also Free electronic resources
  censorship, 125–26
  history, 203–4
  preservation of, 154
Internet access and digital divide, 18
Internet Archive, 154
Internet sites, reviews of, 105–6
Intner, Sheila S.
  on access vs. ownership, 255
  on print vs. nonprint materials, 109
inventories
  as protection against theft, 161
  and withdrawals, 140
inventory profiling. See Conspectus method

J

Jackson, Mary, on document delivery services, 257
Jewett, Charles C., on collection analysis, 269
job responsibilities for collection development, 32–39
Joint Committee on Intellectual Cooperation, 241
JSTOR, 147
"just-in-time" inventory management, 255–56

K

Kachel, Debra E., on school libraries, 241
Kahle, Brewster, Internet Archive, 154
KB (Koninklijke Bibliotheek), 148
Keller, George, on planning, 66–67
Kent, Allen
  on circulation, 142
  on collection use, 275
Koninklijke Bibliotheek (KB), 148
Koop, James J., on bibliographic utilities, 247
Kotler, Philip, on marketing, 178–79
Kryzs, Richard, on collection development courses, 15

L

LAN (local area networks), 202
language of materials, as collection categories, 103
leases, definition, 219
legal issues. *See also* Intellectual property rights; License agreements and contracts
    electronic resources, 212, 218–23
    trends, 21
levels of collection. *See* Conspectus method
liability in licensing agreements, 222
liaison
    benefits and hazards, 191–93
    definition, 172–73
LibLicense web site, 218–19
LibQual+ survey instrument, 288
librarian as mediator to remote users, 22
librarians
    as arbiters of quality, 10–12
library automation, cooperative, 245
"Library Bill of Rights"
    in collection development policies, 75
    text of, 120
Library Binding Institute Standard for Library Binding, 155
library of record, in collection development policy, 84
library school curricula, 15, 50–53
license agreements and contracts
    and access to back files, 258–59
    as challenge for electronic resources, 201
    definition, 219
    in e-resource collection development policies, 83
    in selection process, 111
    terms and conditions, 220–23
    trends, 21
Line, Maurice B., on interlending, 8
line-item budgets, 90
list checking method of collection analysis, 280–81
Litman, Jessica, on copyright law, 219
local area networks (LAN), 202
local ownership
    and advances in technology, 19–20
    vs. remote access, 23

Lopez, Martin, on marketing, 174
Louisiana State University, document delivery services, 257
Lynch, Clifford A.
    on e-books, 209
    on electronic resources, 202

M

macro selection, 113
Mancall, Jacqueline C., on research habits, 145
Manoff, Marlene, on hypertext, 204
manuals for employee training, 55
market research, 175–78
market segments, 175
marketing, definitions, 173–75, 178
markup and searching, 201, 204
Martin, Murray, RTSD Collection Development Committee, 14
Marvin, Cornelia, on fiction, 11
master planning model, 67
mastery of skills, 53–54
materials budget
    and electronic resources, 217
    monitoring of, 94–95
    and planning, 85–86
    requests for, 88–90
materials, types of, 102–3
McLuhan, Marshall, on technology and societal change, 16
Measures for Electronic Resources (E-Metrics), 279
MEDLARS (Medical Literature Analysis and Retrieval System), 202–3
MEDLINE, 202
MELVYL shared catalog, 248
Metz, Paul
    on serials cancellations, 160
    on workloads, 39
micro selection, 113
microfilming projects, as collaboration, 246
microforms
    as alternative in retrospective selection, 118–19
    as preservation, 152–53
Midwest Inter-Library Center, 148
migration of data in preservation of electronic resources, 154

Miller v. California, 123
Minnesota Library Access Center, 148
mission statements
    and assessment of collections, 269
    collection development policy, 73–74
    marketing, 173
    planning, 95
models
    collection development policies, 77–80
    cooperative collection development,
        239–47
    of organization. *See* Organizational
        models
    for planning, 67–69
    selection criteria, 103–4
Morrill Act, 5–6, 225–26
Mosher, Paul H.
    on collection analysis, 269
    on collection development, 72, 239
    preconference on collection manage-
        ment, 14
    on withdrawal of materials, 139
Moulthrop, Stuart, on hypertext, 204
multitype library networks, 248–49
mutability of information, 201
mutilation of materials, 161
mutuality in ethical relationships, 46

N
narrative model for collection develop-
    ment policies, 78–80
National Council of Teachers of English,
    126
National Telecommunications and
    Information Administration (NTIA),
    17
National Union Catalog, 238
native format, 200, 203
Naudé, Gabriel, 4
NCIPA (Neighborhood Children's Internet
    Protection Act), 125
needs assessment or needs analysis. *See*
    Market research
Neighborhood Children's Internet
    Protection Act (NCIPA), 125
netLibrary, 207–8
networks, definition, 247
New England Depository, 148, 244

nonprint materials
    preservation of, 153–54
    selection of, 109
    withdrawals, 146
nonprofit organizations, marketing by,
    174
Norman, O. Gene, on marketing, 174
North American Title Count, 252, 274
North Carolina State University, 241
Northern and Southern [California]
    Regional Library Facilities, 148
NTIA (National Telecommunications and
    Information Administration), 17

O
OAI (Open Archives Initiative), 208, 227
obscenity, definition of, 123
OCLC, 247
OEB (Open Ebook) Standards Initiative,
    208
Ohio Wesleyan University, 6
OhioLink, 249
on-the-job training, 53–56
Open Archives Initiative (OAI), 208, 227
Open eBook Forum, 208
Open Ebook (OEB) Standards Initiative,
    208
Open eBook Publication Structure, 208
order preparation, 111
organizational models, 41–44
    as barrier to cooperative collection
        development, 251
    in collection development policy, 79
    consortia, 252
Osburn, Charles B., marketing by, 175
Outagamie Waupaca Library, cooperative
    webliography, 245
out-of-print materials
    on Internet, 106–7
    sources of, 118
outreach, benefits and hazards, 191–93
outsourcing, 25, 114–15
ownership markings, 161
ownership vs. access, 255–59

P
Pankake, Marcia, on collection
    development, 239

paper holdings and electronic resources, 224
paraprofessionals. *See* Support staff
parties to licensing agreements, 221
payment options for e-resources, 215–16
PDF (Portable Document Format), 203
peer review, 225
penalties in licensing agreements, 222
performance evaluation
    of marketing program, 190–91
    of staff, 56–57
periodicals, 109. *See also* Serials
peripheral materials and cooperative collection development, 240–41
perpetual access in licensing agreements, 223
Peterborough Town Library, 6
Philadelphia Library Company, 7
"place" in marketing, 182
planning, 65–72
    budgeting in, 84–85
    and collection analysis, 272
    models for, 67–69
    need for, 71–72
    responsibilities for, 33
    and trends monitoring, 69–71
plenitude, 235
policy. *See* Collection development policy; Collection management policy
Poole, William F., on popular materials, 11
Portable Document Format (PDF), 203
PostScript page description language, 203
power of dominant group, mediated by librarians, 19–20
Pratt, Mary Louise, on contact zones, 19
preprints, 227
preservation, 151–58
    in collection development policy, 83–84
    and collection-based analysis, 271
    e-books, 209
    electronic resources, 224
    microfilming projects, 246
    preservation plans, 157–58
    and storage facilities, 149
    storage of older materials, 150
    trends, 24

"price" in marketing, 181–82
prices of materials and scholarly communications, 226
"Principles for Emerging Systems of Scholarly Publishing," 226
priority setting, in collection development policy, 74
privacy
    in collection development policies, 76
    and collection of use data, 284
    in licensing agreements, 222
    and use of electronic resources, 224
Privacy Guidelines for Electronic Resources Vendors, 284
"product" in marketing, 181
professional associations
    conference exhibits, 106
    directories of, as selection tool, 105
professional pride, as barrier to cooperative collection development, 250–51
program budgeting, 86
programmatic responsibilities, 41, 57
Project Gutenberg, 207
Project MUSE, 147–48, 205
promotion, 182–84
Ps in marketing, 180–84
"public" in marketing. *See* User community
public libraries
    conservation of materials, 154–55
    cooperative collection development, 242
    e-books in, 208–9
    history, 6–8
    and Internet access, 18
    outreach activities, 173
    promotion in, 184
    responsibilities in, 37–38
    serials ratio, 91
    user community, 79, 176
    value of, 180
    withdrawals, 145
Public Library Association, preconference 1984, 15
Public Library Inquiry, 13
publishers announcements as selection tool, 106

publishing industry
  and back files of journals, 24
  competencies required, 51
  trends in, 20–21
purchase decision, 110

Q
qualitative analysis
  definition, 270, 271–72
  history, 275–77
quality of access, 256–57
quality of collection, and withdrawals, 140
quality of information, as challenge for
    electronic resources, 201
quality of service, measurement of, 287–88
quantitative analysis
  definition, 270, 271
  history, 273–75

R
rare book collections, security in, 161
RASD. See Reference and Adult Services
    Division (RASD)
reading, as changed by hypertext, 204
Reference and Adult Services Division
    (RASD)
  on collection development, 15
  "Guidelines for Liaison Work," 173
  markets in, 176
Reference and User Services Association
    (RUSA). See Reference and Adult
    Services Division (RASD)
reference collections, weeding of, 145
reference responsibilities of subject spe-
    cialists, 35
reformatting projects, 152–53, 155–57
remote users. See also Distance education
  technical problems, 201
  trends, 22
Reno v. American Civil Liberties Union
    (Reno I), 125
repair techniques and preservation, 152,
    154–55
replacement copies, acquisition of,
    118–19, 155–57
Research Libraries Group (RLG)
  Collection Management and
      Development Committee
      (CMDC), 15, 247

founding, 8
  as model of cooperation, 246–47
Research Library Information Network
    (RLIN), 246
research practices, quality of, 272, 291
Research Triangle University Libraries,
    241
reserves, course, in licensing agreements,
    221
reserves in budget, 92
resource sharing
  in cooperative collection development,
      237
  definitions, 236
resources budget. See Materials budget
response time of electronic resources, 201,
    209
responsibility-centered management, 68
retrospective files. See Back files of elec-
    tronic resources
retrospective selection, 118–19
review copies, as selection tool, 106
review sources, 11, 105, 303–5
Richardson, Ernest C., on interlibrary
    loan, 236
Rider, Fremont, on research collections, 8
RLG. See Research Libraries Group
    (RLG)
RLG Conspectus, 77–78, 247, 275–76
RLIN (Research Library Information
    Network), 246
Roden, Carl. B., on fiction, 12
Roth v. United States, 123
Rothenberg, Jeff, on preservation of elec-
    tronic resources, 154
routing of journals, 183
RTSD Collection Development
    Committee, 1977 preconference, 14
Runkle, Martin, on autonomy, 250
RUSA Collection Development and
    Evaluation Section, collection devel-
    opment policies for e-resources, 83
Rutledge, Jon, model for selection criteria,
    103–4

S
San Francisco Public Library, weeding
    project, 139, 143

SCAP (Shared Collections and Access
    Program), 248
scenario planning, 68
Schad, Jasper G., on leadership role of
    CDO, 45
scholarly communication, 224–27
    and cooperation, 254
    effect of technology on, 16
scholarly publishing
    history, 6
    scholarly monographs, 226
    trends in, 20–21
Scholarly Publishing and Academic
    Resources Coalition (SPARC), 227
school libraries
    conservation of materials, 154–55
    cooperative collection development,
        242
    curriculum in selection, 108
    faculty relations, 179, 184–85
    Internet access, 17
    mutilation of materials, 161
    outreach activities, 173
    promotion in, 184
    responsibilities in, 38
    serials ratio, 91
    user profiles, 88, 177, 190
    withdrawals, 145
ScienceDirect, 148
security, 160–62
Segal, Joseph P., on withdrawals, 140
selection
    electronic resources, 209–10
    history of, 12–14
    and outreach programs, 192
    responsibilities for, 32–33
    theories of, 10–14
    trends, 23
selection process, 103–5
selection tools, 103, 105–7
    bibliography, 299–305
Senge, Peter M., on mastery, 53–54
serials
    back files, 118, 147–48
    budget ratio with monographs, 91
    cost rises in, 102, 226, 256
    criteria for storage, 150
    selection of, 109–10

serials cancellations, 158–60
    in collection development policy, 76, 84
    and collection-based analysis, 271
    and outreach programs, 192
serials collections, in-house studies, 286
SGML (Standard Generalized Markup
    Language), 204
Shared Collections and Access Program
    (SCAP), 248
shelf availability studies, 288–89
shelf list analysis, 282
shelf list measurement, 252
shelf scanning as weeding technique,
    142–45
shelving and protection of materials, 160
Shreeves, Edward, on cooperation, 240
Sibley, John Langdon, librarian of
    Harvard, 5
skills and competencies, 50–54, 58
Slote, Stanley J., on weeding, 142
small group behavior and consortia,
    253–54
Smith, Lotsee P., on school library collec-
    tions, 108
Smith, Richard, Wei T'o process, 152
Soete, George I.
    on assumed competencies, 50
    on cooperative collection development,
        238
space for collections and withdrawals, 140
SPARC (Scholarly Publishing and
    Academic Resources Coalition), 227
special and corporate libraries
    budget requests, 88
    and market research, 176
    new research programs, 273
    promotion in, 184
    subject specialists in, 38–39
    users of, 184–85, 190
    withdrawals, 145–46
special collections, solicitation of gifts,
    116
staffing for collection management. See
    also Training
    assignment of responsibilities, 34
    storage of materials, 149
    support staff, 40–41, 57
    trends, 24–25

Stam, David H., on library cooperation, 235, 241
Standard Generalized Markup Language (SGML), 204
standards
    for collections and collection analysis, 283–84
    e-books, 208
    electronic resources, 201–2
standing orders, 113
Stanford University, SCAP Program, 248
statistics
    comparison with other libraries, 282–83
    on price trends, 89–90
storage of materials, 146–51
    and collection-based analysis, 271
    cooperative agreements, 244
    journals, 147–48
    off-site storage, 148–50
strategic planning, 95
    definition, 68
    environmental scanning, 69–71
students, as target market, 176–77
Stueart, Robert D., on withdrawals, 140
subject of resources, as collection categories, 102–3
subject specialists
    and outreach activities, 192
    paraprofessionals as, 41
    public libraries, 37
    responsibilities of, 34–37
supplemental costs for e-resources, 217–18
support staff, levels of responsibilities, 40–41, 57. See also Staffing for collection management
surveys of users. See User surveys
Swindler, Luke
    on library cooperation, 241
    model for selection criteria, 103–4
synergistic cooperation, 240–43

T
tax implications of gifts, 117
technology. See also Hardware requirements
    and cooperation, 254

and deskilling of responsibilities, 40–41
    effect on collection development, 16–17, 49–50, 58
Telecommunications Act of 1996, 17–18
tenure and performance evaluations, 57
termination of contract in licensing agreements, 222
theft protection, 161
time-saving for users
    and access vs. ownership debate, 258
    with e-resources, 217
    as value, 182
training
    and collection development policies, 74
    handling materials, 160, 162
    lack of and cooperative collection development, 252
    in licensing agreements, 222
    on-the-job, 53–54
transaction log analysis, 279
transculturation, 19
trends monitoring. See Environmental scanning
Trueswell, Richard N., on circulation, 142
Tuckman, Bruce W., on small groups, 253–54

U
union catalogs, print, 238
United States v. One Book Called "Ulysses," 123
University of California
    collaborative agreements, 248
    Northern and Southern Regional Library Facilities, 148
University of New Mexico Library, on withdrawal of materials, 139
University of North Carolina at Chapel Hill, 241
university presses and scholarly publishing, 226
U.S. Supreme Court on CIPA, 113
use statistics
    electronic resources, 278–79
    serials cancellations, 159, 160
use-centered analysis methods, 284–90

user community
  and assessment of appropriateness, 108
  in budget requests, 88
  in collection development policy state-
    ment, 79
  external users, 176–77
  liaison and outreach activities, 172–98
  and market research, 175–76
  needs of vs. cooperative collection
    development, 249
  requests from as selection tool, 107
  and selection responsibilities, 39
  and storage decisions, 151
user expectations
  effect of technology, 19–20
  and user-based analysis, 271
user instruction for electronic resources,
  201
user profiles, 187–90
user satisfaction
  and document delivery services, 258
  in marketing, 179–80
user support, in licensing agreements, 222
user surveys
  and assessment of electronic resources,
    278
  as collection analysis, 287–88
  faculty profile, 187–90
user-based analysis, definition, 270, 271

V
value, definitions, 179–80
Veaner, Allen B., on staffing, 41
vendors
  in acquisitions process, 111–13
  ethical relations with, 48–49, 58
verification studies, 280

W
Wallace, Karen L., on marketing, 180
WAN (wide area networks), 202
warranties, in licensing agreements, 222
Wayback Machine, 154
web sites
  defined access, 277
  development of, 33–34
  links from catalog record, 116–17
  as promotion, 183
  webliographies, 214
weeding. See Withdrawal of materials
Wei T'o process, 152
wide area networks (WAN), 202
Wiemers, Eugene L., on budgets, 84
William and Mary, College of, 5
Williams, Lynn B., on decision making,
  104
Winsor, Justin, on popular materials, 11
withdrawal of materials, 138–46
  and circulation studies, 286
  in collection development policy, 76,
    84
  and collection-based analysis, 271
  coordinated with other libraries, 244
  criteria for, 139–42
  history, 139
  techniques for, 142–45
  in types of libraries, 145–46
WLN collection development policies, 77
WLN Conspectus, 277
WWW (World Wide Web). See Internet

Z
zero-based budgets, 86
Zubatsky, David, RTSD Collection
  Development Committee, 14

Peggy Johnson is associate university librarian, University of Minnesota Libraries. In addition to holding positions in public and academic libraries, she has consulted on library development in Africa and China. She edits the journal *Technicalities: Information Forum for the Library Services Practitioner,* serves as interim editor of *Library Resources and Technical Services,* and has written and edited several books, including *New Directions in Technical Services* (ALA, 1997); *Collection Management and Development,* coeditor with Bonnie MacEwan (ALA, 1994); *Guide to Technical Services Resources* (ALA, 1994); *Recruiting, Educating, and Training Librarians for Collection Development,* coeditor with Sheila S. Intner (Greenwood, 1994); and *Automation and Organizational Change in Libraries* (Hall, 1991). Johnson served as president of the Association of Library Collections and Technical Services during 2000/2001.